C0-BVO-975

Transportation Economic Analysis

Transportation Economic Analysis

James T. Kneafsey
Massachusetts Institute of Technology

Lexington Books
D.C. Heath and Company
Lexington, Massachusetts
Toronto London

Library of Congress Cataloging in Publication Data

Kneafsey, James T.
Transportation economic analysis.

Bibliography: p.
Includes index.
1. Transportation–United States. 2. Urban transportation–United States. 3. Transportation–Passenger traffic. 4. Freight and freightage. I. Title.
HE151.K57 380.5'0973 74-2203
ISBN 0-669-93211-6

Published simultaneously in Canada.

Printed in the United States of America.

International Standard Book Number: 0-669-93211-6

Library of Congress Catalog Card Number: 74-2203

To my mother and father

". . . the amalgam of logic and intuition and the wide knowledge of facts, most of which are not precise, which is required for economic interpretation in its highest form is, quite truly, overwhelmingly difficult for those whose gift mainly consists in the power to imagine and pursue to their furthest points the implications and prior conditions of comparatively simple facts which are known with a high degree of precision."

John Maynard Keynes
Essays in Biography (1933)

Contents

Part II *The Domestic Transportation Industries*

List of Figures

List of Tables

Preface

Just as each generation of economists incurs the burden of interpreting for itself the history of the discipline, each generation also confronts, tacitly or overtly, the problem of where to apply the methods of economic analysis effectively. In most treatises, the language of the economist is not designed to impress the reader with an exotic blend of cognizant allusiveness and shocking iconoclasm. Rather, beneath this indurated surface lurks the real problem and confusions of the economist attempting to work his way out of a heritage of muddled historical developments in the transportation field. The depth of my concern with these matters is apparent in this book's emphasis on analysis—both prior and concomitant. Economic analysis then in my formulation represents the foundation for further inquiry and for policy prescription. It should be the *sine qua non* for any student of transportation, or for that matter, any other branch of economics.

In writing this material, I have emphasized the belief that transportation economics is a diffuse subject, and that no single selection of topics or techniques can be satisfactory to everyone. My primary intention has been to construct a unified thread of analysis which can be useful to students and readers in understanding a variety of predominantly current activities and problems in transportation. The price paid for this strategy is that more intensive approaches to certain topics have been delineated or, in some cases, omitted. While I have intentionally abbreviated the length of the book so that it can be supplemented with readings that present alternative views or more comprehensive treatments of certain topics, I simply invoked the law of comparative advantage by stressing economic analysis and the significance of contemporary issues in deference to strictly institutional and administrative matters.

No book can be a textbook that will cover all aspects of transportation. One of the persistent complaints from students who have used the standard texts in the economics of transportation is that the material has been too institutionally oriented. While I intentionally omitted lengthy discussions of certain historical facts, stories, and incidents in this book, my purpose was not necessarily to undermine their importance. Interested students should be able to examine rather easily more extensive discussions of any institutional points of intrigue with the assistance of the references provided in this book. A bibliography of selected readings is presented for the reader's benefit at the end of each of the six major parts in the book. The major parts of the book reflect the elements of change in the world of transportation and the relationship of transportation to the national economy. In particular, the subject matter concentrates on the principles of transportation economic analysis, federal regulation, managerial practices, and public policy issues. I also have attempted to illustrate and supplement such principles with materials and information which both refer to classic studies and introduce new developments to the field. During the last few years, events in the transportation field have been progressing very rapidly and probably will continue to do so in the near future. The best approach for the student and the reader to appreciate and improve upon these events is to first learn the theory and the analysis before moving to issues of policy. To the extent that this approach may represent a "new" type of text, I hope that my contribution will be worthwhile.

This book is designed to meet the needs of an introductory graduate level course in transportation economics for students in economics, business administration, and civil engineering programs. In addition, advanced undergraduates with some exposure to microeconomics should find the material beneficial. I should also hope that the material would be useful for students in geography, urban planning, and other disciplines with an interest in transportation economics. In most cases throughout the book, the level of mathematics and statistics has been kept to a minimum—a standard consistent with the author's past experience in using the material in classes.

The original material was developed in a course for senior economics majors and first year graduate students in both the Economics Department and the Graduate School of Business at the University of Pittsburgh. More recent ideas and information have been generated from a course in "Transportation Economics," which I developed at the Massachusetts Institute of Technology. I wish to express my appreciation to Mark Perlman of the University of Pittsburgh and to A. Scheffer Lang, formerly of M.I.T. and now with the Association of American Railroads, for allowing me the necessary latitude in developing the contents of these courses.

I am indebted for constructive comments at various stages of the manuscript development to Richard E. Caves of Harvard University, William H. Dodge of the University of Wisconsin, Gorman Gilbert of the University of North Carolina, and Theodore E. Keeler of the University of California, Berkeley. I wish to thank Paul O. Roberts and Joseph M. Sussman of M.I.T. and H.W. Bruck of the University of California, Berkeley for providing research opportunities in which some of the ideas in this text originated. I acknowledge the support of the U.S. Department of Transportation, the National Science Foundation, the California Department of Transportation and the Southern California Association of Governments under whose auspices some of the original research for this book was conducted; in particular, I thank Frances Banerjee of the Southern California Association of Governments for permission to use selected material which I authored under her agency's sponsorship. In no way do the views represented in this book necessarily reflect those of the above individuals or agencies. Other sections of the book can be attributed to the results of discussions on the issue of transportation systems analysis with members of M.I.T.'s Center for Transportation Studies and Flight Transportation Laboratory, especially Robert W. Simpson, Nawal K. Taneja, Henry Marcus, Wayne

Pecknold, Marvin L. Manheim, Michael Godfrey (now at The Ohio State University), and Richard deNeufville. My deepest thanks is to several colleagues at M.I.T. who have read and commented on different parts of the manuscript: Ann F. Friedlaender, Paul W. MacAvoy, Carl D. Martland, Paul O. Roberts, James Sloss, and Robert M. Solow. On the editorial side, I am indebted to Ephraim Gerber and Martha G. Blalock for their comments. Finally I thank Deborah S. Sylvain for typing the bulk of the manuscript and T.J. Houseman, Philomena Grossman, and Renée E. Todres for assisting on the remainder. Of course, full responsibility for any remaining errors or omissions is mine.

Part I:
Microeconomic Theory and Transportation

1 Introduction to Transportation Economics

Transportation economics has finally become an increasingly important branch of economic analysis and contemporary inquiry. Its importance has been enhanced by the growing public and social awareness of the so-called triple-E's: the problems of energy, environment, and the economy, which have been plaguing the country during the middle 1970s. When students are asked why they study transportation economics, they usually respond that they want to gain insight into urban problems such as pollution, land use, energy conservation, and suburban sprawl—all problems *related* to transportation.

An increasing number of students, however, want to learn about the *details* of transportation: its operating characteristics, industrial structure, economic performance, financing, and the environmental and economic impacts of both passenger and commodity movements on the quality of life. Every newspaper reader should realize that transportation issues appear perennially on the front pages of his or her local tabloid. Every commuter can speak to the claim that transportation ranks as one of our country's more urgent and serious domestic problems. While transportation is a ubiquitous factor in the functioning of the American economy, its true significance has not been acknowledged until recent years.

Transportation economics is a special field within economics in which economists use their tools of analysis to observe, understand, and evaluate transportation economic phenomena. It has developed as a field in two very distinct stages: The first stage extended from the post World War I period through the 1950s, when most of the emphasis was on comprehending and explaining the variety of institutional mechanisms that had previously pervaded all levels of transportation activity; and the second stage came about as a result of the creation of the U.S. Department of Transportation in 1966, where a newer breed of economists, systems analysts, and planners generated a renewed excitement about solving some of the pressing problems in the field. In this second stage the renewed efforts undoubtedly have been aided by two factors: first, the availability of increased federal government funds for sponsoring programs and direct assistance to the transportation sector from 1967 to the present (with further increases projected until at least 1982); and second, substantial and (in some cases) dramatic structural changes in the economy, including a new environmental awareness and the multiple-fold increases in energy costs.

Only recently, since the 1966 creation of the cabinet level department mentioned above, has transportation economics become a recognized specialty within the discipline. Even today, among the approximately 12,000 professional economists in this country, a significantly larger number specialize in labor economics or in monetary theory than in transportation economics. Yet, these differences in the numbers of economists in various specialties can be explained easily by the emphases (and their rewards) recognized in the traditional or classical fields of economics: The mainstream of the economics profession is simply slow to respond to changes in applied areas of study. This shift in emphasis within the profession hopefully will catch up with the increased transportation activity in the real world.

As an important field of inquiry within economics, transportation economics is no different from international trade, monetary theory, labor economics, or any other specialty in which economists have been stimulated to undertake specialized empirical and theoretical studies in order to understand better certain aspects of the economic world. It is different, however, in the substantive sense that transportation economics is a subset of other fields in economics; for example, it draws heavily from industrial organization and public finance and in many ways may be construed as a distinct branch of applied microeconomics.[1] In fact, a central theme to this book is that the emphasis on microeconomic analysis should be a necessary and sufficient condition for effective public policy prescriptions. Too many poor policy decisions have resulted from a lack of analytical abilities or even from the improper use of such abilities when they are available.

Transportation economics then is both a subject of broad interest and imprecise boundaries. In order to limit the scope of analysis, domestic transportation economics narrows the focus to the operations and facilities of urban passenger, intercity travel, and freight movements within the continental United States. Transportation facilities in this country include various types of rights-of-way, terminal operations, vehicles that provide motor power and that contain space for passengers or commodities, communications equipment, and numerous forms of specialized devices designed to improve the flow of transportation

1. Students continually are requesting advice on the best background for studying transportation economics. I repeatedly respond: The more microeconomic theory and econometric methods, the better. Of course, the most pragmatic answer depends on the student's goals, objectives, and capabilities. If the student wishes to become proficient in technical analysis, then courses focusing on quantitative methods are desired. If the goal is to be a generalist, then a program including courses in planning, sociology, and psychology should be stressed. A distinction also should be made between studying *transportation* and studying *transportation economics*: For a long time the former has been dominated by engineers and planners who generally have represented an anathema to economists (and vice versa). With an increased awareness of interdisciplinary needs, however, these barriers are gradually diminishing so that more meaningful and less fragmented results of inquiries into transportation problems should be forthcoming. Transportation economics then is simply the application of economic analysis to problems in transportation. In either case the important ingredient and signifying measure of a student's training is the ability to develop a proper perspective—and here only courses in literature will help.

services or to respond to the needs of special types of passenger or freight traffic. The companies and agencies that provide these domestic transportation services are business *enterprises*, competing for the same financial and resource markets as other business firms. Each enterprise usually has functioned in a particular mode of transportation, although some have expanded into integrated transport or have diversified into nontransport activities where regulation permits such endeavors. It is generally acknowledged that equity problems arise from the fact that motor carriers, water carriers, and airline firms make use of publicly provided facilities, while railroad companies and pipeline firms must provide their own basic facilities.[2] The ways in which these problems and their current impacts have been (and should be) analyzed represent the main thrust of the material in this book.

Organization of the Contents

The book is separated into six parts, each focusing on special topics in domestic transportation economics. At the end of each part appears a selected set of references pertaining to both classic and recent publications germane to the material in the preceding chapters.

The remainder of Part I consists of eight chapters that discuss the economic analysis tools necessary for students as a basis for approaching problems and issues of transportation economics. Too often students either find themselves bored with review sessions on economic theory or discover that their prior training in economics has been inadequate (or both). To help alleviate some of these concerns, Part I is designed to provide an improved foundation for the student with a solid two-semester economic principles background (also including differential calculus). It also presents some new perspectives of the application of economic analyses to transportation for the more advanced student.

Part II is a discussion of the major transportation industries in the United States. As indicated in the preface, the emphasis is on the structures of the motor trucking, railroad, and airline industries. The material in this part is intended to provide the reader with a sufficient understanding of the institutional (and particularly contemporary) features of the major transportation industries.

Part III focuses on problems of urban transportation economics. No attempt is made in this part to discuss the wide body of material available in the general field of urban transportation. A tremendous amount of research has been conducted in the area of urban transportation, but mostly in the fields of urban

2. For a thorough, institutional treatment of these problems, see D. Philip Locklin, *Economics of Transportation*, 7th ed., (Homewood, Ill.: Richard D. Irwin, Inc., 1972), esp. chap. 36.

and city planning, civil engineering, and regional science. The only attempt in this part is to synthesize the significant contributions that may be classified "urban transportation economics."

In Part IV three chapters appear on intercity passenger transportation. Even though private automobile travel constitutes a large number of intercity trips, few data sets exist for examining the characteristics of this important segment of transportation. The emphasis then in this part is on intercity railroad and airline passenger service.

In Part V is a series of chapters that discuss selected economic issues in commodity and freight transportation. Due to the general lack of empirical information on urban goods movements, most of the emphasis in this section is on the intercity and regional aspects of freight shipments. With an increasing significance attached to the energy-related features of freight transportation, the material in this part deserves renewed and special attention.

The final section of the book, Part VI, contains a set of interdependent analyses of selected topics in transportation economics. The principal intention of this part is to indicate certain areas of transportation in which statistical and econometric methods can be applied. The importance of the material and the methods in this part should not be underestimated: Much of the original luster and glamour in the field early in this century was lost simply because of the lack of quantitative investigations of transportation economic problems. Hopefully, this trend has been reversed.

2 The Scope of Transportation Economics

The twentieth century has been called by all the names we know that are related to the phenomenon of change—the age of mobility, the age of communication, the age of acceleration, the age of technological change, and the age of electronic revolution. Not much more than a hundred years ago, people's capacity to move around was restricted because the prevailing technologies of movement had been by animal and by water. Since about 1910, improvements in surface and airborne vehicle technology have accelerated the abilities of people to cover greater and greater areas in shorter and shorter times.

The extent to which transportation, both in its quantitative and its qualitative aspects, has been of paramount importance in developing and shaping large sectors of contemporary economic society is enormous. This movement of people, the interchange of commodities, advances in communications, and the dissemination of the skills and knowledge underlying much of modern civilization have all been possible because of transportation. This dependence on transportation for past progress (in some cases, the lack of it) and for future growth and development should make the study of the methods and principles by which the domestic transportation system functions, and of the ways in which its efficiency can be improved, of interest to individuals in all areas of business, economics, engineering, and planning.

In every specialized area of knowledge there are terms that possess particular and occasionally very specific meanings. Nine terms are used repeatedly throughout this book, namely: industry, firm, enterprise, market, structure, behavior, performance, transportation, and regulation. Consequently, a brief glossary of the meanings attached to these terms should assist the reader.

Industry: An industry usually consists of a group of firms (or establishments) primarily in the same or closely related types of business activity. An ideal classification of an industry should include all firms engaged in the provision of the same type of service or the production of similar services. Since each of the transportation industries is regulated by an independent commission, the definitions of airlines, railroads, and motor carriers are straightforward and are discussed in Part II.[1]

Firm: The firm is viewed as a collection of particular resources that can be

1. In addition, the *1967 Census of Manufactures* classified the output of all manufacturing establishments into 417 industries. The two-digit Standard Industrial Classification (SIC) code for transport is 37, for aircraft production it is 372, and so on. A complete *Census of Manufactures* was published in 1947, 1954, 1958, 1963, and 1967. Also, a separate *Census of Transportation* was published for 1963, 1967, and 1972.

used either for producing output (that is, providing transportation services) or for training new resources. The firm then is the traditional organization, incorporated with a state charter and in business for profit. When the emphasis of an analysis is on the industrial organization aspects of transportation, the firm is the carrier of rail, trucking, or air transport services, respectively, as defined by the entry conditions specified by the relevant regulatory agency.

Enterprise: In many transportation situations business firms simply cannot offer their services in a profitable manner in order to insure their survival. If these situations are deemed crucial or publicly necessary, a government agency of one form or another usually is called on to absorb the provision of the transportation service. Examples of such situations are the urban and local transportation authorities providing mass transit services to Boston, Washington, New York, and other major cities. In addition, there are many regional transportation authorities or agencies that are responsible for providing urban and regional transportation services, like San Francisco, Los Angeles, and Philadelphia. On the national level the provision of most intercity rail passenger service by the National Railroad Passenger Corporation (Amtrak) is the most obvious example. In each of these situations the agency or authority offering transportation services can be viewed along with the list of transportation firms performing the same service as enterprises.

Market: Quite often one refers to the market economy without paying particular attention to the meaning of the word. In this book a market includes all the participants (buyers and sellers), actual and potential, of a particular transportation service or set of services. There are several levels of markets in domestic transportation: fixed (or contractual), local, city-pair, regional, and national. Due to the geographical constraints imposed by the regulatory agencies, an individual enterprise's competition with other firms in its industry and with enterprises in other modes may be limited to specific markets. Other regulatory constraints either may impede any form of competition or may prolong excess competition in certain markets.

Structure: A major effort by economists interested in industrial organization has been devoted to the measurement of structural characteristics of markets or industries. Here structure refers to those factors that will determine and effect the performance of firms in the transportation industries. Market structure is an aggregate concept, referring to certain ways in which each transportation industry is structured or aligned. In his well-known textbook on industrial organization, Joe Bain claims that the salient dimensions of market structure pertain to concentration, product differentiation, and entry conditions. In explaining his choice of a small number of elements, Bain states:

At times, market structure has been defined much more broadly. . . . So construed, market structure could embrace every objective circumstance—psychological, technological, geographical or institutional—that might conceivably influence market behavior. . . . We do not espouse this concept of market structure here because a very loose and frequently ambiguous use of the idea of structure is involved, and also because meaningful intermarket comparisons and meaningful generalizations about the influence of structure on behavior are effectively forestalled if the content of "structure" is made so comprehensive that no two markets can be viewed as structurally alike.[2]

Other researchers prefer to use a larger list of elements to denote market structure and present evidence to substantiate their views.[3] A further discussion of this topic appears in later chapters.

Behavior: In actual markets the expectations, uncertainties, market control, and rate structure are very significant influences on firms' activities. Market behavior (loosely analogous to market conduct) refers to the manner in which firms behave within the context of their market structure; or as Bain, in his earlier monograph, describes it: ". . . patterns . . . which enterprises follow in adapting or adjusting to the markets in which they sell (or buy)."[4]

Performance: A primary societal concern should relate to how an industry performs in terms of its efficiency, progressiveness, stability, and true worth. The concept then of economic performance refers to the economic results that flow from the firms in an industry. Bain, again from his textbook, lists five measures:

1. The height of price relative to the average cost of production
2. The relative efficiency of production so far as this is influenced by the scale or size of plants and firms (relative to the most efficient) and by the extent of excess capacity
3. The size of sales-promotion costs relative to the costs of production
4. The character of the product, including choice of design, level of quality, and variety of product within any market
5. The rate of progressiveness of the firm and industry in developing both products and techniques of production, relative to evidently attainable rates and relative to the costs of progress.[5]

In general, performance criteria reflect economic yardsticks. A detailed discussion of these and other measures of industrial performance appears in the following chapter.

Transportation: As stated previously, the emphasis in this book is on the enterprises that offer transportation services (freight and passenger) in the

2. Joe S. Bain, *Industrial Organization*, 2nd ed. (New York: John Wiley & Sons, 1968), p. 9.

3. For a thorough review of this literature to date, see John M. Vernon, *Market Structure and Industrial Performance: A Review of Statistical Findings* (Boston: Allyn and Bacon, Inc., 1972); and Stanley E. Boyle, *Industrial Organization: An Empirical Approach* (New York: Holt, Rinehart and Winston, Inc., 1972).

4. Joe S. Bain, *Barriers to New Competition* (Cambridge: Harvard University Press, 1956), pp. 10-11.

5. Bain, *Industrial Organization*, p. 12.

domestic markets of the United States.[6] In particular, subsequent chapters examine the determinants of market structure and industrial performance in the airline, railroad, and motor trucking industries in domestic markets. Table 2-1 illustrates and traces the historical development of the major modes of transportation over the last two centuries. Table 2-2 indicates changes in the number of employees in the domestic transportation industries during the 1960s. Finally, Figure 2-1 depicts the allocation of expenditures into each of the modes (including international) for a recent year.

Regulation: Unless it is specified otherwise, regulation will reflect the impacts of domestic intercity freight and passenger movements under the auspices of the appropriately designated federal independent regulatory commission. Usually this commission is either the Interstate Commerce Commission (ICC) in the cases of the railroad and motor trucking modes or the Civil Aeronautics Board (CAB) in the case of the airline industry. For those other situations where alternative jurisdictions prevail, especially at metropolitan and urban levels (where interstate commerce is not involved), the appointed regulatory agency has primary responsibility.

---

6. Traditional textbooks in transportation economics tend to examine transportation from an institutional perspective. See, for example, D. Philip Locklin, *Economics of Transportation*, 7th ed. (Homewood, Ill.: Richard D. Irwin, Inc., 1971); Hugh S. Norton, *Modern Transportation Economics*, 2nd ed. (Columbus: Charles E. Merrill Books, Inc., 1971); Dudley F. Pegrum, *Transportation: Economics and Public Policy*, rev. ed. (Homewood, Ill.: Richard D. Irwin, Inc., 1968); and a more elementary text by Roy J. Sampson and Martin T. Farris, *Domestic Transportation: Practise, Theory, and Policy*, 3rd ed. (Boston: Houghton Mifflin Co., 1975).

Table 2-1
Life Cycle of Modes of Transportation

Period 1. *Experimentation:*	Before a mode is considered practical.
Period 2. *Early Extension:*	General public acceptance and growth.
Period 3. *Rapid Expansion:*	Technical improvements, formation of systems, recognition as a major field for financial investment and speculation, development of intensive internal competition, imposition of restrictive governmental regulations.
Eriod 4. *Maturity:*	Slower rate of construction and extension of service, cooperation and coordination among carriers on rates and service, high levels of efficiency and engineering standards.
Period 5. *Decadence:*	Loss of traffic to competitors, general unprofitableness, decline in utilization of facilities, strenuous efforts (with or without public aid) to regain lost laurels.

Mode of Transport	Period 1	Period 2	Period 3	Period 4	Period 5
River steamboats	1795-1815	1815-1839	1839-1850	1850-1870	1870-1900
Steam railroads	1829-1850	1850-1870	1870-1890	1890-1924	1924-1952
Pipelines	1865-1880	1880-1906	1906-1960	1960-	
Electric railroads (interurbans)	1881-1890	1890-1900	1900-1910	1910-1922	1922-1962
Motor trucks and buses	1884-1908	1908-1938	1938-1953	1953-	
Commercial Aviation	1903-1925	1925-1935	1935-1973	1973-	
Steam and diesel river barges	1920-1930	1930-1945	1945-1960	1960-	
Diesel locomotives	1920-1940	1940-1952	1952-1970	1970-	

Source: Data adapted partially from pp. 39-42 in *Economics of Transportation*, Rev. Ed., by Marvin L. Fair and Ernest W. Williams, Jr. (New York: Harper & Row, 1959).

Table 2-2
Average Number of Full-time and Part-time Employees by Transportation Sector, 1960-71 (in Thousands)

	1960	1963	1966	1969	1970	1971
Total	2,563	2,470	2,614	2,726	2,689	2,639
Railway	883	770	724	643	626	600
Local, suburban, and highway passenger	282	270	272	280	280	277
Motor freight and warehousing	866	902	1,008	1,093	1,080	1,088
Water	234	221	240	227	218	202
Air	192	203	256	356	354	343
Pipeline	23	20	18	18	18	17
Services	83	84	96	109	113	112

Source: Office of Systems Analysis and Information; U.S. Department of Transportation *Summary of National Transportation Statistics*, November 1973, p. 60.

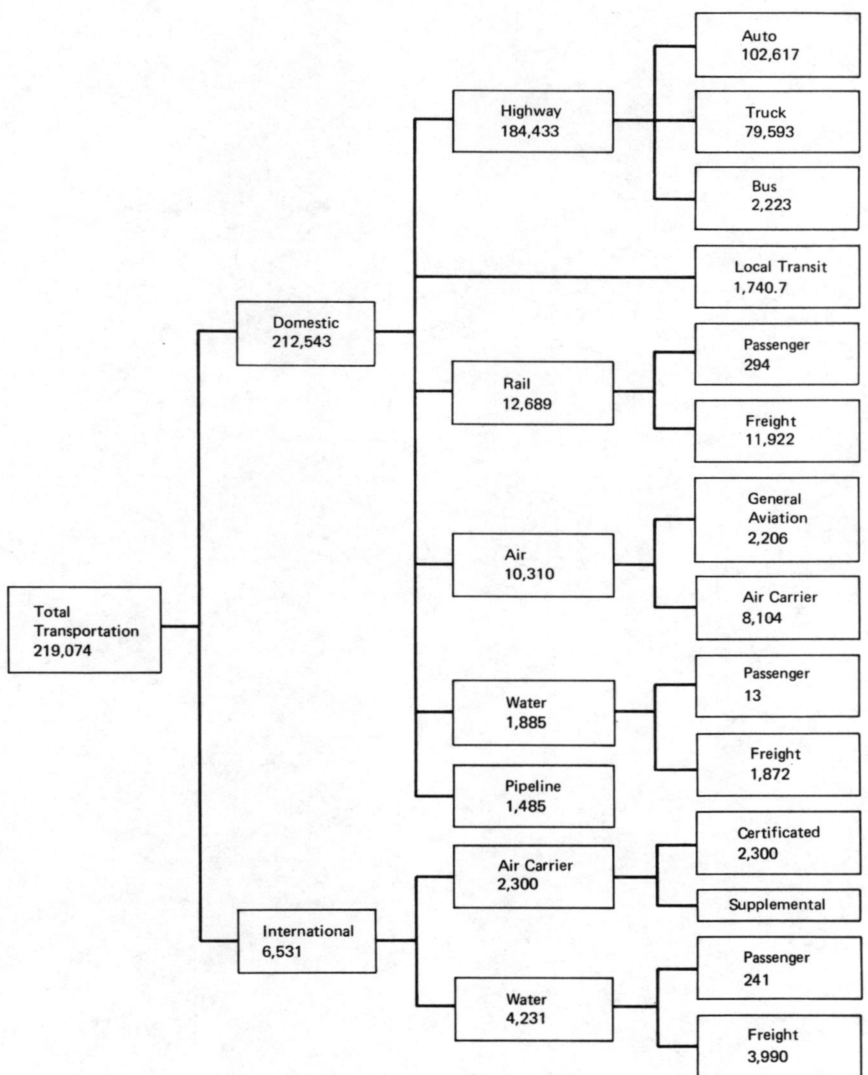

Figure 2-1. Modal Structure of Transportation: Expenditures for Private Modes and Revenues of For-Hire Modes in 1971. Sources: Institute for Defense Analysis, *Economic Characteristics of the Urban Public Transportation Industry* (Washington, D.C.: U.S. Government Printing Office, February 1972); and *Summary of National Transportation Statistics*, Report No. DOT-TSC-OST-73-76 (Washington: U.S. Department of Transportation, November 1973), p. 8. Figures are in millions of dollars.

3 Market Structure and Economic Performance in Transportation

The firms and agencies in the domestic transportation industries are subject to varying degrees of regulation and different types of market structure. The differences in market structure arise both from historical regulatory decisions and from independent factors associated with the internal decisions of the firms' managements. The intention in this chapter is to analyze the effects of these different market structures on market performance, and to offer some specific comments on selected impacts of recent regulatory practices in the transportation industries.

The perennial question arises as to how to evaluate market performance. One way is to emphasize static economic efficiency or the extent to which observed prices and costs correspond to long-run minimum costs. A second yardstick of market performance is the magnitude of technological innovation that is central to any study of costs and production (in any industrial study there will always exist beneath the surface several important relationships among technology, costs, and market performance). Another measure of market performance is the rate of return on investment earned by the industry.

One method of evaluating the static efficiency of an industry is to determine its profits: If the return on investment has been driven down to zero, it might be presented as evidence that prices have approximated long-run minimum average costs. This inference assumes that managements minimize costs; but in the case of the transportation firms in the airline, railroad, and motor trucking industries, cost minimization is unlikely. Yet, this measure of market performance still should reflect the extent to which managements approach cost minimization, as well as the difference between fares (or rates) and minimum costs.

A difficulty with the measurement of minimum costs in the airline industry, for example, is that they depend to some extent on load factors (the proportion of available seats filled by revenue generating passengers). The assumptions of given load factors are to some extent arbitrary, for there is no theory of general load factors.[1] Data from the airline industry over the last decade show that the markup of prices over minimum efficient costs ranged from 15 to 20 percent on the shortest hauls to as high as 90 percent on long hauls.[2] Yet, during this period

1. Crude load factors of 60 percent for air travel and 50 percent for bus and rail passenger service have been adopted in several previous studies; for example, see T.E. Keeler, "The Economics of Passenger Trains," *Journal of Business* 44 (April 1971), pp. 148-74.

2. See T.E. Keeler, "Regulation in Intercity Passenger Transportation," Ph.D. diss., Department of Economics, M.I.T., 1971.

the airlines on the average did not earn higher than normal profits, which would suggest that the relatively poor market performance of the airline industry might be due to low load factors and inefficient operations.[3]

The performance of the California intrastate airlines contrasts sharply with that of the scheduled interstate carriers.[4] For the intra-California markets, fares were calculated to be within 3 percent of estimated minimum efficient costs.[5] The differential between the superior performance of the California intrastate airlines and those of the scheduled interstate carriers is attributed to CAB regulation, which has both excluded new firms and kept fares on high density routes substantially above costs.[6] The relative importance of these two market controls of entry restriction and fare regulation have been quite pronounced and discussed thoroughly in the literature.

The interstate airline industry's relatively poor market performance is coincidental with the facts that the CAB has not permitted entry of any new interstate airlines since its inception in 1938, as well as maintained prices above minimum costs on high-density routes.[7] Yet, even in this industry back-door entry of a peculiar nature has improved the situation more than it appears on the surface. Until the late 1940s passengers did not have the option of flying on an economy class basis. World War II had left a surplus of both pilots and inexpensive aircraft, temporarily lowering the natural barriers to entry into the airline business. Although the CAB could prevent the entry of new scheduled carriers, it could not prevent the new supplemental (nonskeds or charter) airlines from entering the market on unscheduled flights.[8] The supplemental firms entered the most profitable routes and offered low fares with high seating densities to attract passengers from the scheduled flights. The airlines noticed a diversion of business and petitioned the CAB for the right to operate a new, low-cost service. Although the CAB first objected and attempted to obtain a legal injunction against the supplemental carriers, it finally allowed the airlines to implement air-coach service.[9] Another more recent form of entry into certain

3. Ibid.

4. For the most thorough analysis of an intrastate airline situation, see William A. Jordan, *Airline Regulation in America: Effects and Imperfections* (Baltimore: The Johns Hopkins Press, 1970). The evidence that he collects from the intra-California airline markets is used to suggest that CAB encouragement of new and innovative entrants into the interstate markets would be more efficient than the steady expansion of routes of existing carriers. See also a review of Jordan's book by Paul W. Cherington in *Journal of Economic Literature* 10 (June 1973), pp. 496-97.

5. Keeler, "Intercity Passenger Transportation."

6. Jordan, *Airline Regulation.*

7. In 1974, however, the CAB did certify Air New England as a regional air carrier.

8. For a thorough discussion of the charter airlines, see Richard E. Caves, *Air Transport and Its Regulators* (Cambridge: Harvard University Press, 1962), pp. 171-74, 370-71.

9. An extension of air-coach service occurred in 1975 when Eastern Airlines first introduced an economy-class service on its New York-Miami market, and then other trunk airlines offered variations of this "third-class" service.

markets of the airline industry has occurred with the advent of the third-level carriers.[10] Thus, entry of new firms (albeit through the back door) has made the airline industry substantially more efficient than it otherwise would be.[11]

Another standard measure of market performance pertains to the magnitude of technological innovation. This measure raises the issue of whether there are any important differences between market structures conducive to static efficiency and those consistent with a high and effective rate of innovation. In evaluating the market efficiency of innovations, the transportation economist must be concerned with the absolute number of innovations, with the amounts expended on research and development, and with the market success of the innovations. All transportation firms have adopted innovations over the postwar period to some degree. The really interesting question is which carriers have been the most successful in their policies. Although a complete listing of all successful and unsuccessful innovations in the transportation industries is not feasible here, it is possible to sketch a general picture.

In the case of the regulated versus nonregulated airlines, direct comparisons between innovative policies of the interstate and California intrastate carriers have been conducted. For example, William A. Jordan concluded that prior to the late 1950s the interstate carriers had indeed introduced innovations more rapidly than the intrastate carriers that before 1959 did not offer pressurized cabins.[12] After 1959, though, when Pacific Southwest Airlines (PSA) purchased Lockheed Electra aircraft, the intrastate carriers (both PSA and more recently Air California) appear to have been competitively as up-to-date as the interstate carriers. While the California intrastate carriers might have lagged slightly in innovation for a short time in the 1950s, there is at least no evidence that they ever wasted large amounts of money on innovations that were bound to be market failures. The same cannot be claimed for the interstate firms, which in the mid-1950s invested large amounts of money in transcontinental, piston-powered planes that were not only more expensive to operate (on a seat-mile basis) than existing aircraft, but were also to become obsolete within five years because of the introduction of jet aircraft. According to Aaron V. Gellman, this wayward behavior can be traced directly to CAB regulatory policies, which have maintained fares much higher than costs on long-haul routes and have encouraged wasteful service rivalry.[13] The more recent appearance of luxury

10. See Virgil D. Cover, "The Rise of Third Level Air Carriers," *Transportation Journal*, 14 (Fall 1971), pp. 174-87; and J. Cowley, "Air Transportation at Small Cities: Practice, Theory and Policy," M.S. Thesis, Department of Civil Engineering, M.I.T., 1973.

11. The railroad industry did not have any spur of new entry, through the back or front door, because the extremely high fixed costs of the industry precluded entry of new railroads. Furthermore, the ICC policies of forcing continued operation of unprofitable long-haul trains in passenger service slowed (if not blocked) exit.

12. Jordan, *Airline Regulation*, chap. 3.

13. For a full analysis of the effects of CAB regulation on aircraft choice, see Aaron V. Gellman, "The Effect of Regulation on Aircraft Choice," Ph.D. diss., Department of Economics, M.I.T., 1968.

lounges and inflight movies would appear to be examples of the same phenomenon: innovations of questionable value that can be attributed to market imperfections.[14]

On the basis of this brief commentary on innovation policies, it would appear that there is no conflict between market efficiency in the static sense and the effectiveness of innovations. In markets with low-entry barriers, innovations tended to reflect more closely the needs of the market, whereas in those markets subject to higher entry barriers, innovation seems more often to have diverted from the needs of the market. It appears, then, that low-entry barriers play a very decisive role in the efficient operation of markets. This result is quite consistent with microeconomic theory and has certain implications for public policy.[15]

A third measure of market performance relates to the rate of return, a fairly widely used yardstick in the transportation industries. To some extent the rate of return measure is imperfect, since its value depends on the selection of an appropriate denominator. The most frequently used base is investment in fixed plant and equipment, although others appear in the literature from time to time, like annual revenues, stockholders' equity, and net worth. The numerator is usually the same: net income (profit after taxes). Regardless of which measure is used for the transportation industries, one fact remains: Rates of return on the average for the transportation firms have been chronically below those of firms in the unregulated sector. The airline firms have performed best, followed by the motor trucking companies, and then the railroad firms. Perhaps a better utilization of this measure is to compare intraindustry differences among the firms in each transportation industry. The question of why are transportation firm rates of return significantly below the norm needs to be answered in the context of the markets served by these firms.

Regulation and the Transportation Decision Process

From an economic viewpoint very little tangible benefits have resulted from regulation in the intercity passenger transportation markets. Only two reasons for fare regulation in the transportation industries have appeared plausible: first,

14. In the case of railroad passenger service, vistadomes, all-room sleeping cars, and other accoutrements of long-haul luxury trains are a similar example of a collossal mistake in policies of innovation. While the railroads after World War II invested heavily in up-to-date, long-haul equipment, they almost completely ignored the innovations that were suitable to efficient, profitable, short-haul operations, including better signaling for higher speeds and bidirectional equipment to cut short-haul, terminal costs. In the bus industry new features such as rest rooms were popular and adopted by the two large carriers in a relatively short time. Others such as onboard sleeping berths and food service were generally failures and were withdrawn from service quickly in most markets.

15. Joe S. Bain, *Industrial Organization*, 2nd ed. (New York: John Wiley & Sons, 1968).

a natural monopoly situation, with increasing returns to scale in the relevant output area; and second, the need to promote a large transportation system, using profits from high-density routes to subsidize low-density ones. With the exception of the railroad passenger industry, now largely under the responsibility of Amtrak, there is only fragmented evidence of important increasing returns to scale for the carriers, at least on high-density routes.[16] Even in the case of Amtrak, financial statistics show that the short-haul, higher density routes are less costly than the long-haul routes. Cross-subsidization from high-density routes to low-density routes is very common in transportation. It is used by the Highway Trust Fund in applying urban highway profits to subsidize rural roads, by the airlines, and now by Amtrak, which will be using whatever profits it can derive from the short-haul, high-density routes to subsidize long-haul, low-density routes.[17] For low-density airline and rail service, the important question is whether there should be any subsidy at all (most practitioners seem to agree that there should be subsidies for little-used rural highways, such as farm-to-market roads).[18] The large unit of operation in the railroad industry renders its service unsuitable for truly low-density activities. In a global sense it appears that the benefits from fare regulation on high-density routes are very few. On the other hand, the costs of this regulation and entry control are quite substantial. It is this easy to imagine why the demands for the dismantling of this kind of regulation have come to the forefront in recent years.

A popular commentary on the performance of transportation firms is that the further an enterprise (private or public) is away from the rigors of the market, the less likely will it behave efficiently. The bus companies and the intrastate airlines, which are the least regulated and hence closest to the market, appear to have performed with the highest efficiency.[19] The interstate airlines and railroads have displayed some serious shortcomings in terms of efficient performance. The results can be traced partially to regulation and partially to natural barriers to entry.

The highway system, though supposedly controlled to some extent by the rigors of the market (through the Highway Trust Fund), has used the profits of urban roads in order to encourage intercity auto travel at prices well below long-run marginal costs. It is probably in practice the transportation system least

16. These topics are discussed in depth in Chapters 30 and 31.

17. Assuming that subsidies are politically desirable, it is probably preferable to use direct payments from general revenues rather than internal subsidies, the latter essentially the taxation of one good (high-density transportation) to subsidize another (low-density transportation). It has been discussed convincingly in the public finance literature that a general tax is more efficient than a specific tax, yet cross-subsidization entails a specific tax on high-density transportation. Consequently, cross-subsidization would not appear to be so efficient as a subsidy from general revenues.

18. See, for example, Richard A. Musgrave, *The Theory of Public Finance* (New York, McGraw-Hill, 1959), pp. 140-55.

19. Keeler, "Intercity Passenger Transportation."

subject to market controls. In earlier years highway agencies in the United States had a broad mandate to build roads. Highway engineers first were asked to "get the farmer out of the mud," but more recently their job has been to create a network of fast, safe, and efficient highways spanning the country. The new emphasis of these agencies cannot be exclusively or even predominantly on highways. Equal attention should be devoted to the other modes—rail, air, and various technologies of public transportation. The concern should be with the efficient operation of these facilities as a multimodal system to move both passengers and freight, and not simply with their construction. Some relevant options for consideration in future years must include not only capital intensive investments in fixed facilities but also operating, pricing, and regulatory policies, vehicle control strategies, and demonstration projects.

Significant changes are occurring in the *process* by which transportation plans are being developed and decisions made. Transportation agencies have found that their credibility and the confidence of other agencies, officials, and the public are based on the process under which the agency operates. Furthermore, the series of recent environmental laws and associated court decisions relating to highways and other public works projects have contributed to the development of a more legally rigorous process; the largely ad hoc procedures that were satisfactory in the past no longer are acceptable. Some specific process related changes probably should include the following:

1. An increasing concern with the allocation of scarce resources, where decisions would take into consideration the costs of eliminating or minimizing both short- and long-term adverse effects
2. An increased coordination with plans for state, regional, and urban studies
3. A redistribution of decision-making authority with respect to all modes with local and regional institutions being given increased responsibility and a corresponding lessening of the traditional decision-making role for state highway agencies
4. An increasingly active level of the participation by the public in transportation planning, and more than ever before, asking that particular attention be given to providing transportation service tailored to special needs and with a minimum of social and environmental disruption
5. Increased attention to issues of equity, the disaggregate effects of transportation proposals, means of ameliorating negative impacts, and easing the mobility problems of the elderly, the young, the poor, and the disabled.

As a consequence of these changes, agencies' responsibilities are expanding. Social, economic, and environmental studies comprise an increasingly significant portion of their activities, and they are employing increasing numbers of natural and social scientists.[20] A wider variety of alternatives, including policy and operating options as well as facility proposals, are being investigated. Many states have formed separate departments of transportation and are conducting multimodal planning activities. As the transportation field evolves, the objective of simply planning and building roads no longer reflects the breadth and sophistication of the highway agency's activities. In fact, when the "plan and build" objective is carried too far, it can work counter to the best interests both of the highway and the public it serves.

Cynics might argue that politics will always control transportation policy and that considerations of economic efficiency and equitable income distribution will always be in the background (if they are considered at all). One can be certain that these interest groups will continue to press for transport policies that have little justification in terms of either economic efficiency or equitable income distribution. The aviation lobby always will want large subsidies for the development and airports of vertical take-off aircraft (VTOL), which could make short-haul travel for businessmen much faster and easier than it now is. Amtrak will continue to request more subsidies as it erodes its capital on long-haul deficits. The highway lobby will want more intercity highways after the Interstate System is completed. The CAB will want to regulate vertical take-off aircraft fares and entry, and the first VTOL carriers will support such action (as has occurred with air taxis).

More private ownership without subsidy might be advocated as a better method of achieving efficiency, but private ownership of, say, the highways would have many awkward and undesirable aspects. Besides, in industries with high natural entry barriers such as railroads, private ownership is no guarantee of economic efficiency.[21] It may in fact be that public intervention in rail passenger service through Amtrak actually will improve efficiency.[22] The problem is simply that there are many transport agencies (railroads in the private sector and highways and airports in the public sector) that for various reasons have been too distant from market forces. While it is not apparent how these market checks can be integrated into the transportation system in a politically acceptable

20. A good example of these studies would be the large research effort mounted by M.I.T.'s Urban Systems Laboratory over the last five years. The research (funded by the National Cooperative Highway Research Program; Federal Highway Administration, U.S. Department of Transportation; and the California Department of Transportation) resulted in the publication of numerous reports by Marvin L. Manheim and his associates in the areas of community and environmental factors in the transportation planning process, including project, corridor, and systems planning.

21. It is often alleged that if the railroads' rights-of-way were subsidized, similar to the Trust Fund concept prevalent in the motor trucking industry, economic efficiency in the railroad would increase. This point is the thrust of the "Confac" proposal for a Consolidated Facilities Corporation put forth by the United States Railway Association (USRA) in 1975.

22. There is no question that any efficiency gains have been retarded by the cumbersome and costly contractual arrangements between the railroads, which own or lease passenger equipment, and Amtrak, which operates the equipment for the railroads.

manner, one observation is clear: The institutional solutions have serious shortcomings and improvements are critically necessary.

4 Marginal Analysis Models of the Firm

In the field of microeconomics the term *theory of the firm* is a collection of theories about the structure and behavior of firms operating under a special set of environmental conditions known in the aggregate as a market economy. For the most part, neoclassical price theory treats the firm in a holistic way by considering it as a collective economic unit pursuing one or more goals or objectives in a completely rational manner.[1] Holistic models view the firm as a "unified acting entity or organism"[2] in which input and output decisions are made simultaneously in the context of a given objective of the firm and in light of given information on product (service) demand, factor supply, and production technology.[3] The purpose of this chapter is to describe and analyze several alternative economic models of the firm within the general class of "marginal analysis" models. *Marginal analysis* is the heart of neoclassical price theory and reflects models in which choices between alternative input-output combinations are made on the basis of infinitesimal changes in those combinations.[4] The models reflect the integration of the independent neoclassical theories of demand, production, and cost into a unified framework, consisting of alternative market structures like perfect competition, monopoly, and imperfect competition.

The basic hypotheses and notions of standards for industrial and economic performance can be obtained from these models of economic theory. It is necessary to examine the concepts of structure and performance from these models as a precondition to evaluating the public policy issues of industrial organization and transportation economics. These concepts are useful to the economist in analyzing the fundamentals of the economic theory of markets and in providing a linkage between the theory and various empirical studies of market structure. These fundamentals will include brief discussions of the

1. Milton Friedman, *Price Theory* (Chicago: Aldine Publishing Co., 1962).

2. Joseph M. McGuire, *Theories of Business Behavior* (Englewood Cliffs, N.J.: Prentice-Hall, Inc., 1964).

3. Contrasted with holistic models would be behavioral models of the firm that incorporate the empirical features of organizational behavior into their analyses. The classic treatment is provided in Richard M. Cyert and James A. March, *A Behavioral Theory of the Firm* (Englewood Cliffs, N.J.: Prentice-Hall, Inc., 1963).

4. Under marginal analysis the firm's demand, production and cost functions are all continuous; furthermore, the first and second partial derivatives of these functions are assumed to exist; and finally, these models assume static equilibrium, complete certainty, and perfect divisibility of inputs and outputs.

economic models of competition and monopoly and their performance implications. While these two models represent extreme cases of economic models, there may be particular and specialized markets in transportation that conform to their characteristics. Of the two extremes, it is more likely that transportation firms operate in monopoly markets than in perfectly competitive ones. Even more likely is the belief that transportation firms participate in imperfectly competitive markets, like monopolistic competition and a variety of oligopolies. This chapter, then, discusses the cases of perfect competition, monopoly, and monopolistic competition, while the following chapter centers on oligopoly models. The models in this chapter stress the neoclassical objective, which is the heart of the theory of the firm—profit maximization.

Perfect Competition

This market structure consists of firms producing an item Z and selling this product (or service) in a market characterized by: (1) product homogeneity, (2) many firms, (3) many consumers, (4) freedom of entry, (5) perfect information, and (6) no collusion. The market price P for the competitive firm's product is determined by the intersection of the market demand function and the market supply function.[5] The firm's total cost function is assumed to be of the form[6]

$$C = f(Z) \tag{4.1}$$

The firm's profit π is by definition equal to the difference between total revenue R and total cost C:

$$\pi = R - C \tag{4.2}$$

$$= P \cdot Z - f(Z) \tag{4.3}$$

Total profit is maximized when the derivative of profit with respect to output is equal to zero:

$$\frac{d\pi}{dZ} = P - \frac{d(C)}{dZ} = 0 \tag{4.4}$$

or when marginal cost MC is equal to price:

$$MC = P \tag{4.5}$$

5. Therefore, the revenue function *OR* will be linear.

6. It can be of any shape, but the most conventional is one with a double inflection point, as shown in Figure 4-1.

which graphically will hold when the slope of the firm's total cost function is equal to the slope of the total revenue function. In Figure 4-1 total profit (ST) is at a maximum at output Z_0, when the vertical distance between TR and C is a maximum. In examining Figure 4-1, one can find that MC also equals P at output Z_1 but total profit is clearly not at a maximum.[7]

In the short run, when the firm cannot vary its fixed factors of production, it will have no incentive to change its rate of output from the level at which $MC = P$. Total profit will decrease when output is either increased above Z_0 or decreased below Z_0 in Figure 4-1. Hence, the firm is said to be in short-run equilibrium when output is such that $MC = P$. Figure 4-2 suggests an important limitation to the profit-maximization rule: If price falls below average variable cost (AVC), say at price P_3, the firm's profit will be greater (or its loss will be less) if it produces no output at all than if it produces a positive output. In this

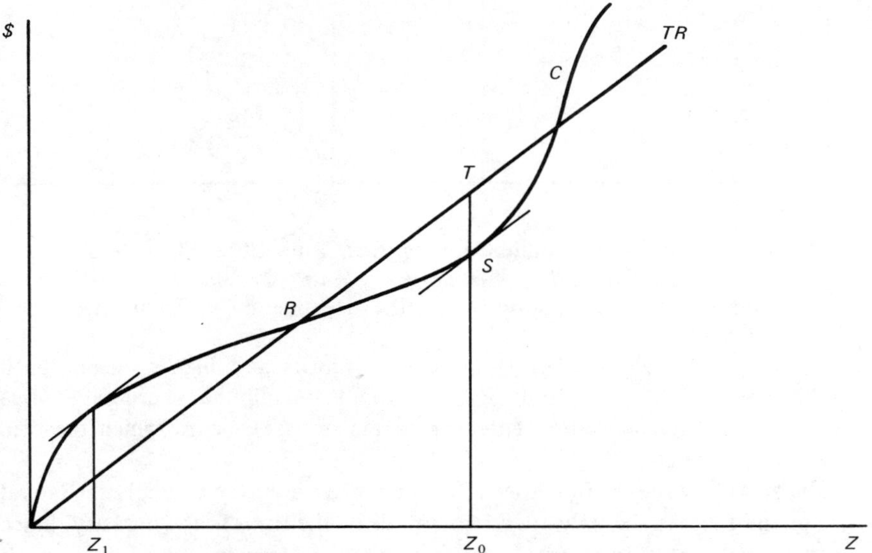

Figure 4-1. Profit Maximization for the Competitive Firm. Source: James T. Kneafsey, *The Economics of the Transportation Firm* (Lexington, Mass.: Lexington Books, D.C. Heath and Co., 1974), p. 38.

---

7. In fact, total profit is negative and at a minimum at output Z_1. To guarantee that total profit is maximized when $MC = P$, the second derivative of profit must be negative:

$$\frac{d^2\pi}{dZ^2} = \frac{-d^2C}{dZ^2} < 0 \text{ or } \frac{d(MC)}{dZ} < 0$$

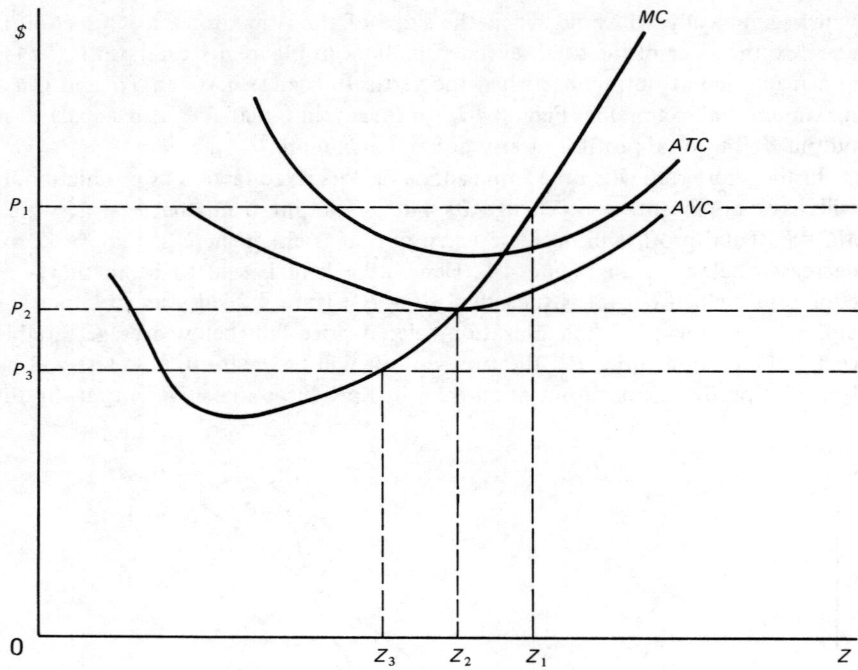

Figure 4-2. Short-run Equilibrium for the Competitive Firm. Source: James T. Kneafsey, *The Economics of the Transportation Firm* (Lexington, Mass.: Lexington Books, D.C. Heath and Co., 1974), p. 39.

figure a price of P_1 will bring temporary profits and higher output until equilibrium price ($\bar{P}$) and output ($\bar{Z}$) prevail. P_2 is the minimum acceptable price (in the case of transportation enterprises, rate or fare), below which the firm should cease operations.

The short-run supply function for a competitive industry is simply the lateral sum of the short-run supply functions for all of the firms in the industry. Since the short-run supply function of each firm in the industry has a positive slope, it follows that the industry short-run supply function is fixed. This is attributable to two factors: First, the supply functions (*MC* functions) of all of the firms in the industry are fixed in the short run; and second, in the short run there are not sufficient time and opportunity for new firms to enter, or for existing firms to leave the industry. In the long run, however, all factors of production are variable. Figure 4-3 shows the long-run marginal cost curve (*MC*) and the average total cost curve (*ATC*) for a typical firm in a competitive industry. Both *MC* and *ATC* are derived from the firm's long-run total cost function, and since there are no fixed factors in the long run, average total cost is equal to average variable cost.

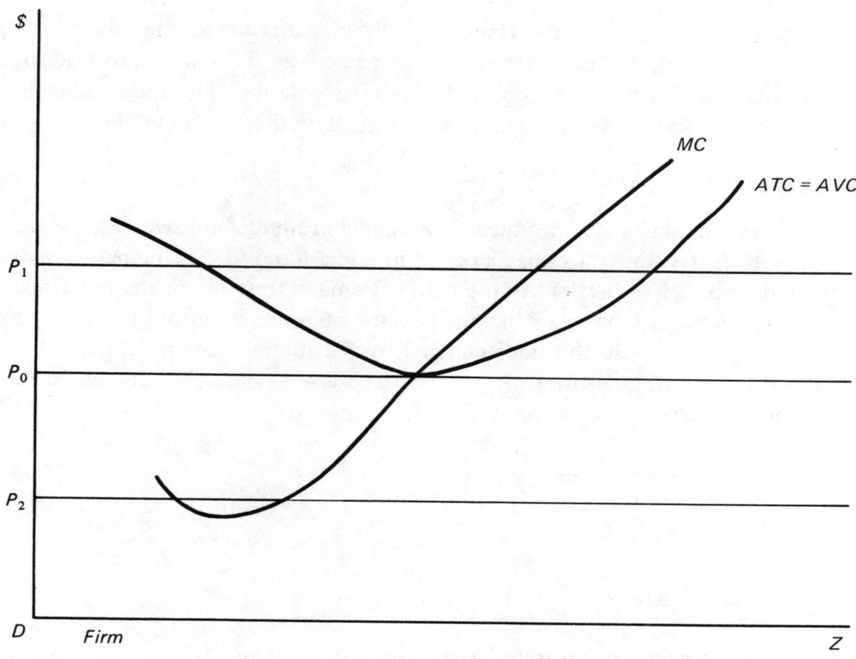

Figure 4-3. Long-run Equilibrium for a Perfectly Competitive Firm. Source: James T. Kneafsey, *The Economics of the Transportation Firm* (Lexington, Mass.: Lexington Books, D.C. Heath and Co., 1974), p. 40.

The long-run equilibrium conditions for a perfectly competitive industry are that every firm in the industry maximizes profit ($P = MC$) and that a long-run minimum ATC (including normal profit) for every firm in the industry be just equal to the market price P. If this latter condition does not hold, then firms will either be entering or leaving the industry. Combining the short-run equilibrium condition $P - MC$ with the long-run equilibrium condition $ATC = P$ yields:

$$P = MC = ATC \tag{4.6}$$

where MC and ATC are now long-run costs rather than short-run. The firm's long-run supply function is simply that portion of its increasing long-run MC curve that lies above long-run AVC (which is equal to ATC). If price falls below minimum ATC then zero output is produced.[8] Since it is an extreme, the model of perfect competition in practice is recognized as an unattractive ideal. Consequently, performance becomes difficult to describe. The most valuable aspect of this market model, though, resides in its hypothetical foundations.

Monopoly

This market model has a sole producer of a unique product Z for which there are no close substitutes. Entry to this market is in effect blocked. The demand curve for the monopolist is equivalent to the market demand function in a competitive market since there may be many buyers. Because increases in output can only be achieved by reductions in the price charged by the monopolist, the monopolist cannot sell unlimited quantities of its output at a given price. The demand curve for a monopoly firm may be expressed as

$$P = P(Z) \text{ where } \frac{dP}{dZ} < 0 \tag{4.7}$$

or

$$AR = AR(Z) \tag{4.8}$$

where AR denotes average revenue. Total revenue is defined as

$$TR(Z) = P(Z) \cdot Z \tag{4.9}$$

For the monopolist, the necessary condition for profit maximization is that

$$\frac{d\pi}{dZ} = \frac{dTR}{dZ} - \frac{dC}{dZ} = 0 \tag{4.10}$$

or, as before,

$$MR = MC, \tag{4.11}$$

the equalizing of marginal revenue and marginal costs.[9]

8. The long-run supply function for the industry is more intricate. An industry characterized by fixed factor prices is called a *constant-cost industry.* An *increasing-cost industry* is one where an increase in the industry's output as a whole may bid up prices of the inputs and/or may cause an unfavorable shift in a firm's production functions, both of which tend to increase the total cost of firms in the industry. A *decreasing-cost industry* is one that increases in output for the industry as a whole lead to favorable technological progress and/or the discovery of cheaper sources of raw materials, both of which tend to reduce the total costs of firms in the industry. These distinctions are quite important in the transportation industries, where estimations of economies of scale have important public policy implications.

9. A sufficient condition for profit maximization is that the firm's profit function be strictly concave over all Z. That is, the second derivative of profit with respect to output must be negative: $d^2\Pi/dZ^2 < 0$. The second derivative of the firm's profit function will be negative if the firm's marginal revenue function is decreasing and if its cost function behaves in a certain prescribed manner.

The optimum level of output $\bar{Z}$ for the monopolist can be found by solving equations (4.10) or (4.11) for Z. It is assumed that $AR(\bar{Z}) \geqslant AVC(\bar{Z})$ or otherwise the firm will produce nothing in the short run. The monopolist's optimum selling price $\bar{P}$ can be found by substituting $\bar{Z}$ into equation (4.8). Figure 4-4 illustrates graphically the monopolist's optimum price-output decision.

The preceding analysis of the behavior of the monopolist has been limited to the short run. However, since entry to the industry is blocked, the analysis of a monopolist's behavior in the long run is of limited interest. The only difference between the long-run and short-run monopolist cases is in terms of the possible shapes of the cost function.

The equilibrium output of the monopolist has the important property that price exceeds marginal cost. This divergence is the usual basis for the policy condemnation of monopolies, since a price-marginal cost gap supposedly represents a misallocation of resources by virtue of the restriction of output. The result of this output restriction is that a marginal dollar's worth of resources produces more than a dollar's worth of output (since price exceeds marginal cost) in a monopoly, whereas in competition the marginal dollar of resources produces exactly one dollar of output (since price equals marginal cost): the inference being that reallocating resources from competitive industries to

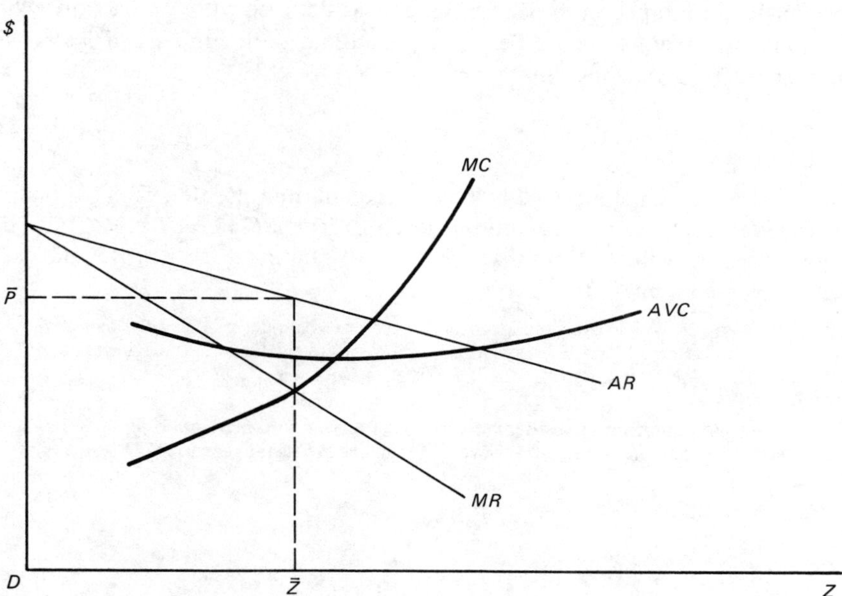

Figure 4-4. The Monopolist's Optimum Price-Output Decision. Source: James T. Kneafsey, *The Economics of the Transportation Firm* (Lexington, Mass.: Lexington Books, D.C. Heath and Co., 1974), p. 42.

monopolies would increase the value of the economy's output. Consequently, performance in the context for monopoly firms is regarded as poor. In the case of the transportation industries, responsibility for insuring adequate performance has been assigned to the independent regulatory commissions.[10]

Imperfect Competition

Imperfect or monopolistic competition is a term used to describe market situations that lie somewhere between the two extremes of perfect competition and pure monopoly. In the theory of "monopolistic competition," five of the assumptions of perfect competition are retained: (1) many firms, (2) many consumers, (3) freedom of entry, (4) perfect information, and (5) no collusion. The assumption of product homogeneity is dropped: That is, each firm is assumed to offer a product or service that is differentiated in some way from that of its competitors. This is a situation that most nearly corresponds to the real world activities of some railroads and motor trucking firms.

The demand curve for a monopolistically competitive firm has a negative slope with the managers of a typical firm assumed to behave as though their actions had no effect on the behavior of competitors. In the short run firms will maximize profit by maintaining an output level at which MC equals MR. This condition is necessary and sufficient for profit maximization if the firm's marginal profit function is decreasing, as was the case with a monopoly. With freedom of entry, as under perfect competition, both profits and losses will approach zero in the long run, that is,

$$AR = ATC \tag{4.12}$$

Figure 4-5 shows graphically the long-run equilibrium position of the monopolistically competitive firm. At output level $\bar{Z}$, $MR = MC$ and $AR = ATC$ with the equilibrium price of $\bar{P}$. Note that the point of tangency between AR and ATC lies above minimum ATC.[11]

10. The extent to which this regulation is effective is a subject of debate. For a review of some of the selected writings on this topic, see my book, *The Economics of the Transportation Firm* (Lexington, Mass.: Lexington Books, D.C. Heath & Co., 1974), chap. 4.

11. It is easy to demonstrate mathematically that the long-run, marginal cost curve in Figure 4-5 intersects MR at the same output level $\bar{Z}$ for which AR is tangent to ATC.

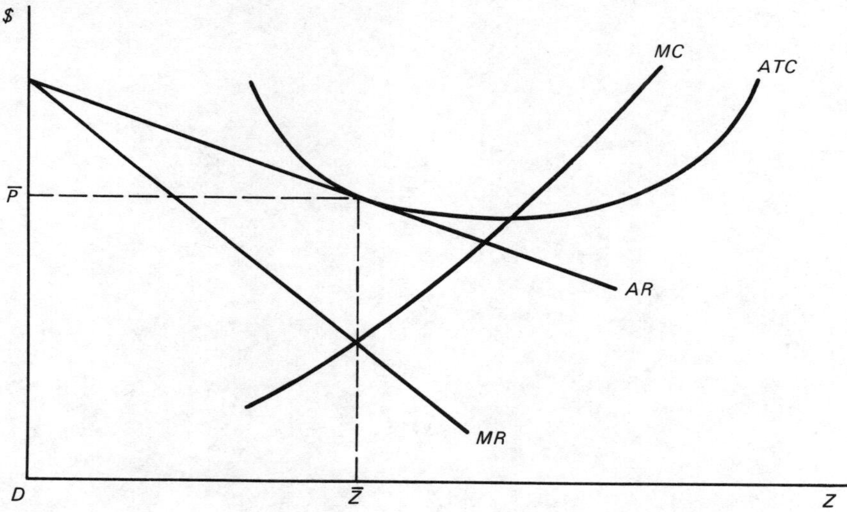

Figure 4-5. Long-run Equilibrium for a Firm Under Monopolistic Competition. Source: James T. Kneafsey, *The Economics of the Transportation Firm* (Lexington, Mass.: Lexington Books, D.C. Heath and Co., 1974), p. 44.

5 Oligopoly Models for Transportation Markets

The cases of pure competition, monopoly, and monopolistic competition discussed in Chapter 4 reflect well-developed and unified theories of market behavior: An important exception to these theories is the case of oligopoly, which essentially is a market structure where the number of sellers is small enough for the behavior of one firm to affect the behavior of the other firms in that market. There is no unique theory of oligopoly, but rather:

> The typical industrial organization economist interested in examining the behavior of firms in market environments characterized by small numbers, does not approach his task with any unified set of analytical tools which one could call "the theory of oligopoly." Instead, he comes armed with a whole smorgasbord of formal models, ad hoc models, case study information, stories, and vague notions concerning the impact of business psychology and sociology. The various theories, whether they be formal or informal, are based on a bewildering collection of *a priori* behavioral assumptions, formal mathematics, hard case study information, casual empiricism, hand waving and as much as possible of the traditional theory of the atomistic competitive firm.[1]

The formal models of oligopoly and duopoly can be traced back to 1838 when Augustin Cournot, a French mathematical-political economist, developed the first explicitly oligopolistic model. Since that time numerous propositions on theories of oligopoly have been advanced but no agreement has been reached among economists on the description of a universal oligopoly model. Part of the difficulty in developing a general theory of oligopoly behavior can be traced to the nature of markets. The other part of the problem is simply due to the lack of adequate analytical tools:

> The oral tradition of industrial organization abounds with many behavioral stories about pricing, entry, R&D, financing, etc., but they have not been incorporated into our theoretical conception of industrial markets. We have spent too much time calculating too many kinds of concentration ratios and running too many regressions of these against profit figures of questionable validity. We have spent too little time analyzing regularities in behavior that arise from structural characteristics other than concentration including the structure of internal organization, the nature of basic learning, diffusion, and information processes. . . . Nevertheless, the essence of the oligopoly problem is behavior, and if the tools are not to be found in the conventional theory of the firm we might consider developing tools that are appropriate.[2]

1. Paul L. Joskow, "Firm Decisionmaking Processes and Oligopoly Theory", *American Economic Review, Papers and Proceedings*, 65 (May 1975), forthcoming.

2. Ibid.

In spite of these conceptual difficulties, this chapter suggests that the most appropriate market model for describing the behavior of the transportation industries is the oligopoly model.

Nature of Transportation Markets

In previous economic studies of scale effects in the airline industry, attempts have been made to relate the total airline system output of a homogeneous item denoted as seat-miles (or ton-miles) to the systems inputs. The results of these studies almost without exception have suggested constant returns to scale. On an individual market basis, however, these studies cannot offer any such guideline. For, as Robert W. Simpson has argued:

> . . . If we look at the individual market, and see the reduction in costs which comes from using larger aircraft, it seems clear that economic efficiency argues that load sizes should be increased, and therefore the number of suppliers reduced. After aircraft sizes of around 300 seats are being used, this effect is not strong—at least for present technology.
>
> One could postulate that at the market level, this economy of scale would probably be true for most forms of transportation where vehicle or train size can be increased. . . . It is difficult to see any 'diseconomies of scale' at the market level. This argues that transportation service is a natural monopoly when systems are operated efficiently.[3]

These questions of scale effects and cost calculations are critical in determining the behavior of the participants in airline and other transportation markets.[4] As will be seen in the discussion of the various modes in Chapters 10 to 12, the market structures of the major transportation industries are quite different from one another. Nonetheless, these industries do appear to pursue business practices that might be characterized as oligopolistic. In only a minority of instances are transportation markets characterized by monopoly or competitive situations.

In airline economics the demand function is usually specified for given city pair markets, but the supply function characterizes the behavior of operators who offer a scheduled (sometimes demand responsive) transportation system

3. Robert W. Simpson, "A Theory for Domestic Airline Economics," *Proceedings of the Transportation Research Forum* 15 (October 1974), p. 305.

4. In general, the cost function for a transportation service, like intercity airline operators, consists of fixed costs (*FC*) and variable costs (*VC*). The latter are costs which vary when the quantities of output (Z) or the level of service of output or quality of service (Q) are changed. The Civil Aeronautics Board collects and publishes data that can be used to describe with reasonable accuracy the average costs of domestic airlines operating a fleet of jet subsonic aircraft and to relate these costs to the causal input factors like crew hours, fuel, maintenance, ground operations, and so on.

over a whole network. While the operators (suppliers) may be optimizing over their network of services, they may not be optimizing in any given city pair market.

In order to measure economies of scale, one must be able to estimate long-run average costs for the mode offering transportation services (Chapters 30 and 31 focus on this issue). In the same manner, transportation analysts need to estimate marginal cost–the derivative of cost with respect to quantity or $\partial C/\partial Z$. The difficulty in this situation is that marginal cost may be a very elusive term: It will be dependent on numerous scheduling and routing functions of the transportation firm so that the marginal cost of providing transportation service will vary over time of day, length of haul, and the network of markets. Since each transportation system should be maximizing system profit by equating its marginal revenue and marginal cost, it should be useful to briefly describe typical situations where marginal cost depends on scheduling and routing of vehicles. From the following discussion, the reader will notice that it is difficult to determine marginal cost for a transportation system in any generalized way. In spite of this difficulty, reasonable approximations to marginal cost are usually sufficient in most economic analyses of markets.

Figure 5-1 is a depiction of the four most frequently observed types of transportation markets. Any single transportation firm may face one or more of these markets in scheduling and routing its fleet of operating equipment or rolling stock. These markets thus can be segmented into problems and requirements for the backhaul, the repositioning, the tag end, and the shuttle.

Backhaul

This phrase is used quite widely in each of the transportation modes. It applies to the motor carrier who needs a return loading after hauling its cargo from point *A* to *B* (in Figure 5-1); it applies in the same way to railroad car utilization. It can occur in scheduled passenger systems, for example, the famous "Red Eye" flights to reposition aircraft arriving on the West Coast in the evening back to the East Coast for following morning utilization. In its simplest form, a service is performed from *A* to *B*, and since the vehicle is based in *A*, it must return to *A*. What is the marginal cost of supplying space (cargo or seats) in the market *BA*? What is the marginal cost of supplying space in market *AB*? Should prices be lowered in market *BA* to make efficient use of the return trip? Even with currently available empirical information, these questions are difficult to answer.

Repositioning

This is a generalization of the backhaul problem illustrated in Figure 5-1 where the vehicle is dispatched onward to *C* rather than returned to *A* so that services

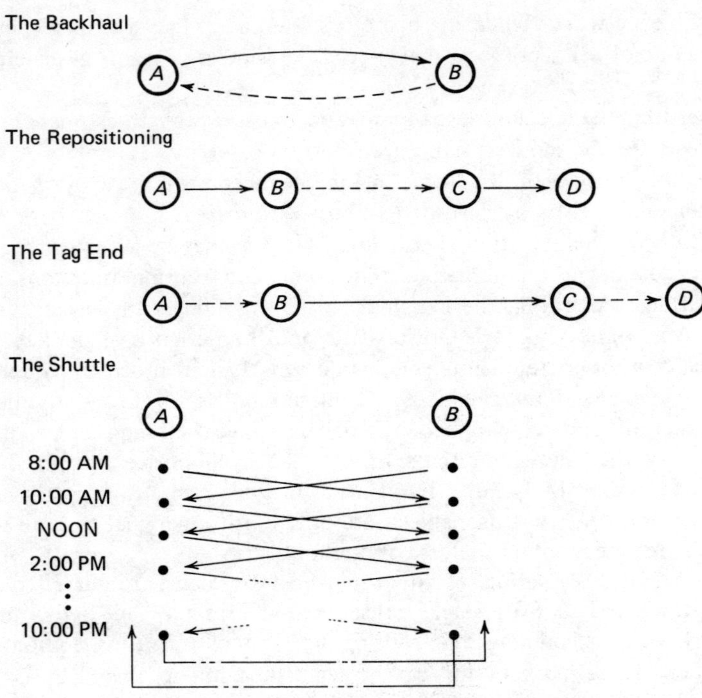

Figure 5-1. Types of Transportation Markets.

C to *D* may be provided. This repositioning of the vehicle is caused by a desire to obtain revenue in market *AB* and then market *CD*. How should the costs of repositioning be split over these two markets? Should prices in markets *AC*, *BC*, and *BD* be lowered in order to generate additional demand to the empty *BC* under the aegis of economic efficiency? What would be the reactions by competitors to a single carrier's reduction in price?

Tag End

Another variation is the tag-end operation that is found most often in the airline industry. In this situation the flight is routed *ABCD* to provide services over a long haul between *B* and *C*. The four markets intended to be served are *AC*, *AD*, and *BC*, *BD*. Incidental markets are *AB* and *CD*, which may be served rather inefficiently by a large capacity, long-range aircraft. What then are the marginal costs of supplying services in the primary four markets?

Shuttle

To display a similar point in a time of day routing example, consider a shuttle pattern between cities *A* and *B*. The map in Figure 5-1 represents the time of day routing pattern for two vehicles that supply services in a short-haul market. Two overnight "arcs" return the vehicles to the top of the pattern for the following day's operations. It is apparent that the marginal revenue and marginal cost depend upon the complete pattern of daily services in such a market. In its Boston-New York (Newark)-Washington shuttle service, Eastern Airlines operates its equipment as a separate fleet, independent of its other routes.

To determine the true marginal cost and marginal revenue of adding or deleting seats in markets, a profit optimizing model for the scheduling function needs to be developed. It should be clear that the marginal cost for one carrier in a market may be quite different from another depending upon the situation of that market in the network of each carrier, and depending upon how the carrier decides to combine its services. The point to be stressed in this discussion is that there does not exist any unique marginal cost for a given market that can be used in the usual classical microeconomic analysis. In spite of this statement, one can and should continue to analyze isolated markets or even hypothetical markets where we assume known marginal cost values or empirically derived approximations of marginal cost.[5] Also, in spite of these barriers, transportation firms and agencies still must make decisions on the bases of limited information. Some knowledge of marginal cost and marginal revenue must be available, especially in markets characterized by a few, large sellers of transportation services (or other industrial products).

Models of Oligopoly Behavior

Given the description of the demand and cost functions in the previous chapter, it is now possible to develop formal models that can explain the likely behavior of sellers in transportation markets as they seek equilibrium among price and cost, quantity demanded and quantity supplied, and quality of service. When the number of participants in a market is small enough for the behavior of one firm to affect the behavior of other firms in the market, a plethora of models can be offered to explain the interdependence of firms and the possibilities of collusion.[6] Within the framework of neoclassical economics, the following

5. Chapters 28 and 29 focus on the estimation of cost functions.

6. A useful discussion of extensions in oligopoly theory appears in Thomas H. Naylor and John M. Vernon, *Microeconomics and Decision Models of the Firm* (New York: Harcourt, Brace and World, Inc., 1969), chaps. 5, 17, and 18.

section identifies and discusses three general classes of oligopoly behavior: first, conjectural variation models; second, price-leadership models; and third, behavioral oligopoly models. In order to provide a general scope of the neoclassical oligopoly models, the following discussion initially outlines the basic structure of six conjectural variation models: (1) the Cournot model, (2) the Edgeworth model, (3) the collusion model, (4) the Stackelberg model, (5) the market-shares model, and (6) the kinked-demand model. Following this is a summary of the underlying logical structure of two price-leadership models and one important behavioral model of oligopoly.

Concept of Conjectural Variations

For purposes of our discussion, let us consider a three-firm oligopoly as being characteristic of many transportation markets. The analysis can easily be extended to a monopoly or to an *n*-firm oligopoly as conditions warrant. The purpose of this discussion is to illustrate the concept of conjectural variations that lies at the heart of neoclassical oligopoly theory. Assume here that the three firms offer transportation services at the same average revenue or price P.[7] Let Z_1, Z_2, and Z_3 denote the output of the three firms, respectively, so that the total output offered (regardless of its empirical dimensions) is

$$Z = Z_1 + Z_2 + Z_3 \tag{5.1}$$

The industry demand function can be specified as $P = P(Z)$ and the total revenue for the ith firm then will be

$$TR_i = P(Z_i) = TR_i(Z_1, Z_2, Z_3) \tag{5.2}$$

Total profit, Π_i, for the ith firm would be

$$\Pi_i \equiv TR_i - TC_i(Z_i) \text{ for } i = 1,2,3 \tag{5.3}$$

where TC_i is the total cost function of the ith firm. To determine the profit maximization level for *each* firm, equation (5.3) must be differentiated with respect to each firm's output and the resulting derivatives set equal to zero:

$$\frac{d\Pi_1}{dZ_1} = \left(\frac{\delta TR_1}{\delta Z_1} + \frac{\delta TR_1}{\delta Z_2} \cdot \frac{dZ_2}{dZ_1} + \frac{\delta TR_1}{\delta Z_3} \cdot \frac{dZ_3}{dZ_1}\right) - \frac{dTC_1}{dZ_1} = 0 \tag{5.4}$$

7. This assumption involves some flexibility with the systems of rates and fares adopted by the carriers. To the extent that average revenue for unit of output reflects price, this assumption should be satisfactory.

$$\frac{d\Pi_2}{dZ_2} = \left(\frac{\delta TR_2}{\delta Z_1} \cdot \frac{dZ_1}{dZ_2} + \frac{\delta TR_2}{\delta Z_2} + \frac{\delta TR_2}{\delta Z_3} \cdot \frac{dZ_3}{dZ_2}\right) - \frac{dTC_2}{dZ_2} = 0 \quad (5.5)$$

$$\frac{d\Pi_3}{dZ_3} = \left(\frac{\delta TR_3}{\delta Z_1} \cdot \frac{dZ_1}{dZ_3} + \frac{\delta TR_3}{\delta Z_2} \cdot \frac{dZ_2}{dZ_3} + \frac{\delta TR_3}{\delta Z_3}\right) - \frac{dTC_3}{dZ_3} = 0 \quad (5.6)$$

These three equations then can be solved for Z_1, Z_2, and Z_3 if we know either the function forms or the values of:

$$\frac{dZ_1}{dZ_2}, \frac{dZ_1}{dZ_3}, \frac{dZ_2}{dZ_1}, \frac{dZ_2}{dZ_3}, \frac{dZ_3}{dZ_1}, \text{ and } \frac{dZ_3}{dZ_2}$$

These six derivations are the conjectural variations of the three-firm oligopoly market.

Cournot Model

The behavioral assumption in the Cournot model is that each firm optimizes its profit by varying the *quantity* of supply while assuming that the quantities supplied by other competitors remain constant. This assumption suggests that the conjectural variation derivatives in equations (5.4), (5.5), and (5.6) are zero. This further implies that each firm in the industry offers output at the level at which marginal revenue and marginal cost are equalized, or when

$$MR_i = MC_i \text{ for } i = 1,2,3 \quad (5.7)$$

If the second order conditions for each firm holds, that is, if

$$\frac{\delta^2 \Pi}{\delta Z_i^2} < 0 \text{ for } i = 1,2,3 \quad (5.8)$$

or

$$\frac{d(MR_i)}{dZ_i} < \frac{d(MC_i)}{dZ_i} \text{ for } i = 1,2,3 \quad (5.9)$$

then equation (5.7) can be solved for the equilibrium levels of Z_1, Z_2, and Z_3 for the transportation market with three firms.

Another term of significance in the conjectural variations framework is that of a reaction function, which expresses the output of each firm as a function of the other competing firms in the market. Reaction functions for the three-firm market can be obtained by solving for Z_1 in the first equation in equation (5.7), for Z_2 in the second equation, and for Z_3 in the third equation:

$$Z_1 = g_1(Z_2, Z_3) \tag{5.10}$$

$$Z_2 = g_2(Z_1, Z_3) \tag{5.11}$$

$$Z_3 = g_3(Z_1, Z_2) \tag{5.12}$$

Firm 1's reaction function in equation (5.10) yields a relationship between Z_1 and the output levels for firms 2 and 3 with the requirement that for any specified values of Z_2 and Z_3, the corresponding value of Z_1 will be a profit maximizing level for firm 1. Similar interpretations apply to the reaction functions associated with Z_2 and Z_3. An equilibrium solution is reached when there exists a set of values for Z_1, Z_2, and Z_3 that satisfy all three reaction functions.

Edgeworth Model

The Edgeworth model focuses on conjectural variations in terms of *price* changes rather than output changes. It has limited applications in transportation markets, principally because rate and fare levels are usually prescribed by regulatory agencies. However, with the general tendency presently toward a relaxation of fare and rate standards, various price experimentations in the near future (by airlines in particular) may render this model more useful.

Collusion Model

The solution to the collusion model occurs when the aggregate profit for all suppliers in the market is maximized. All agree to supply quantities to the market equivalent to assuming that the firms merge into a single monopoly, and then some agreement is made concerning cross-payments to each other from the excess profit that occurs. This class of solutions in international airline markets has been called *pooling.*[8] It has also occurred in various ways in the United States under the name of *capacity agreements*. These agreements generally involve the scaling down of flights offered in selected city-pair markets. While some carriers' practices have raised questions of antitrust statute violations, the capacity agreements to date have received the blessings of the CAB.

8. Simpson, "Domestic Airline Economics."

Stackelberg Model

The concepts of leadership and followership were introduced long ago into duopoly theory by Heinreich von Stackelberg. If all market participants are passive, or "followers," the Cournot solution is merely a special case of the Stackelberg model. However, if any participant becomes aggressive and knows the reaction functions of the competitors, the leadership firm can solve for a position where profit is maximized, with the effect that this firm can lead the market to that position. Assuming that the competitors remain passive followers, they will find a solution if the leading firm is supplying the optimum amount. If any follower also decides to be aggressive, there is no equilibrium solution. Instead, economic warfare occurs until the firms adopt compatible leader-follower roles or establish collusion. As long as one firm behaves like a leader and the other (or others in the case of oligopoly) like a follower, then stable solutions will result if the first- and second-order conditions for profit maximization are satisfied.

Market-share Model

Rather than maximizing profit, a firm may simply try to retain a given market share. The firm can use this strategy to be a leader in the market, or it can be a follower whose reaction pattern is to retain market share. Even as a follower, such a policy for a high-cost competitor can be fruitful if it causes the profit seeking leader to proceed to a different solution. In the duopoly case the market-share model requires one of the firms to maintain a constant share (k) of the total market (perhaps in revenues, or in revenue passenger-miles, or in passengers, etc.):

$$k_1 = \frac{Z_1}{Z_1 + Z_2} \tag{5.13}$$

Solving for Z_1 and assuming that firm 1's conjectural variation derivative is zero $(dZ_2/dZ_1) = 0$, firm 1's output will be:

$$Z_1 = \frac{k_1 Z_2}{(1 - k_1)} \tag{5.14}$$

The other firm will maximize its own profit, utilizing the knowledge of the first firm's market-share goal. The other firm's profit function becomes, upon substitution from equation (5.14):

$$\Pi_2 = f_2 \left[Z_2, \frac{k_1, Z_2}{(1 - k_1)}\right] \tag{5.15}$$

Firm 2 then maximizes Π_2 with respect to Z_2. Through the use of this strategy, the firm with the constant market share thus attempts to derive the long-range advantages associated with a stable portion or share of the market.

Kinked-demand Curve Model

The kinked-demand curve is a classic textbook model of oligopolistic firms. It assumes that the oligopolistic firm's demand curve consists of two portions of separate average revenue functions that intersect at a point which looks like a kink. Notwithstanding the empirical deficiency of failing to explain how the intersecting point B was originally reached, the general form of the kinked-demand curve model is illustrated in Figure 5-2.

Dominant-firm Model

The dominant-firm model assumes that one firm is so strong that it is clearly a market leader and other firms follow along. It thereby avoids the special

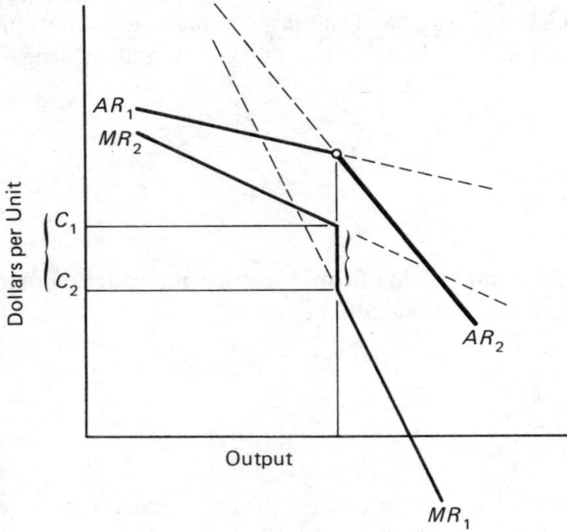

Figure 5-2. The Kinked-demand Curve.

assumptions involving the conjectural variations of different firms in particular markets.[9]

Barometric-firm Model

The barometric-firm model refers to cases where one firm conventionally makes policy or output changes that are usually followed by competitors in the market. The firm need not be so powerful as in the dominant-firm model, but it must reflect some consistent form of market leadership.[10]

Corporate-organizational Model

A major advance in the theory of the firm has been contributed by Oliver Williamson who has developed a model based on a utility analysis of the firm that yields more meaningful trade-offs and results than prior traditional analysis.[11] Williamson's analysis involves a utility model of the firm that structures the effects of internal organization on managerial goals and the internal efficiency of the firm. The theory of the firm developed by Williamson is specifically designed to explain the behavior of large corporations (presumably oligopolies) and can be applied to transportation firms with the appropriate modifications. Williamson investigated the interaction of control loss and corporate size in the context of unitary form organization[12] by postulating a model of the corporation that maximizes net revenue and yields expressions that determine the optimal number of hierarchical levels and the optimal size of the corporation.[13] A brief exposition of this model follows.

Suppose that a transportation firm can pursue a number of managerial objectives, such as net revenues, sales, utility (welfare), or market share, subject to any constraints imposed either by its jurisdictional regulatory agency or by itself. Assume, for example, that it chooses to optimize its own welfare (U) subject to the regulatory agency's requirement that taxes and a minimum profit be earned ($\Pi_R \geqslant \Pi_0 + T$). Then the problem becomes

$$\text{Maximize } U = f(S, M, F, Q) \tag{5.16}$$

subject to

$$(\Pi - M) \geqslant \Pi_0 = T \tag{5.17}$$

9. See Kalman J. Cohen and Richard M. Cyert, *Theory of the Firm: Resource Allocation in a Market Economy* (Englewood Cliffs, New Jersey: Prentice-Hall, Inc., 1965) p. 241.

10. Ibid., p. 244.

11. Oliver E. Williamson, *Corporate Control and Business Behavior: An Inquiry into the Effects of Organization Form on Enterprise Behavior* (Englewood Cliffs, New Jersey: Prentice-Hall, Inc., 1970).

12. As distinct from the multidivisional organization.

13. Ibid., chap. 2.

where:

U = utility or internal welfare of the firm

S = span of control

α = fraction of work done by a subordinate ($0 < \alpha < 1$); an internal efficiency parameter or *compliance* factor

N_i = number of employees at the ith hierarchical level $= S^{i-1}$

n = number of hierarchical levels (decision variable)

p = price of output (avg. rates)

w_o = base wage rate of workers

w_i = wage rate of employees at the ith hierarchical level $= w_o \beta^{n-1} (\beta > 1)$

r = nonwage variable cost per unit output

Q = output (ton-miles) $= \theta (\alpha S)^{n-1}$

R = revenue $= PQ$

C = total variable cost $\sum_{i=1}^{n} wN_i + rQ$

F = staff expense

M = emoluments

Π = actual profits $- R - C - F$

Π_R = reported profits $= \Pi - M$

Π_0 = minimum (after tax) profits demanded

T = taxes (where $\bar{t}$ = tax rate)

discretionary profits $= \Pi_R - \Pi_0 - T$

Since actual profits, Π, equal $R - C - F$, the left-hand side of the constraint becomes

$$R - C - F - M = PQ - \sum_{i=1}^{n} w_i N_i - rQ - F - M \tag{5.18}$$

$$= P(\alpha S)^{n-1} - \sum_{i=1}^{n} w_o \beta^{n-1} S^{i-1} - r(\alpha S)^{n-1} - F - M$$

Taking the first- and second-order conditions, one can find an optimal n^* (number of hierarchical levels) as a function of S, F, and M. Associated with this n^* is an optimum performance characteristic of the organization structure of the company (see Chapter 32 for an implementation of this concept). If this structure were to change (for instance, by a merger or an acquisition), then both the firm(s) and the regulatory agency should be able to use this model to predict more accurately its organizational and market impacts.

Summary

This chapter has described briefly a variety of oligopoly models that might depict the behavior of firms in the transportation industries. While these models are not so theoretically rigorous as models of competition and monopoly, oligopoly models do possess a special appeal in being able to capture a larger amount of realism in the real world. Even though some oligopoly models have appeared in the literature for a long time, substantial research in this area should be forthcoming:[14]

> Attempts to relate characteristics of the organizational structure to decisionmaking in the oligopoly situation have been quite limited . . . (but it) is nevertheless of great interest. . . . Organizations with complex hierarchies and centralized decisionmaking are likely to respond more slowly and more routinely to changes in costs, demand, and actions of rivals and potential entrants than would a less hierarchical and more decentralized decisionmaking structure. . . . It would be interesting to see how much of the relative price rigidity often associated with concentration is really determined by differences in organizational structure. To the extent that organizational structure influences the nature and speed of a firm's responses, further analysis along these lines may also be useful in designing effective antitrust remedies.[15]

In order to suggest some additional alternatives for describing the behavior of firms in the transportation industries, the following chapter outlines several variations on the profit-maximization objective believed to be pursued in practice by most transportation firms.

---

14. Two theoretical examples of such research would be papers by Jerry R. Green, "Vertical Integration and Assurance of Markets," Harvard Institute of Economic Research, working paper number 383, Harvard University (October 1974); and Roy Radner, "A Behavioral Model of Cost Reduction," Center for Research in Management Science, Technical Report OW-2, University of California, Berkeley (October 1974).

15. Joskow, "Firm Decisionmaking Processes."

6 Variations on the Profit-maximization Objective in the Theory of the Firm

Most models of pricing strategies in the economics literature have adhered to the assumption that business firms seek to maximize profits. Newer models of the behavior of large corporations have included a variety of assumptions about business motivation and nonmaximizing behavior in the traditionally static framework. The developers of these new models have paid increasing attention to the nature and determinants of the forces governing the size and growth of the companies of which they are composed. As a result the newer theoretical models of the growth of the firm have rapidly become more rigorous, comprehensive, and widely accepted.

Since firms in the transportation industries compete in money and capital markets with numerous other firms in both the regulated and unregulated sectors of the economy, these models of firm behavior can be applied directly to each of the transportation industries. In fact, one often forgets that airlines, railroads, and motor trucking companies are *business* firms with problems and frustrations similar to industrial firms. Since many of the characteristics of all firms are identical, the focus in this chapter is on the alternative formulations of managerial goals that transportation firms may be pursuing in practice, especially the consideration of different objective functions that the companies may be following in lieu of profit maximization.[1] Since these models can reflect the behavior of any single firm in any mode, each of the following analyses is one of partial equilibrium that assumes the current activities of all other competitors as given.

This chapter has two general purposes: It is intended mainly to provide a frame of reference from which alternative hypotheses can be stated concerning the objectives that managers and executives in a transportation industry may be pursuing. It also incorporates as comprehensive a list as possible of alternative objective functions and demonstrates graphically that each separate objective may result in its own unique price (fare or rate) and output (volume) combination when equilibrium occurs.

This material has been extracted to a large extent from my book, *The Economics of the Transportation Firm* (Lexington, Mass.: Lexington Books, D.C. Heath and Co., 1974), pp. 102-10.

1. For recent evidence that some railroad firms are pursuing different objective functions see George C. Eads, "Railroad Diversification: Where Lies the Public Interest." *Bell Journal of Economics and Management Science* 5 (Autumn 1974), pp. 595-613.

Specifications of Alternative Objective Functions for Transportation Firms

Using the neoclassical goal (objective) of profit maximization as a base, one can analyze the following alternative objective functions:

1. Short-run profit maximization
2. Revenue maximization
3. Sales maximization (break-even)
4. Volume maximization
5. Cost minimization
6. Constrained sales maximization
   a) Minimum value profits
   b) Ascending buffer
   c) Descending buffer
7. Other specifications
   a) Utility maximization
   b) Growth maximization
   c) Stockholder equity maximization
   d) Security maximization
   e) Market share equalization

Each case will determine the resulting price-output combination that optimizes its respective alternative objective function. By nature these models are simplistic; yet, the underlying importance of the basic demand-supply relationships is reflected in the sharply different results of each model. In essence, the shapes of the revenue and cost functions (or demand and supply) determine the optimal price-output combination for each alternative. With the appropriate modifications for regulatory practices, the analysis can be applied to any of the major domestic transportation industries.

Short-run Profit Maximization

Revenues are derived from the demand function and are depicted in Figure 6-1 as a concave function (to the origin), that is, $RR = P \times Z$ where P can be fare and Z represents output (or volume of passengers). Assuming that fares can be changed and that the law of demand applies ($\partial Z/\partial P < 0$), R reaches a maximum at point B.

However, to generate profits, a knowledge of costs is necessary. If costs are a function of volume, they can be depicted typically as CC in Figure 6-1. Profits are simply the algebraic difference between RR and CC at each alternative level of Z, and are maximized when RR exceeds CC by the greatest amount (point A

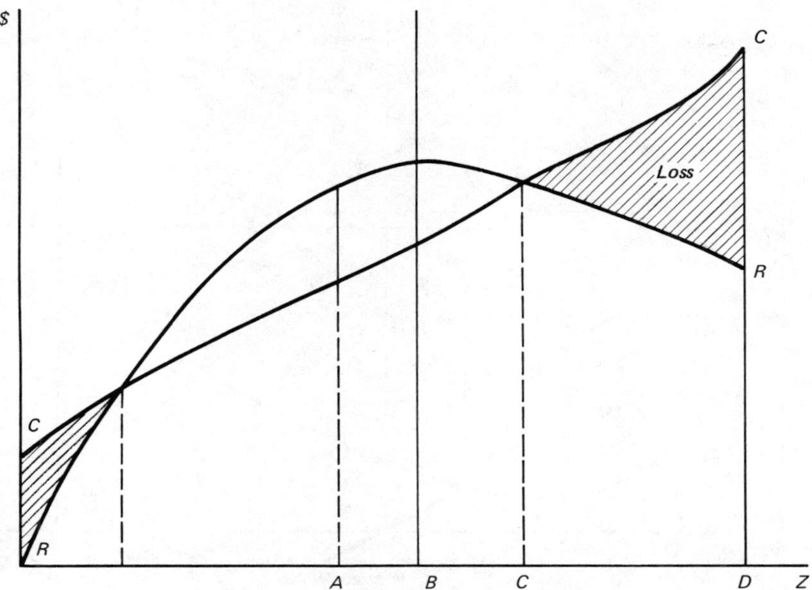

Figure 6-1. Typical Revenue and Cost Curves in the Transportation Industries. Source: James T. Kneafsey, *The Economics of the Transportation Firm* (Lexington, Mass.: Lexington Books, D.C. Heath and Co., 1974), p. 104.

in Figure 6-1). This point is also the maximum of the profit curve, as displayed in Figure 6-2 (top); finally, the equating of marginal costs (*MC*) and marginal revenue (*MR*) in Figure 6-2 (bottom) also occurs exactly at point *A*.

Revenue Maximization

With the shape of the present *RR* curve, revenues are maximized at its peak (point *B* in Figure 6-1). This result also obtains where $MR = 0$ in Figure 6-2 (bottom) because additional *Z* can only occur with a decline in revenues as a result of the law of demand in operation. *MR* is simply the slope of the *RR* curve ($\partial RR/\partial Z$).

Sales Maximization (Break-even)

There are different variations of the sales maximization hypothesis. In this case we are referring simply to carrying as many passengers (*Z*) out to the break-even

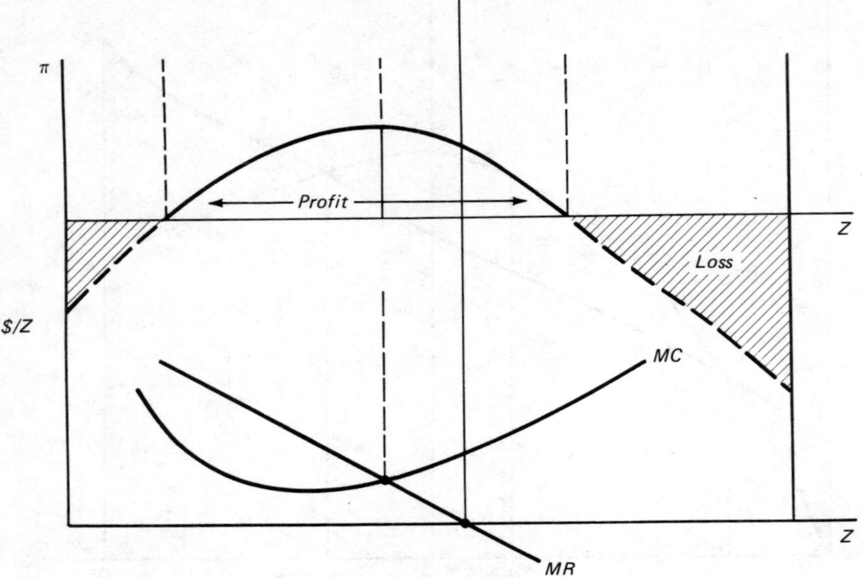

Figure 6-2. Total Dollars ($), Profits ($\pi$), and Dollars per Unit ($/$Z$) Plotted Against Output (Z). Source: James T. Kneafsey, *The Economics of the Transportation Firm* (Lexington, Mass.: Lexington Books, D.C. Heath and Co., 1974), p. 104.

point *C*. For reasons of market penetration, the firm may neither be interested in short-run profits nor in revenues but rather in attracting more customers as long as no losses are incurred.

Volume Maximization

An extension of the sales maximization hypothesis is that the transportation firm may wish to carry as many passengers as possible, even if it results in a short-term loss. The result is in effect an objective of maximizing all available capacity (point *D* in Figure 6-1). Note that a large loss would be incurred with the pursuit of this objective function with the present revenue and cost relationships.

Cost Minimization

Sometimes companies become extremely cost conscious and pursue the goal of cost minimization (point *E* in Figure 6-3). This output level occurs at the

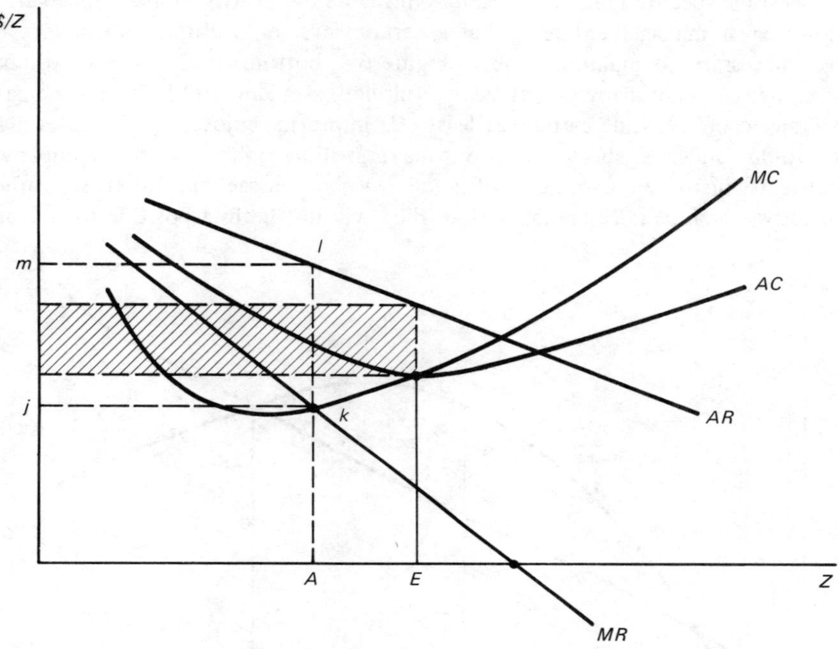

Figure 6-3. Dollars per Unit ($/Z) Plotted Against Output (Z). Source: James T. Kneafsey, *The Economics of the Transportation Firm* (Lexington, Mass.: Lexington Books, D.C. Heath and Co., 1974), p. 106.

bottom of the average cost curve (*AC*) where $MC = AC$. It is an objective completely independent of demand influences, unlike the objective discussed above. A danger which companies occasionally and regrettably experience is that they may minimize themselves to death if revenue considerations are ignored. If the demand curve (*AR*) lies far below where it does in Figure 6-3, then cost minimization as a corporate objective still would not help. As it turns out in the present case, total profits are depicted by the hatched area in Figure 6-3 (as compared with *jklm*, the total profits accruing from an objective of profit maximization).

Constrained Sales Maximization

Minimum Value Profits. This hypothesis has been advanced by a number of economists with William J. Baumol in the vanguard. In the most complete statement of this proposition, Baumol argued that firms with market power tend to maximize sales subject only to the condition that profits not fall below some specified minimum value.[2] In Figure 6-4 profits are maximized at *A*. However, if management feels that a certain level of profits is satisfactory or even necessary to maintain (*OM* in Figure 6-4, bottom) irrespective of volume (*Z*), then the company's goal is overfulfilled at volume *OA*. It can increase volume to 0(*F*1) while earning at least *OM* in profits, enjoying higher sales than it would under a short-run, profit-maximization policy. If the company's managers insist on earning profits of *ON* before seeking to satisfy other objectives such as sales maximization, they will not be in a position to increase

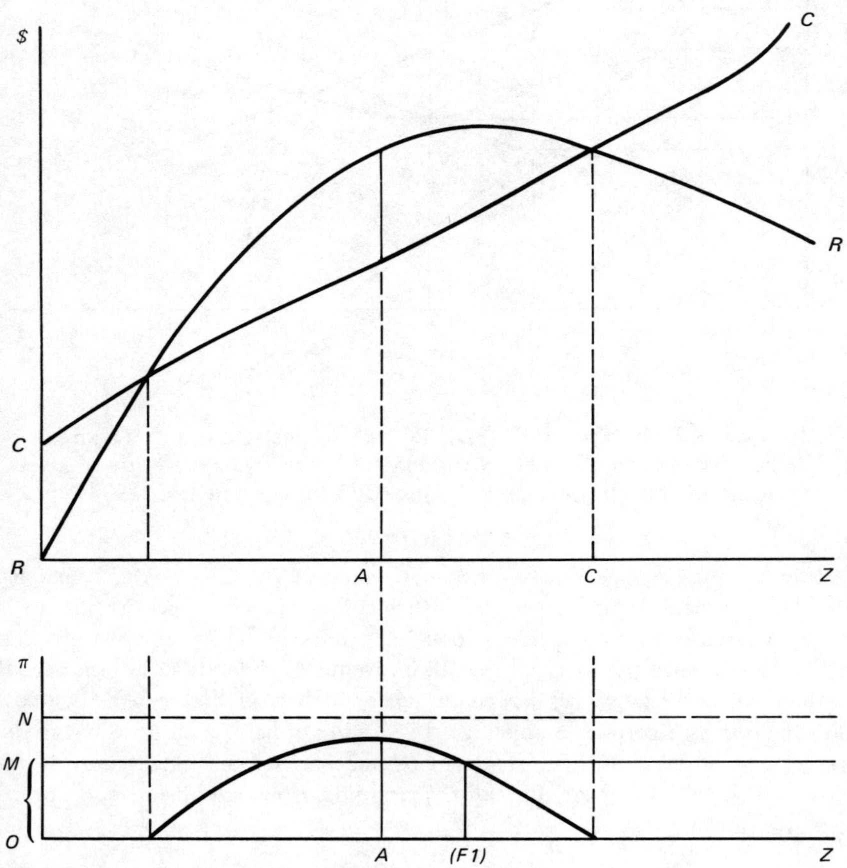

Figure 6-4. Constrained Sales Maximization. Source: James T. Kneafsey, *The Economics of the Transportation Firm* (Lexington, Mass.: Lexington Books, D.C. Heath and Co., 1974), p. 107.

2. William J. Baumol, *Business Behavior, Value and Growth*, rev. ed. (New York: The Macmillan Company, 1967), pp. 45-82 and 86-104.

revenue beyond the short-run, profit-maximizing level since the profit objective lies out of reach. The most important implication of this analysis is that if firms in any transportation industry in fact strive to increase revenue and if they require less profit to meet capital needs (for example, *OM* in Figure 6-4), then they can charge lower fares and offer more volume than they would under the goal of profit maximization. Two variations on this particular objective are the ascending and descending buffer objectives.

Ascending Buffer. In Figure 6-4 *OM* represents a buffer of profits that the firm desires to earn. These profits may be used for unexpected financing purposes, for dividend declarations, or for retained earnings. As long as *OM* is earned, the company will sacrifice additional profits for more sales. In Figure 6-4 *KK* represents a buffer stock of profits that increases with volume (*Z*). With more and more volume, presumably the firm should be in a stronger position to increase dividends or to finance additional expenditures. An allowance for this growth is reflected in the rising slope of *KK*. In this case the firm will select volume (*F*2) in Figure 6-5, where sales are maximized subject to the buffer (*KK*) constraint.

Descending Buffer. Alternatively, firms may be willing to sacrifice substantial short-run profits in order to generate volume that would result in a buffer stock *LL* that varies negatively with volume. If volume during a given period is decreased sharply, say as a result of a strike, the company may wish to have a

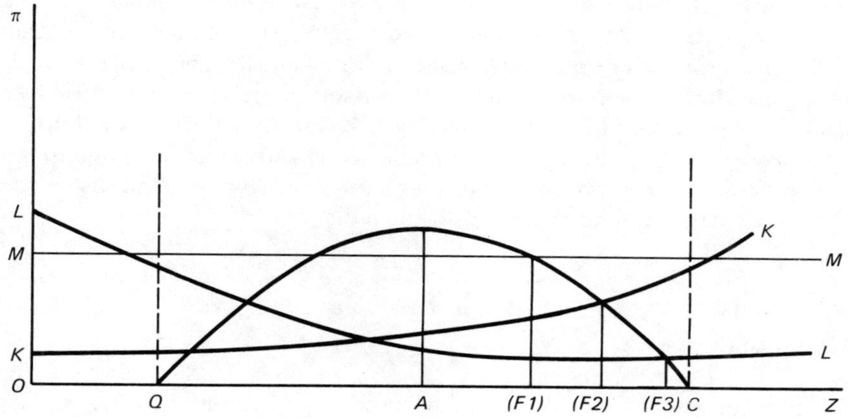

Figure 6-5. Ascending Buffer and Descending Buffer, and "Satisficing" Objectives. Source: James T. Kneafsey, *The Economics of the Transportation Firm* (Lexington, Mass.: Lexington Books, D.C. Heath and Co., 1974), p. 108.

larger profit buffer at low ranges of Z. As volume increases, though, the trade-off with profits becomes apparent and the company would opt for output ($F3$) in Figure 6-5.

"Satisficing"

In the early 1960s several economists in the Graduate School of Industrial Administration at the Carnegie Institute of Technology (now Carnegie-Mellon University) developed the "behavioral" theory of the firm. At the heart of this theory lies the concept of "satisficing," usually attributed to the work of Herbert Simon.[3] Essentially, *satisficing* refers to the fact that firms may not be maximizing at all, but rather may be pursuing a number of goals simultaneously resulting in accepting a "satisfactory" level of profits. Graphically, this means that the firm can select any volume in Figure 6-5 as long as some satisfactory level of profits is attained. In the case of pursuing any profit at all, the range would be QC within which the firm would be satisfied.

Other Specifications

Numerous other objectives could be pursued by firms in practice either individually or jointly. These goals might include the maximization of a firm's utility function, of its rate of growth of output, or of its stockholders' equity. Since ownership and management are separate functions of airlines and other large companies, an important objective to analyze might be the maximization of the management's own security and stability. Also, the companies might be satisfied with maintaining or increasing market shares as an objective independent of any other one. Since these objectives are more difficult and intricate to display graphically, the above discussion should suffice for present purposes.

For those objectives which have just been discussed above, a summary version of each alternative volume appears in Figure 6-6.

Objectives in the Theory of the Firm: Additional Comments

No one has yet succeeded in demonstrating conclusively whether airlines, railroads, motor carriers, or other business firms behave in the ways and for the reasons postulated in the above models of selecting alternative objective functions. One obstacle to enlightenment is that the behavioral differences between long-run profit maximization and various short-run alternative goals are

3. Herbert A. Simon, *Models of Man* (New York: John Wiley & Sons, Inc., 1957).

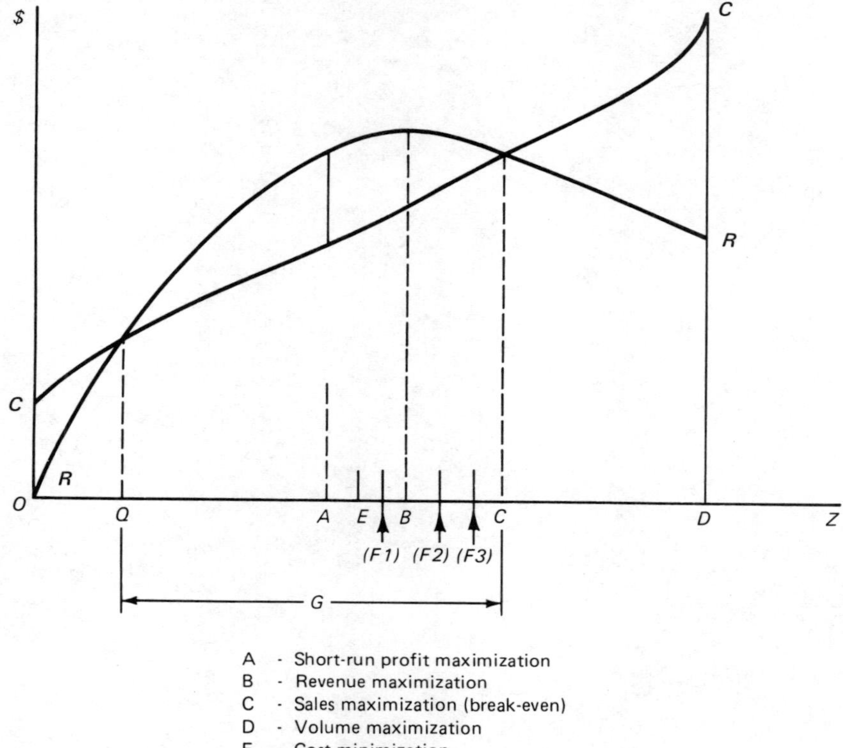

A - Short-run profit maximization
B - Revenue maximization
C - Sales maximization (break-even)
D - Volume maximization
E - Cost minimization
F1 - Minimum value profits
F2 - Ascending buffer
F3 - Descending buffer
G - "Satisficing"

Figure 6-6. Objectives of the Airline Firm–Summary
Source: James T. Kneafsey, *The Economics of the Transportation Firm* (Lexington, Mass.: Lexington Books, D.C. Heath and Co., 1974), p. 110.

so subtle that econometric tests with existing data are not sufficiently powerful to discriminate among the contending hypotheses. Since it is clear that transportation firms do pursue one or more of these objectives in practice, the present state of knowledge certainly must be extended through more sophisticated econometric research and by more detailed case studies than any heretofore attempted.

7 Market Demand Characteristics for Transportation

The demand for transportation services is a derived demand. In the freight sector it is based primarily on the final demands of the commodities hauled, and in the passenger sector it is based on the preferential and economic characteristics of travellers who need to move from one place to another. The demand for a particular mode, like rail services, is a function of the demand for transportation service, and the cost and service characteristics of rail vis-à-vis alternative transportation services (primarily barge or truck operations). The demand for a specific railroad's services will depend in turn on the locations it serves and on its prices and service in relation to any intraindustry and intermodal competitors. This chapter briefly reviews some of the significant demand characteristics for rail transportation service as an example of one of the major modes of domestic transportation. A later chapter (Chapter 20) will examine the demand characteristics of passenger transportation.

Demand for Commodities

The demand for transportation service is affected by the final demand conditions for commodity (or passenger) movements, particularly suited to each transportation technology. Railroad transportation, for example, has proven efficient in hauling frequent regular movements of carload quantities of many manufactured goods. Structural changes in the economy and in the economic base of many communities can result in a shift in the demand (market share) for rail services. As a case in point, the commodity and tonnage mix carried by the railroads in the Northeast region of the United States is substantially different from the mix transported 30 years ago. For some commodities the change has been gradual, while for others the mix alteration occurred in a relatively short period. By way of example, a brief examination of several key commodity groups is presented.

Coal

While total United States coal production increased by 16 percent between 1965 and 1970, the coal tonnage produced in the Northeastern region increased by only 5 percent. The relative decrease in this demand between 1965 and 1970 can be most closely identified with the environmental impacts of burning coal; because of its high sulphur content coal was beginning to lose favor as a source of energy for use by utilities. This had a considerable impact on the northeastern railroads and particularly on the Penn Central since the coal mined in its region had a higher sulfur content than even that of the southern Appalachian states served by the Chesapeake & Ohio Railway and the Norfolk & Western Railway.

Iron and Steel

Another important source of revenue for the northeastern railroads has been iron and steel products transportation. For this commodity group, total iron and steel rail tonnage decreased nationwide by 15 percent between 1965 and 1970, although the Penn Central revenues surprisingly increased by 29 percent from these products. This aberration indicates that while iron and steel production had been decreasing in relation to total production of domestic goods, the railroads, particularly the Penn Central, have compensated tonnage loss with increased rates.

Automobiles and Auto Parts

During the early 1960s the introduction of the tri and bilevel auto rack cars, together with high-cube auto parts cars reversed the railroads' losing trend in the shipment of automobiles and auto parts. Between 1960 and 1963 the class I rail tonnage of automobiles hauled increased by 165 percent, and revenues increasing by 93 percent. Between 1960 and 1975 railroads' share of this traffic in terms of revenues increased from 15 percent to 52 percent, while the motor carriers' market share decreased from 84 percent to 48 percent. Clearly, the movement of automobiles and auto parts traffic is now a well established commodity for rail transportation.

Manufactured Commodities

In the area of manufactured commodity traffic a significant portion of the railroads' share of intercity traffic shifted to motor carriers. As an example, in 19 of the 24 manufacturing product classes defined by the 1967 Census of Transportation, the volume of goods transported increased in terms of ton-miles between 1963 and 1967; of these 19 class increases, the railroads experienced absolute ton-mileage declines in 13 of them. In the remaining six classes the railroads increased their absolute volume, but their market shares relative to other modes fell. In the eastern United States the decline of the railroads' market share of manufacturing items was especially pronounced.

On the basis of the above discussion one may conclude that the demand for transportation service can be affected significantly by the changing conditions in commodity markets and locational patterns of production and consumption. Such changes have been dramatically apparent in the East and have affected the Penn Central traffic base, which has contributed substantially to the railroad's recent financial dilemma. To a large extent these changes are independent of actions taken by railroads: More aggressive marketing and pricing strategies alone cannot significantly revive this type of traffic loss. Nonetheless, there are traffic losses, such as the auto traffic, that are dependent on competitive modal costs and levels of service. Often in these instances the improved performance of rail technology and operations suited to the shipper needs can improve the market penetration of railroads.

Levels of Service

During the last decade shippers' reactions to rail freight service have generally been on the negative side. Many shippers claim that if railroads improved their level of service, traffic not only would be recaptured from the other modes, but further deterioration in rail plant and equipment caused by recent modal shifts would be halted. Shippers also have expressed an almost universal belief that the most important requirement of service is time reliability. When a shipper is dealing with bulk commodities of a relative low value per ton, such as coal or gravel, the cost trade-offs between transportation and inventory may be such that the variability in transit times are economically acceptable although perhaps not desirable. If the shipment is also a large one and flows continuously throughout the year between specified points, the cost of variabilities in individual shipments would become smoother. On the other hand, shippers with high valued semifinished or finished products without a large annual volume but with consistent year-round shipments have experienced extremely high inventory (with safety stock) costs that result partially from the attempts to counter transit time variability. Motor carriers, which can offer lower transit times in total and can produce significantly decreased transit time variability, have generally met the needs of this latter group much more effectively than the railroads.

If improved levels of service by rail carriers would make railroads more competitive for increased market penetration, the unanswered question remains as to why this event has not occurred over the last few decades. In addition to the lack of an adequate financial base to undertake service improvement programs, several additional factors appear to have contributed to declining service.

Train Performance

Because of the lower operating expenses assumed to be characteristic of longer trains, shipments can become delayed when terminal operating policies involve holding a train for additional tonnage rather than permitting it to depart on its normal schedule. As a result, connections are often missed and shipments are delayed usually by 24-hour increments. For this reason, statistics showing on-time train performance can be misleading: The trains can show up as on-time, but the freight cars may be several days late.

It is generally claimed that increasing train length has the overall effect of decreasing levels of service, assuming constant volume of tonnage. The decrease in service results from the longer trains' increased probabilities of knuckle or drawbar failures and the increased probabilities of derailments. The Denver and Rio Grand Western Railroad has been a pioneer in offering shorter trains with faster service. While these kinds of trains may lose some of the possible efficiencies of the very long train with one "consist" (set of locomotives),[1] the overall levels of service appeared to have improved since the service is more responsive to the needs of the shippers served.

Number of Cars in Service/Car Utilization

Another perennial shipper complaint has involved freight car shortages. The inability of railroads to deliver empty cars is another form of unreliable service. This problem can be analyzed in terms of car utilization. In response to a 2 percent increase in rail tonnage originated and a 32 percent increase in revenue ton-miles between 1951 and 1974, the number of freight cars in service decreased by 16 percent while the average car capacity increased by a third. Increased car capacity simply is not a direct substitute for increased number of cars in terms of the potential level of service provided. Although the average freight car now produces 53 percent more ton-miles per day than it did in 1951 because the car is large and its mileage is greater, its number of trips per time period has remained almost constant. Consequently, with the decrease in the total number of units in the freight car fleet, car availability for loading has deteriorated.

Track and Roadbed Condition

Track and roadbed condition is an important variable in the determination of freight service levels. On account of the policy of deferred roadway maintenance

1. A consist refers to the available horsepower, represented by a group or cluster of compatible locomotives, required to move a given tonnage.

adopted by many carriers over the years (not necessarily by choice), the condition of the track and roadbed for rail service has deteriorated alarmingly. This has occurred to the point where FRA track standards have been introduced in the early 1970s to protect the general public. Not only do lower speed limits and slow orders cause reductions to the transit times in the obvious ways, but they complicate the process of train dispatching, especially in single track territory. Between 1964 and 1967 the total mileage of track restricted under slow orders increased by a factor of five; also in 1974 more than 8,000 miles of Penn Central track had a speed limit of eight miles per hour or less. Furthermore, track which has been allowed to deteriorate becomes extremely rough riding for the rolling stock, resulting in extensive damage to the lading and, to a lesser degree, the equipment. Finally, the number of derailments increases substantially by virtue of the cumulative effects of broken rails and spread gauge, misalignment, and poor surface.

Loss and Damage

The damages caused to lading because of rough track, poor car handling, and derailments are substantial in the domestic railroad industry. While the magnitude of this damage is normally considered proprietary information, the value of merchandise damaged in transit is believed to be substantial. In summary, a deterioration in the level of service, ceteris paribus, is the equivalent of an increase in the cost of providing the service.

Intramodal Competition

The actual and potential competition of other railroads that are located in a given railroad's region of operations has a significant impact on the level of demand for its transportation services. Intramodal competition among railroads takes two general forms: competition in rates and competition in service. In theory, intramodal competition is expected to be quite strong in most industries, but in practice it is not evident in the railroad industry.

Rate Competition

Because of the high degree of interchange traffic and joint rate making practices among railroads, rate competition ordinarily is limited. The practice of undercutting competing railroads can be risky unless a sound cost data base exists and interchange traffic is well protected from diversion. The limited degree to which rates can be used as a competitive force is a result of the present collective rate-making mechanism of the railroad industry. If this mechanism is altered in any way, the competition in rates among railroads could become more active.

Service Competition

Railroads are also limited in service competition because of their significant volume of interchange and bridge traffic. This means that quality control in transit time and reliability is difficult to achieve if the traffic is handled by more than one railroad. Individual railroad firms do attempt to compete, however, by purchasing specialized equipment and thereby reducing car shortages to shippers. Nonetheless, it is the shippers' decision to select the railroad(s) over which their traffic is routed.

Intramodal competition exercised by railroads thus is presently limited because of the high degree of interdependence among railroads in their operations and in the collective rate-making mechanism. Shippers, on the other hand, can indirectly stimulate competition by selecting routings according to their individual performance requirements.

Intermodal Competition

Intermodal competition historically has been a much stronger market force affecting railroads than has intramodal competition. From the data to be presented in Tables 11-3 and 11-4 in Chapter 11 on tonnage, ton-miles, and revenues, the position of the railroads with respect to competition from other modes has been generally weak. As can be noted from these tables, between 1945 and 1973 the rail share of tonnage decreased from approximately 65 percent to 39 percent, while the rail share of revenues decreased from 74 percent to roughly 42 percent. One can then conclude that substantial rail share has been captured by the trucking and pipeline modes over this long period, and that, although trucks produce only 60 percent of the current ton-miles of railroads, the motor trucking carriers receive a higher percentage of the revenues.[2] Assuming that railroads do have a relative advantage over trucks in the average length of haul, it is illustrative to examine the extent to which this advantage has been exploited in the past. From 1945 to 1973 the average rail length of haul increased from 415 to 497 miles; during the same period, the average truck length of haul increased from 220 to 270 miles. Even though the railroads increased their average length of haul during this period relative to trucking, a significant modal shift occurred.

A second indicator of the relative weakening in the rail transportation market

2. Even between 1963 and 1967 the railroads' market share for manufactured commodities declined in most major markets, as Table 7-1 suggests.

Table 7-1
Share of Transport Market in Selected Production Areas for Manufactured Commodities, Railroads, and For-hire Motor Carriers

	1963		1967	
Production Area	Rail	Motor Carrier	Rail	Motor Carrier
Boston, Mass.	28.7%	50.0%	17.4%	73.4%
New York City	25.7	49.2	22.2	59.0
Philadelphia, Pa.	41.0	42.3	40.2	45.4
Pittsburgh, Pa.	55.6	23.8	45.2	24.0
Harrisburg, Pa.	53.8	30.7	48.3	41.3
Allentown/Bethlehem, Pa.	58.8	34.3	37.7	47.7
Cleveland, Ohio	56.9	35.3	52.2	39.1
Detroit, Michigan	73.6	20.4	71.5	23.6
Newark, N.J.	29.3	44.9	34.6	46.3

Source: *U.S. Census of Transportation* (1967).

can be seen in the analysis of costs to the shipper. Between 1945 and 1973 the revenue collected per ton-mile for rail increased by 38 percent while the truck rates increased by 65 percent. Thus, even though the rail haul increased substantially relative to trucking, and the truck rate increased relative to rail, the railroads still lost a large portion of the intercity freight. Some additional reasons for explaining the modal shift, both from the perspective of trucking and the other modes, is presented in the following paragraphs:

Motor Trucking Competition

The most pervasive competing modal transportation service for railroads is the motor trucking industry. It offers complete point to point service throughout the country and possesses excellent service characteristics: fast, reliable door-to-door service and adaptable to carrying a broad range of freight. The comparative advantage of trucks is very strong for short hauls (up to 200 or 300 miles) of packaged freight.

Water Competition

Barge competition on the inland waterway system and on the Great Lakes are significant alternatives to rail service in movements where rail otherwise has a strong market position: bulk products with large annual tonnage movements.

However, water competition is limited to the natural paths of lakes and rivers which service a limited number of points, often require feeder movements, and can involve substantial circuity. Water transportation companies will typically offer lower costs for large annual tonnage movements where origin and destination are on the waterway and the length of movement exceeds several hundred miles.

Air Cargo

Air cargo usually is a premium cost, high level of service form of freight transportation. In general, air competition does not affect a significant amount of the tonnages carried by the rail, truck, water, or pipeline modes.

It should also be indicated that railroads are not merely competitive with other modes. They are indeed complementary to both trucking and water operations. The complementary relationships are very significant and fall into three broad categories:

Feeder and Distribution

Motor trucking is the mode most commonly used to collect and distribute freight locally. Perhaps the most common form of rail/truck complementarity is rail line-haul to warehouses with local truck distribution. Rail can act as a feeder and distributor of bulk commodities in the same way with water line-haul operations.

Intermodal Line-Haul

Combination rail/water movements have been common in many bulk commodities for years. Overseas export movement of grain commodities reflects by nature this form of movement.

Intermodal Systems

Containerization concepts have led to the design of intermodal systems specifically aimed to optimize the characteristics of each mode in providing transportation service while lowering the cost of shifting from one mode to another during the movement. TOFC/COFC is the most successful intermodal system and one of the most significant innovations in the transportation industries. It has drawn rail, trucking, and water operations in most cases into a truly integrated transportation system.

Expected Demand

While the railroads' market share of tonnage has decreased since World War II, the absolute tonnage of railroads has increased markedly. Students of transportation economics should wonder about the expected change in the future insofar as it would affect the various modes. In general changes in tonnage are correlated with changes in the level of gross national products. The projected growth in rail tonnage for the decade beginning in 1970 and ending in 1980 was estimated in a recent study performed by the U.S. Department of Transportation. A portion of the results of this study are summarized in Table 7-2, which forecasts that the overall rail freight tonnage is expected to increase by 2.3 percent annually until 1980 and that, although the absolute rail tonnage is expected to increase, the rail market share is expected to continue to decline, as evidenced by the lower growth of rail compared with that of other modes.

Price Elasticities

The effect of an increased price on the quantity of rail (or other modes) transportation services demanded is a key decision parameter in a discussion of market demand characteristics for transportation. These estimates from empirically tested demand models can take the form of direct price (rate) elasticities for an individual mode or of cross-elasticities of demand with respect to other modes (competitors). The general indications of previous empirical studies are that short-haul freight traffic is more price elastic than long-haul traffic. There also exists the traditional view of price elasticity associated with the value of service concept of pricing. This concept focuses on the *share* of transportation in the final delivered price of the product and attributes a high share to more elastic price elasticities and a low share to more inelastic price elasticities. In this instance the result is to consider bulk commodities more elastic and manufac-

Table 7-2
1972-80 Projected Growth Rates of the Freight Modes

Transportation Sector	Annual Growth Rate in Percent	
	Ton-Miles	Revenue
Railroads–freight	2.3	2.4
Domestic water–freight	2.6	3.2
For-hire trucking–intercity	4.0	4.2
Private trucking–intercity	5.0	5.0
Pipelines	2.5	2.4

Source: U.S. Department of Transportation, *Transportation Projections 1970-1980* (Washington, D.C.: 1973).

tured commodities more inelastic. With changes that have occurred in transportation markets since 1945, one might conclude that very little confidence can be placed in the application of prior research or traditional views to current and future transportation markets. It is essential and perhaps even compelling that transportation research efforts in the future develop both better demand (also cost and interactive) models and data sets with which the models can be calibrated and verified.

The general determinants of market demand may be classified into an activity system and the absolute and relative levels of service of the transportation product. It is desirable to know the impacts of changes in the activity system and/or the level of service so that one can predict the volume of passengers or shippers who will demand transport service. The activity system may be characterized in terms of population, employment, income, family size, cars per household, or any other of a wide range of socioeconomic variables. The level of service would include the convenience variable, travel time, frequency, or other operating efficiency variable. In disaggregate terms, since individual consumers have different indifference functions over the level of service variables, the demand functions will vary for different social and economic groups, for different trip purposes, and for different time periods. For example, the demand function for home-to-work trips by high-income workers during week-day peak hours will be different from the demand function for shopping and recreational trips by low-income workers on weekends. These differences in the behavior of various market segments are reflected in differences in the values of parameters of the demand functions, as well as in differences among the forms of the functions.

There are many different forms of possible demand functions. Among the more common forms are the following, where c is travel cost (the price variable) and t is travel time:

1. *Linear* $V = \alpha C + \beta t$ where $\frac{\partial V}{\partial C} < 0, \frac{\partial V}{\partial t} < 0$

2. *Product* $V = Ct$

3. *Exponential* $V = \alpha e^{\beta t}$

4. *Logistic* or *Logit* $V = \frac{\alpha}{1 + e^{\beta t}}$

These forms are simple to handle algebraically and are particularly straightforward for calibration by standard statistical techniques. For example, linear regression techniques can be used to estimate the coefficients of the linear form of the demand model directly. To estimate the coefficients of the product and exponential forms, logarithms are taken to transform the equation into a linear form, and then regression techniques are used on this transformed equation. The logit form is particularly useful for disaggregate functions, which are used to describe in more detail the expected actions of travelers and passengers by combining them into smaller groups that possess similar characteristics, such as income or household composition.

One particularly useful characteristic of a demand function is its "elasticity." The motivation for this concept is as follows: Consider the demand function $V = f(L)$, where V is the volume of traffic demanded and L is the level of service variable (reliability, travel time, etc). An important need in transportation engineering (and in economics) is to express the relative rate of change of volume with respect to changes in the level of service. One useful measure would be to take the ratio $\Delta V/\Delta L$ as an absolute measure, or the partial derivative $\partial V/\partial L$. However, one problem with either form of this measure is that it depends on the dimensions of V and of L. It may be more desirable to have a dimensionless concept, like an elasticity, which can be defined as the percentage change in V for a given percentage change in L. Thus the elasticity of volume with respect to level of service is:

$$\epsilon_L(V) = \frac{L}{V} \cdot \frac{\partial V}{\partial L}$$

where $\epsilon_L(V)$ = elasticity of demand, V, with respect to the level of service, L.

To see the significance of the elasticity, consider two examples: the first

$V = \alpha \cdot L^{\beta}$ such that the elasticity of demand is

$$\epsilon_L = \frac{L}{V} \cdot \frac{\partial V}{\partial L} = \beta$$

This example indicates another advantage of the product form of demand model: The elasticity is a constant and is equal to the exponent of the level of service variable. Thus the simple product form demand model suggests that, for each percentage change in the level of service, L, there will be a β percent change in the volume demanded. The second example is

$V_k = \alpha \cdot L_k^{\beta} L_r^{\gamma}$ where k and r are alternative modes, such that

$$\epsilon_{kk} = \frac{L_k}{V_k} \cdot \frac{\partial V_k}{\partial L_k} = \beta \text{ and that}$$

$$\epsilon_{kr} = \frac{L_r}{V_k} \cdot \frac{\partial V_k}{\partial L_r} = \gamma$$

This example illustrates a more complex use of elasticity where there are defined two "cross-elasticities." ϵ_{kk} is the elasticity of the volume choosing alternative k as a function of a change in the level of service of alternative k, and we see that this elasticity is β again. ϵ_{kr} is the elasticity of the volume choosing k with respect to the service of some other competing alternative r; we see that this is equal to γ. In this demand model we have volume as a function, not only of alternative k, but also of the competing alternative r. The cross-elasticity indicates how the volume choosing one alternative is influenced by the characteristics of another. In this example, ϵ_{kk} is often referred to as the *direct elasticity*—that is, elasticity with respect to itself—while ϵ_{kr} is the *cross-elasticity*, the effect on one alternative of a change in the characteristics of another alternative.

Listed below in consistent notation are the functional forms of the four most widely documented direct demand models: (1) the Kraft-SARC model developed by Gerald Kraft and the Systems Analysis Research Corporation in 1963; (2) the Baumol-Quandt abstract-mode model developed by William Baumol and Richard Quandt at Mathematica, Inc. in 1965; (3) the McLynn model developed by James McLynn in 1965; and (4) the standard linear model. The listed forms omit the frequency variable, which is ordinarily presented as an explanatory variable along with travel time and cost in each demand model.

1. *Kraft-SARC*

$$V_{klm} = \phi_{m0}(P_k P_l)^{\phi_{m1}}(Y_k Y_l)^{\phi_{m2}}(t_{kl1}^{\theta_{m11}} c_{kl1}^{\theta_{m12}})$$

$$(t_{kl2}^{\theta_{m21}} c_{kl2}^{\theta_{m22}})(t_{kl3}^{\theta_{m31}} c_{kl3}^{\theta_{m32}})$$

2. *Baumol-Quandt*

$$V_{klm} = \phi_0 (P_k P_l)^{\phi_1} (Y_k Y_l)^{\phi_2}\, t_{klb}^{\theta_2} \left(\frac{t_{klm}}{t_{klb}}\right)^{\theta_2} c_{klb}^{\theta_3} \left(\frac{c_{klm}}{c_{klb}}\right)^{\theta_4}$$

3. *McLynn*

$$V_{klm} = \phi_0 (P_k P_l)^{\phi_1} (Y_k Y_l)^{\phi_2} \cdot \frac{(t_{klm}^{\theta_{m1}} c_{klm}^{\theta_{m2}})}{\sum_{9}(t_{klq}^{\theta_{q1}} c_{klq}^{\theta_{q2}})} \cdot \left[\sum_{9}(t_{klq}^{\theta_{q1}} c_{klq}^{\theta_{q2}})\right]^{\delta}$$

4. *Linear*

$$V_{klm} = \phi_{m0} + \phi_{m1} P_k P_l + \phi_{m2} Y_k Y_l + (\theta_{m11} t_{m12} + \theta_{m12} c_{k11})$$

$$+ (\theta_{m21} t_{m12} + \theta_{m22} c_{k12}) + (\theta_{m31} t_{k13} + \theta_{m32} c_{k13})$$

where:

V_{klm} = volume between k and l by mode m

P_k = population in zone k

Y_k = median income in zone k

t_{klm}, c_{klm} = travel time and fare between k and l by mode m

t_{klm} = travel time by fastest mode (q refers to alternative modes)

c_{klb} = fare by cheapest mode (not necessarily the fastest)

ϕ, θ, δ = parameters of the model; subscripts indicate whether mode-dependent (e.g., θ_{ml}) or, mode-independent (e.g., θ_1)–"abstract mode."

Each of these models is based on fundamental behavioral assumptions describing the demand for transportation.[3] These models and the newer set of disaggregate, behavioral models that rely on qualitative choice theories reflect the assortment of tools available to predict travel demand. In the future, better data sets will allow transporation analysts and planners to consider the full social aspects of transportation facilities, and to develop a deeper understanding of the characteristics of travel demand.

3. See Richard E. Quandt, ed., *The Demand for Travel: Theory and Measurement* (Lexington, Mass.: Lexington Books, D.C. Heath and Co., 1970); *Urban Travel Demand Forecasting*, Highway Research Board Special Report 143 (Washington, D.C.: 1973); Moshe Ben-Akiva, *Structure of Passenger Demand Models*, unpublished Ph.D. diss., Department of Civil Engineering, M.I.T., 1973; and *Behavioral Demand Modelling and Valuation of Travel Time*, Transportation Research Board Special Report 149 (Washington, D.C.: 1974). In practice most transportation forecasting models have been based on the structure of the traditional Urban Transportation Model System (UTMS) that has been used by metropolitan planning agencies throughout the world. The structure of the UTMS consists of a sequential application of separate models: land use, automobile ownership, trip generation, trip distribution, modal split, and network assignment. The expected levels of service are assumed at the outset and are usually not revised to determine a true equilibrium of supply and demand characteristics. In the trip generation step the total number of trips by all modes from each traffic zone is forecast. Trip distribution models are then used to forecast the matrix of trips by origin and destination. In the modal split phase the shares of transit and automobile use for each origin-destination pair are predicted, and finally, in the network assignment portion the actual volumes on the links of the transportation system are forecast.

8 Forecasting Methods for Transportation Studies

One of the most crucial factors in transportation systems planning is forecasting. In virtually every decision facing the transportation planner, whether it be in the area of passenger travel or in the area of commodity flow analysis, some type of forecast is required. The complexities and variety of each decision have increased with the broadening of the scope and technical requirements of transportation problems. Until recently the forecasting methods available were able to address the earlier issues that were important several years ago. These methods attempted to predict the magnitude of travel volumes to be used in designing major highways, transit facilities, port facilities, and airport locations. Now, however, the transportation planner must develop and use improved methods of forecasting the demand for transportation at all levels and by all modes. Even though significant contributions have been made in recent years to the development of improved methods in forecasting, the state of the art in forecasting methods is still not consistently satisfactory in providing the transportation planner with more accurate and timely information to handle the wide range of contemporarily pressing problems, like: the estimation of social, economic, and environmental impacts; equity issues; investment options; and the determination of facility requirements for commodity flow movements. Of course, in many situations the empirical support to existing forecasting methods is the dilemma.

The purpose of this chapter, then, is to present a brief overview of the current and emerging transportation forecasting methods with the aim of identifying the areas that seem most appropriate in handling existing data sets for both passenger statistics and commodity flows.

Three basic types of forecasting methods are available to assist the transportation planner in his decision-making arena. These types are: (1) causal models, (2) time series analysis and projections, and (3) qualitative methods. The first type, the causal model, uses specific and highly refined information to depict the numerous interrelationships within the transport system. Usually a theoretical model is postulated a priori and then it is tested and calibrated with historical data. Once the model is refined, various extrapolations can be made to yield a set of forecasts. The structure of the models can range from highly aggregate models that use national (or even international) data to quite detailed disaggregate models that require very specific microeconomic data. A full listing of the causal models which may be used in the analysis of commodity flows is presented, along with the other basic types of forecasting methods, in Table 8-1.

Table 8-1
Basic Types of Forecasting Methods for Transportation Studies

Causal Methods
1. Regression analysis
2. Econometric models (simultaneous equation systems)
3. Input-output models
4. Anticipation surveys
5. Diffusion indices
6. Leading indicators
7. Economic base studies
Time Series Analysis and Projections
8. Moving averages
9. Box-Jenkins method
10. Exponential smoothing
11. *X*-11 (Census Bureau)
12. Trend projections
13. Motionary triangles
Qualitative Methods
14. Delphi method
15. Market research
16. Panel consensus
17. Historical analogy
18. Visionary forecasts
19. Factor analysis

The second type of forecasting method involves time series analysis and projections. These rely primarily on the observation of patterns and changes in patterns. As a result, this method makes complete use of historical information as a prelude to extending a trend or extrapolating a configuration. Qualitative methods represent the third basic type of forecasting method and are based on the use of nonquantitative information on special events or "one-shot" situations into the decision-making process. Because of their endemic characteristics, qualitative methods may or may not take into account historical data. In spite of their lack of using hard or scientific data, these methods may be quite important in evaluating a situation where very little historical data exist or where existing data are questionable or inconsistent. Transportation planners will quickly discover that this is the case with most data sets relating especially to commodity flows.

The following sections discuss the general functions of each of the three basic types of forecasting methods in more detail. A synopsis of some techniques appropriate for commodity flow analysis is presented for each type. See Tables 8-2, 8-3, and 8-4 for a sketch of each type of model, including its accuracy of prediction, its estimated cost,[1] and the average time required to develop a forecast. In addition, a general reference is provided should the reader be interested in more elaborate discussions of the methods.

Causal Methods

When historical data are available and sufficient prior analysis has been conducted to indicate explicit and valid relationships between the factor to be forecast and other variables, the transportation planner can construct a causal model. This type of model is the most sophisticated forecasting method. It expresses mathematically the relevant causal relationships and may also directly incorporate the results of other forecasting methods.

Practically all statistical and forecasting methods are based on the assumption that existing patterns and historical proclivities will continue in a similar way into the future. Since this assumption is usually only valid in the short run, most forecasting methods can provide reasonably accurate forecasts for the immediate future but perform quite poorly when the estimation is more than two or three years away. Also, these methods are limited in forecasting turning points in a trend, that is, when the rate of growth of a trend will change significantly (and sometimes abruptly). If a long range forecast is required, however, the best method to utilize in this case is the causal model. From Table 8-2:

1. *Regression Analysis*: The ordinary least squares method can be applied to any single-equation model that is hypothesized to capture a one-way flow of causality from a set of independent variables to a dependent one. The dependent variable is the one to be forecast, using the specified historical relationship as the foundation. This method has been applied extensively to demand models in both urban and intercity passenger transportation; it also has been applied to numerous classes of demand and cost models, ranging from highly aggregate models to disaggregate, behavioral models that use logit, probit, and discriminant analysis specifications.

2. *Econometric Models*: (Simultaneous equation systems): These are systems of independent regression equations that describe some sector or region of economic or transportation activity. As a rule, these models are relatively expensive to develop and operate, *but* they are more effective in expressing the causalities involved than ordinary regression models and consequently will forecast turning points more accurately. In general, they represent the most attractive and potentially necessary modeling framework to handle regional and statewide commodity flows.

1. These costs are based on the author's own experience, using the M.I.T. Computer Center Equipment (IBM 360-30, 360-40, and 1130 systems). The estimates are necessarily rough and are designed only to be exemplary. They also omit any overhead or markup costs that external users may be required to pay.

Table 8-2
Causal Models in Transportation Studies

	Accuracy	Applications	Data Requirements	Estimated Cost[a]	Time Required to Develop Forecast	General Reference
Regression analysis	Usually quite good	To any single equation model with one-way causality	Usually more than 10 observations: either time series, cross-sectional, or pooled data	Can use canned programs; \$100-\$200 per run	Usually less than one man-month per model, assuming data available	J. Johnston, *Econometric Methods* (New York: McGraw Hill, 1972); Henri Theil, *Principles of Econometrics* (New York: John Wiley & Son, 1971)
Econometric models (simultaneous equation systems)	Very good	To capture interactions within more complex systems	Not less than above	Depends on size of the model; for a 10 equation model, in the range of \$5,000 +	Six man-months +	Michael Evans, *Macroeconomic Activity: Theory, Forecasting and Control* (New York: Harper & Row, 1969)
Input-output model	Fairly good	To capture regional economic impacts and interaction	Extremely detailed data at the SIC 2-digit level at minimum	Depends again, but not less than \$50,000	One to two man-years	Wassily Leontief, *Input-Output Economics* (New York: Oxford University Press, 1966)
Anticipation surveys	Fair	To reflect intentions of shippers	Questionnaires or on-site surveys	\$5,000-\$10,000	Three man-months +	Survey Research Center, University of Michigan
Diffusion indices	Fair	To reflect current business trends	Secondary sources	\$1,000	One month	U.S. Department of Commerce
Leading indicators	Fair	To reflect aggregate business indicators	Secondary sources	\$1,000	Two weeks	National Bureau of Economic Research
Economic base studies	Good	To capture short-term changes in industrial composition	Local or regional data	\$1,000 for a small study	One month	Harry W. Richardson, *Regional Economic Analysis* (New York: John Wiley & Son, 1972)

Table 8-3

Time Series and Projections in Transportation Studies

	Accuracy	Applications	Data Requirements	Estimated Cost[a]	Time Required to Develop Forecast	General Reference
Moving averages	Poor	General statistical checks	Quarterly or monthly data	Less than $100	1 day	A Hadley, *Introduction to Business Statistics* (San Francisco: Holden-Day, Inc., 1968)
Box-Jenkins method	Fair	Assigns smaller errors to historical data with a mathematical model	Quarterly or monthly data	$500	2-3 days	Box-Jenkins, *Time Series Analysis: Forecasting and Control* (San Francisco: Holden-Day, Inc., 1970)
Exponential smoothing	Poor	Simply weights recent data points more highly	Quarterly or monthly data	$200	1-2 days	Any general statistics text
X-11 method	Good	Decomposes time series into seasonal, trend, cyclical and irregular elements	At least 12 quarters of data	$500-$1,000	2-4 days	U.S. Bureau of the Census
Trend projections	Variable	Extrapolating an equation	Variable	$100	Less than 1 day	Any general statistics text
Motionary triangles	Fairly good	To predict short-term movements based on technical factors	Monthly data	$500-$1,000	2-4 days	Bache & Co., *Statistical Reports*

Table 8-4
Qualitative Methods in Transportation Studies

	Accuracy	Applications	Data Requirements	Estimated Cost[a]	Time Required to Develop Forecast	General Reference
Delphi method	Fair	To collect expert opinion from a panel of specialists; uses cumulative questionnaires	Tabulation of views; consensus of opinion; rankings	$500 per specialist	2-3 days	Motor Vehicles Manufacturers Association
Market research methods	Good	To forecast longer range developments, especially in shifts of commodity flows	Personal interviews	$8,000 +	3-6 man-months	Consumer Survey Center, University of Michigan; Report to SCAG, 1974 (by M.I.T.)
Panel consensus	Fair	To check with experts' views	Mail questionnaire; or one-day meeting	$2,000 +	2-3 days	
Historical analogy	Poor	To relate present or future events to historical patterns	Long-term historical data	$1,000 +	1 month +	
Visionary forecasts	Variable	To evaluate alternative future scenarios, without the existence of necessary data	A set of realistic future scenarios	$500 +	1 week +	
Factor analysis	Good	To attempt rankings of subjective characteristics or attributes of commodities	Rankings of attributes plus computer program	$2,000	1 month +	J. Johnston, *Econometric Methods* (New York: McGraw-Hill, 1972)

[a]See footnote 1 on p. 73.

3. *Input-Output Models*: These reflect the interindustry or interregional flows of goods and services in the regional (or national) economy and its markets. Considerable effort must be expended to use these models properly and additional detail, not normally available, must be obtained if they are to be applied to specific regions. Caution must be exercised regarding its cost of usage; for example, a simple matrix inversion may be quite expensive for a standard set of industrial data.

4. *Anticipation Surveys*: These surveys of various groups of shippers, carriers, and users of different classes of commodities and freight are quite useful for short range forecasts. The surveys are usually quite brief and are geared to the respondent's immediate decision-making needs. In the case of general consumer surveys, however, the questionnaires are occasionally quite lengthy.

5. *Diffusion Indices*: A diffusion index is a composite of various business and economic indicators. Its purpose is to capture the general flow or trend of all the leading, coinciding, and lagging indicators normally used to reflect general business conditions. To the extent that the demand for travel and the demand for commodities are derived from more aggregate demands, this method should be useful in some areas of transportation planning.

6. *Leading Indicators*: A leading indicator is a particular index that has been estimated by the National Bureau of Economic Research to reflect changing aggregate economic conditions by preceding or "leading" the change. It is particularly useful in forecasting turning points in the rate of growth in various categories of economic and monetary data.

7. *Economic Base Studies*: To some extent, economic base studies are the heart of classical regional location theory. These studies reflect the changing economic and industrial base in local areas and regions. They are extremely useful in capturing the industrial mix of a local community and in generating employment information on its industries.

Time Series and Projections

The oldest and in many cases still the most widely used methods of forecasting the demand for transportation belong in the area of time series analysis and projections. In some situations this area is more simply known as trend-extrapolation or correlative analysis. It differs from causal models to the extent that less "explanatory power" or causation is imbedded in the analysis of time series or in the smoothing of trends. It is quite useful as long as there are no basic changes in trends of the series under study. The method is often used where both time and data are limited such that a forecast of a single variable (like tonnage) is produced through the use of historical data for that particular variable. From Table 8-3:

8. *Moving Averages*: This method is one of the most basic statistical exercises; it uses quarterly or monthly data ordinarily to generate a moving trend.

9. *Box-Jenkins Method*: This method assigns probability weights to a series of historical data with the assistance of a quantitative model. It is more cumbersome than using moving averages, but its accuracy in forecasting short-term movements is much higher.

10. *Exponential Smoothing*: In some ways this method is merely a special case of the Box-Jenkins method. It assigns progressively higher weights in an exponential fashion to the more recent points of observation in a time series.

11. *X-11 Method*: Originally developed at the U.S. Bureau of the Census, this method decomposes time series into the classic distribution of trend, cyclical, seasonal, and irregular components.

12. *Trend Projections*: This in some ways is the simplest forecasting method in usage. The analyst or planner needs only to take an existing series or equation and extrapolate the value of the dependent variable. This extrapolation can be done in many ways; for example, by a range or band of extrapolations, or by applying a known statistical distribution to generate the extrapolation.

13. *Motionary Triangles*: These are among the most complex of the statistical methods. Essentially, there is a wide range of techniques available for plotting or charting short-range movements in a particular indicator. Some of the movements are calculated with different "triangle" configurations, such that a "break-out" on either side of the apex of the triangle could be forecast.

Qualitative Methods

The third group of forecasting methods is qualitative in nature. The methods in this group can be used either when no information or very little historical data exist. In some circles, these methods are referred to as "technological forecasting techniques," largely because they consider new forms of technology for which no current data are ever available. Their main usage, then, is in those situations where some type of forecast is required (especially long range) and when only preference information exists. Usually the methods are coupled with discussions of alternative future scenarios that a capable analyst can present as feasible for a particular project. Long-range passenger and commodity transportation planning are two such projects. Furthermore, these methods are far more effective if they can be linked with one of the causal models discussed above. From Table 8-4:

14. *Delphi Method*: This method is a fairly well-defined procedure for using cumulative questionnaries to solicit expert opinions from a group of carefully selected panelists.

15. *Market Research Methods*: This method uses personal and on-site interviews with shippers, carriers, agencies, and users of commodity transportation. The principal intention is to forecast the longer range developments or shifts in the flows of commodities or in the contributions of the critical industries.

16. *Panel Consensus*: This is simply an organized approach to appraising the

consensus of a panel of individuals on a specific set of issues. The approach is quite useful to generate fairly quick and accurate short-range predictions.

17. *Historical Analogy*: This method requires the use of an analyst who is familiar with previous patterns of behavior or who can associate a trend in current events with some historical configuration. One must be very cautious, however, about its use in forecasting.

18. *Visionary Forecasts*: Quite often, it is valuable to hire a reputed "visionary" in the field, someone who has a track record of providing feasible insight to a particular problem or issue. In a sense, this method is a control or an anchor against which the forecasts of other methods can be compared.

19. *Factor Analysis*: This is the most mathematical method among the set of qualitative ones. It incorporates the preferences of individuals and experts by ranking their views, either with cardinal or ordinal measures. The end product is a set of important factors or attributes that are regarded as explaining a particular event.

Although the preceding classification scheme is consistent with the approach by which many analysts might differentiate forecasting methods, it is by no means unique. Other and perhaps superior classification schemes exist.[2] Some methods have not been discussed at all, such as control theory models, simulations, and computer models.[3] The principal reason that they were not considered herein reflects the belief that they are not appropriate for immediate usage in either passenger demand models or commodity flow analysis, given the current state of the art. In this context, the methods discussed in this chapter were chosen on the basis that each could show the greatest feasible potential for improving our short-run capabilities of modeling transportation activities.

The past two decades have witnessed the development and implementation of a number of large scale econometric models. It was the intention of the architects of these models that they be useful tools in the analysis of the economic impacts of various policy alternatives, thereby allowing for more informal policy choices. Inevitably, these models have also come to be used as economic forecasting tools, with the consequence that questions have been raised as to which of the existing models and competing hypotheses are more accurate. An important research need in the near future is for a study to construct a framework for general application based on an explicit testing methodology. This task is especially important when econometric modeling is extended to the transportation field. For an initial guideline to the existing stock of econometric models, the *International Economic Review* published in three

2. See, for example, John C. Chambers, S.K. Mullick, and Donald D. Smith, "How to Choose the Right Forecasting Technique," *Harvard Business Review* (July-August 1971), pp. 45-74.

3. See D.S. Garvett and N.K. Taneja, "New Directions for Forecasting Air Travel Passenger Demand," Flight Transportation Laboratory, Massachusetts Institute of Technology, Report R74-3 (Cambridge, Massachusetts: July 1974).

issues in 1974 and 1975 the results of a symposium on "Econometric Model Performance," sponsored by the National Bureau of Economic Research and the National Science Foundation. The existing models include:

1. Bureau of Economic Analysis Model (BEA)
2. Brookings Model
3. Michigan Quarterly Econometric Model (MQEM), University of Michigan
4. Data Resources, Inc. Model (DRI-71)
5. Princeton Short-Run Model
6. Federal Reserve Bank of St. Louis Model (FRB St. Louis)
7. MPS Model, University of Pennsylvania
8. Wharton Mark III Model, University of Pennsylvania
9. Wharton Annual Model, University of Pennsylvania
10. Chase Econometrics Associates, Inc. Model (CEA)
11. Hickman-Coen Annual Model, Stanford University
12. Liu-Hwa Monthly Model, Cornell University

Each of these models forecasts a wide range of macroeconomic variables, which in turn affect transportation or regional activities. A major challenge facing the transportation economist during the next decade is to provide the appropriate, simultaneous linkages between these large macroeconomic models and the transportation sector of the economy.

9 Regulation of Transportation

Since the turn of the century various pieces of Congressional legislation have required that certain industries, in which competition was deemed not fully effective, must be regulated by agencies of the federal government with the purported intention of protecting the public interest. Those industries directly subjected to public regulation are collectively referred to as the regulated industries. As commonly used, the phrase *regulated industries* refers to a diverse group of business operations responsive by statutory requirement to local, state, and federal regulation on matters of rates and services.[1] These industries typically are divided into two major classes: first, the public utilities–those enterprises supplying energy in the form of electricity and natural gas, communications services (telephone and telegraph), broadcasting, and water; and second, the transportation industries–those firms and agencies providing local, statewide, and interregional transportation, such as airlines, railroads, motor freight carriers, bus companies, gas and oil pipelines, and water carriers.[2]

These two groups of industries differ in some generic ways from other industries in the economy. The principal historical difference is that the firms in the first category of regulated industries allegedly operate more efficiently as monopolies.[3] Firms in the transportation industries historically have been absorbed under this umbrella of monopolies, or in the case of the railroads, as "natural monopolies."[4] Within the scope of the regulated industries, the transportation firms empirically have not displayed the same kinds of monopoly tendencies as public utilities, especially in the cases of motor trucking and domestic water transportation. In fact, the extent to which the domestic transportation industries should be treated as regulated industries is a contemporary political issue over which there is considerable disagreement.

No one can dispute that there is a strong degree of public interest attached to the services provided by the transportation industries. In practice, the public interest criterion is the primary legal basis for regulation in this country. The

1. One of the best sources on this topic is Charles F. Phillips, Jr., *The Economics of Regulation: Theory and Practice in the Transportation and Public Utility Industries*, rev. ed. (Homewood, Ill.: Richard D. Irwin, Inc., 1969).

2. There are several other industries and activities that also are subject to varying degrees of regulation, notably: banking, corporate securities, radio and television broadcasting, and atomic energy at the federal level; and insurance and milk distribution at the state level.

3. The issue of efficiency in the public utilities is a very complex topic and is beyond the scope of this book.

4. Again, see Phillips, *The Economics of Regulation*, pp. 4 ff. and p. 21.

uniqueness of the transportation industries in the United States contrasts with most other countries that have nationalized large segments of their industries. In this country there are two common characteristics that distinguish the transportation industries from all others: First, private ownership and management predominate; and second, there exist varying degrees of public regulation in conjunction with the independent regulatory commissions at the federal and state levels. This combination of private ownership and public control leads inevitably to conflict. The transportation firms over the years have been attempting to offer profitably services that are deemed socially necessary for the economy and in effect are quasi-public in nature.[5] Public regulation of the transportation industries became necessary because public policy required a restriction of monopoly forces at the same time that it insisted on a continuation of private ownership. As the years have passed, the role of regulation grew substantially in response to pressures brought to bear on legislatures by different interest groups. A basic public policy problem concerning transport regulation is how to disentangle the cumbersome regulatory practices and statutory requirements that have become imbedded in the regulatory process—in other words, how to deregulate.

The critics of regulation in domestic transportation contend that the economy has suffered from substantial resource misallocation and a suboptimization of transportation performance.[6] The practitioners have been faced with an increasing workload of regulatory practice cases and issues, but they still remain unwilling to support a dismemberment of the present regulatory and institutional apparatus (partially because of their vested interests). On the executive level, a succession of presidents and the U.S. Department of Transportation have demonstrated a consistent inclination toward deregulation and have sponsored legislation requesting institutional changes to accommodate partial deregulation.[7]

Goals of the Economic Regulation of Transportation

Transportation regulation is concerned in practice primarily with the twin issues of entry conditions and rate (price) control. The statutory goals, to which the

5. In the famous *Smyth v. Ames* case, Justice Harlan argued that "a railroad is a public highway . . . and performs a function of the State." 169 U.S. 466, 544 (1898).

6. Several studies have calculated a resource misallocation cost to the economy. As samples of these studies, Peck estimated the annual cost of third degree price discrimination (because of the existence of regulation) to be almost $3 billion: see Merton J. Peck, "Competitive Policy for Transportation," in Paul W. MacAvoy, ed., *The Crisis of the Regulatory Commissions* (New York: W.W. Norton and Co., 1970), p. 73; also Moore estimated that value-of-service pricing cost the economy as much as $12 billion annually: see Thomas Gale Moore, *The Feasibility of De-regulating Surface Freight Transportation* (Washington, D.C.: The Brookings Institution, 1974).

7. For one of the earliest evaluations of the U.S. Department of Transportation, especially of its structure, see Grant M. Davis, *The Department of Transportation* (Lexington, Mass.: Lexington Books, D.C. Heath and Co., 1970).

carriers must comply, have been stated in one form or another as the following: reasonable rates, reasonable service, no undue discrimination, and no undue preference. The National Transportation Policy (1940) preamble to the 1887 Act to Regulate Commerce proclaims various regulatory goals for the ICC to follow in administering the intent of the act.[8] This preamble mandates the ICC to regulate the industries over which it has jurisdiction in such a way that the inherent advantage of each carrier be maintained and that a viable national common carrier system be developed to meet the needs of national defense, commerce, and the postal service. The Federal Aviation Act[9] and the U.S. Shipping Acts[10] contain similar policy statements pertaining to the administration of aviation activities and maritime interests, respectively.

The interpretation of "inherent advantage of each carrier" remains a controversial point in the prescription of policy by the ICC. Inherent advantage can indicate anything from a minimum cost firm to a maximum level of service operation. Perhaps the best theoretical treatment of this intricate issue appears in a recent article by Rosalind S. Seneca.[11] At the foundation of this issue lies the traditional marginal cost–marginal revenue paradigm. If the long-run marginal costs of all the participating firms in a given set of transportation markets are equal, then the social resource costs of providing the optimal amount of transportation will be minimized. This inference, however, raises many empirical problems that reflect the source of the controversy: How should such marginal cost curves be derived empirically?[12] How would regional differentials in marginal costs be handled? How are de facto prices related to marginal costs? How are the indirect transportation costs (like loss and damage,

8. See Grant M. Davis and Jack J. Holder, Jr., "Does the United States Have a Cohesive National Transportation Policy?–An Analysis," *ICC Practitioners' Journal* 41 (March/April 1974), pp. 332-49.

9. Stat. 760 (1938), 49 U.S.C. 1374(a).

10. 46 U.S.C. Sec. 1101 (1964).

11. Rosalind S. Seneca, "Inherent Advantage, Costs, and Resource Allocation in the Transportation Industry," *American Economic Review* 63 (December 1973), pp. 945-56.

12. In the absence of time, marginal cost is a simple concept: It is just the derivative of total cost with respect to a particular output. The introduction of time complicates the analysis by requiring the specification of the nature of the output (service); the timing of the change in marginal cost; the timing of the decision to change marginal cost; and the date to which cost changes are discounted or compounded in calculating their net worth. The result is a multiplicity of marginal costs whereby it is necessary to specify which of them are relevant for pricing. Suppose that there are no constraints, externalities, income distribution issues, or second-best considerations so that prices (rate) should reflect marginal costs. The question "which marginal costs?" then can be answered by remembering that the purpose of marginal-cost pricing is to insure that the cost incurred (saved) by a customer as a result of a decision reflect the cost incurred (saved) by the company. One way to guarantee this outcome would be the requirement of an individual long-term contract with a single customer. (Such contracts may only be worthwhile with a few large customers as long as discriminating pricing practices do not result). This principle also has been posited in relation to British public enterprises where "a customer's demand is large enough to justify the effort, a separate costing ought to be made of the demand he offers. Its amount and timing depend on him and it will not be marginal in the strict sense of relating to a tiny increment in output." See Ralph Turvey, *Economic Analysis and Public Enterprises* (London: George Allen & Unwin, 1971), p. 57.

unreliability, and delay costs) treated? How are the demands for transportation services and for individual mode's services determined? The regulatory commissions must consider these questions in the context of their enforcing the appropriate rate levels and rate structures[13] that allow traffic to be distributed in the most efficient way.[14] Unfortunately, the ability of the regulatory agency to determine costs unambiguously with past techniques has been limited, and the information necessary to perform estimates of such cost has not been made generally accessible.[15]

Theories of Regulation

What is regulation? Why do we have it in transportation? The answer to the first question is not straightforward at all. There appear to be three general explanations of regulation in the domestic public utility and transportation industries:

> . . . the first is that regulation is instituted primarily for the protection and benefit of the public at large or some large subclass of the public. In this view, the regulations which injure the public—as when the oil import quotas increase the cost of petroleum products to America by $5 billion or more a year—are costs of some social goal (here, national defense) or, occasionally, perversions of the regulatory philosophy. The second view is essentially that the political process defies rational explanation: "politics" is an imponderable, a constantly and unpredictably shifting mixture of forces of the most diverse nature, comprehending acts of great moral virtue (the emancipation of slaves) and of the most vulgar venality (the congressman feathering his own nest).[16]

Posner offered a third view:

> . . . In my opinion neither view, at least as thus far formulated, explains an important phenomenon of regulated industries: the deliberate and continued provision of many services at lower rates and in larger quantities than would be offered in an unregulated competitive market or, *a fortiori*, an unregulated monopolistic one. This phenomenon can be explained, I believe, only if we modify existing views by admitting that one of the functions of regulation is to perform distributive and allocative chores usually associated with the taxing or

13. The rate (or fare) level pertains to the average yield of a set of rates whereas the fare structure pertains to the relationship one fare has to another.

14. Care must be exercised in distinguishing between "efficiency-in-the-small" or cost minimization (to a firm) and "efficiency-in-the-large" or allocative efficiency. The concept of efficiency is generally expressed to characterize the utilization of resources. Efficiency is a statement about the economic performance of processes transforming a set of inputs into a set of outputs. It is a word that is easy to use, but quite difficult to pinpoint a precise meaning. For an interpretation of alternative efficiency measures, see Finn R. Forsund and Lennart Hjalmarsson, "On the Measurement of Productive Efficiency," *Swedish Journal of Economics* 76 (June 1974), pp. 141-54.

15. See James T. Kneafsey, *The Economics of the Transportation Firm*, (Lexington, Mass.: Lexington Books, D.C. Heath and Co., 1974), chap. 4.

16. George J. Stigler, "The Theory of Economic Regulation," *The Bell Journal of Economics and Management Science* 2 (Spring 1971), p. 3.

financial branch of government. And we shall see that an analysis of taxation by regulation explains other perplexing phenomena. But it would be error to think that the analysis compels rejection, as distinct from modification, of the existing views of regulation. I hope to show that any theory that conceives the function of regulation to be to approximate the results of competition, or to enrich the regulated firms, or to do sometimes the one and sometimes the other, is incomplete. But it does not follow that a broadened public-interest approach (one that accommodated certain subsidy elements) or a broadened effective-political-group approach (one that viewed certain customer classes as effective political groups) might not be tenable.[17]

Posner thus assigns the term "taxation by regulation" to the function of regulation, particularly in the cases of "internal subsidization," whereby unremunerative services (or cross-subsidies) are provided out of the profits from other services. Examples of the view abound in transportation: long-haul airline fares being based primarily on distance rather than on cost, resulting in the long-haul flights subsidizing the unprofitable short-haul ones;[18] railroad rates;[19] local and regional airline service;[20] and the flat rate characteristic of most urban transit systems.[21] The issues of internal subsidization, predatory price discrimination, and marginal cost pricing are quite intricate and beyond the scope of this discussion.[22] Suffice it to say, there are many deficiencies in the present arrangements of transportation regulation. Perhaps the best summary of these deficiencies has been provided by Clair Wilcox who identifies three general problems: First, regulation has been employed as a substitution for competition; second, many regulators are unflinchingly regulation minded; and third, many regulatory agencies possess large amounts of power but lack responsibility.[23] In summary, then, regulation possesses an inherent and continuing dilemma in the administration of rate determination:

In any economic setting, a central problem in the regulation of price discrimination is found in the need for accommodating what often appears to be the irreconcilable claims of efficiency, as an economic value, and equality, as a political value.[24]

---

17. Richard A. Posner, "Taxation by Regulation," *The Bell Journal of Economics and Management Science* 2 (Spring 1971), pp. 22-23.

18. Richard E. Caves, *Air Transport and Its Regulators* (Cambridge, Mass.: Harvard University Press, 1962).

19. Ann F. Friedlaender, *The Dilemma of Freight Transport Regulation* (Washington, D.C.: The Brookings Institution 1969).

20. George C. Eads, *The Local Service Airline Experiment* (Washington, D.C.: The Brookings Institution, 1972).

21. John R. Meyer, John F. Kain, and Martin Wohl, *The Urban Transportation Problem* (Cambridge, Mass.: Harvard University Press, 1965).

22. Discussions of "value-of-service" pricing in the railroad industry, for example, appear in most standard transportation economics textbooks.

23. Clair Wilcox, *Public Policies Toward Business*, 4th ed. (Homewood, Ill.: Richard D. Irwin, Inc., 1971), pp. 476-78.

24. J.J. Hillman, *Competition and Railroad Price Discrimination: Legal Precedent and Economic Policy* (Evanston, Ill.: The Transportation Center at Northwestern University, 1968), p. 1.

Independent Federal Regulatory Agencies

Regulation then may be regarded in a general way as a measure designed to alleviate any gaps between private and public interests that might arise. Traditionally, the regulatory agencies have operated via a system of rules concerning items such as rates, depreciation methods, rates of return, and so on. Yet, the problem remains that the rules allegedly have not provided any inducements to superior performance on the part of the firms under their jurisdictions. Quite frequently the rules or methods do not tell how or with what instruments a company could induce superior dynamic performance, such as its managerial decisions involving increased risk taking, cost reduction, service innovation, and new market development.[25] In consequence of the inherent limitations of regulation it functions more as a restraining influence than as a positive impetus to good performance. These restraining influences exercised by the regulatory agencies can be interpreted in relation to the cartel stabilization features of regulation.[26] In practice the ICC has devoted the major part of its efforts toward regulating selective competitive rate cutting,[27] but this fact is not surprising, since this should be the primary duty of a cartel-stabilizing agency.

One appealing view of the origin of the Interstate Commerce Commission is that it grew out of the joint railroad industry and grain shippers needs to stabilize the rate-making cartel in the 1880s.[28] The ICC was created by the 1887 Act to Regulate Commerce and thus is by far the oldest of the independent federal regulatory commissions. The other major regulatory agencies in transportation are the Civil Aeronautics Board and the Federal Maritime Commission. On special matters of interest, both the Securities and Exchange Commission and the Federal Power Commission are involved in transportation matters. In Table 9-1 is a set of information on these five agencies, depicting selected characteristics insofar as they relate to transportation.

U.S. Department of Transportation

One purpose of the 1966 legislation creating the U.S. Department of Transportation (DOT) was to circumvent the tendencies of the independent regulatory

25. The most striking example of a regulatory agency being a hindrance to the adoption of an innovation by a firm is the case of the Southern Railway's "Big John" hopper cars and the ICC. For a discussion, see Aaron J. Gellman's essay in William F. Capron, ed., *Technological Change in Regulated Industries* (Washington, D.C.: The Brookings Institution, 1971).

26. See Paul W. MacAvoy, *The Economic Effects of Regulation: The Trunk-Line Railroad Cartels and the Interstate Commerce Commission before 1900* (Cambridge, Mass.: M.I.T. Press, 1965).

27. Phillips, *The Economics of Regulation*.

28. MacAvoy, *The Economic Effects of Regulation.*

Table 9-1
Selected Data on the Federal Independent Regulatory Commissions

Agency	Year Established	Number of Members	Length of Term (Years)	Staff Size	1974 Fiscal Budget (Millions of Dollars)	Jurisdiction
Interstate Commerce Commission	1887	11	7	2,150	$39.8	Railroads; motor carriers; inland waterways; oil pipelines; express companies; freight forwarders
Civil Aeronautics Board	1938	5	6	1,253	23.4	Airlines
Securities and Exchange Commission	1934	5	5	1,742	23.2	Securities and financial markets; electric and gas utility holding companies.
Federal Power Commission	1920, 1930	5	5	1,545	20.5	Electric power; natural gas and natural gas pipelines; water-power sites.
Federal Communications Commission	1934	7	7	1,829	30.3	Radio; television; telephone; telegraph; cables

Source: The Budget of the United States Government, Fiscal Year 1975, Appendix (Washington, D.C.: U.S. Government Printing Office, 1974).

commissions to promote their own industries (namely, those industries over which the commissions have jurisdictional authority). Unfortunately, this purpose has failed. In less than a decade the Department of Transportation has become an extremely cumbersome institution with all the predictable (and unfortunate) consequences of a bureaucracy. Not only have problems arisen within the department, but other complications have resulted from the multiplicity of congressional interests which lie beneath the organization and support of the modal interests. The principal "modal agencies" within the U.S. Department of Transportation are the Federal Railroad Administration (FRA), the Federal Aviation Administration (FAA), Federal Highway Administration (FHWA), and the Urban Mass Transportation Agency (UMTA). In addition to the modal agencies within DOT are the special offices, including the Office of the Secretary, the Office of Policy and Development, Office of Research and Development, and so on–each being responsible for particular problems, issues, and policies that cross all modal boundaries. As Paul W. Shuldiner has pointed out, numerous House and Senate committees and subcommittees exercise legislative oversight with respect to transportation authorizations.[29] Figure 9-1 illustrates the maze of relationship that exists. Again, as Shuldiner states: "If broken down to subcommittees, where most of the action takes place, . . . (the situation) would be totally incomprehensible–a not inappropriate depiction of the real world."[30]

The department itself is quite large; its budget is $9 billion and it employed 71,000 workers in 1975. To show the relative position of DOT with the other executive branches, Table 9-2 lists the shifts in the employee counts for each of the executive branch agencies for the period 1970-73. The share of DOT in the total budgetary outlay program is still small, as Table 9-3 indicates, but it is expected that the role of DOT in procuring congressional funds will increase during the next decade. The major problem, then, becomes one of using these funds most effectively.

State and Local Regulatory Agencies

In addition to the federal independent regulatory commissions and the U.S. Department of Transportation, regulation of intrastate transportation activities is usually administered by a variety of state and local regulatory agencies. In particular, the state public utility or public service commissions are quite influential in effectuating state transportation policy. States like California with its Public Utilities Commission and Massachusetts with its Departments of

29. Paul W. Shuldiner, "Institutional Constraints on Comprehensive Transportation Planning at the Federal Level," *Proceedings of the Transportation Research Forum* (October 1974), pp. 285-89.

30. Ibid., p. 286.

Transportation and Public Works are especially active in transportation matters. In addition, most states now have developed their own departments of transportation. Cities and metropolitan agencies have created primarily planning agencies to assist in the development of planning mechanisms to administer a variety of economic and environmental plans involving transportation, and to qualify for federal funds that may be available for specific transportation projects.

In general, regulatory commissions reach final decisions in cases brought before their jurisdictions by examining the presentations of the parties, deciding the relative merits of their arguments, and possibly making adjustments and modifications whenever special conditions arise. In a special study of the decision-making process of a state regulatory commission, Paul L. Joskow postulated the following model:[31]

$$R^* = H(P_f, P_I, J, E, U)$$

where

R^* = allowed rate of return

P_f = presentation of the firm in the hearing

P_I = presentation of intervenors

J = judgment of the commission

E = performance characteristics of the firm: subjective judgment by the commission concerning the efficiency of the particular firm (the commission might reward firms that performed well)

U = random distrubance factors

His empirical evidence suggested that the rate of return allowed by the commission depended on the size and relative reasonableness of the firm's request, the presence or absence of intervenors presenting conflicting rate-of-return testimony, the type of firm itself, and a subjective evaluation of the efficiency of the firm making the request. Joskow's results also suggested that the behavior of the commission shifted in response to problems characterized by rapid inflation. Additional research on the impacts of regulation, both at the federal and state levels, appears warranted.

31. Paul L. Joskow, "The Determination of the Allowed Rate of Return in a Formal Regulatory Hearing," *The Bell Journal of Economics and Management Science* 3 (Autumn 1972), pp. 632-44.

Conclusion

Regulation in transportation has been criticized adversely because of resource misallocation effects, the lack of viable competition, and a general insensitivity regarding the changing needs of the consuming public. The defenders of

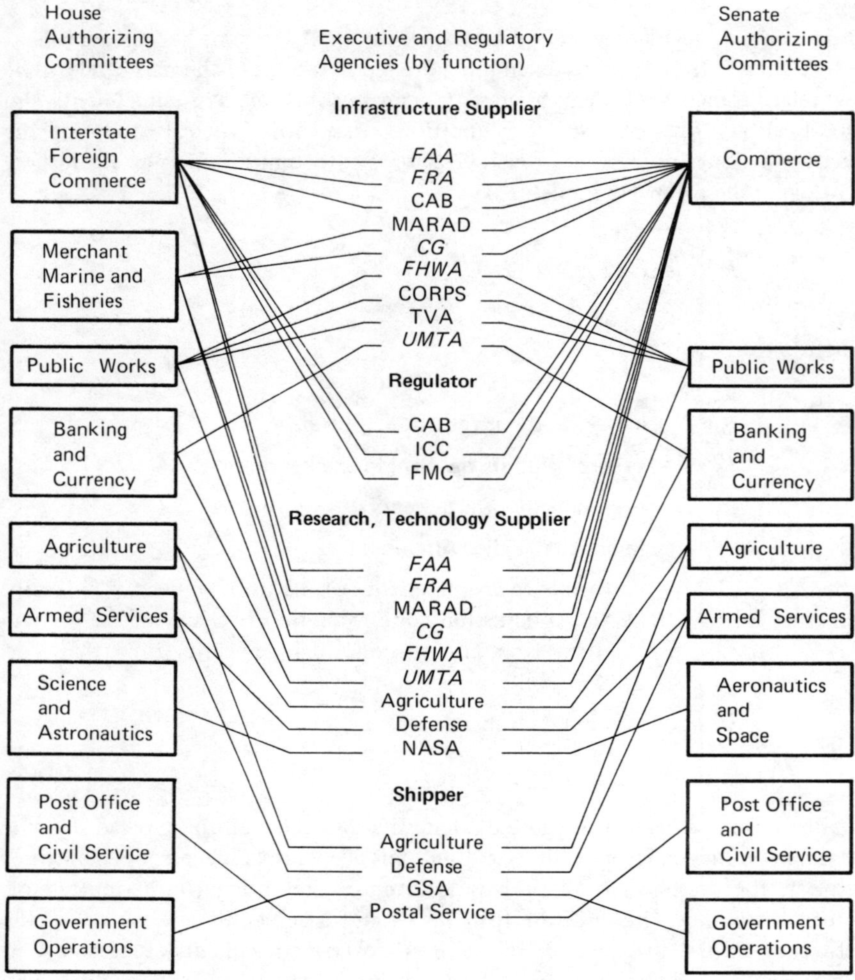

Figure 9-1. Congressional-Executive Relationships for Transportation Authorizations. Source: *Report on a Long-Range Transportation Planning System*, National Academy of Sciences (March 1972); and Paul W. Shuldiner, "Institutional Constraints on Comprehensive Transportation Planning at the Federal Level," Proceedings of the Transportation Research Forum (October 1974), p. 287.

transportation regulation point to the overall stability of rates, generally dependable services, shipper participation in the establishment of rates, and the reduction of uncertainty as indicative of the beneficial attributes of regulation. In theory, a decision on a given case by the independent regulatory commissions must be based on a practical solution to numerous facts and

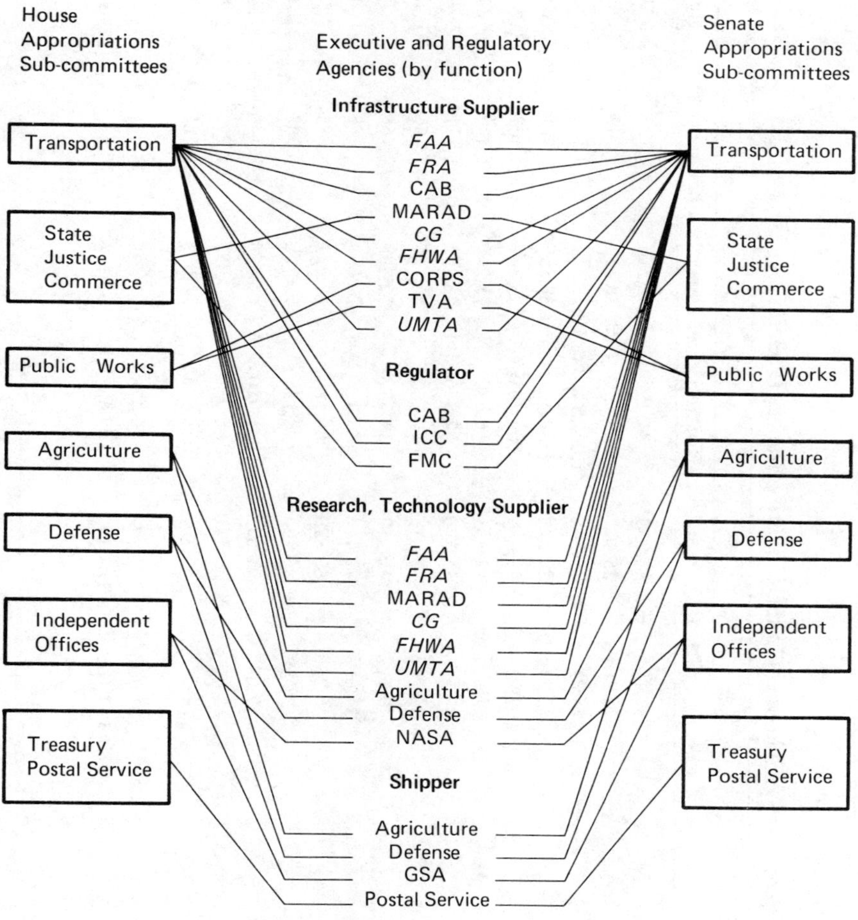

Figure 9-1. (cont.)

Table 9-2
Summary of Full-time Permanent Employment in the Executive Branch, 1969-75

Agency	As of June 30						
	1969 Actual[a]	1970 Actual[a]	1971 Actual[a]	1972 Actual[a]	1973 Actual	1974 Estimate	1975 Estimate
Agriculture	83,425	82,553	84,252	82,511	81,715	80,200	80,200
Commerce	25,364	25,427	28,435	28,412	28,300	28,600	29,100
Defense–military functions	1,225,877	1,129,642	1,062,741	1,009,562	957,310	996,600	995,900
Defense–civil functions	31,214	30,293	30,063	30,585	29,971	28,700	29,100
Health, Education, and Welfare	102,941	99,667	104,283	105,764	114,307	123,900	126,200
Housing and Urban Development	14,307	14,661	16,030	15,200	15,820	14,800	14,200
Interior	58,156	56,570	57,570	56,892	56,771	58,900	59,400
Justice	35,106	38,013	42,662	45,446	45,496	48,900	51,000
Labor	9,723	10,217	11,352	12,339	12,468	12,700	13,000
State	24,658	23,618	23,398	22,699	22,578	23,400	23,400
Transportation	60,386	63,879	68,489	67,232	67,885	69,500	71,300
Treasury	79,982	86,020	90,135	95,728	98,087	104,700	111,400
Atomic Energy Commission	7,047	7,033	6,920	6,836	7,145	7,400	7,800
Environmental Protection Agency	--	5,778	5,959	7,835	8,270	9,200	9,200
General Services Administration	36,176	36,400	38,076	36,002	35,721	37,200	38,000
National Aeronautics and Space Administration	31,733	31,223	29,478	27,428	25,955	25,000	24,600
Veterans' Administration	147,606	148,497	158,635	163,179	170,616	173,400	181,800

Other:							
Agency for International Development	15,753	14,486	13,477	11,719	10,108	9,900	9,500
Civil Service Commission	4,970	5,214	5,324	5,260	5,911	6,100	6,300
Selective Service System	6,584	6,665	5,569	5,791	4,607	3,100	2,200
Small Business Administration	4,099	4,015	4,004	3,916	4,050	4,100	4,300
Tennessee Valley Authority	11,987	12,657	13,612	14,001	13,995	14,000	14,400
Panama Canal	14,731	14,635	13,967	13,777	13,680	14,000	14,100
United States Information Agency	10,500	9,989	9,773	9,255	9,048	9,100	9,100
Miscellaneous	29,056	29,801	31,332	33,494	34,603	37,300	37,600
Subtotal	2,071,381	1,986,953	1,955,536	1,910,863	1,874,417	1,940,700	1,963,100
Contingencies	--	--	--	--	--	2,000	5,000
Subtotal	2,071,381	1,986,953	1,955,536	1,910,863	1,874,417	1,942,700	1,968,100
Postal Service	562,381	565,618	603,782	594,834	547,283	537,900	534,700
Total	2,633,762	2,552,571[b]	2,559,318	2,505,697	2,421,700	2,480,600	2,502,800

[a]Compiled from budget documents.

[b]Adjusted to include 39,000 Postal Service employees previously classifed as temporary.

Table 9-3
Budget Expenditures by Federal Agency, 1973-75

Department or Other Unit	Fiscal Year Outlays[a]		
	1973	1974	1975
Legislative branch	540	658	734
The judiciary	183	213	310
Executive Office of the President	49	112	121
Funds appropriated to the president	3,733	4,603	4,414
Agriculture	10,028	9,311	9,184
Commerce	1,368	1,519	1,712
Defense–military	73,297	78,400	84,600
Defense–civil	1,703	1,621	1,649
Health, Education, and Welfare	82,040	96,768	110,959
Housing and Urban Development	3,592	4,983	5,550
Interior	–2,253	–3,774	–2,657
Justice	1,531	1,938	2,106
Labor	8,639	8,590	10,043
State	591	743	793
Transportation	**8,183**	**8,444**	**9,059**
Treasury	30,960	35,849	37,633
Atomic Energy Commission	2,393	2,328	2,886
Environmental Protection Agency	1,114	2,559	3,991
General Services Administration	468	–306	–883
National Aeronautics and Space Administration	3,311	3,177	3,272
Veterans Administration	11,968	13,241	13,594
Other independent agencies	11,449	13,343	14,528
Allowances	––	300	1,561
Undistributed intragovernmental transactions:			
Employer share, employee retirement	–2,927	–3,543	–3,577
Interest received by trust funds	–5,436	–6,420	–7,140
Total Budgeted Outlays	246,526	274,660	304,445

[a]Figures are in millions of current dollars.

Source: U.S. Budget of the Federal Government, Fiscal Year 1975, Table 5, p. 54.

allegations, reflecting purely economic reasoning on the one hand and vested interests of individual participants on the other. The result inevitably leads to what Ann F. Friedlaender calls a "dilemma" and what Paul W. MacAvoy labels a "crisis."[32] Perhaps economic analysis simply has reached the limit of its application to issues of regulation:

32. Friedlaender, *Freight Transport Regulation* and MacAvoy, *Crisis*, p. 73.

(The technique of) marginal social costs/marginal social benefits does provide some theoretical justification for regulating the industry in addition to the traditional arguments of balancing competition, avoiding monopolies, controlling prices, providing reasonable services, *ad infinitum*. Critics of the domestic transportation industry essentially want to change the industry, particularly that part dealing with trucking, but as Professor Stigler so eloquently stated, they should use political processes—not economic analyses.[33]

33. Grant M. Davis and Charles S. Sherwood, "Transportation Regulation: Another Dimension," *ICC Practitioner's Journal* 42 (January/February 1975), pp. 164-74 (the reference in the quote to Stigler is from Stigler, "The Theory of Economic Regulation," p. 18).

Selected Bibliography: Microeconomic Theory and Transportation

Air Cushion Vehicles for Use in Developing Countries (New York: Department of Economic and Social Affairs, United Nations, 1974).

Barger, Harold. *The Transportation Industries: 1889-1946* (New York: National Bureau of Economic Research, Inc., 1951).

Davis, Grant M., and Linda J. Combs. "Some Observations Regarding Value-of-Service Pricing in Transportation." *Transportation Journal* 14 (Spring 1975), pp. 49-58.

Deakin, B.M., and T. Seward. *Productivity in Transport: A Study of Employment, Capital, Output, Productivity and Technical Change* (London: Cambridge University Press, 1969).

Environmental Protection Agency. *Working Papers in Alternative Futures and Environmental Quality* (Washington: May 1973).

Fair, Marvin L., and James R. Nelson. *Criteria for Transport Pricing: Air-Land-Water* (Cambridge, Md.: Cornell Maritime Press, 1973).

Fair, Marvin L., and John Guandolo. *Transportation Regulation*, 7th ed. (Dubuque, Iowa: William C. Brown Co., Inc., 1973).

Faulks, R.W. *Elements of Transport*, 2nd ed. (London: Ian Allan, Ltd., 1969).

Friedlander, Ann F. *The Dilemma of Freight Transport Regulation* (Washington: The Brookings Institution, 1969).

Fromm, Gary, ed. *Transport Investment and Economic Development* (Washington: The Brookings Institution, 1965).

Harbeson, Robert W. "Toward Better Resource Allocation in Transport," *Journal of Law and Economics* 12 (October 1969), pp. 321-38.

Haritos, Z. "Theory of Road Pricing," *Transportation Journal* 13 (Spring 1974), pp. 53-64.

Heaver, Trevor D. "The Structure of Liner Conference Rates," *Journal of Industrial Economics* 21 (July 1973), pp. 257-65.

Hilton, George W. "The Basic Behavior of Regulatory Commissions," *Papers and Proceedings of the American Economic Association* 62 (May 1972), pp. 47-54.

Hollander, Stanley C., ed. *Passenger Transportation* (East Lansing, Mich.: Graduate School of Business Administration, Michigan State University, 1968).

Johnson, James C. *Trucking Mergers: A Regulatory Viewpoint* (Lexington, Mass.: Lexington Books, D.C. Heath and Co., 1973).

_______. "Section 22: Panacea or Parasite?" *Transportation Journal* 13 (Summer 1974), pp. 34-40.

_______. "Deregulation of Transportation: Its Probable Ramifications," *Pro-*

ceedings of the Transportation Research Forum 15 (October 1974), pp. 133-38.

Johnson, James C., and Donald V. Harper. "The Potential Consequences of Deregulation of Transportation." *Land Economics* 51 (February 1975), pp. 58-71.

Jordan, William A. *Airline Regulation in America: Effects and Imperfections* (Baltimore, Md.: The Johns Hopkins Press, 1970).

Kahn, Alfred E. *The Economics of Regulation: Principles and Institutions:* vol. 1: *Economic Principles* (New York: John Wiley & Sons, Inc., 1970).

Kneafsey, James T. *The Economics of the Transportation Firm* (Lexington, Mass.: Lexington Books, D.C. Heath and Co., 1974).

Kraft, Gerald. "Free Transit Revisited," *Public Policy* 21 (Winter 1973), pp. 79-105.

Lackman, Conway L. "Implication of Conglomerates for Transportation in the 1970's," *Transportation Journal* 14 (Fall 1974), pp. 30-45.

Ladenson, Mark L., and Stoga, Alan J. "Returns to Scale in the U.S. Trucking Industry," *Southern Economic Journal* 40 (January 1974), pp. 390-96.

Lane, R., T.J. Powell, and P. Prestwood-Smith, *Analytical Transport Planning* (London: Duckworth, 1971).

MacAvoy, Paul W., ed. *The Crisis of the Regulatory Commissions* (New York: W.W. Norton and Co., Inc., 1970).

Meyer, John R., and Mahlon R. Straszheim. *Techniques of Transport Planning:* Vol. I: *Pricing and Project Evaluation* (Washington: The Brookings Institution, 1971).

Meyer, John R., Merton J. Peck, John Stenason, and Charles Zwick. *The Economics of Competition in the Transportation Industries* (Cambridge, Mass.: Harvard University Press, 1960).

National Bureau of Economic Research. *Transportation Economics* (New York: Columbia University Press, 1965).

Nelson, James R. "Motor Carrier Regulation and the Financing of the Industry," *ICC Practitioners' Journal* 41 (May/June 1974), pp. 436-57.

Nove, Alec. *Efficiency Criteria for Nationalized Industries* (London: George Allen & Unwin, 1973).

Phillips, Charles F. Jr. *The Economics of Regulation: Theory and Practice in the Transportation and Public Utility Industries* (1965; rpt. Homewood, Ill.: Richard C. Irwin, Inc., 1969).

Quandt, Richard E., ed., *The Demand For Travel: Theory and Measurement* (Lexington, Mass.: Lexington Books, D.C. Heath and Co., 1970).

The Ralph Nader Study Group. *The Interstate Commerce Omission* (New York: Grossman Publishers, 1970).

Sampson, Roy J. "Inherent Advantages Under Regulation," *Papers and Proceedings of the American Economic Association* 62 (May 1972), pp. 55-61.

Sampson, Roy J., and Martin T. Farris. *Domestic Transportation: Practice, Theory and Policy* (1966; rpt. Boston: Houghton Mifflin, 1971).

Seneca, Rosalind S. "Inherent Advantage, Costs, and Resource Allocation in the Transportation Industry," *American Economic Review* 63 (December 1973), pp. 945-56.

Spychalski, John C. "Criticisms of Regulated Freight Transport: Do Economists' Perceptions Conform with Institutional Realities?" *Transportation Journal* 14 (Spring 1975), pp. 5-17.

Thomson, A.W.J., and L.C. Hunter. *The Nationalized Transport Industries* (London: Heinemann Educational Books, 1973).

Transportation Association of America. *Transportation Facts and Trends* (Washington, 1974).

Trebing, Harry M., ed. *Essays on Public Utility Pricing and Regulation* (East Lansing, Mich.: The Institute of Public Utilities, 1971).

U.S. Department of Transportation, Office of the Secretary. *Summary of National Transportation Statistics* (Washington, D.C., November 1973).

Waters, W.G., and D.G. Hildebrand. "Road Costs and Government Revenues from Heavy Vehicles in Canada," *Canadian Journal of Economics* 6 (November 1973), pp. 608-12.

Watson, Peter L. "Homogeneity of Models of Transport Mode Choice: The Dimensions of Trip Length and Journey Purpose," *Journal of Regional Science* 14 (August 1974), pp. 247-57.

_______. *The Value of Time: Behavioral Models of Modal Choice* (Lexington, Mass.: Lexington Books, D.C. Heath and Co., 1974).

Wohl, Martin. *Transportation Investment Planning* (Lexington, Mass.: Lexington Books, D.C. Heath and Company, 1972).

Part II: The Domestic Transportation Industries

10 The Airline Industry

A member of the Rothschild family is claimed to have once advised on the three most dependable ways to lose money: "... put it on horses—the fastest way; spend it on women—the pleasantest way; or invest it in aviation—the surest way."[1] Although this prescription for the airline industry is a hyperbole, there are occasional periods when it is true. The airline industry is the newest of the major modes and in many ways the most glamorous. As a result, many investment decisions within the industry have been criticized rather adversely, especially in the timing of aircraft purchases. With a change in national priorities in the United States during the early 1970s from an economy with a heavy commitment to aerospace and military productions to one less so, the importance of accurately forecasting aircraft purchases by the airline firms becomes quite compelling. Since more than three-quarters of their capital stock is in aircraft equipment, the airline firms will experience red ink on their income statements very quickly with a single major purchasing mistake.

The overall airline industry consists of several sectors: the international carriers; the domestic trunk lines; local service or regional airlines; third level air carriers or air taxis; and supplemental or nonscheduled airlines. Each sector contains its own special features regarding entry conditions, profitability, and the level of service.

The international airline industry includes Pan Am plus several of the trunk airlines that participate in selected international routes. Most of the international airline industry consists of each country's flag carrier competing with one another on the major international routes. Regulation is of the self-imposed variety and falls under the doctrines of the International Air Transport Association (IATA), the industry's cartel. The best reference for detailed information on this sector of the airline industry is provided in Mahlon R. Straszheim's[2] book, *The International Airline Industry*.

The domestic portion of the airline industry is characterized by large private investments in equipment and facilities, coupled with public financing for airports and many supporting airway features. The modern fleet of aircraft represents expensive outlays for equipment and requires an elaborate array of instrumentation and technical personnel to maintain its operation at maximum

1. "Productivity: The Key to Success," *Technology Review* 76 (October/November 1973), p. 66.

2. Mahlon R. Straszheim, *The International Airline Industry* (Washington, D.C.: The Brookings Institution, 1969).

levels of safety and convenience. As an example of equipment costs, examine Table 10-1, which shows the early 1975 purchase prices for selected commercial aircraft.

The major classes of domestic air carriers are the trunklines, local service carriers, air commuters, and supplementary or charter carriers.[3] The trunks dominate the industry, with the Big Four (American, Eastern, TWA, and United) accounting for roughly two-thirds of all revenue passenger-miles.[4] The best source for the names and initial routes of the United States domestic airlines is Phillips' monograph,[5] which lists all the carriers analogous to the domestic trunklines that entered scheduled operations prior to 1938. An excellent source on the development of the local service carriers is a recent book by George C. Eads.[6] The local service carriers (originally called "feeders" and sometimes "regionals") were created by the CAB after World War II for the specific purpose of furnishing local feeder air service. While 19 carriers were originally certificated as local service carriers, only nine remain, following the absorption of Mohawk Airlines by Allegheny Airlines in 1972 and the certification of Air New England in 1974.[7] A narrow definition of the domestic airline industry then would include the trunk carriers and the local service carriers. Clearly this segment of the industry is dominant in terms of any market structure proxy for size,

Table 10-1
Purchase Prices for Selected Commercial Aircraft

	($ Millions)
DC-9-30	5-7
B727-21	7-9
DC-10/L-1011	18-22
B747	24-28
Concorde	60-100
U.S. SST[a]	100 +

[a]Based on a renewed effort to revive the original B2707 version of the SST.

3. This classification excludes helicopter carriers, seaplane service, and all-cargo lines.

4. The trunk carriers are those certificated in 1938 under the "grandfather" provisions of the Civil Aeronautics Act (Section 401(e)(1)). Table 10-2 shows the changes in the trunklines from that time to the present; and Table 10-3 indicates four of the more important performance measures among the trunklines, namely, operating ratio, debt ratio, rate of return, and profit margin.

5. Almarin Phillips, *Technology and Market Structure: A Study of the U.S. Aircraft Industry* (Lexington, Mass.: Lexington Books, D.C. Heath and Co., 1971).

6. George C. Eads, *The Local Service Airline Experiment* (Washington, D.C.: The Brookings Institution, 1972).

7. Ibid.

Table 10-2
Domestic Trunk Airlines, 1938-75

Carrier	Year of Trunk Line Operations[a]
American Airlines	1938-
Eastern Air Lines	1938-
Trans-World Airlines	1938-
United Air Lines	1938-
Braniff Airways	1938-
Continental Air Lines	1938-
Delta Air Lines	1938-
National Airlines	1938-
Northwest Airlines	1938-
Western Air Lines	1938-
Capital Airlines[b]	1938-60
Chicago and Southern Air Lines[c]	1938-52
Colonial Airlines[d]	1938-55
Inland Air Lines[e]	1938-51
Mid-Continent Airlines[f]	1938-51
Northeast Airlines[g]	1938-72
Pan American Airways[h]	1974-

[a]From 1938 to last full year of operation; names given are of most recent vintage.
[b]Absorbed by United Air Lines, June 1961.
[c]Absorbed by Delta Air Lines, May 1953.
[d]Absorbed by Eastern Air Lines, June 1956.
[e]Absorbed by Western Air Lines, April 1952.
[f]Absorbed by Braniff Airways, August 1952.
[g]Operated as Boston-Maine Airways, 1936 to 1938; absorbed by Delta Air Lines, August 1972.
[h]Pan Am was certified as a domestic trunk airline (in addition to its international operations) by the CAB in June 1974.
Sources: U.S. Civil Aeronautics Board, *Air Carrier Financial Statistics, 1958-1973*; Air Transport Association of America, *Air Transport* 1974.

whether it be operating revenues, passenger-miles, or assets. Table 10-3 shows the trunk and local service airlines with their rates-of-return for the period 1965-72.

A third sector of the domestic airline industry pertains to the synonymous terms: commuter air carriers, third-level carrier, or air taxi. The commuter air carrier industry has played an increasingly significant role in the provision of air transportation to small cities. Part 298 of the Civil Aeronautics Board's *Economic Regulations* designates "air taxi operators" as a class of air carriers

Table 10-3
Average Financial Statistics for the Trunk Air Line Firms, 1960-72[a]

	Operating Ratio[b]	Debt Ratio[c]	Rate of Return[d]	Profit Margin[e]
American	93.7	62.5	6.5	3.2
Braniff	93.3	59.3	7.6	3.0
Continental	88.6	62.7	9.7	4.5
Delta	85.9[f]	42.5	15.8[f]	7.5
Eastern	100.3	69.6	2.7	0.1
National	89.8	51.0	11.0	5.8
Northwest	86.7	38.0[f]	13.3	10.6[f]
TWA	98.8	66.5	5.8	1.5
United	95.2	56.8	5.9	2.6
Western	90.5	51.8	10.4	3.8

[a]Calculated as the average (mean) *ratio* for each firm for the period 1960-72.

[b]The ratio of operating expenses to operating revenues.

[c]The ratio of long-term debt to total capital (long-term debt plus common equity).

[d]The ratio of net income to invested capital, as defined by the CAB.

[e]The ratio of net income (profits) to sales.

[f]Indicates the best performance in each column category.

Source: Richard D. Gutta, "Risk and the Fair Rate of Return in Air Transportation," *Transportation Journal* 13 (Summer 1974), pp. 41-45. Reproduced with permission from the *Transportation Journal*, a quarterly publication of the American Society of Traffic & Transportation, Inc., 547 W. Jackson Blvd., Chicago, IL.

that, among other things, "do not directly or indirectly utilize in air transportation large aircraft (other than turbojet aircraft authorized for use under certain conditions), and "do not hold a certificate of public convenience and necessity or other economic authority issued by the Board." "Commuter air carrier" is defined as "an air taxi operator that either performs at least five round trips per week between two or more points and publishes flight schedules that specify the times, days of the week and places between which such flights are performed, or transports mail by air pursuant to a current contract with the Post Office Department." Air taxi operators therefore are exempted from economic regulation.[8]

8. Since Part 298 became effective in 1952, several changes have occurred. Originally air taxi operators were not permitted to carry mail or to provide frequent service on markets that were served by certificated carriers with small aircraft or by helicopter airlines. Of course, this has changed over the years; in fact, as of September 1972 the CAB's definition of "large aircraft" was changed from one with maximum gross takeoff weight exceeding 12,500 pounds to an aircraft having a maximum passenger capacity of more than 30 seats or a maximum payload capacity of more than 7,500 pounds. The 12,500 pounds weight limitation and the limitation as to the markets that air taxis could serve were intended to protect the certificated airlines from competition (Eads, *The Local Service Airline Experiment*). Also during the last several years, under certain circumstances the CAB allowed a number of commuter airlines to use equipment exceeding the 12,500 pound limit (usually DC-3 aircraft).

During the 1960s the commuter air carrier industry experienced tremendous growth as they began serving the markets that were being neglected by the local service airlines who became more interested in serving denser, longer haul markets. In 1960 there were 10 scheduled air taxis (or commuter airlines); in April 1971 the National Air Transportation Conferences reported 144 commuter airlines in service. The numbers vary due to the relative instability of the industry, but the facts are that the commuter air carrier industry has undergone a dramatic growth since 1960 and that it is becoming more stable and mature. The CAB reports that during 1973, 72 commuter air carriers registered with the board (in one or more quarters),[9] and that during 1974 the number was 185. The dramatic rise in commuter air firms that provide service to low-population density areas has occurred as a result of the gradual retreat of the large carriers from this type of service.[10] In many low-density areas, however, air service can hardly be self-sustaining even at the commuter air carrier level. (Table 10-4 depicts the range of air service available to cities with population less than 100,000 in 1970.)[11] The continual reassessment of CAB policy in short-haul air service to communities of light traffic density is necessary to bring about a stronger common carrier distribution in the airline industry. The reassessment is important from a policy viewpoint when the users of such service are discovered to be concentrated into a relatively few major hubs (like New York, Chicago, and Houston) and tourist areas (like Puerto Rico, Southern California, and Southern Florida).[12]

In examining particular airline markets, two broad classifications should be considered: scheduled and nonscheduled service. *Scheduled service* is that available to the public at a fixed price and according to a published timetable or at sufficiently regular times as to constitute a systematic service. *Nonscheduled service* refers to the remainder of domestic air service: in effect, charter operations. Airline firms that offer charter service are tenderly referred to as "supplementals." One might ask: Why bother to study the supplemental air carriers? The whole supplemental industry accounts for only 7 percent of the

9. During 1971 only 107 commuter air carriers registered for all four quarters. Source: U.S. Civil Aeronautics Board, *Commuter Air Carrier Traffic Statistics*, year ended December 31, 1971.

10. See Jorge Cowley, "Air Service to Small Communities: Practice, Theory and Policy," M.S. Thesis, Department of Civil Engineering, M.I.T., June 1973.

11. The most interesting arrangement in this sector of the industry is between Allegheny Airlines and a group of lessees, who provide air commuter services. The nine Allegheny Commuter operators are the following: AeroMech, Air East, Atlantic City Airlines, Crown Airways, Fischer Brothers Aviation, Henson Aviation, Pocono Airlines, Ransome Airlines, and Vercoa Air Service. The 15 cities served by these operators are the following: Altoona, Pa.; Atlantic City, N.J.; Danville, Ill.; DuBois, Pa.; Elkins, W. Va.; Franklin, Pa.; Hagerstown, Md.; Hazletown, Pa.; Johnston, Pa.; Mansfield, Ohio; Muncie, Ind.; North Philadelphia, Pa.; Salisbury, Md.; Trenton, N.J.; and Wildwood, N.J. In addition to the main hubs, these cities originally were served by Allegheny Airlines and now are served by Allegheny Commuters. For additional background material, see Eads, *The Local Service Airline Experiment*, pp. 168-69.

12. See James T. Kneafsey, *The Economics of the Transportation Firm* (Lexington, Mass.: Lexington Books, D.C. Heath and Co., 1974). table 2-10.

Table 10-4
Air Service in 1970 at Cities with 1960 Population of Less Than 100,000

Service	Number of Cities	Percent of Total
Trunk only	11	2.2
Local only	185	36.3
Commuter carrier only	152	29.9
Trunk and local	30	5.9
Trunk and commuter	21	4.1
Local and commuter	89	17.5
Trunk, local, and commuter	21	4.1
	509	100.0

Source: U.S. Civil Aeronautics Board, Bureau of Operating Rights, Service to Small Communities, Pt. II, March 1972.

airline industry's annual gross revenue and is not quite as large as Northwest Orient, the seventh largest trunk airline. The supplementals are dismissed as insignificant in some studies because it is contended, for the most part correctly, that excluding about 20 percent of the industry (supplementals, all cargo air carriers, and air taxi operations) will not impair research conclusions.[13] Indeed, these carriers operate differently and might distort the results of certain studies, but these differences, especially those of the supplementals, should not be brushed aside so easily. In spite of the uncertainty of their existence, the supplementals have proved not only tenacious but have grown over the past decade. Table 10-5 briefly describes some of the characteristics of this section of the industry. Even though most of their operations are international in scope, the supplemental carriers are mentioned here as an important sector of the industry, especially in view of their capacities to haul freight.[14]

Rate of Return

The issue of the appropriate level of a fair rate of return has been quite controversial and thoroughly documented, irrespective of the industry. The issue has been no less serious for transportation firms even though they have been relatively immune from the imposition of regulatory constraints like those in the utility industries. In the airline industry the first standard established was a fair rate of return on capital investment and was designed for ascertaining reasonable fare levels.[15]

13. Eads, *The Local Service Airline Experiment.*

14. Straszheim, *The International Airline Industry*, pp. 217-19.

15. U.S. Civil Aeronautics Board, *General Passenger Fare Investigation Economic and Safety Enforcement Cases*, vol. 23 (Washington, D.C.: 1960), p. 291ff.

Table 10-5
Supplemental Air Carriers

Airline[a]	Commercial Area Authority[b]
Trans International Airlines	Transatlantic, Transpacific, Central & South America, Caribbean
Overseas National Airways	Transatlantic
World Airways	Transatlantic, Transpacific, Central & South America, Caribbean
Universal Airlines	Canada, Mexico
Capital Airways	Transatlantic, Caribbean
Saturn Airways	Transatlantic, Caribbean
American Flyers Airline	Transatlantic, Caribbean, Canada, Mexico
Modern Air Transport	Canada, Mexico
Southern Air Transport	Caribbean, Transpacific
Purdue Airlines	Canada
McCullock International Airlines	Canada, Mexico
Johnson Flying Service	Canada

[a]Airlines ranked by 1972 gross revenues.

[b]All airlines have Domestic and Hawaii Civilian authority and worldwide military charter authority.

In the early 1960s the trunk airline industry adopted a rate of return based on capital investment standard that was established by the CAB for ascertaining reasonable fare levels.[16] The airlines had argued unsuccessfully for the adoption of the "operating ratio" (the ratio of operating revenue to operating expense) as the most appropriate standard because they asserted it provided a better measure of the degree of risk involved in obtaining external investment funds.[17] The fair rate of return (after taxes but before interest rate deductions) was set at 10.5 percent. This figure represented a weighted average of those rates thought to be needed by the Big Four carriers (10.25%) and the smaller carriers (11.125%) to maintain financial integrity and access to external investment funds and reflected the "cost of capital" approach used by most public utilities.[18]

The 1960 general fare investigation settled some, though by no means all, of the problems associated with standards of reasonable fares. There was testimony

16. U.S. Civil Aeronautics Board, *General Passenger Fare Investigation, Economic and Safety Enforcement Cases.*

17. Ibid., pp. 294-95.

18. In the 1960 "General Passenger Fare Investigation," the CAB restricted the capital base to operating property and equipment used in rendering actual airline service and therefore excluded such airline assets as hotels and television stations. Deferred tax allowances, reserves accumulated by charges to operating expenses, and cash outlays for undelivered orders of new flight equipment were other items excluded so that carriers would not be able to artificially inflate their capital stock estimates. Finally, the capital structure was to consist of the actual mixture of debt and equity prevailing in the industry, instead of some hypothetical ideal mixture.

early in the hearings on the need to establish an efficient pricing policy for particular fares like discount fares, but no concrete decisions resulted. Nor was there consideration given to change in the fare structure in order to reflect lower average costs being experienced over longer route segments. The hearings even brought out those weaknesses inherent in the adopted resolutions. The rate-of-return standard implied that the CAB would henceforth have to treat the individual trunklines as if they were a single unit. Thus, the fare level would necessarily have to be set high enough to recover revenue that covered the costs of both efficient and inefficient operators.

Due to a prolonged economic recession in 1961, trunkline profit levels continued to decline. This period was especially acute for the industry because of the substantial transformation from piston- to jet-engine aircraft fleets then underway. The CAB approved a 2.5 percent, plus one-dollar-per-ticket, general fare increase in July 1960, expressing the belief that the resulting improvement in revenues would allow the carriers to achieve a 10.5 percent rate-of-return on their investments over the next few years. When airline income statements did not show an appreciable improvement in earnings in the second half of 1961, another 3 percent fare level increase was granted in February 1962.[19] Beginning in late 1963 prosperity returned to the industry, with most of the trunk airlines experiencing record high rates-of-return during the next few years. At this point the CAB notified the airlines that the general fare level would be revised downward unless discount fares were reduced and the level of service was improved.[20] The firms immediately cut "family-plan" and "Visit USA" fares, and introduced off-season "group," along with various other excursion, discount packages. Although the board was generally satisfied at the end of 1965 with these changes and decided not to order an overall fare level reduction, it still continued to apply pressure for more discount rate experimentation, and inaugurated new competitive route investigations.[21] The result was an unprecedented sequence of new route awards, beginning with the "Pacific Northwest-Southwest Service Case."[22]

Beginning in 1967 the combined effects of inflated labor wage settlements, a decline in the rate of traffic growth caused by the slowdown in general economic activity, greatly intensified airline competition, and record financial commitments for new wide-body jet aircraft induced another sharp deterioration in trunk carriers' income. Whereas trunkline carriers reported pre-tax profits of $416 million or a 11.2 percent rate-of-return on their investments in 1965, only

19. U.S. Civil Aeronautics Board, "Fares and Rates in U.S. Transport: 1926-1970," *Handbook of Airline Statistics* (Washington, D.C.: 1971 edition), pp. 501-2.

20. James R. Ashlock, "Airline Initiative to Determine Fare Action," *Aviation Week and Space Technology* 83 (August 9, 1965), pp. 35-36.

21. James R. Ashlock, "Downward Pressure on Fares to Continue," *Aviation Week and Space Technology* 84 (March 6, 1966), pp. 173-78.

22. U.S. Civil Aeronautics Board, "Major Civil Aeronautics Board Actions: 1938-1970," *Handbook of Airline Statistics* (Washington, D.C.: 1971 edition), p. 491.

$16 million or a 1.5 percent rate-of-return was evident in 1970. Furthermore, when one takes into consideration after-tax profits, the industry suffered in 1970 its first net loss in history, amounting to a $40 million deficit.[23] During this period the CAB came under severe airline criticism for its over-enthusiasm in approving competitive route awards. When no general agreement could be reached between the board and the airlines as to the specific remedial steps to be taken, a second general passenger fare investigation was ordered in late 1969. The fare level phase of this investigation ended on April 9, 1971, whereby the CAB reaffirmed both the appropriateness of the rate-of-return standard and its policy that the fare levels must be regulated to produce a reasonable return over an extended period of time. The fair rate-of-return was raised from 10.5 percent to 12 percent because of the increased instability in airline earnings, and a fare hike of 12 percent over the 1970 average revenue yield was deemed necessary for the achievement of a 12 percent rate-of-return.[24]

The rate-of-return in the airline industry has improved slightly since 1970 but it consistently has remained below the 12 percent standard, as Table 10-3 has indicated.[25] Only with the major cutbacks in capacity linked with sharply higher fares during 1974 did the domestic airlines begin to be normally profitable. In fact, the situation was so profitable at the beginning of 1975 (even with large declines in revenue-passenger-miles partially as a result of the economic recession) that the airlines originated a new set of fare decreases. Instead of countercyclical fare policies, the airlines have aggravated their own dilemmas with the imprudent timing of their fare change requests.

Air Cargo

The air cargo side of the airline industry is a separate topic. Only recently have the trunk lines been purchasing aircraft with the intention of utilizing them for all-cargo service.[26] Previously the airlines would convert the seating configuration of a B707 or a DC-8 to an all-cargo spacing plan so that certain backhaul trips could carry freight to supplement the passenger generating potential of the original trip. A large portion of the currently moving air freight, however, is

23. U.S. Civil Aeronautics Board, *Handbook of Airline Statistics* (Washington, D.C.: 1971 edition), p. 210.

24. U.S. Civil Aeronautics Board, *Domestic Passenger Fare Investigation: Phase 7 Fare Level, Docket 21866-7* (Washington, D.C.: 1971), pp. 70-85.

25. The 12 percent rate of return is the weighted average of the costs of debt (6.2%) and common equity (16.75%), using as weights an ideal or optimal capital structure mix of 45 percent debt and 55 percent equity.

26. The addition of an L-1011 or a DC-10 to an airline's fleet is the equivalent of adding two-thirds of a conventional jet freighter, even when the wide-body aircraft carries a full load of passengers and baggage. The result has been a doubling of the industry's cargolift capacity between 1971 and 1975.

shipped in the belly compartments of the larger capacity aircraft, like the B747, DC-10, and L-1011. The air freight market has displayed a more rapid growth rate than the air passenger market during the first 15 years of the commercial jet era.[27] Scheduled airlines in 1973 carried more than 4.7 billion ton miles of freight, an 11 percent increase from the preceding year. Operating revenues exceeded $1 billion, a gain of more than 800 percent since 1958. One of the principal reasons for this sustained growth has been the introduction of the wide-body passenger aircrafts to provide additional capacity for shippers. As air freight also has received increased shipper acceptance, it has become a significant factor in several key industries, such as electronics, auto parts, and wearing apparel. Table 10-6 represents the most important commodities moving in air freight on the high density North Atlantic routes.

The traditional method of identifying potential air commodities is to first consider the high-value shipments. This is to be expected for several reasons: First, air transport usually costs more, and high-value commodities can absorb this higher cost more easily; also, high-value shipments often benefit from air

Table 10-6
Leading Commodities in Air Trade Between the United States and Europe, 1970

Exports	Air Tonnage	% Air
Office machines (including parts)	15,348	75
Electronic computers	7,028	74
Phonograph records & other sound media	6,185	49
Aircraft parts and accessories	5,786	67
Motor vehicle & tractor parts & accessories	5,378	5
Grand total to OECD countries	210,728	0.3

Imports	Air Tonnage	% Air
Footwear (new)	24,854	26
Clothing and accessories	6,847	65
Textile machinery	6,256	10
Yarns and cotton thread	4,699	6
Textile fabrics	4,440	53
Grand total from OECD countries	175,372	0.6

Source: Based on The Boeing Company, *U.S.-Europe Air Cargo* (Renton, Wash., April 1972), p. 64.

27. A good reference on this topic is Lewis M. Schneider, *The Future of the U.S. Domestic Air Freight Industry: An Analysis of Management Strategies* (Boston: Graduate School of Business Administration, Harvard University, 1973).

transport in other ways, such as smaller losses from damage, reduced inventories, and increased productivity; finally, high-value commodities usually possess higher basic growth rates than low-value and bulk commodities—which is an appealing factor in the generation of new business. Although the average value of present air cargo exceeds that of surface shipments and thereby appears to confirm the importance of value, this method has shortcomings in predicting the potential air market penetration of a commodity. In other words, a positive relationship appears to exist between value per kilogram and that commodity's market share for air transport, but usually with a large variance. To test this hypothesis, the Boeing Company examined the eastbound U.S.A.-West Germany market for air and ocean shipments of 71 commodities for which at least 100 air tons were carried eastbound in 1972.[28] After tabulating commodity air market share, defined as the percent of total tons moving by air, the Boeing analysts concluded that there was only a slight tendency for air market share to increase with product value and then went on to suggest better indicators of air eligibility, such as composites of value per kilogram, commodity density, fragility, market time sensitivity, and market growth.[29]

Can the domestic air freight industry attract substantial volumes of divertible traffic? Lewis M. Schneider's analysis suggests that truck feeder plus TOFC line haul service will continue to maintain substantial cost advantages, even over B747 type freighter aircraft.[30] On several topics of air cargo service, Schneider claimed the following:

1. Growth per se will not necessarily produce profits, particularly in the air freighter service segment of the industry.
2. Technology was not the major factor in unprofitable freight operations.
3. The problems were underpricing and overcompetition.
4. The domestic freighter carriers during the 1965-69 period were divided into two camps, the optimists and conservatives. The optimists (American and United) poured on capacity with little or no return. The conservatives (Trans World and Flying Tiger) lagged behind in additions to capacity, but usually suffered deficits, albeit on less investment.
5. The excessive competition and low-load factors may have stemmed from the hope that increased capacity shares would produce disproportionately high-market shares and profits. In fact, market shares were proportionate to capacity, and profits were not correlated well with capacity shares.
6. Economies of scale were somewhat evident in the traffic service (terminal) account, but overall freighter economies of scale were not readily apparent, given a generation of equipment.
7. During 1965-69, the period of intensive growth of air freighter operations,

28. The Boeing Company, *U.S.-Europe Air Cargo* (Renton, Washington: April 1972).

29. Ibid.

30. Schneider, *U.S. Domestic Air Freight Industry.*

freighter service exhibited the poor capital productivity of the railroads, and the high operating ratio of the motor carriers.

8. Perhaps the financial malaise of the general airline industry prevented it from making a serious financial blunder during 1970-71. If precedent had been followed, it might well have invested in jumbo freighters, cut prices, overcompeted, and generated even greater losses. Today the industry has been granted a short reprieve–a time to take stock and plan more rational strategies for the future. Otherwise, once financial health is restored to the passenger sector, it will invest again in a new generation of aircraft in the hope of lowering operating costs and prices.[31]

From the period 1965 to 1970 the rewards for increased investment were minimal or nonexistent profits. In 1969 the domestic trunk and all-cargo carriers suffered on cargo an operating loss before taxes for the year of $27.6 million. In 1970 this loss climbed to $45.2 with United being the largest loser ($19.8 million). Part of this loss can be attributed to the inefficiencies of the quick change (QC) jet.[32] Unlike the railroads, the airlines are experiencing difficulties in earning money from cargo operations. But also unlike the railroads, the airlines have discovered ways to realize profits by offering attractive services to passengers.

31. Ibid., pp. 143-44.

32. See Harold D. Watkins, "Sagging Cargo, Economy Cut Use of QC's," *Aviation Week and Space Technology* (August 2, 1971), p. 27.

11 The Motor Trucking Industry

The motor trucking industry encompasses a very large number of firms, as Table 11-1 indicates. Some of these firms are relatively huge, as suggested by an array of the 10 largest trucking firms, ranked by operating revenues in Table 11-2. The motor trucking industry, then, has the interesting features of both a large number of sellers and fairly high concentration. The industry in the broadest sense includes almost 20 million trucks. In addition to the intercity carriers, there are thousands of motor carriers engaged in intrastate commerce, in hauling exempt agricultural commodities, and in private carriage.

The American Trucking Associations, the industry lobby group, estimated that motor carriers in 1973 moved 505 billion ton-miles of freight, accounting for 22.8 percent of the total of freight transport, as illustrated in Table 11-3. Of these 505 billion ton-miles, approximately 212 billion represented the intercity portion of freight transported by the class I, II, and III motor carriers.[1] Note that the market share of motor carriers in comparison to that of the railroads has been rising steadily since 1945; the stabilization of the motor carriers in comparison to that of the railroads has also been rising steadily since 1945. The stabilization of the motor carriers' ton-mile market share with respect to all modes around the 22 percent figure during the last decade is influenced by the increased movements of oil by the pipeline companies.

The revenue distribution among the regulated freight carriers is more revealing. Table 11-4 shows that the operating revenues of motor carriers (class I, II and III) in 1973 were estimated at $21 billion, which represents a market share of 55.3 percent of all modes' revenues. Unlike the ton-mile distribution, the revenue market share of motor carriers has been increasing sharply during the last decade both with respect to all modes and especially to that of the railroads. The railroads and the motor carriers clearly are the principal revenue generators in freight transport—together they are responsible for 93 cents of every freight transport revenue dollar.[2] While the data in Tables 11-3 and 11-4 are not perfectly aligned, aggregate comparisons are useful. The revenue distribution data show the benefits of relatively high-value commodities to the

1. The larger remainder includes the intercity ton-miles of all private trucks and for-hire trucks not subject to economic regulation by the ICC and the intercity ton-miles of local ICC carriers.

2. While the combined market share of railroads and motor carriers for freight revenues has remained invariant over the years around the 93 percent level, the same two modes combined share for ton-miles has declined gradually to its present level of about 61.7 percent.

Table 11-1
Number of Trucking Carriers by Size Class[a]

Year	Class I $1,000,000 or More	Class II $200,000 to $1,000,000	Class III Under $200,000	Total
1957	933	2,055	14,779	17,767
1960	1,053	2,276	12,947	16,276
1963	1,175	2,533	11,910	15,618
1966	1,298	2,675	11,453	15,426
1967	1,389	2,769	11,238	15,396
	$1,000,000 or more	$300,000 to $1,000,000	Under $300,000	
1968	1,421	2,082	11,617	15,120
1969	1,503	1,998	11,706	15,207
1970	1,571	2,061	11,468	15,100
1971	1,597	2,169	11,351	15,117
1972	1,771	2,202	11,165	15,138
1973	1,738	2,026	11,380	15,144

[a]Size refers to annual revenues, as reported by the firms to the ICC.
Source: Interstate Commerce Commission Statements No. 589 and 6406 and American Trucking Associations, Inc., *American Trucking Trends 1974*, p. 12.

motor carrier industry: In 1973 these carriers generated 55.3 percent of all freight revenues stemming from carrying only 22.2 percent of the total volume. The impacts of high value freight also are displayed by examining the airlines' share of revenues for 1973: $880 million in revenues (or 2.3 percent of all freight revenues) were generated from just 3.5 billion ton-miles of air freight (or only 0.2 percent of all ton-miles). The converse side of the domestic freight market is the bulk, low-value area where the pipelines and inland waterways firms together account for 39.1 percent of all ton-miles but generate only a combined 4.7 percent of freight revenues.[3]

From the revenue side of the freight picture, the most important trend over the years has been the increasing dominance of the motor carrier industry.[4] This is especially important in view of the shifts in composition of the industry. Two trends stand out: (1) a large increase in the number of class I carriers; and (2) a concomitant absolute decline in the number of the small carriers (Cf. Table 11-1). The industry as a whole in 1974 encompassed more than 15,000 firms, of

3. However, the revenue market share of the pipeline companies might very well increase during the next few years if regulatory constraints are relaxed.

4. For a thorough classification of the detailed laws and regulations governing specific vehicles, length, weight and speed limitations, see *Trucking Business* 67 (October 1973).

Table 11-2
Operating Revenues of the Ten Largest Motor Trucking Firms[a]

Firm	Operating Revenues
Consolidated Freightways	$591.1
Roadway Express	373.5
Leaseway Transportation	363.1
National City Lines	285.5
Yellow Freight System	258.6
McLean Trucking	195.1
Allied Van Lines	187.3
Associated Transport	143.7
Transcon Lines	128.7
Bekins	126.9

[a]In millions of dollars for 1972; includes those revenues from nontransportation activities and sales from discontinued operations when they are published; all companies derived at least 85 percent of their operating revenues from carrier operations.

Source: Computed from "The 50 Largest Transportation Companies," *Fortune*, July 1973, pp. 130-31.

which 1,738 were class I carriers and only 75 were publicly owned companies.[5] The largest eight firms in the motor trucking industry account for approximately 11 percent of the intercity tonnage carried by trucks, 18 percent of the gross revenues earned by all classes of trucking firms, and 26 percent of the total net income earned by all trucking firms.

During recent years various pieces of legislation have been introduced to the Congress with the intention of "opening up" numerous city-pair markets to a larger number of competitors. Needless to say, the large-sized trucking companies do not favor the tenor of this legislation and have been lobbying strongly against it.[6] The lobbying effort has been conducted by the firms themselves and through the American Trucking Associations, which presumably shares all trucking interests but in practice represent the interests of the larger companies.[7] The rationality of certain portions of the rate structure in the motor

5. These 75 carriers include those whose stocks are publicly owned or are subsidiaries of corporations whose stocks are listed on a national security exchange or traded over-the-counter. The average operating revenues for these 75 carriers in 1973 amounted to $87.4 million. Sources: *Transport* Statistics, Moody's Transportation Manual and Trincs Red Book–Trucking Industry.

6. See "Trucking Industry Largest Nixon Donor," *New York Times* (November 7, 1973), p. 34. This article depicts the industry as the largest contributor to the 1972 Nixon campaign by virtue of its legal solicitation of company contributions which totaled $600,000.

7. As of January 1975 federal weight limits on interstate vehicles were increased from 73,000 lbs. to 80,000 lbs.

Table 11-3
Ton-Mile Distribution Among Intercity Freight Carriers

Year	Railroads		Motor Carriers		Inland Waterways		Pipelines (Oil)		Airways		Total
	Ton-Miles[a] (Billions)	% of Total	Ton-Miles[b] (Billions)	% of Total	Ton-Miles[c] (Billions)	% of Total	Ton-Miles (Billions)	% of Total	Ton-Miles[d] (Billions)	% of Total	Ton-Miles[e] (Billions)
1940	379	61.30	62	10.03	118	19.08	59	9.58	--	.002	618
1945	690	67.26	66	6.52	142	13.90	126	12.32	--	.009	1,027
1950	596	56.17	172	16.27	163	15.37	129	12.16	0.3	.030	1,062
1955	631	49.53	223	17.51	216	16.98	203	15.94	0.4	.038	1,274
1960	579	44.06	285	21.72	220	16.76	228	17.40	0.7	.059	1,314
1965	708	43.25	359	21.92	262	16.01	306	18.70	1.9	.120	1,638
1967	731	41.43	388	22.01	281	15.95	361	20.46	2.5	.150	1,764
1968	756	41.16	396	21.55	291	15.85	391	21.28	2.8	.160	1,838
1969	774	40.84	404	21.32	302	15.98	411	21.69	3.2	.170	1,895
1970	768	39.74	412	21.32	318	16.46	431	22.30	3.4	.180	1,932
1971	742	38.45	430	22.26	307	15.90	448	23.20	3.7	.190	1,931
1972	781	38.05	470	22.90	330	16.08	468	22.80	3.8	.190	2,052
1973	860	38.80	505	22.78	340	15.36	507	22.87	4.2	.190	2,216

[a]Class I and class II railroads.

[b]Include class I, II, and III intercity ICC regulated common and contract motor carriers, the intercity portion of local ICC carriers, and intercity private and for-hire trucks not subject to ICC regulations.

[c]Including Great Lakes, but excluding deep sea ton-miles between mainland and Alaska, Hawaii, and territories.

[d]Scheduled domestic service, including mail and subsidy, express freight, and excess baggage. Comparability of early data with 1950 and later years is limited due to the inclusion since that time of additional domestic air carrier services. Effective January 1, 1970, all travel between 48 mainland states, Alaska, and Hawaii, was reclassified as domestic operations.

[e]Components may not add to total due to rounding.

Sources: Interstate Commerce Commission, Bureau of Economics, *Transport Economics, ICC Annual Reports*; Federal Aviation Agency, *Statistical Handbook of Aviation*; Air Transport Association of America, *Facts and Figures about Air Transportation*; Civil Aeronutics Board, *Handbook of Airline Statistics* (various years).

carrier industry (and in the railroad industry) is a well known and well documented topic. Whether the ICC, or indirectly the Congress, will loosen these markets in the near future is a matter of conjecture.

Since freight rates are determined by averaging the total carrier costs within the designed rate-making territories, unilateral decisions by any state can have an impact on any through rate. For example, 65-foot twin-trailer combinations are permitted in all states through which Interstate road I-94 passes between Detroit and Seattle, with the exception of Wisconsin, which has banned these double bottom trucks. Large interstate general commodity carriers, like Consolidated Freightways Corporation and Raymond Motor Transportation, Inc., are forced either to divide (and/or unload) their twin trailers at Wisconsin's borders to enable the loads to pass through the state or to use circuitous routes around the state. The large carriers also allege that twin-trailers are cheaper and have a lower accident rate per vehicle-miles than single semi-trailer combinations presently in use on interstate roads.

In the motor trucking industry common carriers were required under the provisions of the Motor Carrier Act of 1935 to display a certificate of public convenience and necessity. Contract carriers were required to purchase certificates; even private carriers were included under the aegis of the legislation. The economic characteristics of the regulated motor trucking industry may be summarized as follows:

1. Most motor carrier assets are geographically highly mobile.
2. Motor carrier equipment units are very small relative to the size of the industry.
3. Motor carrier equipment is quite standardized, and is subject to relatively continuous and predictable technical changes.
4. Motor carrier equipment is subject to the kind of rapid depreciation one would expect for over-the-road vehicles whose operation is based on moving parts.
5. The industry of motor carriage of commodities is, by definition, concerned with the transportation of commodities and not people.[8]

In the sense that motor carriers are both numerous and quite often large, competition in the aggregate does prevail. However, on certain routes a few large carriers can adhere to oligopoly practices and may even resort to nonpricing policies reminiscent of cartel behavior. A cartel may be defined as a collection of firms in an industry held together in some fashion by a common bond in order to maintain the product's (or service's) price above its competitive level.[9] A

8. See James R. Nelson, "Motor Carrier Regulation and the Financing of the Industry," *ICC Practitioners' Journal* 41 (May/June 1974), pp. 438 ff.

9. Usually cartel behavior is imputed to firms in the railroad industry, especially before the creation of the ICC in 1887.

Table 11-4
Revenues Distribution Among Regulated Freight Carriers[a]

	Railroads Class I & II		Motor Carriers Class I, II, & III		Water Carriers Class A, B, C, & Maritime[b]		Pipelines (Oil)		Airways[c]		Total
	Millions of Dollars	% of Total	Millions of Dollars	% of Total	Millions of Dollars	% of Total	Millions of Dollars	% of Total	Millions of Dollars	% of Total	Millions of Dollars
1940	$3,686	75.43	$867	17.74	$85	1.75	$225	4.62	$22	0.46	$4,887
1945	6,748	78.65	1,406	16.39	74	0.87	304	3.55	48	0.55	8,580
1950	8,134	64.09	3,737	29.44	259	2.04	441	3.48	119	0.95	12,692
1955	8,888	57.04	5,535	35.53	321	2.06	677	4.35	158	1.02	15,581
1960	8,390	49.39	7,213	42.47	335	1.97	770	4.54	278	1.64	16,987
1965	9,286	44.15	10,068	47,86	314	1.49	903	4.30	463	2.20	21,036
1967	9,591	42.29	11,229	49.51	313	1.39	994	4.38	550	2.43	22,678
1968	10,247	41.22	12,655	50.91	319	1.29	1,023	4.11	615	2.47	24,860
1969	10,876	40.34	13,958	51.98	330	1.23	1,103	4.09	690	2.56	26,958
1970	11,100	39.93	14,400	51.80	400	1.44	1,188	4.27	709	2.55	27,797
1971	12,200	38.82	16,700	53.14	413	1.32	1,284	4.09	766	2.44	31,429
1972	13,500	38.89	18,700	53.87	445	1.28	1,300	3.74	770	2.22	34,715
1973	14,223	37.48	21,000	55.35	476	1.26	1,363	3.59	880	2.32	37,943

[a]Figures are in millions of dollars and are derived from gross operating revenues of freight transportation. Included are revenues of Federally regulated carriers only: a major portion of the traffic handled by motor and water carriers is not subject to this regulation–for example, local, and exempt for-hire and private motor carriers; if included, the total value of all motor carrier services would approximately triple the $21 billion shown in 1973.

[b]Includes only regulated water carriers and excludes domestic traffic of regulated maritime carriers in coastal and intercoastal service for the years 1939-1947 (data not available for period); because of changes of various kinds of regulation, reporting requirements, and statistical publication procedures, comparison of early data with 1951 and later years is not strictly valid.

[c]Domestic service, including freight, mail, express, excess baggage, and freight charter revenues of the certificated airlines. Comparability of early data with 1950 and later years is limited because of the inclusion since that time of additional domestic air carrier services. Effective January 1, 1970, in accordance with the new 50 states definition of "domestic operations," operations between 48 states and Alaska/Hawaii were reclassified as domestic. Data of 1969 and later years have been adjusted to the new definition.

Sources: Interstate Commerce Commission, Bureau of Economics, *Transport Economics, ICC Annual Reports*; Federal Aviation Agency, *Statistical Handbook of Aviation*; Air Transport Association of America, *Facts and Figures about Air Transportation*; Civil Aeronautics Board, *Handbook of Airline Statistics*; American Trucking Associations, Inc., *American Trucking Trends 1974* (various years).

cartel may function by setting minimum prices, by allocating production quotas among member firms, or by restricting entry. To the extent that the motor trucking industry consists of 60 percent of the carriers being free of federal regulation, it is surprising to some that a cartelization might still exist. In fact, the dominant labor union (Teamsters) in that industry may be able to expropriate any excess profits accruing to cartelization:

> Although it is clear that such inflated wages are not "excess profits" per se, the effect on the allocation of resources is much the same. Indeed, the effect is probably more deleterious than explicit profit accrual by the cartelized firms in that these expropriated profits are effectively hidden from public view.[10]

Perhaps the best solution lies in determining the appropriate level of concentration for both selected city-pair markets and for the industry as a whole.

Many discussions of industrial concentration distinguish between overall concentration in a broad industrial sector, such as manufacturing (often measured by the share of the 100 largest firms), and concentration in a specifically defined industry like motor trucking, which more adequately reflects the concept of a market in microeconomic theory.[11] Whereas the first indicator suggests broad political issues raised by the control of an absolutely large amount of economic resources by a relatively small number of individuals or executives, the second measure focuses on the existence of market power. One way to link the two measures is to estimate the extent to which the largest firms in a broad industrial sector are also among the largest firms in specific markets. In other words, what is the probability that in a specific market chosen at random from the broad sector, a particular leading firm will be one of the largest 100? Statistical information relating monopoly (market) power or scale economies to measurable firm attributes has important policy implication.[12] As a result, applied economists, regulators, and students of industrial organization should address the challenge of providing additional empirical tests of hypotheses pertaining to these relationships, especially in the motor carrier industry.

---

10. James E. Annable, Jr. "The ICC, the IBT, and the Cartelization of the American Trucking Industry," *The Quarterly Review of Economics and Business* 13 (Summer 1973), p. 44.

11. For example, see M.A. Utton, "Aggregate Versus Market Concentration," *Economic Journal* 84 (March 1974), pp. 150-55.

12. See Richard B. Manche, "Causes of Interfirm Profitability Differences: A New Interpretation of the Evidence," *Quarterly Journal of Economics* 88 (May 1974), pp. 181-93.

12 The Railroad Industry

Railroads are classified by the Interstate Commerce Commission (ICC) into two sizes: class I railroads, those with annual operating revenues exceeding $5 million; and class II railroads, the remainder. Table 12-1 shows some selected statistics for the class I railroads over a five-year period, 1968-73; the table also allows comparisons among the three major districts into which the ICC divides the class I roads. By far, the class I roads are the most important: In 1974 there were 67 class I and 205 class II railroads, but the class I companies accounted for 99 percent of the industry's line-haul traffic and 97 percent of total operating revenues. Even within the class I scheme, concentration is high; the large railroads, as depicted in Table 12-2, controlled nearly 80 percent of the mileage operated and collected over 60 percent of the freight revenues. If one includes total operating revenues, the absolute size of the largest railroads is substantial, as Table 12-3 indicates.

From a competitive point of view, most efforts are intramodal and related to city-pair markets, where usually the participating railroads are few. This fact suggests that the market structure of the railroad industry is one of oligopoly, with intramodal competition occurring only over the major city-pair markets.

From a financial point of view, at least 25 of the class I railroads are in difficulty. The situation is especially serious in the Northeast. One can quickly notice from Table 12-1 that the rates-of-return are less than competitive with other industries. It is not therefore surprising that several railroads in the Northeast are bankrupt. Among the more frequently stated explanations for this dilemma is the federal government support from general funds in the federal budget for airports, waterways, and the merchant marine and their support systems—competitors in the broad sense to the railroads. Table 12-4 shows the amounts of government expenditures on intercity transport systems and facilities for all the modes. The railroad industry is conspicuous by its relatively miniscule share. Also, the bitter polemics of featherbedding have perpetuated and deepened traditional rifts between management and labor. Management itself either has been mediocre in quality or simply unable to cope with the irretrievable chain of circumstances that have beset the industry. Furthermore, some claim that property taxes have been inordinately high, resulting in an erosion of each company's solvency. Table 12-5 suggests that the costs and right-of-way taxes paid by the railroad industry far exceeds that of any other mode. Finally, there is the ubiquitous imputation of blame to the ICC for forcing the railroads to maintain uneconomic services far beyond their justified retention.

Table 12-1
Selected Railroad Statistics, 1969-73

Year	District	Operating Revenues[a]	Operating Expenses[a]	Net Railway Operating Income[a,b]	Rate of Return[c]	Revenue Ton-Miles[d]	Freight Car Miles[d]
1969	U.S.	$11.4	$9.1	0.65	2.36	768	30.3
	Eastern	4.3	3.5	0.12	1.10	260	9.7
	Southern	1.9	1.4	0.18	4.17	139	5.1
	Western	5.2	4.1	0.35	2.81	369	15.5
1970	U.S.	11.9	9.6	0.49	1.73	764	29.9
	Eastern	4.5	3.8	(0.10)	def.	254	9.5
	Southern	2.0	1.5	0.21	4.50	140	5.1
	Western	5.4	4.3	0.38	3.02	370	15.2
1971	U.S.	12.7	10.1	0.70	2.47	739	29.2
	Eastern	4.6	3.9	(0.03)	def.	225	8.7
	Southern	2.2	1.6	0.24	4.93	140	5.3
	Western	5.9	4.6	0.49	3.92	374	15.2
1972	U.S.	13.4	10.6	0.84	2.96	778	30.3
	Eastern	4.8	3.9	0.04	0.37	231	8.8
	Southern	2.3	1.7	0.26	5.32	149	5.6
	Western	6.3	4.9	0.53	4.24	398	15.9

1973	U.S.	14.8	11.6	0.86	3.08	852	31.2
	Eastern	5.2	4.2	0.06	0.56	245	8.8
	Southern	2.5	1.9	0.27	5.40	158	5.7
	Western	7.1	5.5	0.53	4.21	449	16.8

[a]In billions of dollars.

[b]Net railway operating income is the remainder of operating revenues after deducting operating expenses, taxes, and rents for equipment and joint facilities, but before recording nonoperating income and deducting fixed charges, such as interest or debt and rents for leased lines.

[c]In percent: the relationship of net railway operating income to net investment in transportation property.

[d]In billions.

Source: Association of American Railroads, *Yearbook of Railroad Facts* (1974 edition).

Table 12-2
Operating Freight Revenues of the Class I Railroads for 1972[a]

	Large Size Railroads		
Atchison, Topeka & Santa Fe	794.0	Louisville & Nashville	447.5
Baltimore & Ohio	484.8	Missouri Pacific	434.6
Burlington Northern	956.2	Norfolk & Western	765.3
Chesapeake & Ohio	566.2	Penn Central	1,606.5
Chicago & Northwestern	322.7	Seaboard Coast Line	546.6
Chicago, Milwaukee, St. Paul & Pacific	292.2	Southern	455.9
Chicago, Rock Island & Pacific	288.2	Southern Pacific	1,092.3
Erie Lackawanna	233.0	Union Pacific	743.8
Illinois Central Gulf	446.3		
	Medium Size Railroads[b]		
Boston & Maine	64.3	Reading	90.2
Central of Georgia	79.1	St. Louis-San Francisco	221.3
Cincinnati, New Orleans & T.P.	73.7	St. Louis Southwestern	150.5
Denver & RioGrande Western	109.9	Soo Line	137.5
Grand Trunk Western	86.6	Texas & Pacific	104.7
Kansas City Southern	101.4	Western Pacific	85.5
Missouri-Kansas-Texas	76.3		

Small Size Railroads[b,c]

Alabama Great Southern	48.2	Elgin, Joliet & Eastern	48.3
Bangor & Aroostook	13.1	Florida East Coast	38.4
Bessemer & Lake Erie	43.9	Fort Worth & Denver	9.9
Central of New Jersey	29.8[d]	Lehigh Valley	49.2
Central of Vermont	9.6	Long Island	8.6[d]
Chicago & Eastern Illinois	39.0[d]	Maine Central	27.7
Clinchfield	39.8	Monon	8.3[d]
Colorado & Southern	26.5	Norfolk Southern	15.0[e]
Delaware & Hudson	40.9	Northwestern Pacific	14.0
Detroit, Toledo & Ironton	40.6	Pittsburgh & Lake Erie	35.5
Duluth, Missabe & Iron Range	42.3	Richmond, Fredericksburg & Potomac	23.7
		Western Maryland	45.8

[a]Dollar amounts are in millions.

[b]Some class I railroads reported here are operated as subsidiaries of larger companies.

[c]The table excludes 12 other very small class I railroads.

[d]Represents a decline in revenues from 1968.

[e]Acquired by Southern Railway, November 1973.

Sources: Interstate Commerce Commission, Forms OS-A, OS-B and OS-C; American Association of Railroads, *Operating and Traffic Statistics: 1972* (Washington, D.C.: June 1973).

Table 12-3
Operating Revenues of the Largest Railroad Firms[a]

Firm	Operating Revenues
Penn Central Transportation	$1,825.5
Southern Pacific	1,449.4
Burlington Northern	1,195.0
Seaboard Cost Line Industries	1,122.1
Union Pacific	1,094.4
Chesapeake & Ohio Railway	1,025.4
Santa Fe Industries	972.8
Norfolk & Western Railway	850.8
Southern Railway	723.8
Missouri Pacific System	642.9

[a]Figures are for 1972 and are in millions of dollars.
Source: Computed from "The 50 Largest Transportation Companies," *Fortune*, July 1973, pp. 130-31.

It may be more surprising that there are profitable railroads in the region, for example, the Chesapeake and Ohio Railway, the Baltimore & Ohio Railroad, and the Norfolk and Western Railway. Even in the bankrupt companies the survival of the operations is a tribute to the portion of the industry that is inherently efficient and to that segment of labor and management to which railroading is a way of life rather than merely a job. Even so, the survival of the bankrupt firms without external assistance is not assured unless the complicated, impending legislation is effective over the long run. Various proposals have been put forth to resolve the current dilemma in the structure of railroad companies in the northeastern United States. While each of these proposals may have contained specific advantages for certain segments of the industry, it is possible that none of them actually will provide any practical remedies for returning the northeastern companies to viability in the long run. The central theme of all the proposed legislation is to "rationalize" the insolvent northeastern railroads by discontinuing service on or by abandoning approximately 15,000 miles of low-density trackage. The drift of the current congressional restructuring program appears to lean toward the establishment of a large, single rail system to be called the Consolidated Railroad Corporation (or ConRail), which would survive the financially troubled yet still competitive northeastern railroads. The direct and peripheral impacts of the new system on the profitable railroads, both large and small, contiguous to the Northeast are unknown. Without additional empirical evidence, there still may be a niche in the national rail network for small, closely managed and competitive companies.

In the railroad industry the largest percentage of revenues derives from the

Table 12-4
Government Expenditures for Intercity Transportation Systems and Facilities in 1974[a]

	Federal	State and Local	Total
Airways[b]	$1,654	--	$1,654
Airports	258	$1,200	1,458
Airline cash subsidies	73	--	73
Highways	5,119	19,718	24,837
Waterways[c]	532	540	1,072
High-speed ground transportation (including rail research and development)	45	--	45
Total	$7,681	$21,458	$29,139

[a]Dollar amounts are in millions. The data for 1974 are for the fiscal year in some instances and for the calendar year in others. Government expenditures do not include programs of federal and local loans and grants to public bodies in support of local mass transportation; some railroads providing suburban passenger service have participated in such projects, which are not related to intercity transportation. Also, under the Rail Passenger Service Act of 1970, federal grants amounting to $155 million were programmed to be paid to Amtrak in fiscal 1974. Under the Regional Rail Reorganization Act of 1973, interim operating subsidies not to exceed $85 million for a two-year period were authorized for bankrupt railroads so that essential transportation services may be continued. The rail programs referred to herein do not include federal loans or loan guarantees.

[b]Refers to obligations for the establishment, administration, maintenance, and operations of the Federal Airways System and for the Federal Aviation Administration.

[c]Includes navigation and terminal facility expenditures for inland waterways, intracoastal waterways, Great Lakes, and coastal harbors.

Source: Association of American Railroads, *Government Expenditures for Highway, Waterway, and Air Facilities and Private Expenditures for Railroad Facilities* (Washington, D.C.: May 1974), p. 2.

freight sector. In fact, approximately 99 percent of all railroad revenues in 1974 were derived from this source. For all practical purposes, private railroads really are not in the passenger business. The Rail Passenger Service Act of 1970 (Public Law 91-518) authorized the creation of a National Railroad Passenger Corporation (Amtrak), which assumed responsibility for providing rail passenger service over a designated intercity network, commencing May 1971. Only four railroads chose to continue offering their own passenger service and therefore did not join the Amtrak system.[1] Revenues from passenger operations had been declining for decades until the fuel crisis in the winter of 1973-74, when patronage of passenger trains began to increase.

1. These included the Southern; Denver and Rio Grande Western; Chicago, Rock Island and Pacific; and the Georgia companies.

Table 12-5
Costs and Taxes for Right-of-Way of the Regulated Intercity Carriers for 1972[a]

Item	Class I Railroads		Class I Intercity Motor Carriers: Carriers of Property		Class I Intercity Motor Carriers: Carriers of Passengers		Total Domestic Airlines		Class A and B Water Carriers	
	Amount	Ratio to Revenues	Amount	Ratio to Revenues	Amount	Ratio to Revenues	Amount	Ratio to Revenues	Amount	Ratio to Revenues
Total Operating Revenues:	$13,409	100.0%	$15,169	100.0%	$775	100.0%	$8,651	100.0%	$432	$100.0%
Right-of-Way Costs and Taxes:										
Annual carrying charge on investment in way[b]	1,198	8.9	--	--	--	--	--	--	--	--
Maintenance expenses–way	1,729	12.9	--	--	--	--	--	--	--	--
Crossing protection and drawbridge operation	22	0.2	--	--	--	--	--	--	--	--
Payroll taxes (applicable to items 4 & 5)	76	0.6	--	--	--	--	--	--	--	--
Property taxes–way[c]	185	1.4	--	--	--	--	--	--	--	--
User Taxes:										
Gasoline, other fuel and oil taxes	d	--	275	1.8	15	2.0	15	0.2	--	--
License, registration fees, mileage tax, etc.	--	--	237	1.6	7	1.0	--	--	--	--

Tolls: bridge, tunnel, highway, ferry[e]	--	--	108	0.7	5	0.7	--	--	--	--
Other federal excise taxes[c]	--	--	46[f]	0.3	2[f]	0.4	581[g]	6.7	--	--
Total Costs and Taxes for Right-of-Way	$3,211	24.0	$667	4.4	$31	4.1	$596	6.9	--	--

[a]Dollar amounts in millions.

[b]Calculated at 7.99 percent (Moody's average yield on railroad bonds) on investment in roadway and track (exclusive of stations, shops, office buildings, and other facilities not forming part of roadway, tracks, yard tracks, and appurtenances), estimated at 55 percent of total depreciated investment in road and equipment.

[c]Estimated at 45.8 percent of local taxes.

[d]Not available. Fuel taxes paid by railroads are charged to cost of materials and are not reported as taxes.

[e]Apportioned to class I motor carriers of property on the basis of Bureau of Public Roads' estimate of toll receipts in 1972.

[f]Estimated at 49.8 percent of federal fuel taxes, based on such ratio shown for typical four-axle tractor semitrailers in "Supplementary Report of the Highway Cost Allocation Study," House Document No. 124, 89th Congress, 1st session, table 82, p. 315.

[g]Treasury receipts from federal excise tax (8%) on domestic airline tickets of $548,633,000 and (5%) on freight of $32,717,000 as reported by IRS. According to the United States budget, total user taxes from all sources received into the Airport and Airway Trust Fund (established by Public Law 91-258) amounted to $758,159,000 in fiscal 1973.

Source: Association of American Railroads, *Government Expenditures for Highway, Waterway, and Air Facilities and Private Expenditures for Railroad Facilities* (Washington, D.C.: May 1974), table 11.

Amtrak has relieved the companies of their strictly legal burden of providing intercity passenger service but there still remain the problems of reimbursements and operations conflicts.[2] The commuter business is a totally separate problem: There is no conceivable reason why a railroad would naturally choose to offer this type of service, except for tax purposes or from the burden of past regulatory imposition.[3]

2. This situation remains particularly acute in the Northeast, especially with the Penn Central.

3. Commuter rail operations were indeed profitable several decades ago.

13 Major Problems of Railroad Service

Freight Service

It is not surprising that several railroads in the Northeast have filed for bankruptcy proceedings.[1] Among the more frequently stated explanations for some portion of this dilemma has been the unbalanced federal government subsidy program from general funds in the federal budget for airports, waterways, and the merchant marine and their support systems—competitors in the broad sense to the railroads. It is also claimed that a fundamental cause has been the general protection and continuity of funds generated by the Highway Trust Fund for the motor carrier industry. Also, within the railroad industry, the bitter polemics concerning featherbedding has perpetuated and deepened traditional rifts between management and labor. Management itself has either been quantitatively mediocre or simply unable to effectively handle the irretrievable chain of circumstances that have beset the railroad industry. Some critics claim that property taxes have been inordinately high, resulting in an erosion of each company's solvency. Finally, there is the ubiquitous imputation of blame to the ICC for forcing the railroads to maintain uneconomic services far beyond their justified retention.[2] While each of these factors have affected the railroad industry on the whole, the eastern region of the United States (or the ICC Official Territory) has suffered proportionately more than the rest of the country.

The extent to which any of the bankrupt railroads are dismembered or sold on a piecemeal basis to solvent railroads remains a matter of conjecture and of the United States Railway Association (USRA) recommendations. Synthesizing these proposals, a recent article suggested a more comprehensive solution containing the additional advantage of reliance on market forces.[3] The outstanding feature of a market-oriented approach is that continuous adjustments to future economic changes can always be insured and promoted by the mechanisms of supply and demand. With this approach it should not be necessary for

1. The bankrupt class I railroads in the Northeast in 1975 were the following: Penn Central (including New Haven), Lehigh Valley, Reading, Central of New Jersey, Erie Lackawanna, and Boston and Maine.

2. A recent statement of this imputation appears in John C. Spychalski, "Imperfections in Railway Line Abandonment Regulation and Suggestions for their Correction," *ICC Practitioners' Journal* 40 (May/June 1973), pp. 454-69.

3. See J.T. Kneafsey and M.E. Edelman, "A Market-Oriented Solution to the Northeast Railroad Dilemma," *ICC Practitioners' Journal* 41 (January/February 1974), pp. 174-89.

Congress or the regulatory agencies to be periodically called upon to revamp the rail network whenever new crises arise. The recent national surge to conserve and to preserve energy dictates that careful social and economic considerations be afforded to the implementation of the restructured railroads whatever shape they may take.

To a large degree the resolution of some of the railroad problems in the eastern United States depends on the ways in which "excess capacity" in the industry is eliminated. The ways or mechanisms in turn depend on the ICC, USRA, and ConRail.[4] This institutional apparatus of course raises the whole question of the effects of regulation on the performance of the industry. In fact, a general view is that railroad rates, as administered by the ICC historically have been geared more to protecting railroads than protecting motor trucking firms from rail competition. If indeed the cross elasticity of demand on the average between rail and truck transportation is low, railroad profits will be maximized by maintaining high rail rates on high-value commodities. While it is true that in some instances truck transportation will benefit by maintaining these high rail rates, it is also true that there should be downward pressure on rates from railroads in many instances as a result of intraindustry competition. Nevertheless, one might still ask, exceptions do not disprove the basic point; if, for example, ICC regulation is geared towards maximizing railroad profits, why have most railroads fared so poorly on that count in recent years? There are numerous possible answers to this question, but the most important cause of low railroad profits would appear to be redundant capacity. In a recent article Theodore E. Keeler has claimed that as of 1969 the total cost of excess capacity in the railroad industry was between two and three billion dollars.[5] The existence of this excess capacity can be attributed directly to the ICC (or its political pressures), which historically has taken a hard line against abandonments, both in the case of redundant parallel lines and in the case of lightly used branches.[6] Why then is it considered necessary to maintain such a large railroad system? It would appear to be due to the political pressures brought to bear on the ICC by small communities on parallel lines and on lightly used branch lines. It can be argued that the main purpose of the ICC-imposed rate structure is to provide revenues to support the national railroad network, which has not shrunk much since the turn of the century in spite of drastic changes that have occurred in overall transportation operations.[7]

4. The term "ConRail" may not be a prudent choice in the eyes of some observers, who have pointed out the undesirable implications of the sound of (or meaning of) "con".

5. Theodore E. Keeler, "Railroad Costs, Returns to Scale, and Excess Capacity," *Review of Economics and Statistics* 56 (May 1974), pp. 201-8.

6. For a complete discussion of ICC abandonment policies, see Michael Conant, *Railroad Mergers and Abandonments* (Berkeley: University of California Press 1964), chap. 6.

7. The notion that regulation exists primarily as a method of cross-subsidization is of course not new at all. For a complete discussion of this issue, see Richard A. Posner, "Taxation by Regulation," *The Bell Journal of Economics and Management Science* 2

A system of rates, however, is basic to transportation economics. This system should have been established and maintained at levels that would encourage the continuing development of better levels of service provided by the carriers to a shipping public, which itself has been growing more demanding and diverse. One of the problems is that shippers have used many ploys to avoid or minimize the effects of rate-adjustments. The result has been an increased number of rate cases crowding the ICC's docket.[8] So the process goes on and the adverse effects of such proceedings become cumulative.

Passenger Service

This chapter has, so far, centered on the problems of the railroad industry in the freight sector; but there is also the passenger sector, which involves both intercity and commuter operations for the railroad industry. The structure of the passenger sector has changed drastically during recent years with Amtrak taking over most of the intercity service and with individual class I railroads continuing to offer commuter services (mostly with deficits).

Until late 1973 one of the major national transportation crises was the gradual demise of rail passenger service in the United States. Beginning soon after the end of World War II, this has been attributed generally to the ascendancy of other modes of intercity passenger transportation, particularly air and automobile, again to the operating conditions imposed on the railroads by inflexible Interstate Commerce Commission constraints, and also to mismanagement, even neglect, on the part of the railroad companies themselves. These factors, among several others, combined over the years to make rail passenger service in the United States essentially less attractive than other modes of intercity passenger transportation. Most railroads accumulated massive passenger service deficits throughout the 1960s and in 1970, when the Penn Central Railroad, which provided approximately 40 percent of the rail passenger service, petitioned for bankruptcy, national intercity rail passenger service in the United States was on the verge of complete collapse.

As a result of this crisis a quasi-public agency, the National Rail Passenger Corporation (NPRC or Amtrak), was established and assumed the operation of intercity rail passenger service in May, 1971.[9] The existence of this agency and the

(Spring 1971), pp. 22-50; a recent discussion of this issue in the context of the railroad industry may be found in George W. Hilton, "The Basic Behavior of the Regulatory Commissions," *American Economic Review, Papers and Proceedings* 62 (May 1972), pp. 47-54.

8. For a shipper's perspective on the obsoleteness of the present system of commodity rates, see Charles T. Golden, "A Flaw in the Fabric," *ICC Practitioners' Journal* 41 (September/October 1974), pp. 667-75.

9. Only the Southern Railway Company, the Chicago, Rock Island, and the Pacific, and the Denver and Rio Grande Western continue to operate non-Amtrak passenger trains. The Georgia offers periodic mixed trains with passenger service and the Toronto, Hamilton and Buffalo (jointly owned by the Penn Central and the Canadian Pacific) offers passenger service between Buffalo and Toronto.

contract relationship between Amtrak and the railroad companies is unique in the transportation industries, adding still another dimension to the provision of transportation service in the United States.

Although the Rail Passenger Service Act states that "Insofar as practicable, the Corporation (Amtrak) shall directly operate and control all aspects of its rail passenger service," the corporation does not, in fact, exercise much direct control over the railroads that run the Amtrak trains. Amtrak has taken over responsibility for travel agent transactions and reservations, it owns about 500 passenger train cars and 350 locomotives, it employs some 1,200 station and terminal personnel, and it has assumed certain onboard functions such as the work done by stewards, cooks, waiters, and sleeping car attendants, but this hardly constitutes direct control over the actual operation of rail passenger service in the United States.[10] While, theoretically, the railroads are responsible to Amtrak, the relationship between the National Rail Passenger Corporation and the railroads is not hierarchical from a management perspective.

The existence of Amtrak has not significantly increased or improved the data available or the operation of rail passenger service. One of the most important and long standing issues concerning data for rail passenger transportation service measures is simply the way in which passenger costs are allocated. Over the years the ICC has developed elaborate formulae to determine the costs assignable to rail passenger service. In some cases the allocation of costs is clear, but in most cases (such as in the operation of a station that provides both freight and passenger service) an accurate allocation of costs is hardly possible. As a result the ICC allocation formulae are suspect. The problem on rail passenger data is compounded further because the current contract relationship between the railroads and Amtrak does not provide an incentive for the railroads to minimize the cost of rail passenger operations. While the ICC may collect a vast amount of information on the annual Form A documents, only a minor portion of the data is relevant to ascertaining costs and performance for passenger service. Because of budgeting constraints imposed by Congress, Amtrak has not significantly increased the amount of information reported by the railroads or improved on the quality of the information reported. Neither the ICC nor Amtrak collects information vital to establishing a measure of the quality and efficiency of rail passenger service in the United States. An obvious example of such a data gap is the lack of information on the condition of roadbeds, track, and rights-of-way. As Amtrak slowly assumes more and more direct responsibility for the operation of rail passenger service in the United States, it will need to construct an information system that reflects the true indication of costs and performance. This requirement becomes all the more compelling in view of the spectacular increases in intercity rail ridership demand experienced in 1974.

It is frequently alleged that railroad passenger service represents the most

10. See National Railroad Passenger Corporation, *1973 Annual Report* (Washington, D.C.: February 1974).

appealing energy saving mode of transportation. This argument is not unambiguous, however, because it depends on the conditions of the comparisons. For example, if the operating conditions can be normalized, there may be very little significant difference between the performance of railroad passenger and bus transportation equipment. If one examines the latest representative estimates of fuel consumption per seat mile for railroad passenger trains, buses, automobiles and passenger aircraft, the average seat miles per gallon of fuel generated by various configurations of rail equipment are only marginally superior to those of buses, although they both are substantially higher than for the other modes. On this issue much additional research is warranted, especially as a foundation for public subsidy programs.

Problems in Railroad Yards

Perhaps the most significant source of waste and inefficiency in the railroad industry (especially freight) stems from the utilization of yards.[11] This section then introduces the reader to the major types of railroad yards and terminals that serve important functions in railroad operations.[12]

Railroad yards may be categorized in various ways: by operating function, by traffic and commodity flow characteristics, by size and capacity, by type of switching, by layout, and by their importance relative to flow characteristics of the network of which they are a part. Seven general types of yards and terminals are discussed:

1. Classification
2. Interchange
3. Storage
4. Local switching
5. Support function
6. Piggyback terminals
7. Other yards and terminals

The basic questions of yard utilization rest on determining what a yard is and how is it utilized? These questions can be best answered by tracing the process of a freight-car movement from its original demand to its final usage. In essence, this process may be described in the following way:

1. The shipper places an order for a car with the railroad's agent.
2. The yard office receives the order and selects the car.

11. See the M.I.T. *Studies in Railroad Operation and Economics*, Vols. 1-15.

12. This section is based on discussions with and material provided by Kenneth J. Belovarac of the U.S. Department of Transportation, Transportation Systems Center.

3. The car is inspected by the car inspector (it must be mechanically sound and must also be suitable for the special requirements of the shipper).
4. The car is switched to the industry track (an industrial switch-run engine will take a group or cut of cars covering a specified portion of the industrial district).
5. The shipper loads his car and notifies the agent or yard office that it is ready for "pulling".
6. A bill of lading and waybill is prepared for the shipment.
7. A switch engine takes the car from the industry's tracks to the assembling or classification yard.
8. The car is classified into a train of cars having a generally similar destination.
9. After the train is completely built, the road movement begins.
10. During the line haul the car may pass through one or more intermediate classification and interchange yards so that the car eventually is placed in a train going directly to its final destination.
11. On arrival at its destination the train is broken up in another classification yard and the processes of steps 4, 7, and 8 are repeated in reverse until the car finally comes to rest on tracks of the consignee.
12. The consignee unloads the car and notifies the freight agent of its release.

It should be noted from this series of events that the classification yard is the most used yard with respect to a freight car movement.

Classification Yard

A classification yard is designed to receive incoming trains and reassemble the cars into outbound trains that will bring the cars closer to their destinations. Three major functions are performed in the classification yard: receiving, classification, and departure. The receiving function consists of an incoming train being placed in the receiving yard to await classification; the classification function is the breaking up of the train and placing each car onto a classification track corresponding to its general destination; and departure function is the making-up of a train comprised of one or more classification blocks according to destinations. In some cases a modern classification yard complex is segmented into receiving, classification, and departure yards as Figure 13-1 illustrates. Yards may also reflect many types of layout; receiving, classification, and departure yard segments are combined into a single yard. Each yard layout has particular advantages and disadvantages that may affect intrayard switching operations and must therefore be evaluated on a case by case basis by considering individual operating variables.

The classification yard segment of a yard may be separated into a "flat" yard and a "hump" yard. The difference between the two is that a flat yard is

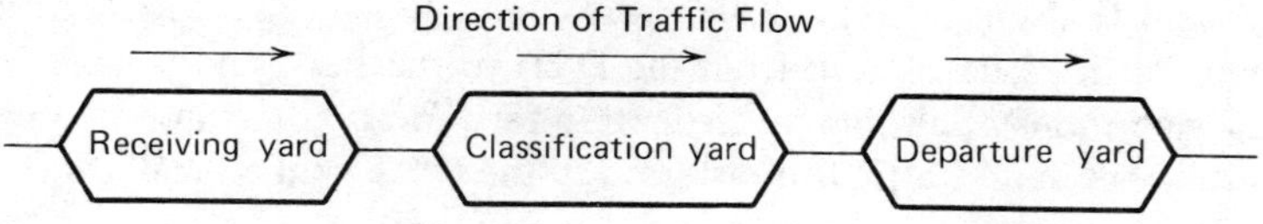

Figure 13-1. A Modern Railroad Classification Yard Layout.

generally constructed on level ground or on a slight grade; freight cars are pushed by a switching locomotive and then released, coasting to their respective tracks. In a hump yard, there is a steep incline or hump leading into the classification yard segment; freight cars are pushed over the hump and roll downhill to their proper track, with their speed controlled by mechanical retarders built into sections of track to keep the average car speed at coupling below four miles per hour.

Most new major classification yards in the railroad industry are hump yards. The principal advantage of a hump yard over a flat yard is that cars can be processed faster and with fewer switch engine movements. The economic trade-off between flat yards and hump yards is not measured in the volume of cars moved daily; rather, it should reflect the balance between capital costs and operating expenditures: in general, hump yards are more expensive to construct than flat yards, but offer a lower cost per car handled. An efficient hump yard can handle up to 3,500 cars per day with an average hump rate of three to five cars per minute; a flat yard on the average usually does not handle more than 1,000 cars daily. Some freight cars are likely to be humped more than once for several reasons: because of cars without waybills (no bills), cars needing repair (rips), or cars sent to the wrong classification tracks, which must be reclassified onto the proper tracks (misroutes). Regardless of the complications, classification yards are important facilities in a rail network because most rail traffic at some time will have to be stopped to be classified in the course of a trip.

Interchange Yard

Interchange yards handle freight cars being transferred from one railroad to another. Cars moving from one railroad to a connecting railroad ordinarily will be placed on an interchange or connecting track. A switching locomotive from the receiving railroad will then pick up the car at that point. The interchange yard can range from a single track to a large classification yard where cars are blocked into trains at the transfer point.[13] An example is the interchange yard at Mechanicsville, New York, which is a major connecting point between the

13. Blocking refers to arranging cars in groups according to their destinations.

Delaware and Hudson (D&H) and the Boston and Maine (B&M) Railroads; here eastbound traffic is transferred from the D&H to the B&M and is classified by the B&M into trains according to destination for various points in New England, and similar westbound traffic is transferred to the D&H by the B&M.

Storage Yard

Storage yards are yards where cars, generally empty, are stored until needed. Storage yards can also be an inventory stock of old locomotives, bad order cars, unused rolling stock, and any other equipment awaiting downgrading, retirement, or shifts in assignment. In certain situations these yards hold freight cars loaded with a commodity such as coal or grain, which are being stored pending shipment on short notice.

Local Switching Yard

Local switching yards are small yards located in towns, industrial areas, and junctions and are used for the handling, sorting, and storage of traffic related to local freight service for industries, interchange movements, large shippers, and general local car handling needs. Unlike classification yards, a local yard is not a place to assemble and break up main-line road trains.

Support Function Yard

Support yards serve purposes such as caboose storage, engine maintenance, storage for bad order cars needing repair, and maintenance-of-way equipment storage and service tracks. Support yards can be located at major junctions, local yards, interchange points, or at classification yards, depending on the needs of the rail network that they serve.

TOFC Terminal

A TOFC or piggyback[14] terminal is a specially designed yard where truck-trailers are loaded on and unloaded from flat cars. This is an unique terminal because piggyback trains are often dispatched and received in these special facilities,

14. Piggyback is a term depicting a service whereby highway truck trailers are loaded onto rail flatcars and transported by train, making rail service available to shippers who do not have access to rail car facilities and who would usually only transport by motor carrier.

thereby bypassing the usual classification process for the majority of freight cars.

Miscellaneous Yards and Terminals

In addition to the yards listed above, there are also various yards and terminals designed to handle specific commodities. Examples of such facilities are special loading and unloading terminals for coal, ore, and automobiles.

14 Rail Freight Rates

Pricing patterns in both the railroad and motor trucking industries are functions of rates and service. The current rate structure is a complex assortment of rates that reflect elements such as detailed commodity classifications, shipment volume price differentials, and specific origin and destination considerations. A rail rate generally represents the total charge for a shipment, excluding demurrage and accessorial services.[1] The structure of rail rates reflects two different pricing approaches: class rates and commodity rates.

Class Rates

One form of pricing utilized by the rail industry is class rates. Under this rate-making approach, each commodity is placed into one of 31 major commodity classes, with the rates charged the shipper being based on the commodity class and movement distance. The class rate structure is relatively straightforward and serves to reduce the total number of rates published. However, much traffic does not move under class rates and their relative importance in the overall pricing of rail transportation has never been substantial.

Commodity Rates

Charges made under commodity rates account for more than 80 percent of total rail freight charges. Under this pricing scheme each specific commodity is assessed a unique rate for movement between two specific points and will normally include volume price differentials, such as LCL, carload, or multiple car rates. These rates are normally filed individually with the ICC through a rail freight bureau. Needless to say, the number of rail commodity rates in force today is substantial.[2]

1. Accessorial services are any services "in addition to" those "normally" provided in the rail movement of goods; examples are export lighterage and mechanical refrigeration services.

2. There are some 43 trillion railroad rates on file with the ICC (see Charles F. Phillips, Jr., *The Economics of Regulation*, 2nd ed. (Homewood, Ill.: Richard D. Irwin, Inc., 1969), p. 314. The railway rate structure is currently so complex that there is an industry of rate specialists employed by rate audit firms acting as independents who are experts in obtaining the most favorable rate applicable to a movement. These firms audit past freight bills for a percentage (usually 50 percent) of the savings realized from filing claims against rail carried on improperly rated movements.

As the largest railroad in the United States, the Penn Central rate structure reflects the complexity and the pricing approach used by railroads throughout the country. Table 14-1 summarizes the average rate per revenue ton-mile received by the Penn Central in 1973 for regular freight traffic. Note that the data generally substantiate the relationship of declining rates per ton-mile as mileage (length of haul) increases. Of course, part of this relationship can be explained by the fact that for some specific commodities these average rates per ton-mile reflect lower movement rates when large annual tonnages occur. From the data in Table 14-1, several other features appear: Revenue per ton-mile for interchange traffic, when compared to local traffic, is somewhat lower for a number of the mileage blocks; revenue per ton-mile for bridge traffic generally lower than either interchange or local traffic; and in several instances lower revenue per ton-mile, often out of pattern in relation to the mileage of the movement, is associated with larger annual tonnage classifications.

Rate Setting

A rail rate, as published in a freight tariff, then identifies the charge for hauling a specific commodity or a class of commodities. The tariff also identifies the services that are applicable for that rate. The charges for services not covered by the rate, but which could be used by the shipper, are also published in the

Table 14-1
Revenue per Ton-Mile for the Penn Central System by Mileage Block and Traffic Class for Regular Movements, 1973[a]

Mileage Block	Penn Central Revenue per Ton-Mile (Cents)			Ton-Miles (Millions)		
	Local	I/C[b]	Bridge	Local	I/C	Bridge
0 to 49	8.2	9.0	2.2	13.1	13.4	14.0
50 to 150	3.5	3.4	2.3	22.7	23.3	17.8
151 to 250	2.4	2.0	1.6	22.1	31.6	45.3
251 to 350	2.0	2.2	1.1	19.2	17.5	45.5
351 to 500	2.0	1.9	1.1	12.8	17.8	41.7
501 to 750	2.6	1.7	1.5	7.4	13.5	12.1
751 to 1,000	2.0	1.4	1.3	2.9	11.6	18.7
1,001 to 1,500	2.2	1.4	0.9	0.2	3.9	5.7

[a]The rates do not include TOFC/COFC traffic or traffic in transit.

[b]I/C refers to interchange traffic with other railroads.

Source: A.T. Kearney, Inc., *Pricing Strategies for Conrail* report prepared for the United States Railway Association (Washington, D.C.: October 1974), p. 11-44.

freight tariff. The establishment of transportation prices and services and changes in prices and service levels are implemented by either the railroad or by petition of a shipper or a group of shippers. The process for setting a rail rate is usually initiated by a rail carrier submitting the proposed rate to the corresponding freight bureau, which is a consortium of carriers established for the purpose of setting and publishing rail rates. The freight bureau reviews the proposed rate and conducts hearings regarding its acceptability to both intramodal and intermodal competitors and shippers. If the proposed rate is approved by the freight bureau, the bureau publishes it as approved in its freight tariff. If the freight bureau disapproves the proposed rate, the carrier may unilaterally take independent action to publish it in the freight tariff. At the present time nearly 90 percent of railroad rates are made collectively through tariff bureaus. While collective rate making can be considered necessary for through-freight shipments involving several railroads, the setting of rates in general by employing approaches closely analogous to "price-fixing" techniques has been publicly questioned by both governmental and private interests.

Once a rate is published it becomes effective 30 days after publication and public notice. Upon publication the rail rate is simultaneously forwarded to the ICC, which may invoke actions to determine its reasonableness relative to existing regulation. If the ICC decides to investigate the proposed rate, or if shippers or carriers file a protest regarding the rate, the commission is empowered to suspend the rate for a period of seven months. If during this period the commission finds the proposed rate to be reasonable and lawful, the rate then becomes effective. If, however, the rate is found to be unreasonable or unlawful by the commission, it may then prescribe a rate to replace the proposed rate that in their opinion will meet the conditions of regulation.

The Role of Costs

The role of costs in establishing rail rates has been generally passive rather than active. This situation has resulted from the fact that neither the railroad industry nor the ICC currently possesses the capability of accurately measuring the cost of performing a particular set of transportation services. As a result, cost systems that have been utilized tend to apportion rather than to trace the costs incurred to specific cause and effect relationships. The numerous deliberations concerning branch line abandonments and the discontinuance or curtailment of passenger train services and the related costs and revenues of these operations are excellent examples of the impact of inadequate cost information.

Most railroad firms today apply a modified ICC Rail Form A variable costing system to evaluate costs associated with the movement of a commodity between two destination areas. It is a well known fact that rail carriers, except in a very few circumstances, do not actually know what the real cost of an individual movement is on their road.[3] The cost presented by Rail Form A are the average costs incurred by general cost centers of a railroad. These costs are accepted by the ICC as being the determinants of the cost justification for a proposed rate.

The deficiency in railroad costing is generally attributable to two factors: first, the reluctance of rail carriers to initiate innovative costing systems in view of the fact that the commission has traditionally "clung" to the ICC Rail Form A costing as a basis for rate setting in defense of proposed rates; and second, the relatively new state of large-scale management information system applications for the railroad companies. Until the systems become operative, the data gathered by the railroads will continue to be deficient, both in validity and degree of detail, for supporting cost research.

When cost estimates are used in the analysis of a proposed rate,[4] the cost statistics are many times overruled by other factors. These include the total amount of business that the shipper gives the rail carrier (even though the quantity on the proposed movement might be relatively small) and the historical rate pattern applicable to this type of movement. Often an arbitrary amount is added to the variable cost estimate in order to establish the rate. This arbitrary amount may reflect a judgment of obtaining an amount that will generate the traffic for the railroad and is typically as compensatory as is possible, given competitive conditions. Although the ICC has not recognized Rail Form A as prima facie evidence in regulatory proceedings, it has been regarded as such in a practical sense. Any alternative costing method requires the applying party to indicate its superior quality. Even though Rail Form A is known to be only an average or broad indicator of costs, it has been utilized historically in the determination of the reasonableness of rail rates, resulting in an overall constraint in many instances on the ability of carriers to price efficiently.

The principle of general ex parte price increases also poses a traditional constraint upon railroad pricing flexibility. In agreeing on a specific percent to be requested by all rail carriers, initial increase percentages exhibit a high degree of variability among geographical areas and individual carriers. Due to "higher costs of living," the western and northeastern roads in many instances have wanted to ask for a higher percentage than southern roads. After a lengthy period of time in intraindustry negotiations, a single "across-the-board" percentage is agreed upon. Thus, general rate increases are constrained to a rail industry negotiating process that may not adequately provide for the needs of individual

3. This problem has been source of much inquiry on the part of the author; see James T. Kneafsey, *The Economics of the Transportation Firm*, chapts. 3 and 4; and my volume 13 of the M.I.T. Studies in Railroad Operations and Economics, entitled "Costing in Railroad Operations: A Proposed Methodology," March 1975.

4. To understand better the terminology of identifying particular kinds of rates the student is referred to Roy J. Sampson and Morton T. Farris, *Domestic Transportation: Practice, Theory and Policy*, 2nd ed. (Boston: Houghton Mifflin Company, 1971), chapts. 12 and 13; and Charles F. Phillips, Jr., *The Economics of Regulation*, 2nd ed. (Homewood, Ill.: Richard D. Irwin, Inc., 1969).

carriers. It is extremely difficult for a railroad to "go its own way" in establishing price and service independent of the pattern of the industry.[5] Ultimately the ICC has the authority to require interchange and joint rates for through movements over any road. In addition, the ICC can establish reasonable rate divisions between participating roads on through movements if the roads cannot themselves determine an appropriate division.

Regulatory Constraints on Rates

The largest source of regulation of rail rates is the original Act to Regulate Commerce of 1887 and various amendments thereto. The ICC is empowered by the act to determine the legality of a rail rate. Although states do have regulatory powers over the railroads, the effect of this regulation is minor relative to the effect of the ICC on rail rates. State regulation has further lost its impact under the Transportation Act of 1920, which empowered the ICC to regulate intrastate rates that may impact interstate commerce.

The ICC uses two primary considerations in determining the legality of a rail rate; first, *reasonableness*: a rail rate must be reasonable in and of itself and must be justified by costs; the rate may only deviate from cost and still remain reasonable if the rate was established as a reaction to the competition faced by the railroad, if the commission allows such a consideration; and second, *discrimination*: rail rates may not be discriminatory, that is, a rail rate may not be set that results in the discrimination of one of many similar shippers or one of many similar commodities; rates that do not treat shippers or commodities equally must be justified by differences in the cost of moving like goods or providing rail transportation to similar shippers.

The Importance of Costs

Costs in the rail industry, as in many other industries, are defined in several differentiated ways depending on the unit of output under consideration or the singularity or multiplicity of service elements drawing on given resources. The general cost elements that are discussed most widely in transportation are: variable, joint, constant, full, and unit cost.

Variable Cost

This element is defined as the cost that changes as the quantity of output changes. Other terms that are generally synonymous with variable costs are

5. Occasionally one or more railroad firms will not go along with the industry sentiment for a rate increase. The most recent example occurred in January 1975 when the Chessie System, Seaboard Coast Line, and Florida East Coast railroads actually influenced the ICC to disapprove a 7 percent general rate increase. See "ICC Rejects a Bid for Rail Rate Rise," *New York Times* (January 31, 1975), p. 43 ff.

prime, traced, separable, assignable, direct, and out-of-pocket costs. Variable cost levels may be different depending upon the definition of output and the period over which variation is defined.

The specification of how costs actually vary with output levels has been the source of more historical disagreement than perhaps any other economic topic in the rail industry. Most analysts would say that the cost categories should be assigned a point estimate only within a finite output range; yet, the ICC has used in its formulae a constant percent variability level on costs. Until 1970 rail operating expenses, rents, and taxes (excluding federal income tax) were assumed by the commission to be 80 percent variable at *all* levels of output.

The original 80 percent variability rule was derived from the arithmetic mean of estimated variability levels of individual (or groups of individuals) accounts as calculated in a study two decades ago. In an important article on rail cost variability, Zvi Griliches recomputed the total variability of the individual elements of the ICC's study, weighting each group's variability by the percent of total operating expenses (accounted for) by that group.[6] Since his analysis yielded a variability percentage that was extremely close to 100 percent, more doubt was heaped on the ICC costing approach.

Joint Cost

Joint cost refers to the consumption of resources in a single operation where two or more products or services result and where resource consumption cannot be individually distinguished. Many costs incurred by railroad firms are considered to be joint. An example of such a joint cost is the rail communications system, which is designed to support train dispatching, maintenance of way coordination, record maintenance and verification, and general managerial functions. The resources used by this process cannot be directly assigned to each individual output: They are joint costs and are apportioned, often in an arbitrary manner.

Constant Cost

Constant cost is generally synonymous with indirect, fixed, or overhead costs. They consist of those costs that are unaffected by increases or decreases in production. Constant costs are unavoidable within normal operating ranges, are incurred for the operation in total and are a function of time. The shorter the period, the greater the quantity of costs that are constant. In an extremely short period a high percentage of rail costs are constant. In a longer period there are

6. Zvi Griliches, "Cost Allocation in Railroad Regulation," *The Bell Journal of Economics and Management Science* 3 (Spring 1972), pp. 26-41.

few costs that do not become amenable to change due to the turnover of real capital employed.[7]

Full Cost

This element is the sum of variable, joint, and constant costs. Variable costs play the dominant role in railroad rate making but full costs are relevant, primarily in two areas: to provide a standard by which to measure deviation from cost-of-service rates and thus help maintain these deviations within reasonable limits; and for use by the ICC in intermodal rate comparisons when establishing the lowest cost mode. The terms fully allocated and fully distributed are synonymous with full cost.

Unit Cost

Unit cost is used to indicate the average cost of an identifiable unit of output, such as train mile, car mile or ton-mile, and is usually expressed in terms of variable expenses only. In practical application the marginal cost per unit is seldom utilized in the rail industry.

Concluding Comments

The application of these cost concepts by the railroad industry and by the ICC has concentrated on the use of accounting data sources and therein lies the problem. The historical emphasis has been on attributing costs to specific operations on an "after the fact" basis; thus, for example, interest charges and capital costs of all types are allocated to operations throughout the system in development of the Form-A costs typically used for costing out movements.[8] It is important in developing contemporary pricing strategies for the railroads to distinguish between concepts of cost that are applied in an historical accounting

7. An example of a constant cost is freight car investment relative to a particular car or homogeneous group of cars. Once a purchase or capital investment decision has been made, the capital recovery associated with that investment over the life of cars is constant. As the time-frame lengthens and the point is reached where a reinvestment decision is required, this cost loses its rigidity. Other costs, such as corporate staff salaries are constant for a shorter period and become subject to change at more frequent time intervals than freight car investment. In the extremely long-run period, all costs become variable.

8. It is interesting to note that there is still an emphasis on establishing accounting cost systems in the regulated transportation field. On the basis of current econometric evidence, however, it is hoped that this emphasis will shift to more functional systems of economic data.

context and concepts of costs that are applied to an estimation of future costs. While the concept in each instance may sound similar in application, they clearly differ in substance.

15 Capacity in Transportation

In the transportation industries it is important to discuss the structural characteristics that make capacity unique relative to that of a typical manufacturing firm. Such a discussion should serve as background to understanding some of the problems involved in specifying the concept and deriving measures of transportation capacity. It should be acknowledged that many of the unique characteristics described below do not apply to all modes of transportation; where they do apply, the effects will be reflected in different degrees.

Quality of Service

In many of the transportation industries costs do not rise appreciably after the minimum point on the short-run average cost curve. Typically, however, the quality of service declines. More specifically, as additional output is demanded, it can only be supplied at a marginally higher cost as the quality of that output deteriorates. Such a situation is prevalent in the airline industry; for example, if the load factor were to increase from 60 to 80 percent, variable cost would increase only slightly. Slight additional costs would be incurred for food, jet fuel, and perhaps additional crew members, but the overwhelming costs of depreciation, maintenance, reservations ticketing, and pilot salaries would remain constant. However, travelers on the average might now have to wait in line longer for the purchase of tickets, to check baggage, and perhaps fly less optimal routes.[1] A decline in the quality of service could also take place in many of the other transportation modes. In the railroad industry, for example, peak operating conditions might not raise the rates of the commodities hauled, but would rather increase the shipping time from origin to destination. Similar situations often exist for trucking, water, and pipeline transportation.

In evaluating both the theoretical and empirical properties of transportation capacity, one should be cognizant of their impact on service quality. In a theoretical sense, one method to reflect such costs is to impute the cost of this congestion (deterioration of service quality) to the shipper (consumer) and add it to the costs incurred by the carrier (producer). In other words, any congestion above some normal amount is a cost being borne by the consumer instead of the

1. A less optimal route could mean a longer stop-over at an intermediate stop or flying a less direct route to make the necessary connections due to absolute capacity being reached on the optimal flight.

producer. If these imputed consumer costs were aggregated with the producer costs, then a new short-run average cost curve would be reflected where the minimum point may not coincide with the original (without the imputed) consumer costs. Figure 15-1 shows that the short-run average cost curve for the individual producer is given as *SRAC* while the curve that reflects both the imputed costs to the consumer and the producer costs is presented as $\overline{SRAC}$. For output *OB* in the diagram, the producer unit costs are *AB* while there are no imputed consumer costs since the quality of service is equal to or greater than the expected "norm." At *OE* output, however, the quality of service has decreased substantially and now costs *CD* per unit of output in addition to the producer unit costs of *ED*. Another approach is to reflect the impact of lower levels of service in the demand function. Obviously, the effects of changes in any of the important variables can be imputed to the cost or price dimension. This price change could be thought of as the cost to the consumer of a different level of service.

Interpretations of Capacity

In general terms, capacity refers to the amount of output or service that can be produced by a given stock of plant and equipment in a discrete period. While, on the surface, this definition appears quite straightforward, further investigation indicates that some of the terms are subject to interpretation. From our earlier discussions, the term output can be interpreted to mean either a quantity or constant dollar value measure. Although normally it is believed that a quantity measure of output would be more reliable, in the transportation industries the choice may not be so salient. Due to the uniqueness of some types of operating equipment and the special handling required for certain commodities, the capacity of the given capital stock will change as the demand shifts for service by

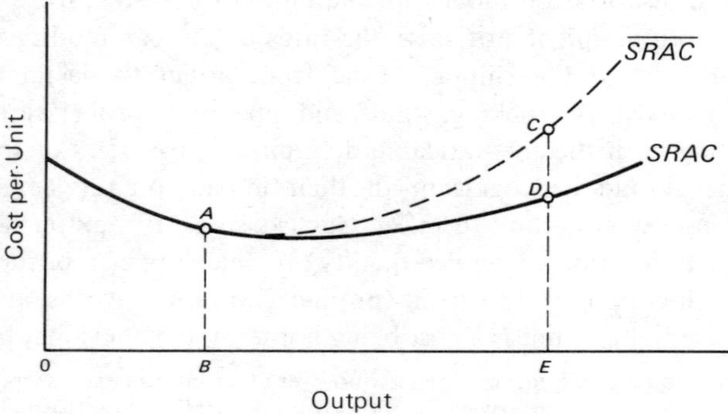

Figure 15-1. Producer and Imputed Consumer Average Costs.

type of commodity. This suggests that a physical ton-mile measure may be less appropriate than the constant dollar measure that weights the tons by their respective base period values.

The part of the definition that is the most open to question are the words "can be produced by." A given stock of plant and equipment producing a maximum output with an operation of 24 hours a day for 7 days a week would differ considerably from one in operation only 8 hours a day during weekdays. In order to eliminate some of the ambiguity of the time problem, three approaches are considered.[2] The first approach is to define capacity as the most efficient rate, or the point at which the marginal cost (*MC*) intersects the minimum of the short-run, average cost (*SRAC*) curve. This economic measure is appealing since its minimum unit cost characteristic has desirable resource allocation implications. Furthermore, the restriction that capacity is the point where the short-run unit cost is a minimum produces a conceptually clear and useful measure. In considering this economic concept of capacity, it is worth noting the following problem. At any specific time, economic capacity (or minimum cost output) depends on the following three factors: the size of the capital stock, embodied technology, and the prices of the factors of production. Since both the size of the capital stock and its embodied technology only change in the long run, they should not cause any shift in short-run economic capacity. On the other hand, any change in the price of variable inputs may actually shift the short-run economic capacity of the given plant and equipment: For example, a change in the wage rate of labor would shift *SRAC* and therefore a new minimum point and consequently a new economic capacity would be designated. This suggests that shifts in the average cost curve (and consequently capacity) can be generated by external factors as well as by changes in the size or technical character of facilities.

A second interpretation of capacity is that of some *absolute* maximum in a physical sense. More specifically, it could mean the output that could be sustained in the short run by operating the plant and equipment constantly (with allowance for normal maintenance and repair). As this absolute capacity output is approached, marginal cost will begin to rise rapidly and will approach infinity.

A third but not so acceptable approach would be to use the highest number of operating hours per week over some historical period as an indicator of capacity. The main limitation of this so-called "normal" approach is that the conceptual meaning of capacity may now become obscure. Specifically, the highest historical rate may not represent capacity if the decision process of the individual firms in that particular industry is not reliable, that is, firms may always have excess capacity and never operate at their most efficient rate due to

2. These approaches and their discussions are extracted from Jack Faucett Associates, Inc., *Transportation Capacity, vol. 5* (Washington, D.C.: U.S. Department of Transportation, August 1973).

errors in planning or expectations. The quantification of such a measure is easy relative to others but its uses are more limited than those of economic or absolute capacity. On the other hand, such a measure might serve as a proxy to assist in the evaluation of either the efficiency (economic) or the absolute maximum concept. If all the assumptions regarding competition, profit maximization, and rationality are made, then the normal operating rate should be reasonably close to the most efficient rate. In practice, however, the two may differ significantly.

Figure 15-2 graphically depicts several of these currently accepted definitions of capacity. The traditional economic capacity, that is, the output consistent with the minimum point on the *SRAC*, is point *A* while the measure of absolute maximum capacity is point *C*. For the latter, regardless of the applications of variable input, no increases in output are attainable: Costs increase while output remains constant (*MC* becomes vertical at that point). A variant of the marginal cost measure is to visualize capacity as a point between the minimum point on the *SRAC* and full capacity, or where *MC* is substantially above the *SRAC*.[3] Although the point would have to be quite arbitrary the concept is meaningful as the *MC* may not increase sharply until some output substantially above the minimum unit cost. If there is a point of inflection, then such a measure would be easier to specify. Point *B* in the diagram depicts this alternative measure. Although the point is somewhat arbitrary, it is indicative of an output where the unit costs begins to increase substantially.

Other measures of economic capacity may have some relevance to certain

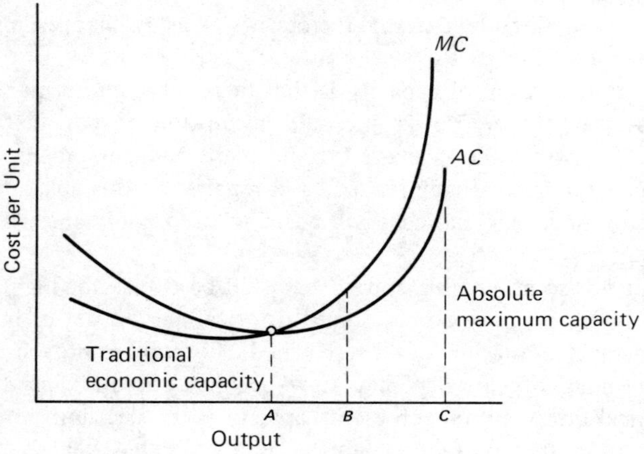

Figure 15-2. Measures of Capacity.

3. See Frank de Leeuw, "The Concept of Capacity," *Proceedings of the Business and Economic Statistics Section*, American Statistical Association (1961).

types of problems. For example, the point of tangency between *SRAC* and the long-run average cost is meaningful for estimating economies of scale since for any output beyond this point there should exist a more optimal size plant. Such a situation can be easily depicted in Figure 15-3. Two short-run, average cost curves are presented for two different plant sizes. It is assumed that the plant is currently operating at point *A* on $SRAC_1$ producing output *OX* at a unit cost of *OM*. Due to a change in demand, the new most efficient output should be *OY*. Such an output can be produced only in the short run by a movement down the *SRAC* to point *B* at a unit cost of *OQ*. In the longer run, however, it is better for the firm to build a new plant or expand its present plant (with $SRAC_2$), which could also produce output *OY* but with a unit cost of only *OR*. Therefore, the point of tangency between the long-run and short-run average cost can be considered a special type of economic capacity, that is, it is a point beyond which there is a more optimal plant for that output. Such a measure is used predominantly as a planning horizon indicating cost possibilities where firms can alter plant size as well as the number of plants.

If there were interest in capacity for some social optimum long-run sense then the minimum point on the long-run, average cost curve would become relevant. Since firms always operate in the short run, interest would be essentially in the minimum point on the *SRAC* that coincides with the same point on the *LRAC*.[4] In Figure 15-3 such a measure is indicated by point *D*; alternatively stated, the ideal output that parallels this socially optimum capacity would be *OZ*. This point represents, however, more of a theoretical reference point than a practical decision consideration.

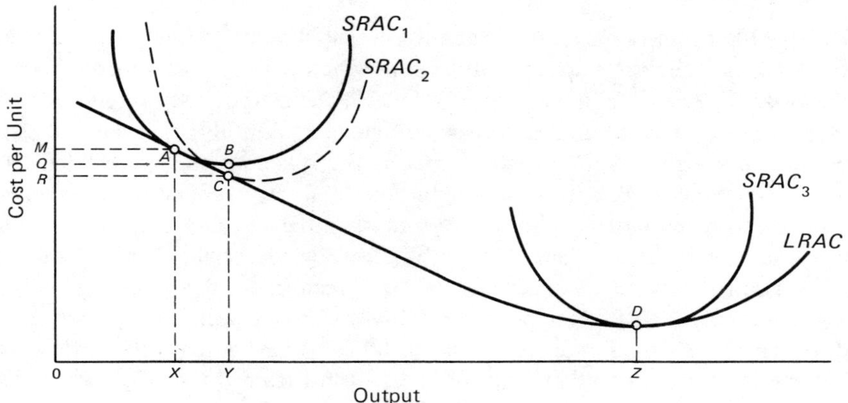

Figure 15-3. Alternative Measures of Capacity.

4. For this social optimum point to be meaningful it would have to be assumed that there were enough demand to support plants that produce such a quantity of output.

One other less important measure of capacity is worth noting. Specific reference is made to a very short-run measure of absolute capacity that differs from the previously described absolute capacity in that the latter is sustainable in the long run while the former is not. The essential cause of the difference is that certain maintenance and repairs can be put off for only a given period. Consequently, it is possible for a given industry to produce temporarily an output above the maximum. Such a measure would be useful in the analysis of a given transportation industry's capacity during some limited national emergency. For example, the impact on the economy of a two week rail strike would depend substantially on this short-run capacity of the trucking, air, and water modes.

Empirical Measures of Capacity

Given the difficulty in defining and measuring capacity, it is not surprising to find that there are few generally accepted conventions for the standardization of capacity measures. There are several alternative measures that follow quite different approaches and approximate somewhat different concepts. In general, the currently available measures can be neatly classified according to their measurement methodology: by the use of peak output measures, surveys, and capital stock measures.

Trend-Through-Peaks

Perhaps the simplest measure of capacity available is that developed in deriving the Wharton Index of Capacity Utilization, which is used in several equations of the Wharton Econometric Forecasting Model.[5] The method used is referred to as "trend-through-peaks" and is derived as follows:[6] Monthly seasonally adjusted physical output series are averaged into quarterly values and are plotted on a graph over time; peak outputs are connected by linear lines and these points are assumed to be potential or capacity output; then the percentage of capacity that is utilized is estimated as the actual output over the potential or capacity output.

Difficulties arise in the mechanics of the procedure for the following reasons: The determination of which peaks are actually capacity peaks may be extremely difficult especially if the series is unstable. Also, it may be difficult to extrapolate the series either forward or backward from the previous peak. The main conceptual problem with the method is the assumption that the peaks are

5. The utilization estimates are used in the investment, price, hours worked, and production function equations of this quarterly model.

6. For a complete explanation of this concept, see Lawrence R. Klein and Robert Summers, *The Wharton Index of Capacity Utilization*, University of Pennsylvania, 1966.

similar: The major question is clearly whether the output at each of the cyclical peaks represents the same degree of utilization. The Wharton group assumed that the peaks represent minimum points on the short-run, average cost curves, but since different peaks need not coincide with this minimum point, the measure suffers an important limitation.[7] One may also be critical of the application of straight lines due to the fact that capital formation is not a smooth process. Generally, additions to plant and equipment are more concentrated during the up-phase of the cycle so that the "trend-through-peak" method most likely underestimates capacity during expansion and overstates it during contraction. Perhaps some normalization with respect to the rate of investment might reduce this possible source of error. A final criticism of this method is the fact that the peak may not represent plant and equipment capacity, namely, the peak may have been restrained by the absence of qualified labor or materials and not capital.

Survey Method

The survey approach is essentially an ex-post evaluation of capacity and its utilization during the previous year by plant managers and other knowledgeable persons who are in direct contact with the actual production unit. Perhaps the best known example of this approach is the McGraw-Hill measure that has been in existence since 1947. A questionnaire is mailed to manufacturing industries (representing 40 percent of total manufacturing employment) in which executives are asked to indicate their past and present operating rate as a percentage of capacity. McGraw-Hill does not present a definition of capacity but does ask the companies to be consistent through time. In general, the companies follow a practical definition of capacity such as the maximum output under normal work schedules. Industry indices are then constructed from company returns using employment as weights.

While this measure overcomes one of the basic criticisms of the Wharton measure, it also has some limitations. First of all, the replies are on a company and not an establishment or plant basis. Then, without a clear definition of capacity there is undoubtedly great variation across industries and even over time as executives' concepts of capacity differ. In addition, McGraw-Hill presents very little information on the sample size for each industry or the distribution across small, medium, and large firms.[8]

The best measure may be the recently devised Federal Reserve Board survey

7. An attempt is made to check on which peaks really constitute capacity by fitting production functions. The result, however, was that the improvement in the measures was negligible. See L.R. Klein and R.S. Preston, "Some New Results on the Measurement of Capacity Utilization," *American Economic Review* 57 (March 1967), pp. 34-58.

8. It is generally held that the survey is concentrated among the large firms, which may also cause some distortion.

on capacity, which will eventually become an integral part of the *Census* and *Annual Survey of Manufacturers.* This survey is substantially different from other approaches in that it attempts to derive an economic measure of capacity, namely the minimum point on the short-run, average cost curve. Specific definitions are presented and the degree of sampling error is indicated. Although this new measure is restricted to manufacturing industries, it is a very valuable new addition to capacity information.

Capital/Output Ratios

This approach to the measurement of capacity is based on the technological relationship between the stock of capital and the output derived from capital. In general, the procedure is to compute capital/output ratios in constant dollars over time and then examine these ratios for cyclical peaks. From independent evidence a bench mark year is then selected to indicate the capital/output ratio that reflects "virtually full capacity" utilization. This ratio is then used to determine the extent to which the other output rates depart from the capacity output.

Several problems are apparent from this type of measure. First, the derivation of adequate measures of the value of the capital stock are extremely difficult. Second, there are problems in forecasting inflation and in determining the appropriate method of capital depreciation. In addition, as time passes, there is more of a movement toward social or nonproduction capital, for example, environmental control equipment, which would be valued in the capital stock and, consequently, present an upward bias in the capacity output. Finally, over certain ranges, technological change might be exceptionally capital intensive, which may distort interpretations of capital/output ratios.

Peak Loads

A salient feature of transportation capacity is that the demand for transportation services is rather volatile and the transportation industries have chosen to provide capacity for the peaks. In other industries the consumption of many commodities may be seasonal in nature, but the production may in turn be smooth. Because the production and consumption of transportation services must coincide both with respect to location and to time, the transportation industries do not have the option to store these services.

Since the transportation industries have chosen not to smooth the demand by some variant of marginal cost pricing (against the will of many economists), the very nature of the service induces substantial excess capacity at certain times and consequently substantial excess capacity on the average.[9] Such a situation also contributes toward making the industry more capital intensive, and therefore fixed costs are larger than they should perhaps be. To the extent that a firm can not shift revenue equipment from one location to another to meet these regional peaks, the amount of national excess capacity may be greater since each individual company may maintain capacity for its individual peaks.[10] Consequently, if there is no type of a national pool from which companies can lease revenue equipment on a short-term basis, the amount of excess capacity would depend to some extent on the degree of geographic mobility of this equipment.

The peaking problem is very severe on an hourly basis for many of the local modes of transportation such as bus, taxi, and rapid transit. It is quite important for the airline industry with respect to time of day, week, and season and much less important for domestic water and railroads. It is far less important in the pipeline, motor trucking, and international water industries. In very general terms, the modes of transportation that are designed primarily for passenger use seem to face a much greater peaking problem than those which are largely carriers of freight. However, motor carriers and railroads do face peaks, especially in seasonal operations for an industry like agriculture.

Public Capital

The existence of a large amount of public capital over which the individual transportation carriers have little control suggests that transportation capacity may be unique relative to that of other industries. Capacity may be imposed on an industry through the public decision process, which is exogenous to the investment decision process of the individual carriers that comprise a given transportation industry; for example, the capacity of the airline industry may be X passenger-miles due to the inability of either airport or airway capital to accommodate any additional demand. The capacity restraint imposed upon the airline industry by this public capital may be either above or below that of the private capital of the individual firms.

In measuring the capacity of those transportation modes that utilize public capital, one must therefore at least be cognizant that it is possible for the capacity of the public capital to be reached prior to that of the private capital. Public capital is currently found in airports, airways, highways, waterways, and to some extent, local bus transportation and rapid transit. With the general

9. The domestic airline industry has introduced some very minimal amount of marginal cost pricing by instituting various discount fare packages, which from time to time unfortunately are rescinded by the CAB.

10. Individual companies do not always maintain capacity for individual peaks; as an example, railroad companies pool freight cars so that individual carriers can utilize one another's equipment at fixed rates.

exceptions of the rail and pipeline modes, all modes currently utilize substantial public capital.[11] In theory, regardless of which capacity measure is desired, one should include the public costs associated with this capital because it could change both the position and shape of the average cost for providing transportation service. In other words, if this capital had to be provided by the individual industries rather than the public in general, it would be reflected in the cost schedules of the individual firms and therefore of the industry.[12] For this reason, at least in the measurement of capacity, it would seem most appropriate to develop short-run costs associated with supplying a given transportation service. The main problem encountered in attempting to include the costs associated with public capital is that much of the public capital is used by several transportation modes and consequently an allocation problem exists. General aviation, domestic, and international airlines jointly use airway and airport capital; waterway capital is used by domestic and international water; and highways are used by several transportation modes—autos, trucking, taxicab, and bus. Therefore, the costs associated with public capital must be allocated among the individual modes prior to their inclusion with private costs.

Indivisibility of Capital

Another characteristic that prevails in transportation is that capital is indivisible. When the operating equipment is brought on line, it must be supplied in rather large aggregates rather than in specific units to meet the demand for a unit of service. For example, if an air carrier is to meet the demand for several passengers, it can only do so by supplying an aircraft with its designed seating capacity.[13] The identical situation may exist for buses, ships, and even railroad cars. This indivisibility of capital increases the possibility that a particular industry will have excess capacity. The impact of this indivisibility of operating equipment on the capacity and its utilization is accentuated by the fact that there are many carriers that service numerous routes. At any one time, therefore, the carriers are faced with the decision of how much freight or how many passengers are necessary to warrant adding additional equipment. To the extent that indivisibility does exist in the operating equipment of a given transportation industry, it is a factor contributing to the permanency of excess capacity. As

11. The most notable examples of "public capital" in the railroad industry have been Amtrak and the Consolidated Railroad Corporation.

12. To the extent that user costs are imposed on a given industry (like fuel taxes, landing fees and tolls), the public capital costs may be reflected in the cost curves of the individual firms.

13. For an excellent treatment of the quality of service aspects of this problem, see George W. Douglas and James C. Miller III, "Quality Competition, Industry Equilibrium, and Efficiency in the Price Constrained Airline Market," *American Economic Review* 64 (September 1974), pp. 657-69.

with many of the previously described characteristics, the extent of this indivisibility differs considerably by transportation mode. It is probably most important for air and overseas water and much less important for motor trucking. It is currently a severe problem in the railroad industry, especially in the context of the heroic efforts aimed at rationalizing the railroad system.

Capital Intensity

One of the primary distinguishing characteristics of most transportation modes is the fact that they are extremely capital intensive. As can be noted from Table 15-1, the capital/output ratios for the four major modes of rail, trucking, air, and water range from a high of 12.6 to a low of 2.7 in 1965.[14] All are substantially above the average both for manufacturing and nonmanufacturing industries and at least slightly above that for agriculture.

If transportation capital/output ratios are high, it is very likely that the fixed costs associated with this capital are high relative to the variable costs. This

Table 15-1
Capital Output Ratios for Selected Industries[a]

	Year			
Industry	1947	1953	1958	1965
Agriculture	2.00	2.44	2.65	2.50
Manufacturing	1.09	1.00	1.25	.95
Nonmanufacturing[b]	1.58	1.50	1.53	1.47
Railroads	6.29	6.87	7.90	6.07
Trucking (for-hire)	2.98	2.56	2.74	2.74
Air[c]	6.83	3.81	2.79	2.72
Water[d]	10.56	13.80	13.98	12.58

[a]These capital/output ratios are based on constant 1958 dollar net output (gross product originating) and gross capital stocks. The ratios for the transportation industries are based on an aggregation of both private and public capital; for example, the share of airport and airway capital that is used by United States domestic and international carriers is included in the ratios given for air.

[b]Excludes agriculture and government.

[c]International and domestic airlines.

[d]Domestic and overseas carriers.

Source: Jack Faucett Associates, Inc., *Capital Stock Measures for Transportation*, Report prepared for U.S. Department of Transportation, (Washington, D.C.: June 1972).

14. The mere fact that the capital/output ratios are high does not necessarily imply that the industry is labor intensive since the yearly cost of the flow of services differs depending upon the average age of the capital.

should in turn influence the shape of the short-run average cost curve by making it more horizontal, or less U-shaped than that of a firm whose variable costs are substantial. When the short-run cost curves are horizontal for a substantial range of output, then unit cost changes only slightly as output changes. From a social welfare viewpoint, this means that the misallocation of resources from a firm not operating at the minimum point on the average cost curve would be minimal. This in turn implies that the concept of economic capacity, as a specific point on short-run, average cost curve, may be less important since there would be a large number of outputs where unit costs would be extremely close to that of the minimum point. This would, of course, depend upon the number of units demanded as well as the unit cost differences. Stated alternatively, the more U-shaped the average cost curve, the more meaningful the minimum point becomes since substantial inefficiencies would occur as soon as the firm changes its output level slightly. For relatively horizontal curves, such inefficiencies are slow to be reflected by even a rather marked shift in output demanded.

Summary

Capacity is a very difficult term to define. This chapter has attempted to provide an overview of some alternate interpretations of capacity in the transportation industries which typically are characterized by relatively large amounts of fixed capital and by peak load operating conditions. An accurate estimate of capacity is useful to the transportation economist in order to better understand productivity and to serve as a possible foundation for efficient pricing in transportation.[15]

15. A knowledge of capacity is also useful in analyzing current problems in the reorganization of the railroad industry, for example, in determining how much traffic can be absorbed by the solvent railroads in case the bankrupt railroads are forced to shut down.

Selected Bibliography: The Domestic Transportation Industries

Railroad Economics

Altman, Edward I. "Predicting Railroad Bankruptcies in America," *The Bell Journal of Economics and Management Science* 4 (Spring 1973), pp. 184-211.

The American Railroads: Posture, Problems and Prospects, Staff Analysis for the U.S. Senate Committee on Commerce. Prepared at the Direction of the Honorable Warren G. Magnuson, Chairman, Committee on Commerce, United States Senate, August 28, 1972.

Anderson, John. "Applications of Engineering Analysis of Production to Econometric Models of the Firm," *American Economic Review, Papers and Proceedings* 59 (May 1969), pp. 398-402.

R.L. Banks & Associates, Inc., *Development and Evaluation of an Economic Abstraction of Light Density Rail Line Operations*, prepared for the Federal Railroad Administration, U.S. Department of Transportation (Washington: June 1973).

Baumel, C.P., T.P. Drinka, D.R. Lifferth, and J.J. Miller, *An Economic Analysis of Alternative Grain Transportation Systems: A Case Study*, prepared for the Federal Railroad Administration, U.S. Department of Transportation (Washington: November 1973).

Beckmann, Martin J., Ryuzo Sato, and Mark Schupack. "Alternative Approaches to the Estimation of Production Functions and of Technical Change," *International Economic Review* 13 (February 1972), pp. 33-57.

Belovarac, K., and J.T. Kneafsey. *Determinants of Line Haul Reliability*, M.I.T. Department of Civil Engineering Research Report R72-38, Studies in Railroad Operations and Economics, vol. 3, 1972.

Borts, George H. "The Estimation of Rail Cost Functions," *Econometrica* 28 (January 1960), pp. 108-31.

Daughen, Joseph R., and Peter Binzen. *The Wreck of the Penn Central* (Boston: Little, Brown and Company, 1971).

Dewitt, William J. III. "The Railroad Conglomerate: Its Relationship to the Interstate Commerce Commission and National Transportation Policy," *Transportation Journal* 12 (Winter 1972), pp. 5-14.

Eads, George C. "Railroad Diversification: Where Lies the Public Interest?" *Bell Journal of Economics and Management Science* 5 (Autumn 1974), pp. 595-613.

Felton, John Richard, "Freight Car Shortages: The Problem and Some Proposed Solutions," *Nebraska Journal of Economics and Business* (Spring 1972), pp. 33-44.

Fogel, Robert William. *Railroads and American Economic Growth: Essays in Econometric History* (Baltimore, Md.: The Johns Hopkins Press, 1964).

Friedlaender, Ann F. *The Dilemma of Freight Transport Regulation* (Washington: The Brookings Institution, 1969).

Griliches, Zvi. "Cost Allocation in Railroad Regulation," *The Bell Journal of Economics and Management Science* 3 (Spring 1972), pp. 26-41.

Harbeson, Robert W. "Some Policy Implications of Northeastern Railroad Problems," *Transportation Journal* 14 (Fall 1974), pp. 5-12.

Improving Railroad Productivity. Final Report of the Task Force on Railroad Productivity to the National Commission on Productivity and Council of Economic Advisers (Washington: November 1973).

Joy, Stewart. "Pricing and Investment in Railway Freight Services," *Journal of Transport Economics and Policy* 5 (September 1971), pp. 231-46.

Keeler, Theodore E. "Railroad Costs, Returns to Scale, and Excess Capacity," *Review of Economics and Statistics* 56 (May 1974), pp. 201-8.

Kelejian, H.H. "The Estimation of Cobb-Douglas Type Functions with Multiplicative and Additive Errors: A Further Analysis," *International Economic Review* 13 (February 1972), pp. 179-82.

Kneafsey, James T. "Mergers, Technical Change, and Returns to Scale in the Railroad Industry," *Proceedings–Thirteenth Annual Meeting–Transportation Research Forum* 13 (November 1972), pp. 439-58.

_______. *Costing in Railroad Operations: A Proposed Methodology*, Studies in Railroad Operations and Economics, vol. 13, Department of Civil Engineering, M.I.T., 1974.

_______. *The Economics of the Transportation Firm* (Lexington, Mass.: Lexington Books, D.C. Heath and Co., 1974).

Kneafsey, James T., and Matthew E. Edelman. "A Market-Oriented Solution to the Northeast Railroad Dilemma," *ICC Practitioners' Journal* (January/February 1974), pp. 174-89.

Kullman, B.C. *A Model of Rail/Truck Competition in the Intercity Freight Market*, Studies in Railroad Operations and Economics, vol. 15, Department of Civil Engineering, M.I.T., 1974.

Leibenstein, Harvey, "Allocative Efficiency vs. 'X-Efficiency,' " *American Economic Review* 56 (June 1966), pp. 392-415.

MacAvoy, Paul W. *The Economic Effects of Regulation: The Trunk Line Railroad Cartels and the Interstate Commerce Commission Before 1900* (Cambridge, Mass.: The M.I.T. Press, 1965).

MacAvoy, Paul W., and James Sloss. *Regulation of Transport Innovation: The ICC and Unit Coal Trains to the East Coast* (New York: Random House, 1967).

Martin, Albro. "Railroads and the Equity Receivership: An Essay on Institutional Change," *Journal of Economic History* 34 (September 1974), pp. 685-709.

Martland, C.D. *Rail Trip Time Reliability: Evaluation of Performance Measures and Analysis of Trip Time Data*, M.I.T. Department of Civil Engineering

Research Report R72-37, Studies in Railroad Operations and Economics, Vol. 2, 1972.

Mercer, Lloyd J. "Building Ahead of Demand: Some Evidence for Land Grant Railroads," *Journal of Economic History* 34 (June 1974), pp. 492-500.

Meyer, John R., Merton J. Peck, John Stenason, and Charles Zwick. *The Economics of Competition in the Transportation Industries* (Cambridge, Mass.: Harvard University Press, 1959).

Moore, Thomas G. *Freight Transportation Regulation, Surface Freight and the Interstate Commerce Commission* (Washington, D.C.: American Enterprise Institute for Public Policy Research, 1972).

Nerlove, Marc. *Estimation and Identification of Cobb-Douglas Production Functions* (New York: Rand-McNally, 1965).

Nupp, Byron. "Railroads and the Transportation Problem: Some Thoughts on Strategy and Political Roles," *Transportation Journal* 13 (Winter 1973), pp. 34-37.

The Penn Central and Other Railroads. A Report to the Senate Committee on Commerce, 92nd Cong., 2nd Sess., December 1972 (Washington: USGPO, 1972).

Scheppach, R.C. *Capital Stock Measures for Transportation. Volume 1*, (Chevy Chase, Md.: Jack Faucett Associates, June 1972).

Sharp, Clifford. "The Optimum Allocation of Freight Traffic," *Journal of Transport Economics and Policy* 5 (September 1971), pp. 344-56.

Silbertson, Aubrey, "Economies of Scale in Theory and Practice," *Economic Journal* 82 (March 1972), pp. 369-91.

Sussman, Joseph M., C.D. Martland, and A.S. Lang. *Reliability in Railroad Operations: Executive Summary*, M.I.T. Department of Civil Engineering Research Report R73-4, Studies in Railroad Operations and Economics, vol. 9, 1973.

Tihansky, Dennis P. "Trends in Rail Freight Transport." *Traffic Quarterly* 28 (January 1974), pp. 101-18.

U.S. Department of Commerce, Maritime Administration. *Domestic Waterbourne Shipping Market Analysis: Executive Summary* (Chicago: Kearney-Management Consultants, February 1974).

U.S. Department of Transportation. *Report to the Congress on the Rail Passenger Service Act* (Washington: July 1974).

"USRA Sees Need for Subsidies Even If Bankrupt Roads are Reorganized," *Traffic World* (November 18, 1974), p. 23.

Whitin, T.M. "Output Dimensions and Their Implications for Cost and Price Analysis," *Journal of Business* 45 (April 1972), pp. 305-15.

Airline Economics

Air Transport Association of America, *Air Transport Facts and Figures: The Annual Report of the U.S. Scheduled Airline Industry* (Washington: 1974).

Bain, Donald. *The Case Against Private Aviation* (New York: Cowles, 1969).

Caves, Richard E. *Air Transport and Its Regulators: An Industry Study* (Cambridge, Mass.: Harvard University Press, 1962).

DeVany, Arthur. "The Revealed Value of Time in Air Travel," *Review of Economics and Statistics* 56 (February 1974), pp. 77-82.

Douglas, George W., and James C. Miller, III. "Quality Competition, Industry Equilibrium, and Efficiency in the Price-Constrained Airline Market," *American Economic Review* 64 (September 1974), pp. 657-69.

Eads, George C. *The Local Service Airline Experiment* (Washington: The Brookings Institution, 1972).

Ellison, A.P., and E.M. Stafford. *The Dynamics of the Civil Aviation Industry* (Westmead, England: Saxon House, D.C. Heath Ltd., 1974).

Fruhan, William E. Jr. *The Fight for Competitive Advantage: A Study of the United States Domestic Trunk Air Carriers* (Cambridge, Mass.: Harvard University Press, 1972).

Gritta, Richard D. "Risk and the 'Fair Rate of Return' in Air Transportation," *Transportation Journal* 13 (Summer 1974), pp. 41-45.

Gronau, Reuben. *The Value of Time in Passenger Transportation: The Demand for Air Travel* (New York: National Bureau of Economic Research, 1970).

International Air Transport Association, *World Air Transport Statistics* (Montreal: 1974).

McWhinney, Edward, and Martin A. Bradley, eds. *The Freedom of the Air* (Dobbs Ferry, N.Y.: Oceana Publications, Inc., 1968).

Phillips, Almarin. *Technology and Market Structure: A Study of the Aircraft Industry* (Lexington, Mass.: Lexington Books, D.C. Heath and Company, 1971).

Poirier, Dale J., and Steven G. Garber. "The Determinants of Aerospace Profit Rates 1951-1971," *Southern Economic Journal* 41 (October 1974), pp. 228-38.

Schneider, Lewis M. *The Future of the U.S. Domestic Air Freight Industry: An Analysis of Management Strategies* (Boston: Graduate School of Business Administration, Harvard University, 1973).

Scott, Ronald Dean, and Martin T. Farris. "Airline Subsidies in the United States," *Transportation Journal* 13 (Summer 1974), pp. 25-33.

Simpson, Robert, "A Theory of Airline Economics," mimeo, M.I.T. Flight Transportation Laboratory, 1974.

Straszheim, Mahlon R. *The International Airline Industry* (Washington: The Brookings Institution, 1969).

_______. "The Determination of Airline Fares and Load Factors: Some Oligopoly Models," *Journal of Transport Economics and Policy* 8 (September 1974), pp. 260-73.

Stratford, Alan H. *Air Transport Economics in the Supersonic Era*, 2nd ed. (London: MacMillan, 1974).

Taneja, Nawal. "Financing of the Major U.S. Scheduled Airlines," *Proceedings of the Transportation Research Forum* 13 (November 1973), pp. 451-68.

U.S. Civil Aeronautics Board, *Air Carrier Financial Statistics* (Washington: U.S. Government Printing Office, 1974).

U.S. Civil Aeronautics Board, *Handbook of Airline Statistics, 1973* (Washington: U.S. Government Printing Office, 1974).

Part III:
The Urban Passenger Sector

16 Urban Transit Systems

When one thinks of urban transit, the bus or taxi immediately comes to mind; if it is of urban *mass* transit, then rail transit or subways become the thought. The facts are that many different types of vehicles qualify for performing urban transportation services. A chronological list of urban transit vehicles was prepared by the U.S. Department of Transportation and is presented in Figure 16-1. Note that the latest form of urban transit, PRT or personal rapid transit, is considered operational for 1976.

Especially in lower density population areas major efforts to supplant the automobile and to upgrade the existing mass transportation facilities have produced a wide variety of transit innovations and service improvements ranging from improved marketing-promotion techniques to paratransit approaches like carpooling, subscription bus services, jitneys, and dial-a-bus or demand-responsive vehicles. Spectacular developments have occurred in urban transit in the early 1970s in the area of demand-responsive transportation systems. These systems reflect flexibly routed, personalized transportation services available to serve individual needs.[1] They depict a range of problem transportation services characterized by the flexible scheduling of relatively small size vehicles to provide shared occupancy, usually door-to-door, personalized transportation on demand and at moderate fares. These systems thus are hybrid forms of traditional bus and taxicab services, combining the point-to-point flexibility and convenience of private vehicles with mass transportation. The basic way in which a demand-responsive transportation operates is illustrated in Figure 16-2.

Although the predecessor of demand-responsive transportation services originated more than 60 years ago with touring-car jitneys, the concept was not applied to transit service on a community service until 1964. Since that time demand-responsive transportation systems have mushroomed throughout the world. Table 16-1 presents a chronological listing of most of the known demand-responsive systems in operation throughout the world up to 1975. A comparison of dial-a-bus services with other forms of urban transit in terms of its frequency of service, degree of coverage, and access is presented in Figure 16-3; also, information on selected dial-a-ride systems appears in Table 16-2.

In the decade following the passage of the Urban Mass Transit Act in 1964,

1. The private taxicab is a form of public transportation (but not regarded as a form of urban *mass* transit) that does supply a high quality of service in terms of personalized, demand-responsive transportation, but its fares are usually prohibitively high for many classes of potential users like the elderly, the handicapped, the impoverished, and in many cases the single-car family.

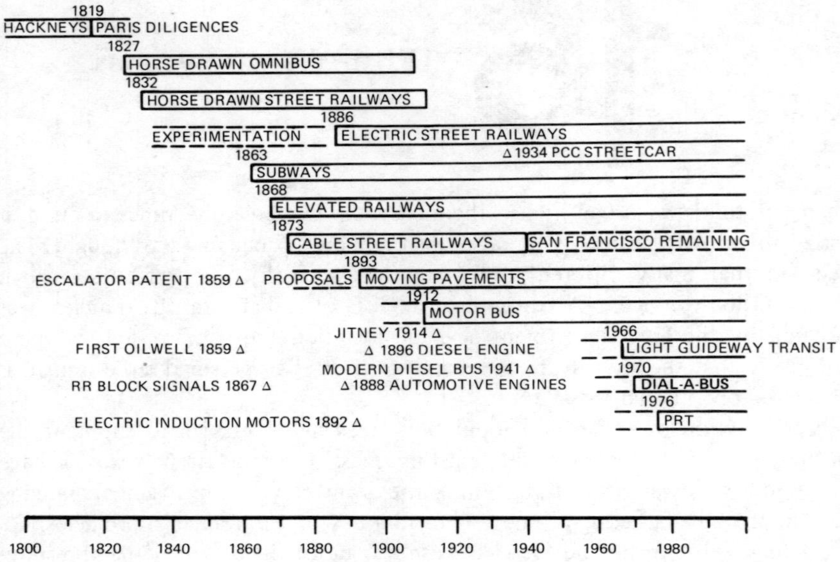

Figure 16-1. A Chronology of Urban Transit. Source: U.S. Department of Transportation, *Demand-Responsive Transportation: State-of-the-Art Overview* (1975), p. viii. Data taken from N.D. Lea Transportation Research, *Lea Transit Compendium* 1, no. 1 (1974).

the federal government had spent approximately $10 billion to improve local transit systems. Every dollar of these expenditures was limited to capital investments. With the legislation passed in 1974, however, funds were allocated over an interim period to cover also a portion of the operational expenses incurred by hard-pressed metropolitan transit systems. The ability of urban mass transportation to function effectively in achieving desired goals is weakened by the operating deficit plaguing the industry. On the whole, the deficit in mass transportation has leaped from less than $1 million in 1963 to more than $680 million in 1973.[2]

Transportation Control Measures

Following the Clean Air Act of 1970 and amendments thereto, the Environmental Protection Agency (EPA) promulgated national ambient air quality

2. See George M. Smerk, "Operating Subsidies for Urban Mass Transportation," *Traffic Quarterly* 28 (October 1974), p. 604.

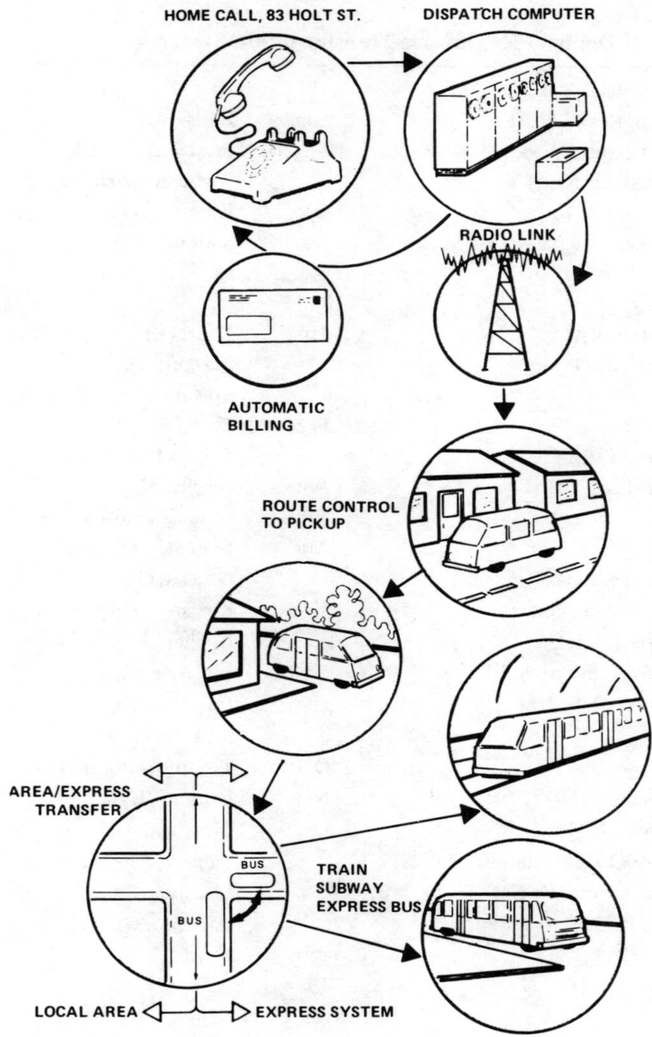

Figure 16-2. Demand-responsive Transportation Service. Source: U.S. Department of Transportation, *Demand-Responsive Transportation: State-of-the-Art Overview* (1975), p. 2. Data taken from Regina Transit System (Saskatchewan), "Regina Telebus Transportation Project: Summary Report" (November 1972).

Table 16-1
Chronology of Demand-Responsive Transportation Systems[a]

1916	Atlantic City, NJ*
1946	Little Rock, AK (E)
1958	Ft. Leonard Wood, MO
1961	Hicksville, NY (E)
1964	Peoria, IL (T)
1967	Gothenberg, Sweden
1968	
Feb:	Reston, VA
Sept:	Flint, MI (T)
1969	
Jan:	Menlo Park, CA
Dec:	Mansfield, OH (T)
1970	
May:	Emmen, Netherlands
July:	Bay Ridges, Ontario
Aug:	Merced, CA
Oct:	Ft. Walton Beach, FL (T)
Dec:	Buffalo, NY (E)
1971	
Jan:	Columbia, MD (E)
	Kent, OH (T)
July:	Scott-Carver Counties, MN
Sept:	Ann Arbor, MI (E)
	Regina, Saskatchewan
Oct:	Batavia, NY
	Columbus, OH (E)
1972	
Jan:	Willingboro, NJ
Feb:	Detroit, MI (E)
	Haddonfield, NJ (E)
	Franklin County, ME
	Toledo, OH (E)
June:	Lincoln, NB
	Medford, OR
Aug:	Klamath Falls, OR (T)
	Rhode Island State
1972 (cont.)	
Sept:	Dallas, TX
	Stratford, Ontario
	West Pal Beach, FL
Oct:	Kingston, Ontario
Nov:	Sudbury, Ontario
1973	
Jan:	Kent, OH
	LaHabra, CA
	Lower Naugatuck Valley, CT
Feb:	Davis, CA
May:	LaMirada, CA
June:	Helena, MT (E)
July:	Grand Rapids, MI (E)
Aug:	Bramalea, Ontario
	Ottawa, Ontario
	Kingston, Ontario
	Rochester, NY
Sept:	Los Angeles, CA
	New Orleans, LA
	St. Petersburg, FL
Oct:	Toronto, Ontario (E)
Nov:	Bensenville, IL
Dec:	Cleveland, OH
	Calgary, Alberta
	El Cajon, CA
	Hartford, CT
1974	
Jan:	Hemet, CA
Feb:	Holland, MI
	Luddington, MI
Mar:	Mt. Pleasant, MI
Apr:	Sault Ste. Marie, MI
	LaMesa, CA
May:	Cambridge, Ontario
	Merced, CA
	Traverse City, MI
June:	Dover, DL
	Fairfax City, VA

Table 16-1 (cont.)

1974 (cont.)			
June:	Midland, MI	Sept:	Benton Harbor
	Isabella County, MI		St. Joseph, MI
July:	Alpena, MI	Fall:	Cleveland, OH
	Houghton-Hancock, MI		Santa Clara County, CA
	Richmond, CA		
Sept:	Washington, DC	1975	Rockville, MD

(E) Subsequently Expanded
(T) Terminated

[a]Not necessarily exhaustive; includes two jitney services, nine taxi-based operations, and 69 bus-based operations.

Source: U.S. Department of Transportation, *Demand-Responsive Transportation: State-of-the-Art Overview* (1975), p. 10.

standards for six classes of pollutants. The act's regulations require each state to enforce procedures to reduce emissions from transportation sources wherever such steps are necessary for the attainment and maintenance of the national standards. Transportation control measures are intended primarily to achieve cleaner air, but their potential benefits extend further. The implementation of transportation control plans may ameliorate a number of urban transportation problems; for example, the need to control the air quality impacts of transportation has been a major lever in strengthening transportation planning and decision-making processes. Other positive effects of transportation control measures include the promotion of more rational use of energy and increased safety through lower average vehicle speeds.

Most urban areas face a complex set of interrelated transportation problems. One obvious problem is the extreme congestion of transportation facilities, both for highways and transit, in the two peak periods of the day associated with the beginning and end of typical working hours. Attempts to relieve peak-hour congestion by increasing capacity have only been partially successful and have aggravated other problems of the urban environment through residential and business displacements, community disruption, and environmental degradation, particularly air pollution, noise, and removal of open space.[3] In addition, when capacities are based on peak demand estimates, facilities are underutilized during off-peak periods, resulting in the inefficient use of manpower and resources.

In recent years the financial difficulties of public transit systems have become especially intense. While energy, material, and labor costs have climbed dramati-

3. See Thomas E. Lisco, "Report of the Workshop on Social, Economic and Environmental Impacts of Transportation Systems," *Highway Research Board Special Report 143*, Highway Research Board (Washington, D.C.: 1973), pp. 90-95.

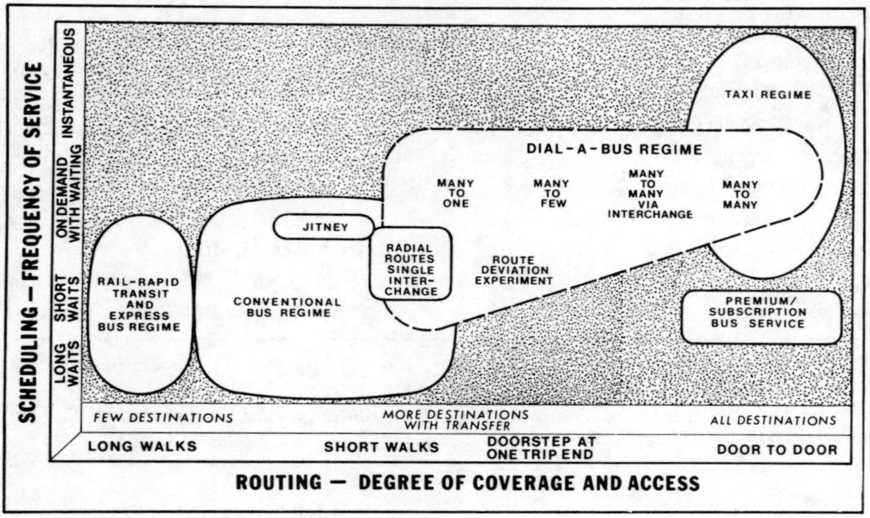

Figure 16-3. A Conceptual Framework for Dial-a-Bus Services. Source: U.S. Department of Transportation, *Demand-Responsive Transportation: State-of-the-Art Overview* (1975), p. 21.

cally, aggregate ridership has declined almost continuously over a long period. Fares have been increased in most cities,[4] but not enough to keep pace with the declining ridership. In most cities service has been reduced such that transit systems have become so unattractive relative to the private auto that most individuals who have a choice between transit and the automobile choose the latter. Even on the New York City subway system ridership declined by 6 percent between January 1974 and January 1975, in spite of an increase in promotional efforts by the Metropolitan Transportation Agency.[5]

Heavy reliance on the private automobile also contributes to the plight of transit by facilitating the decentralization of metropolitan areas. Lower population densities in outlying areas make efficient transit service there difficult to

4. In several major cities the trend as of 1975 has been in the opposite direction. The most famous example is in Atlanta where fares were cut from 40 cents to 15 cents in 1973. Less significant fare reductions have been achieved in Baltimore, Cincinnati, and Los Angeles. Most of these reductions have been offset by new local taxes levied specifically to support transit operations: sales taxes in Atlanta and Los Angeles; an earnings tax in Cincinnati; and in Boston, where the fare has been sustained at 25 cents, special funds were generated through a realty tax on a special transit district.

5. In January 1974 the world's largest bus and subway system carried daily an average of 3.9 million passengers.

accomplish. In many suburbs only the automobile currently can provide the required degree of mobility at a reasonable cost and with acceptable travel times.

A problem in urban transportation related both to the extensive use of automobiles and to the problems of transit systems is the failure to provide adequate mobility for the elderly, the handicapped, and the low-income segments of the population. These groups often cannot rely on the private automobile for essential transportation service. Where transit is available, higher fares and declining levels of service represent a decline in basic mobility; those who cannot drive, do not drive, or choose not to drive pay more money for poorer service. The plight of these groups in areas where no transit exists is, of course, even more serious and the lack of mobility can have economic repercussions in addition to the obvious social welfare problems.

This cluster of urban transportation problems is complex and will not be easily solved. However, there is general agreement that improved transit is a step in the right direction, especially in view of recent commitment by federal and state agencies for increased transit funding. Also, the partial opening of the previously sacrosanct Highway Trust Fund to transit monies is an historically important event. In addition, there is growing agreement that the emphasis on long-term, capital intensive projects must be supplemented by a thorough consideration of lower cost, shorter range options. In response to some of the major unresolved transportation problems, and to the inability of capital intensive projects to solve all of these problems, a number of rather specialized, low-cost, short-range options and control measures have been proposed.[6] These measures are presented in Table 16-3 and can be classified into these major groups: first, measures designed to reduce vehicular miles of travel; second, measures to increase the efficiency of traffic flow; and third, measures that are simply supplementary vehicle emission controls. Virtually all these proposed measures can assist to combat the traditional urban transportation problems discussed above.

Extensive reliance on the automobile as it was used until the mid-1970s has resulted in significant energy consumption. On an annual basis motor vehicles have been consuming approximately 20 percent of the energy used in this country, and 75 percent of the energy required by automobiles is alleged to be wasted due to the inefficiency of the internal combustion engine. In addition, the large size and weight of many domestic autos, coupled with a typical occupancy rate of fewer than two passengers per car, indicates that much of the energy utilized is moving machinery rather than people. There are conflicting data and considerable debate on the extent to which emissions devices for automobiles impose a penalty in fuel economy. The loss in fuel economy may be partially offset by a move toward smaller cars, particularly in urban areas. On an overall basis, however, there is virtually no disagreement that actions which

6. "Highways and Air Quality," *Highway Research Board Special Report 141*, Highway Research Board (Washington, D.C.: 1973).

Table 16-2
Information on Selected Dial-a-Ride Systems

	Ann Arbor	Batavia	Columbia	Davenport	Haddonfield	Regina
Area (sq. mi.)	2.3	4.3	4.3	27.0	8.1	2.5
Population	10,000	18,000	18,000	92,500	27,500	18,000
Population density	4,300	4,200	4,200	3,700	3,500	7,200
Time of service	12 hrs.	12 hrs.	17 hrs.	24 hrs.	24 hrs.	17 hrs.
Nature of service						
Peak	M-F	M-M (Sub)	M-F	M-M	M-M	M-O (Sub)
Off peak	M-F	M-M and a variety of other services	Fixed Route	M-M	M-M	M-F
Equipment: fleet	3	4,1	5,4	23	12	2,1,5
size	10	19,10	10,23	7	17	15,23,45
Equipment on road						
Peak	3	5	--	20	12	8
Offpeak	3	3	--	16	4	4
Transit competition	Bus	None	None	Bus	None	Bus
Patronage/weekday	190	400	--	2,400-3,200	750	1,200
Demand density (D/sq. mile/hr.)	6.9	7.7	--	3.4-4.6	3.8	28.0
Modal split (%)	2	1-2	--	2-3	4-5	6-7
Average productivity	8	10	5	7-9	6-7	15
Maximum productivity	20	12-13	--	10	9	30
Average wait (minutes)	15-20	10-20	--	10-15	15-20	20-30

LOS	--	4.0	--	(lower than bus)	4.0	--
Driver wages ($/hr.)	5.50	3.30	--	2.30-3.50	6.50-7.00	6.00
Drivers	U	NU	--	NU	U	U
Ownership	Pub.	Pub.	Pri.	Pri.	Pub.	Pub.
Cost/vehicle hr. ($)	10.8	7.00	10.5	3.60-4.90	15.00-16.00	--
Vehicle operator cost/ vehicle hr. ($)	6.00	5.00	6.00	3.20-4.50	8.00-10.00	7.00
Average trip revenue ($)	0.45	0.45-0.50	0.50	0.55	0.53	0.32
Total cost/trip ($)	1.35	0.70	2.10	0.40-0.70	2.40	0.73
Vehicle operator cost/ trip ($)[a]	0.70	0.50	1.20	0.35-0.50	1.40	0.47

M-M = Many to many U = Union
M-O = Many to one NU = Nonunion
M-F = Many to few Pri = Private Ownership
Sub = Subscription service Pub = Public Ownership
Productivity defined as passengers/vehicle/hour
LOS = Door-to-door level of service or ratio of dial-a-ride trip time to auto trip time
Data are based on 1973 operating characteristics.

[a]These quantities obtained by dividing the per hour cost by the average productivity.

Source: Based on U.S. Department of Transportation, Office of the Secretary, mimeo (1974).

Table 16-3
Proposed Transportation Control Measures

I. To reduce motor vehicle-miles of travel
- A. Transit operations
  1. Bus lanes on city streets
  2. Bus lanes on freeways
  3. One-way streets with two-way buses
  4. Park-ride, kiss-ride (a situation in which a passenger is driven to a public transportation terminal and dropped off has come to be called a kiss-ride)
  5. Service improvements and cost reductions
- B. Regulation
  1. Parking bans
  2. Automobile-free zones
  3. Gasoline rationing
  4. Four-day, 40-hour week
  5. Congestion passes
- C. Pricing Policy
  1. Parking tax
  2. Road-user tax
  3. Gasoline tax
  4. Car pool incentives

II. To increase efficiency of traffic flow
- A. Freeways
  1. Reverse-lane operations
  2. Driver advisory displays
  3. Ramp control
  4. Interchange design
- B. Arterials
  1. Alignment
  2. Intersection widening
  3. Parking restrictions
  4. Signal progression
  5. Reversible lanes
  6. Reversible one-way streets
  7. Helicopter reports
- C. Traffic improvements
  1. Traffic-responsive control
  2. One-way street operations
  3. Loading regulations
  4. Pedestrian control
  5. Traffic Operations Program to Increase Capacity and Safety (TOPICS)
- D. Staggered work hours

III. To apply supplementary motor vehicle emission controls
- A. Inspection and maintenance
- B. Idling restrictions
- C. Retrofit of emission control devices
- D. Conversion to gaseous fuels

Source: Based on "Highways and Air Quality," *Highway Research Board Special Report 141*, Highway Research Board (Washington, D.C.: 1973).

increase automobile occupancy, reduce vehicle travel, or encourage greater use of more efficient transportation modes (in terms of passenger-miles per unit of fuel consumed) will induce energy savings.

When highway networks are overutilized, or even when partial congestion occurs, one solution which has been offered from the literature is to impose a congestion toll during peak hours so that marginal social cost and private cost are equalized. In practice, though, the implementation of this optimal plan has been discouraged, with the result that "second best" solutions are then proposed. The most fundamental "second best" solution is the subsidization of public transit during peak hours. The reasoning behind this solution is that subsidies allow lower fares to be charged which in turn may induce some urban passengers to switch from auto transportation to public transit. Even though public transit is offered below its average cost, the benefits from reduced highway and street congestion are alleged to result in a net increase in economic welfare. Whether or not these benefits occur are matters of debate and of continued research.[7] Perhaps a better "second best" solution can be generated by the subsidization of improvements of transit levels of service rather than in fares. This particular proposition has been put forth as the strongest attack against the attractiveness of "free transit" schemes.[8] Numerous cities have experimented with reduced fare plans but in 1973 two major cities actually initiated new schedules of free bus service: Seattle's "Magic Carpet" and Dayton's "DASH" (Downtown Area Short Hop). While the prevailing opinion has been that the demand for mass transit is fare inelastic, some recent empirical evidence from the Denver and San Diego bus systems has suggested elasticity coefficients approaching two.[9] If these results are prototypical, then serious questions must be raised about the efficiency of continuing to develop enormously expensive mass-transit systems, especially in sprawling cities (like Los Angeles where the population density is not high). As examples of escalating costs in mass-transit system construction, consider the following: The most recent European system is the Paris Regional Express Network, which is estimated to cost about $10 million per mile; San Francisco's BART (Bay Area Rapid Transit) system may have cost in the range of $30 million per mile; and Washington's METRO system may eventually cost $60 million per mile.

---

7. See Roger Sherman, "Subsidies to Relieve Urban Traffic Congestion," *Journal of Transport Economics and Policy* 6 (January 1972), pp. 22-30; and Raymond Jackson, "Optimal Subsidies for Public Transit," *Journal of Transport Economics and Policy* 9 (January 1975), pp. 3-15.

8. See Gerald Kraft and Thomas A. Domencich, "Free Transit," paper presented at the Transportation and Poverty Conference, American Academy of Arts and Sciences, Brookline, Mass., June 1968; and Lewis M. Schneider, "The Problem of Free Mass Transportation," paper presented at the Annual Meeting, Transportation Research Forum, Kansas City, Mo., September 1968.

9. See James I. Scheiner and Grover Starling, "The Political Economy of Free-Fare Transit," *Urban Affairs Quarterly* 10 (December 1974), pp. 170-84.

"New" Transit Systems

Over the past decade, a whole new spectrum of surface transportation systems has moved from the conceptual stage into development, and, in some cases, into the implementation of productive applications. These developments have taken place, not only because of the necessary technological advances, but also because of changing perceptions about "needs" in urban transportation. The evolution of surface transportation during the last several decades has been dominated by the explosive growth of automobile use, and the transformation of intercity travel by the airplane. During the same period, public surface transportation has largely been destroyed as an attractive alternative. Recently, however, signs of a reversal of this trend have appeared, due in part to greater environmental sensitivities, to air quality legislation, to the energy crisis, and to other factors. The result has been a much greater emphasis on viable and attractive public transportation.

Even as it has become recognized that the automobile is generally unable to provide further required mobility improvements and sometimes is even unable to maintain present levels of urban mobility, it has also become clear that conventional public transportation is often ill-suited, too expensive, or inefficient. Attention then has increasingly turned to the consideration of new types of transportation systems, even with their inherent developmental uncertainties. Various "new" transit systems promise to provide door-to-door service; service times competitive with the automobile, and with less negative esthetic, environmental, and energy impacts; and lower operating costs and associated deficits, considerably higher ridership, and more ubiquitous coverage in route and in schedule than conventional transit. For these reasons, these new technologies are worthy of serious and detailed consideration, even though they are not ready for immediate implementation to the same degree as those conventional transit technologies which have been around for many years.

As discussed in Chapter 7, the critical functional characteristics of transportation innovations are the service characteristics, the costs, and the environmental impacts. The service characteristics include total door-to-door travel time, time reliability, walking time and distance, waiting time, transfers, uncertainty in system performance, degree of privacy, security, and difficulty of understanding and usage. The costs include capital and operating costs and the environmental impacts include esthetic impacts, energy consumption, noise, and air pollution. There is a wide range of technological features which have been the focus of much discussion, such as: rubber tires vs. magnetic levitation vs. air levitation; rotary vs. linear motors; and mechanically connected vs. electronically controlled individual vehicles. In fact, in many cases these technological features may effectively produce only relatively small differences in the functional characteristics identified above. However, the technological features that *do* produce critical differences in system functional characteristics include: work rules and degree of automation; vehicle size, train length and occupancy policy (e.g., whether standees are allowed); network topology and routing/scheduling strategy; the degree of dedicated right-of-way; and the quality of guideway network integration with demand sources and with the roadway collection/distribution modes, such as local bus transit, auto use for park and ride, and so on.

The primary issue in any new transit system is the service that it provides to prospective users as reflected in the above service characteristics. New transit systems should be described primarily in terms of the service levels that they provide to users, rather than by their specific techniques. The nature of the propulsion, control, suspension, and other subsystems (whether steel or rubber, air cushion or magnetic levitation) is of secondary interest from a user perspective, though important in determining costs, environmental consequences, and other nonuser impacts.

To specify the technology as simply a "personal rapid transit system" (PRT) or "mass rapid transit system" (MRT) is not sufficient to provide a basis for a preliminary screening of alternative system concepts. Within each such technology there is in actuality a variety of different systems that can be provided, with very different levels of service, costs, and environmental consequences. For example, for a PRT system, the available options include: vehicle size, standees allowed, minimum headways, cruise speeds (which may differ in "expressway," "arterial," and "collector-distributor" links), system operating policies (demand-responsive or prescheduled or mixed; peak and off-peak policies; if prescheduled, one-to-one, many-to-one, or many-to-many route structures), nature of transfers provided, pricing policy, fare collection procedures, mixture of on-line and off-line stations, network coverage of area (dense, sparse), network geometry, guideway lanes on each link, station locations and sizes, and so on.

A method to clarify these issues is to define the concept of a "generic mode" for new transit systems. A generic mode consists of those specific transportation system concepts which have approximately similar functional characteristics. Though somewhat arbitrary, the following generic mode categories appear appropriate to differentiate and serve as a basis for discussion of the major policy options. These categories are separated into "batch" systems (1-8), moving way continuous systems (9-11), and dual mode vehicles (12-13).

1. High speed ground system
2. Commuter Rail Transit
3. Mass Rapid Transit (MRT)
4. Light Rail Transit (LRT)
5. Bus Rapid Transit (BRT)
6. Monorail
7. Small Group Rapid Transit (SGRT)
8. Personal Rapid Transit (PRT)
9. Mechanically Connected Seats
10. Accelerating Moving Sidewalk

11. Constant Speed Moving Sidewalk
12. Dual Mode Bus
13. Dual Mode Car

While each of these systems has its own guideway and unique technology, there exist rubber tire versions of MRT, BRT, Monorail, SGRT, and PRT. Most vehicle-guideway designs can be scaled up or down over the whole spectrum of generic modes. Air levitation, magnetic levitation, and steel rail technologies, as well as rotary and linear propulsion, are being applied to high speed ground and to PRT systems, which are at opposite ends of the spectrum of "batch" generic modes. Most of the combination of technological features have been designed or constructed in some form or another. A majority of the major manufacturers would probably be able to bid on and construct all of the technological types of systems, if necessary, provided that the functional specifications permitted flexible proposals. Some combinations of technological features will prove, over the years, to be superior to others, but the differences are likely to be relatively small compared to the differences in functional characteristics of the different generic modes.

From the policy point of view, transportation agencies around the country will be making significant changes in the level and mix of public transit services offered over the next few years. Public responses to these services will substantially influence the fundamental long-term issues: Will the public respond to higher levels of local community services? To long-distance commuter services? To off-peak services? How important will the frequency of service, or the fare, or the provision of demand-responsive services be? What will be the actual costs, the actual revenues, the actual management problems and opportunities, in providing these services? Equally important are the following questions: How will the public's priorities for urban transit improvements change? What will be the relative priorities to be placed on peak versus off-peak services, community versus metropolitan or regional services, demand-responsive versus scheduled services? Which portions of the public should be given priority for particular services?

Most areas of the country have now entered a period of substantial improvement and many experiments in public transit: reduced fares, flat fares, changes in services, jitney and dial-a-ride services, and even some demonstration projects. The results of these experiments may substantially change the public's views as to what they want from urban transit systems and how much they are willing to pay for it. The latter, of course, is the fundamental economic question.

17 The New Urban Economics

There are two general types of pressures operating in urban areas. The first is the pressure on the community to develop a city size at which public services are produced at minimum average cost; and the second is to determine the optimal city size in which all firms can maximize profits. A recent article has raised several questions of interest pertaining to these pressures:

> (i) To what extent may . . . (city sizes) diverge? That is, under what circumstances would a conflict appear between the city size which the urban planner finds optimal and that which is optimal to the private decision-maker?
>
> (ii) What set of historical events would serve to produce a divergence between optimal city size as perceived by a representative firm and *actual* city size, and what role would this phenomenon play in determining growth paths of cities?
>
> (iii) Finally, what set of exogenous forces operating on the conditions for optimal plant location might be construed as accounting for the observed increased concentration in the distribution of city sizes prior to the mid-twentieth century?[1]

As a result of these inquiries, a controversial issue in the literature of urban economics is whether contemporary cities are too large, with the inference that optimum size cities should be smaller.[2]

Since the idea of "optimality" for cities represents a concept of static efficiency, some critics have claimed that the issue may not be relevant for public policy purposes. Several reasons are often proposed to support this claim. First, it is empirically difficult to even describe meaningful boundaries of a city or urban area;[3] second, density may be a more important determinant of scale

1. Joseph A. Swanson, Kenneth R. Smith, and Jeffrey G. Williamson, "The Size Distribution of Cities and Optimal City Size," *Journal of Urban Economics* 1 (October 1974), p. 401.

2. A proponent of this view is J. Sandquist, "Where Shall They Live?" *Public Interest* 18 (January 1970), pp. 88-100; an excellent discussion, but with no position being taken, appears in Edwin S. Mills and David M. de Ferranti, "Market Choices and Optimum City Size," *Papers and Proceedings of the American Economic Association* 61 (May 1971), pp. 340-45; and a rejection of this view is given in J.V. Henderson, "Optimum City Size: The External Diseconomy Question," *Journal of Political Economy* 82 (March/April 1974), pp. 373-88.

3. For example, it is argued that for business firms, the optimal city size is one that maximizes the difference between agglomeration economies and the costs of urban services plus agglomeration diseconomies. See Edwin von Boventer, "Optimal Spatial Structure and Regional Development," *Kyklos* 23 (December 1970), pp. 903-24.

economies and diseconomies than city size;[4] third, it may be more illuminating to consider different ranks of the urban hierarchy rather than a single optimal size for the whole city;[5] and finally, it may not be politically possible to redistribute population among urban areas in order to achieve optimality.[6] Nevertheless, while the determination of an optimal size for urban areas is a difficult (if not fruitless) task, there does remain imbedded, at least implicitly, in the concept of urban planning the notion that certain areas are "too large" or "too congested." This notion usually suggests that the areas' sizes impose undesirable externalities on these populations. On the other hand, some areas may be deemed "too small" because their actual size may raise the unit cost of social infrastructure significantly above the economic minimum.[7] In general, however, one might infer that the continuation of the search for optimal city size in the literature suggests that the topic may not be at all irrelevant.[8]

In the early 1970s an interesting development occurred in the literature of urban economics when several illustrious economists, reputed in other fields, produced papers that were characterized by significantly higher mathematical rigor than most earlier studies.[9] While this event may have increased the intrinsically important value of urban economics, it (predictably) spurned lengthy debates on the relevance of the mathematical studies in question.[10] In spite of these debates the result has been a new genre of mathematical models, most of which are unrelated to those of an earlier era (the 1960s) on the spatial organization and growth of urban areas. The distinguishing feature of these new urban models is the reliance on fairly sophisticated mathematical tools, such as the calculus of variations and optimal control theory.[11]

4. Jerome Rothenberg, "The Economics of Congestion and Pollution: An Integrated View," *American Economic Review* 60 (March 1970), pp. 114-21.

5. This suggestion relates to central place theory with its association between city size and the number of service functions performed.

6. See G.C. Cameron, "Growth Areas, Growth Centres and Regional Conversation," *Scottish Journal of Political Economy* 17 (January 1970), pp. 19-38.

7. Ibid.

8. As an example, see William F. Lever, "A Markov Approach to the Optimal Size of Cities in England and Wales," *Urban Studies* 10 (October 1973), pp. 353-66.

9. See Robert M. Solow and William S. Vickrey, "Land Use in a Long Narrow City," *Journal of Economic Theory* 3 (December 1971), pp. 430-47; Edwin S. Mills, "Markets and Efficient Resource Allocation in Urban Areas," *Swedish Journal of Economics* 74 (March 1972), pp. 100-117; J.A. Mirrlees, "The Optimum Town," *Swedish Journal of Economics* 74 (March 1972), pp. 114-35; and Robert M. Solow, "Congestion, Density and the Use of Land in Transportation," *Swedish Journal of Economics* 74 (March 1972), pp. 161-73.

10. Harry W. Richardson, "A Comment on Some Uses of Mathematical Models in Urban Economics," *Urban Studies* 10 (June 1973), pp. 259-70 (including replies by Robert M. Solow and J.A. Mirrlees).

11. Good urban economists do practice economies of agglomeration. Nearly all the papers pertaining to this topic can be found in four journals: *Journal of Economic Theory*, the March 1972 issue of the *Swedish Journal of Economics*, the Autumn 1973 issue of the *Bell Journal of Economics and Management Science*, and the new *Journal of Urban Economics.*

This development in the urban economics field has been labeled the "new" urban economics by Edwin S. Mills and James MacKinnon in a recent symposium on urban problems.[12] Although the models of the new urban economics are different from each other in many respects, they generally characterize the city in a similar way:

The city is built on a flat plain and travel is assumed to be equally costly in all directions. The city has a well-defined and predetermined central business district (CBD), and may have a pie slice of land removed from it to allow for natural features such as harbors or mountains. The CBD is usually assumed to be of fixed size and to employ a fixed number of workers, most typically the city's entire labor force. . . .

In virtually all models, the only travel is commuting trips of the labor force between places of residence and work places in the CBD. Travel within the CBD is usually ignored. Thus, the only spatial characteristic of any location in the city that matters is distance from the CBD or, equivalently, from the city center. This is very important because it means that the residential area of the city can be treated as if it were one-dimensional. A one-dimensional representation of location seems to be crucial if the calculus of variations or control theory is to be used. Distance from the city center plays the role of time in more conventional applications of these techniques.[13]

It is anticipated that these urban economic models will offer more realistic interpretations of urban growth and structure. A particularly important need in the near future will be to modify these models to incorporate congestion and various other issues of urban transportation systems:

Further study is also needed of the transportation sector. It should be possible to establish general conclusions about the urban size and structure that justify particular modal mixes.[14]

Congestion

One would think that analyses of peak and off-peak phenomena should be at the very heart of urban transportation studies: in most cities the rhythm of urban traffic movements occurs daily, is predictable within very fine limits, is extremely pronounced in many instances, and incurs high social costs, confusion, and congestion. It primarily affects passenger transportation to and from work and is therefore a rich source of daily irritations and complaints. In fact, peak-hour commuter service may be regarded as the major underdeveloped area of operations among the entire transportation industries. Realistic projects need

12. Edwin S. Mills and James MacKinnon, "Notes on the New Urban Economics," *The Bell Journal of Economics and Management Science* 4 (Autumn 1973), pp. 543-601.

13. Ibid., p. 594.

14. Ibid., p. 597.

to be sponsored but so far little systematic attention has been given to this core problem. Contemporary metropolitan studies mention it only in passing; notably lacking in these studies, both in the initial statements and in their final reports to the funding agencies, has been any extensive analysis of the development of congestion over time. On the other hand, one of the more important contributions by the new urban economics writers is the analysis of congestion costs by Robert M. Solow.[15]

In the traditional analysis of automobile congestion, various authors have hypothesized that the imposition of congestion tolls raises the price of travel, decreases congestion and lowers the number of users.[16] With tolls, auto drivers will switch to alternative modes of transit, or, in other words, they will shift their consumption pattern to goods without externalities. In practice, though, the travel decision for the consumer involves two aspects: the mode choice and the time of day to travel; but most studies focus only on the first aspect. In a recent article, however, J.V. Henderson has shown that the imposition of congestion tolls affects the relative prices of different travel times and reorders them in an efficient pattern, with the results that there may be a reduction in the price of travel, a decrease in congestion, and an increase in the number of users.[17]

A distinction should be made between vehicle (auto, bus, truck) costs incurred by the road user and road costs that are the legal responsibility of the road commission or agency. Variations of vehicle operating costs with the type of highway is a well known and thoroughly documented topic.[18] There is, however, an obvious interaction between the maintenance standards of the highway and the operating costs of vehicles using that highway. The measurement of such an interaction and its consequences on optimum maintenance expenditures and on traffic flows are questions of plausible highway engineering interest.

The important aspect of vehicle operating costs for the purposes of analyzing congestion is their variation with the level of traffic. In other words, the primary interest would be congestion effects as traffic is increased on a given highway. Obviously cost is not the easiest variable to observe since it is conceptually difficult to define and requires detailed surveys of accounts. Consequently, speed can be used as a surrogate for cost. This approach then would require a

15. Robert M. Solow, "Congestion Cost and the Use of Land for Streets," *The Bell Journal of Economics and Management Science* 4 (Autumn 1973), pp. 602-18.

16. See Alan Walters, "The Theory and Measurement of Private and Social Cost of Highway Congestion," *Econometrica* 29 (October 1961), pp. 676-99; M.B. Johnson, "On the Economics of Road Congestion," *Econometrica* 32 (January 1964), pp. 137-50; and William Vickrey, "Optimization of Traffic and Facilities," *Journal of Transport Economics and Policy* 1 (January 1967), pp. 123-36.

17. J.V. Henderson, "Road Congestion: A Reconsideration of Price Theory," *Journal of Urban Economics* 1 (July 1974), pp. 346-65.

18. Jan deWeille, *Quantification of Road User Savings* (Washington, D.C.: World Book Staff Occasional Papers No. 2, 1966).

transformation from speed to cost. Many such transformations are available and there does not appear to be any enormous variation among them. In a study conducted in the mid-1960s, Jan de Weille showed that the following equations gave good approximations to the cost-speed relationship:

$$c = 4.4 + 93/v \quad \text{Up to 37 miles an hour}$$

$$c = 5.0 + 71/v \quad \text{Between 37 and 45 miles an hour}$$

where

c is the total average cost per vehicle-mile in cents net of taxes

v is the average running speed of traffic in miles per hour.

These results were obtained for a "normal" composition of traffic, but they excluded any element of the valuation of nonworking time.[19] These relationships pertain to primary roads; however, many researchers have constructed "synthetic" costs for lower quality roads by using the de Weille methodology.

The use of statistical methods in making congestion cost estimates must be justified on the same grounds as in any other scientific endeavor. Basically, statistical methods are a substitute for experimental controls in attempting to establish and measure causal relationships, statistical techniques being used when controls are either unavailable or too expensive. Unfortunately, the statistical estimate is usually not so precise or intellectually satisfying, especially to the lay observer, as that obtained in a control experiment.

Urban Spatial Structure

Urban spatial structure has been an intriguing problem to economists and regional scientists for a long time. It is a problem that focuses on the location and density of residential and nonresidential activity in urban areas and their spatial linkages. Because of the general availability of demographic data, much of the attention has focused on population density and the distance from the city center. Colin Clark provided the first systematic empirical analysis of these density gradients and suggested the use of a negative exponential function to describe the decline in population densities with distance from the city center.[20] Numerous authors after Clark have attempted to provide theoretical explanations and to use density functions to test their models of urban spatial

19. Ibid.

20. Colin Clark, "Urban Population Densities," *Journal of the Royal Statistical Society* 114 (1951), pp. 375-86.

structure.[21] Some of these estimates vary sharply, depending on the city selected, the time period, and the dimensions of the parameters (see Figure 17-1).

In recent years the simple concept of the central business district (CBD) has attracted considerable attention from urban economists and economic theorists alike.[22] Studies that examine the optimal allocation of urban land to transportation in CBDs also have been receiving increased attention. The paper by Robert M. Solow and William S. Vickrey was one of the first to analyze this problem by focusing on an operationally one-dimensional, long, narrow city.[23] This paper analyzed long narrow and annular cities. Their cities are operationally one-dimensional, that is, transportation is assumed to be costly in only one direction. No issue of trip-pricing need arise in their cities because the elasticity of demand for trips between O-D pairs was zero.

In transportation, distance represents costs to the users in terms of time,

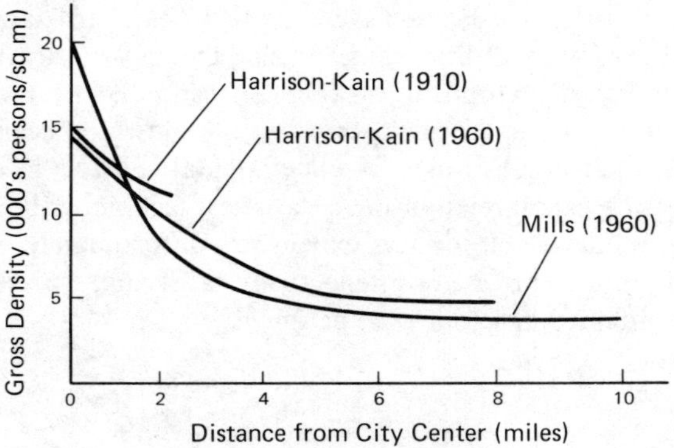

Figure 17-1. Selected Estimated Density Functions for Denver, 1910 and 1970. Source: David Harrison, Jr. and John F. Kain, "Cumulative Urban Growth and Urban Density Functions," *Journal of Urban Economics* 1 (January 1974), pp. 81-83.

21. See William Alonso, *Location and Land Use* (Cambridge, Mass.: Harvard University Press, 1964); Martin J. Beckmann, "On the Distribution of Urban Rent and Residential Density," *Journal of Economic Theory* 1 (January 1969), pp. 60-67; Edwin S. Mills, "Urban Density Functions," *Urban Studies* 7 (February 1970); Richard Muth, *Cities and Housing* (Chicago: The University of Chicago Press, 1969); Robert M. Solow, "Congestion, Density and the Use of Land in Transportation," *Swedish Journal of Economics* 74 (March 1972), pp. 161-73; and David Harrison, Jr. and John F. Kain, "Cumulative Urban Growth and Urban Density Functions," *Journal of Urban Economics* 1 (January 1974), pp. 61-98.

22. See Mirrlees, "The Optimum Town"; Mills and de Ferranti; "Market Choices"; and John G. Riley, "Optimal Residential Density and Road Transportation," *Journal of Urban Economics* 1 (April 1974), pp. 230-49.

23. Solow and Vickrey, "Land Use."

money and opportunities lost. To that extent it tends to act as a barrier to social interaction. On the average, the greater the spatial separation between two places or individuals, the smaller the contact between them. The degree to which automobiles are used for optional purposes like social activities and personal pleasure has been considered the least calculable, and therefore most stochastic, of traffic flows. Nonetheless, there has been a small but growing body of literature that views social trips, by reflecting personal interactions, as both reflecting and influencing the social topography of urban areas.[24]

To provide a synthesis, models of urban structure can be classified into at least four major types: (1) large-scale numerical models of existing cities;[25] (2) analytical models of theoretical cities, where land is usually treated as a continuous variable indexed by its distance from the city center;[26] (3) linear programming models of theoretical cities, where the city is composed of a finite number of discrete sections of land;[27] and search algorithms applied to purely theoretical cities.[28]

Location

The commitment to build the 42,500 mile interstate highway system is the most expensive public works program ever undertaken in the United States.[29] To the extent that its construction has been taking place throughout the past two decades, a legitimate topic of research inquiry has been the impacts of this system on the economy of local communities, land development, and regional travel patterns. One important area of research has centered on the development of land use around interchanges. On this issue, the recent evidence seems to suggest that the majority of interchanges, built on previously low-density land, experienced very little transformation of land to urban uses.[30] With a few exceptions, it appears that interchange areas generally have experienced an initial

24. See F.P. Stutz, "Distance and Network Effects on Urban Social Travel Fields," *Economic Geography* 49 (January 1973), pp. 134-44; and James Forrest, "Spatial Aspects of Urban Social Travel," *Urban Studies* 11 (October 1974), pp. 301-13.

25. See David Kendrick, "Numerical Models for Urban Planning," *Swedish Journal of Economics* 74 (January 1972), pp. 45-67.

26. See Avinash Dixit, "The Optimum Factory Town," *Bell Journal of Economics and Management Science* 4 (Autumn 1973), pp. 637-51 and Robert M. Solow, "Congestion, Density and the Use of Land in Transportation," *Swedish Journal of Economics* 74 (March 1972), pp. 161-73.

27. Mills and MacKinnon, "New Urban Economics."

28. See James MacKinnon, "Urban General Equilibrium Models and Simplical Search Algorithms," *Journal of Urban Economics* 1 (April 1974), pp. 161-83.

29. For an extensive discussion of the economics of the interstate highway system, see Ann F. Friedlaender, *The Interstate Highway System* (Amsterdam: North-Holland Press, 1965).

30. Thomas M. Corsi, "A Multivariate Analysis of Land Use Change: Ohio Turnpike Interchanges," *Land Economics* 50 (August 1974), pp. 232-41.

increase in land use (for example, gasoline stations, motels and restaurants) immediately following the construction of a nearby interstate highway segment, but afterwards very little changes have occurred.[31] This conclusion is particularly important since it opposes the general tenor of earlier studies which suggested that land development might gravitate to interchange communities or small cities with the passage of time.[32] Certainly, some interchange communities have prospered, following the completion of the interstate highway construction, but the reasons for this do not support the belief that economic growth was influenced by the construction of the interchange: usually on account of proximity to large and small urban centers, land uses at these interchange sites probably would have experienced rapid transformation in any event.[33]

The ABC highway program has been a system of federal government matching grants for the construction of federally aided primary highways (the A system), secondary roads (the B system), and extensions of these into urban areas (the C system). This program is one of the oldest of federal matching grant concepts with the primary programs structure having been set up in roughly its present form in 1921.[34] The declared purpose of the program has been to build a system of federally aided primary and secondary highways that the states would not (or could not) construct with federal assistance.[35] The interstate program was added to the ABC program in 1956 with the general intention of allowing freer access to markets for individuals and for industrial firms.

Cobb-Douglas production functions have been used to measure economies of scale in several urban studies, some of which also attempted to provide theoretical explanations of industrial location.[36] Manufacturing firms located within urban areas often occupy sizeable areas of land and represent substantial investments in buildings and equipment. Historically, then, there have been strong forces of inertia associated with industrial location in urban areas. Coupled with a tendency by firms to cluster in a few concentrated industrial zones, the attractiveness to study industrial growth within cities has been

---

31. Ibid.

32. For example, see Richard D. Tward, "A Predictive Model of Economic Development at Non-Urban Interchange Sites on Pennsylvania Interstate Highway," Ph.D. diss., The Pennsylvania State University, 1967.

33. Corsi, "Land Use Change."

34. See Philip H. Burch, *Highway Revenue and Expenditure Policy in the United States* (New Brunswick, N.J.: Rutgers University Press, 1962).

35. A study that examines the amounts states spend on primary and secondary highway construction compared with the minimum amounts they would have had to spend to utilize fully their federal grant money appears in Edward Miller, "The Economics of Matching Grants: The ABC Highway Program," *National Tax Journals* 27 (June 1974), pp. 221-24.

36. See M.J. Goldberg, "An Economic Model of Intra-Metropolitan Industrial Location," *Journal of Regional Science* 10 (February 1970), pp. 75-80; M. Bradfield, "A Note on Location and the Theory of Production," *Journal of Regional Science* 12 (April 1972), pp. 243-48; and M.T. Daly and J.J. Webber, "The Growth of the Firm within the City," *Urban Studies* 10 (October 1973), pp. 303-17.

lacking. In fact, the study of firm distributions within urban areas has been relatively ignored when compared with the numerous analyses of residential and retailing location.

In any particular area the effects of general economic growth will be conditioned by local aspects such as its land and infrastructural resources. The local comparative advantages and industrial mix are likewise important. As a statistical fact, strong economic growth in certain regions of the country has placed stress on the land resource, raised the price of land, and pushed a proportion of new or relocating firms into suboptimal locations. The implications of these firms' uses and requirements for transportation rights-of-way and facilities at present and in future years should become an important inquiry for the new urban economic models to resolve.

A Concluding Point

With the advent of urban economic analysis in recent years, the existence of a satisfactory urban economics text has been openly questioned:

> Urban economic theory is still in an embryonic and turbulent state, there are too many, not gaps but massive voids in our empirical knowledge, and urban economists in general are pulling in too many different directions at the same time rather than marching along together towards a shared goal.[37]

It may be several years before the availability of a text that not only clearly demarcates the field of urban economics but also selects the most appropriate concepts and tools. Since urban transportation economics is a subset of the field of urban economics, students of the former must rely on the disparate views of the current research until this much-needed urban economics text comes along. In the meantime there are still numerous materials for both students and researchers to review, especially in the area of the "new" urban economics.

37. Harry W. Richardson, "A Guide to Urban Economics Texts: A Review Article," *Urban Studies* 10 (October 1973), p. 399.

18 Urban Transportation Economics

The conventional wisdom in the field of the economics of urban (and regional) transportation for passengers and commodities suggests that the pressing problems affecting urban areas can be best understood only if the complex interdependencies of such areas are explicitly considered. To capture these interrelationships one must develop a large simultaneous equation model in which the significant problems are contained in a broad group of interactive functions. Such an endeavor involves many intricate and difficult problems, such as deciding the variables to be included or excluded in specific equations; determining the appropriate levels of aggregation; specifying the relationships accurately; and estimating the parameters correctly. Because the analytical and empirical requirements are so formidable, no urban model of this scope heretofore constructed has been regarded totally satisfactory.

An important issue in applied transportation economics concerns the use of cross-sectional data to estimate the probability that an individual or a firm will pursue a particular action in a binary choice situation. Among the models used in such cases have been the linear probability model and the probit, logistic, and Gompertz models.[1] In particular, the logistic model appears to be the most popular in its application to urban passenger situations and more recently to local and intercity commodity movements. One of the major problems with binary choice models, however, is that they are designed to explain the behavior of individuals, while the predictions that are more intriguing to transportation analysts relate to the behavior of aggregates rather than to that of particular individuals.

Closely allied with the prediction problem is a model transferability problem of determining how to use binary choice models estimated on one population to make predictions about other populations.[2] For example, the impacts of introducing a commuter bus line into a new area (or corridor) may only be predicted by extrapolating information in other areas where modal choices had existed. Unless the socioeconomic characteristics of the new area are identical to the area for which the model was estimated, caution must be exercised in summarizing the effects of changes in the distribution of individual characteristics on modal choice.[3]

1. For a study that discusses the selection of alternate statistical models, see Morley Gunderson, "Retention of Trainees: A Study with Dichotomous Dependent Variables," *Journal of Econometrics* 2 (May 1974), pp. 79-93.

2. See Richard B. Westin, "Predictions from Binary Choice Models," *Journal of Econometrics* 2 (May 1974), pp. 1-16.

3. Ibid., pp. 8-12.

In spite of the large volume of articles presently available on the topic of residential location behavior, nowhere is there a satisfactory theoretical model that includes both environmental amenity and accessibility so as to deduce an operational framework. While a part of this problem is due to a possible overconcern with accessibility, another part may be due to the difficulties of defining residential amenity. Some authors even have regarded residential amenity impossible to evaluate because it is considered a subjective good evaluated in the minds of the consumers and not in the marketplace.[4] On the other hand, there are studies using factor analysis and principal components analysis to provide some indication of the effects of household size and income on housing expenditures and amenities.[5]

Measuring the effectiveness of a transport policy action is one of the most difficult estimation problems facing economists and government analysts. Even in the case of measuring an analogous activity like advertising expenditures, almost every conceivable difficulty of econometric methodology is present: an inadequate theoretical foundation, complex lag structures, simultaneous relationships, multicollinearity, and insufficient data of questionable quality.[6] In attempting to define the boundaries of urban transportation economies one might conclude that it is very difficult to do so and that the choice depends on various considerations such as the type of problem under analysis and the availability of requisite data. In a sense this conclusion places the transportation economist at a disadvantage relative to his other colleagues who analyze national economic problems. Be that as it may, the need to construct an economic theory of the principal transportation processes within a particular geographic area does remain. The ideal for the transportation economist is Keynesian macroeconomic theory, which explains economic processes within the geographical area of the country. If such a model could be borrowed, and if a unified macroeconomic theory of the transport economy could be developed (even at the urban level),

4. See R.H. Nelson, "Housing Facilities, Site Advantages and Rent," *Journal of Regional Science* 12 (August 1972), pp. 215-25.

5. See R.K. Wilkinson, "House Prices and the Measurement of Externalities," *Economic Journal* 83 (March 1973), pp. 1-39; and Graham Davies, "An Econometric Analysis of Residential Amenity," *Urban Studies* 11 (June 1974), pp. 217-25. The latter article is based on the characteristics or wants provided by goods in their production process. Utility to the consumer is only indirectly related to the goods by virtue of the relationship between goods and characteristics. This relationship is often described in the literature as the "consumption technology" and has a long history and excellent pedigree in the history of economic thought, beginning with the recent contributions of Ironmonger and Lancaster and traced back to the writings of Alfred Marshall. See D.S. Ironmonger, *New Commodities and Consumer Behavior* (Cambridge: Cambridge University Press, 1972); and Kelvin J. Lancaster, "A New Approach to Consumer Theory," *Journal of Political Economy* 74 (August 1966), pp. 132-57.

6. In the case of advertising expenditures, a study that presents a comprehensive treatment of estimation techniques for measuring advertising effectiveness is one by Richard Schmalensee, *The Economics of Advertising* (Amsterdam: North-Holland Publishing Company, 1972).

the result should be theoretically and empirically valuable. The basic question then is: How likely is it that transportation economics, and in particular urban transportation economics, can follow national economics in this way?

Urban economic models, in which transportation is a subsector, can be separated into two general classes: land use models of the urban economy and nonspatial models of employment, income, and structural change.[7] Work to date on these models has been generally deficient for a variety of reasons, the most important being that the techniques employed have been quite sophisticated relative to the quality of information available. To give the reader some flavor for the range of models presented in the literature, the following paragraphs are discussions of selected regional and urban economic models that have contributed to the foundation on which the next generation of transportation models must be based.

F.W. Bell estimated in a 1967 paper a regional econometric forecasting model for the state of Massachusetts.[8] This model is essentially recursive and stems from economic base theory combined with concepts of neoclassical growth theory. The economic reasoning works in unidirectional chains starting with exogenous GNP growth, which determines, via the multiplier process, the level of aggregate demand and income in the region. These income components along with some exogenous variables determine the demand for capital via the investment function(s), which in conjunction with the production function yield the demand for labor. The model was formulated primarily to handle long-run forecasts; it also appears to do well for short-run fluctuations in the demand for labor.

Norman Glickman in 1971 developed an econometric forecasting model for the Philadelphia SMSA.[9] The Philadelphia model is an annual macroeconomic structure consisting of 26 interdependent equations, with the first 24 equations belonging to the main block, in which the local economy was divided into three sectors: manufacturing, wholesale and retail trade and selected services, and all other. For each sector equations were specified for output, employment, and average annual wages. In addition, gross regional product, personal income, consumer prices, labor force, and population were determined for the 1949-66 sample period. The government block consisted of the final two equations for local government revenues and local government expenditures. Some statistical

7. One of the largest efforts along these lines has been occurring in a series of projects at M.I.T. beginning with a paper by Robert F. Engle III, Franklin M. Fisher, John R. Harris, and Jerome Rothenberg, "An Econometric Simulation Model of Intra-Metropolitan Housing Location: Housing, Business, Transportation and Local Government," *American Economic Review Papers and Proceedings* 62 (May 1972) pp. 87-97.

8. See F.W. Bell, "An Econometric Forecasting Model for a Region," *Journal of Regional Science* 7 (April 1967), pp. 109-27.

9. Norman Glickman, "An Econometric Model for the Philadelphia Region," *Journal of Regional Science* 11 (April 1971), pp. 15-32; see also Owen P. Hall and Joseph A. Licari, "Building Small Region Econometric Models: Extension of Glickman's Structure to Los Angeles," *Journal of Regional Science* 14 (December 1974), pp. 337-53.

problems facing small sample models were noted, like few statistical degrees of freedom and misspecification.

Lawrence R. Klein presented a strong case for the use of regional econometric models based on Keynesian-type national models.[10] Quite often users of economic forecasts are not totally satisfied with the prevailing estimates of national GNP, income, employment, and other macroeconomic variables. This results from the unending needs of model users for additional detail, especially for specific regions or industries. In his paper Klein outlined the general structures for industry models and regional econometric models and suggested that an industry model should be at least at the two-digit SIC level such as primary metals, transportation equipment, leather and products, and so on. He proposed that many, if not all, industries be separately modeled and linked consistently to a national aggregative model. In regional model building he suggested analogous lines of reasoning. For the United States he recommended the building of regional macromodels similar to that of the typical national macromodel, containing endogenous regional variables, exogenous regional variables, and national variables. He also recommended that regional satellite models be linked consistently with the national macromodels. It was pointed out that the main problem with this approach is the lack of feedback from the region to the nation or other combined regions.

W.L. L'Esperance, Gil Nestel and Daniel Fromm reported an econometric model for the state of Ohio.[11] The model is developed along Keynesian lines with some of the major sectors identified and their interrelations studied. The model consists of 27 equations or relations, describing consumption and investment behavior, levels of tax revenues, and the effect of the national economy on Ohio. A comparison of four other state econometric models was made and these included models of California, Illinois, Massachusetts, and Michigan.

Harold Moody and Frank W. Puffer used a gross regional product approach and developed a regional econometric model for southern California.[12] The model is primarily an annual expenditure system, and it consists of equations representing the relationship between the following variables: gross regional product, regional personal income, tax payments, employment, labor force, and unemployment. An exogenous demographic sector is added to the model, which allows some exploration of regional interactions.

Robert J. Anderson suggested an approach to regional modeling that may be characterized as a synthesis of the theoretically simple economic base study and

10. See Lawrence R. Klein, "The Specification of Regional Econometric Models," *Papers of the Regional Science Association* 23 (1969), pp. 105-15.

11. W.L. L'Esperance, Gil Nestel, and Daniel Fromm, "Gross State Product and an Econometric Model of a State," *Journal of the American Statistical Association* 29 (September 1969), pp. 787-807.

12. Harold Moody and Frank W. Puffer, "A Gross Regional Product Approach to Regional Model Building," *Western Economic Journal* 7 (December 1969), pp. 391-402.

the more complex regional econometric forecasting model.[13] The fundamental notion of his approach is that multipliers in equations similar to those employed in base studies may be interpreted, under assumptions logically equivalent to those employed in the construction of forecasting models, as coefficients of a reduced form system implied by the structural system of a forecasting model. Generally, by confining attention to reduced form equations for some subset of the endogenous variables in a forecasting model system, data requirements may be considerably attenuated. The approach was tested to predict the short-term economic impact of restrictions on the sulfur content of coal exported from southeast Ohio.

D. Romanoff outlined the structural characteristics of the economic base model and the input-output model, and showed that the former is only a very special case of the latter.[14] From the structural differences of the two models, he pointed out that the analytical capability of the economic base approach is actually well below the expectations of users. In the traditional, open, one-equation economic base model, interdependence is smaller than that obtained by the full, partially closed, two-equation economic base model, which in turn portrays only some of the interdependencies of the input-output model. It is suggested that the binary classification of industries into those that export and those that do not export ought to be expanded to include other components of final demand. Further, more effective analytical insights into regional behavior may be gained if, instead of the preoccupation with the extent to which an industry can export or deliver to final demand, the interest is shifted to the analysis of the proportion of deliveries of each industry to intermediate demand relative to its total output.

Predicting Travel Demand

A key element of any appraisal of transportation and energy policies is the prediction of their consequences on travel patterns and on urban development and life-styles. One of the difficulties in the state of the art in urban transportation is that there is significant uncertainty in predicting these effects. For one reason, the present state of knowledge of consumer behavior is still primitive. Research in travel demand is just beginning to produce results on which some confidence can be placed, but knowledge of behavioral mechanisms of auto ownership choices and of locational choices is still relatively weak. In the second place, even if there were a firm base of historical knowledge, its utility for future predictions would be somewhat questionable

13. Robert J. Anderson, Jr., "A Note on Economic Base Studies and Regional Econometric Forecasting Models," *Journal of Regional Science* 10 (1970), pp. 325-33.

14. D. Romanoff, "An Input-Output Model of a Region," *Journal of Regional Science* 13 (August 1973), pp. 255-66.

for several reasons. Prediction is indeed a very intricate matter.[15] Most transportation and energy policies considered likely would result in transportation costs and service attributes that would move substantially along the relevant demand functions away from typical present conditions. Furthermore, changed consumer attitudes about energy, environment, and related issues might result in actual changes in the relevant demand functions as a result of changes in values even for private consumption.

A demand function can be constructed to describe the typical behavior of consumers in market situations. For predicting travel demand we are interested here only in the markets that are affected by transport characteristics, or the markets that influence the conditions of the transportation system, namely, the transportation and the activity markets.[16] The consumer's behavior in transportation markets can be diagnosed by his consumption of transportation services, or his travel pattern, which on the aggregate level can be expressed by the volumes of trips. The actions of the consumer in the activity markets are

15. The nature of the issue may be illustrated rather broadly by the term "after-image." Closing my eyes after looking out during the noon hour at the Pacific Ocean from Big Sur, I am aware of what might be described as a bright bluish-reddish patch, the so-called "after-image" of the daylight scene. In the sense that a film strip is an "image," the bright patch is a species of image. But what are we to label the image of Boston's Southeast Expressway at rush hour, which appears as I sit detached on a cliff at Big Sur? What can we call the image of the traffic on U.S. 1, north of Boston, five years from now?

These images are separated by all the differences between perception and imagination. For my so-called after-image, the bright bluish-reddish patch was no less an object of perception than the daytime scene that I saw before closing my eyes. However, it was quite evident with regard to the Southeast Expressway that I was not perceiving a situation, but imagining one. It is not quite so evident with regard to the Route 1 example as to what was happening: indeed I was imagining but I was also engaging in "projecting" into the future. The terms should not matter but the psychological distinctions that our language expresses or fails to express do matter, at least within the realms of both economic and psychological theory. Projections or forecasts reflect combinatorial choices of numerous individuals and groups that depend on the future interactions of psychic, economic, social, and political forces. The image of the Route 1 projection reflects what I as an analyst preview (or even wish) the situation to be five years from now. In some cases my projection per se may even guarantee its own accuracy as long as enough people react accordingly. Unfortunately, the extent to which image and projection are interwoven has not yet been worked out in psychological theory.

Whatever words one cares to select, my image from Big Sur of the Southeast Expressway is a type of mental phenomenon radically different from my view of the scene before me, from any after-image, and from my forecast of the traffic situation five years out. The differences are not merely ones of degree, or a matter of convention; rather, they do have far-reaching implications. Insofar as possible, the analyst (in transportation or elsewhere) must initially be able to observe his subject matter in order to characterize it adequately. For this reason, students of railroad economics should actually visit hump and flat yards to observe various cars being classified (and banged around) to "have a feel" for the realism of rail operations. Likewise, in the early stages of their development, students interested in the other modes should experience the actual physical mechanics of their respective characteristics.

16. See Marvin L. Manheim, "Practical Implications of Some Fundamental Properties of Travel Demand Models," paper prepared for presentation at the Highway Research Board (Washington, D.C.: 1972).

primarily his locational decisions and other mobility-related characteristics, such as auto ownership.

From the point of view of an individual trip maker, a trip decision for a specific nonwork trip purpose can be described as consisting of the following set of travel choices: choice of trip frequency, choice of destination, choice of time of day, choice of mode, and choice of route. The actions of an individual consumer in the activity markets can be described as including the following set of mobility choices: choice of residence location, choice of housing type, choice of auto ownership level, choice of mode to work, and choice of employment location(s). Thus, on the individual consumer level, the demand models of interest should explain consumers' travel and mobility choices. The travel choices of an individual trip maker are interdependent: For example, the choice of a mode depends on the choice of a destination, and the choice of the destination may also be dependent on the choice of a mode. Similarly, the mobility choices are interdependent: For example, the choice of residence location influences the choice of auto ownership level, and the choice of auto ownership level may also condition the choice of residence location. In addition, the two sets of choices, mobility and travel, are also dependent on each other. The travel choices that describe the trip-making behavior of the consumer are determined as a function of his mobility decisions along with other factors. The consumer makes his mobility decisions in a longer time frame than that required for his travel decisions. As a result, in a demand model that predicts travel choices, the mobility decisions could be assumed to be predetermined. Mobility choices are essentially long-term decisions that are made relatively infrequently but play a vital role in determining overall trip-making patterns.

The first facet of a theoretical consideration of travel and mobility behavior is the basic behavioral unit that makes these decisions. Clearly, analyses relying on zonal, tract, or even national level aggregations are inappropriate in a behavioral analysis. The issue is whether the behavioral unit for these decisions is the individual or the household. In many cases, individuals within a household have complete independence with respect to some mobility and travel decisions. However, if the household is narrowly defined as one or more individuals sharing a residence and making joint economic decisions, an individual's decision affects the remaining household members. Aside from the obvious possibility of the remaining members being involved in the same decision, the household has also allocated its income to various activities and allocated various activities among members of the household. Thus, it seems appropriate in the repertoire of contemporary demand modeling to consider the household as the basic behavioral unit.

For predicting travel demand, we can distinguish among three possible types of effects as real world conditions change. The first is a shift along the demand function, which can be estimated with historical data. This is simply a reflection of the economic theory stating that as prices increase, the quantity demanded by the consumer of that product or service diminishes. A second possible type of change is a shifting of the demand curve, indicating that the trade-offs among attributes have essentially been affected. This is commonly referred to as attitudinal change and might manifest itself in, for example, a conscious shift in consumer behavior toward conservation of energy per se as an important attribute of transporation alternatives. Such an additudinal change might be measurable in comparisons between demand functions estimated on "prior" data and identical specifications estimated on the new data. The third effect of changing conditions on travel demand is the change in importance (both to the consumer and to the transportation planners) of transportation alternatives. Options that might have been relatively unattractive in the past have become prevalent choices in many areas. With this type of change, planners must address issues pertaining to choices that may not have been observable in previous data samples.

Implicit in the empirical estimation of the parameters is the hypothesis that the underlying preferences which the utility function represents are reasonably stable over the period of inquiry. This hypothesis of stable behavior over time is at the heart of every demand analysis. Without it, reliable estimates of a model's parameters can still be obtained, but any attempt to draw inferences about the impacts of alternative policies in the future are meaningless even if all the relevant policy variables are included in the model. In fact, the requirement for stability of a model is one of the foremost reasons for approaching any analysis from a causal or behavioral perspective. Many existing demand models have relied on correlations between observed dependent and independent variables rather than on a consideration of underlying behavior. On the belief that it is far more likely that these correlations will change rather than the underlying behavioral decision mechanism, a model that is firmly rooted in a behavioral theory should provide more reliable estimates of how various policies will affect mobility and travel choices than a general, correlative model. This is particularly true for policies involving radical changes in the transportation supply characteristics because such changes will likely alter the statistical correlations on which noncausal models are based.

In general, then, a trip decision for a given trip purpose will consist of several choices: choice of trip frequency (how often to go shopping), choice of destination (where to shop), choice of time of day, choice of mode of travel, and choice of route. In a probabilistic choice approach, these relationships can be condensed to predicting the following joint probability:[17]

$$P_t(f, d, h, m, r : FDHMR_t)$$

17. For a full discussion of demand models, see Marvin L. Manheim, *Fundamentals of Transportation Systems Analysis*, forthcoming.

which is defined as the probability that individual or household t will make a trip with frequency f, to destination d, during time of day h, using mode m, and via route r, given a set of alternatives $FDHMR_t$ which includes all possible combinations of frequencies, destinations, times of day, modes, and routes, available to individual t.

Historically, urban travel demand forecasting has been the bailiwick of transportation engineers who have developed over the years a repertory of largely ad hoc models which have proven successful in most applications. Accurate forecasts of travel demand under alternative transportation policies are required for the precise determination of social investment decisions. To be fully satisfactory and to handle the newer developments in travel behavior, these forecasts must be sensitive to the impacts of the changing urban environment in the future. Consequently, the state of the art of urban travel demand forecasting has barely transgressed the developmental stage.[18]

18. A recent synopsis on the dimensions of urban travel demand behavior is provided in Daniel McFadden, "The Measurement of Urban Travel Demand," *Journal of Public Economics* 3 (November 1974), pp. 303-28.

Selected Bibliography: The Urban Passenger Sector

Alonso, William. *Location and Land Use* (Cambridge, Mass.: Harvard University Press, 1964).

Beckmann, M.J. "The Isolated Region: A Model of Regional Growth," *Regional and Urban Economics* 3 (August 1973).

Beesley, Michael E. *Urban Transport: Studies in Economic Policy* (London: Butterworth, 1973).

Bernstein, Samuel J. "Modeling the Urban-Suburban Complex," *Traffic Quarterly* 28 (July 1974), pp. 419-35.

Bronzini, M.S., Henderson, J.H., Jr., Miller, J.H., and Womer, N.K. "A Transportation-Sensitive Model of a Regional Economy," *Transportation Research* 8 (February 1974), pp. 45-62.

Clark, T.N. "Community Social Indicators: From Analytical Models to Policy Applications," *Urban Affairs Quarterly* 9 (September 1973), pp. 3-36.

De Vany, Arthur S. "Capacity Utilization under Alternative Regulatory Restraints: An Analysis of Taxi Markets." *Journal of Political Economy* 83 (February 1975), pp. 83-94.

Edel, Matthew, and Jerome Rothenberg, eds. *Readings on Urban Economics* (New York: MacMillan, 1972).

Evans, A.W. *The Economics of Residential Location* (London: Macmillan, 1974).

Fisch, Oscar. "Impact Analysis on Optimal Urban Densities and Optimal City Size," *Journal of Regional Science* 14 (August 1974), pp. 233-46.

Goodall, Brian. *The Economics of Urban Areas* (London: Permagon Press, 1972).

Gordon, David M., ed. *Problems in Political Economy: An Urban Perspective* (Lexington, Mass.: Lexington Books, D.C. Heath and Co., 1971).

Hansen, W.L., R.T. Robson, and C.M. Tiebout. *Markets for California Products: An Analysis of the Sources of Demand*, prepared for the State of California Economic Development Agency, Sacramento, California, 1956.

Haring, J.E., ed. *Urban and Regional Economics: Perspectives for Public Action* (Boston: Houghton Mifflin, 1972).

Harris, Curtis C., Jr. *The Urban Economies, 1985: A Multiregional Multi-Industry Forecasting Model* (Lexington, Mass.: Lexington Books, D.C. Heath and Co., 1973).

Hartwick, Philip G., and John M. Hartwick. "Efficient Resource Allocation in a Multinucleated City with Intermediate Goods," *Quarterly Journal of Economics* 88 (May 1974), pp. 340-52.

Henderson, J.V. "Congestion and Optimum City Size." *Journal of Urban Economics* 2 (January 1975), pp. 48-62.

Hirsch, Werner Z. *Urban Economic Analysis* (New York: McGraw-Hill, 1973).

Isard, Walter, and Langford, T.W. *Regional Input-Output Study* (Cambridge, Mass.: M.I.T. Press, 1971).

Jackson, Raymond. "Optimal Subsidies for Public Transit." *Journal of Transport Economics and Policy* 9 (January 1975), pp. 3-15.

Jacobs, Jill. *The Economy of Cities* (New York: Random House, 1969).

Kraus, Marvin. "Land Use in a Circular City," *Journal of Economic Theory* 8 (August 1974), pp. 440-57.

McGillivray, R.G. "Binary Choice of Urban Transport Mode in the San Francisco Bay Region," *Econometrica* 40 (September 1972), pp. 827-48.

Mills, Edwin S. "Markets and Efficient Resource Allocation in Urban Areas," *Swedish Journal of Economics* 74 (1972), pp. 100-113.

_______. *Urban Economics* (Glenview, Illinois: Scott Foresman, 1972).

Morrison, W.I., and P. Smith. "Nonsurvey Input-Output Techniques at the Small Area Level: An Evaluation," *Journal of Regional Science* 14 (April 1974), pp. 1-15.

Muth, Richard F. *Cities and Housing* (Chicago: University of Chicago Press, 1969).

Needham, D.B. "Three Ways of Studying the Urban Economy," *Urban Studies* 11 (June 1974), pp. 211-15.

Netzer, C. *Economics and Urban Problems* (New York: Basic Books, 1970).

Paraskevopoulos, Christos C. "Patterns of Regional Economic Growth," *Regional and Urban Economics* 4 (June 1974), pp. 77-105.

Perlman, Mark, Charles J. Levin, and Benjamin Chinitz, eds. *Spatial, Regional and Population Economics: Essay in Honor of Edgar M. Hoover* (London: Gordon and Breach, 1973).

Perloff, Harvey S. "The Development of Urban Economics in the United States." *Urban Studies* 10 (October 1973), pp. 289-301.

Perloff, Harvey S., and Lowdon Wingo, Jr., eds. *Issues in Urban Economics* (Baltimore: The Johns Hopkins University Press, for the Resources for the Future, 1968).

Ray, D. Michael, Paul Y. Villeneuve, and Roger A. Roberge. "Functional Prerequisites, Spatial Diffusion, and Allometric Growth," *Economic Geography* 50 (October 1974), pp. 341-51.

Rasmussen, D.W. *Urban Economics* (New York: Harper and Row, 1973).

Richardson, Harry W. *Urban Economics* (Harmondsworth, Middlesex: Penguin Books, 1971).

_______. *Input-Output and Regional Economics* (New York and Toronto: John Wiley and Sons, Inc., 1972).

_______. *The Economics of Urban Size* (London: Saxon House, 1973).

_______. *Regional Growth Theory* (New York and Toronto: John Wiley and Sons, Inc., 1973).

Riley, John G. "Optimal Residential Density and Road Transportation," *Journal of Urban Economics* 1 (April 1974), pp. 230-49.

Roberts, B.F., Gail Wittels, and M.H. Jorgenson. "The CEFP/CAL 4 Econometric Model of California," working Paper, California Economic Forecasting Project, University of California, Berkeley, November 1972.

Solow, Robert M., and William S. Vickrey. "Land Use in a Long Narrow City," *Journal of Economic Theory* 3 (December 1971), pp. 430-47.

Steinnes, Donald N., and Walter D. Fisher. "An Econometric Model of Intraurban Location," *Journal of Regional Science* 14 (April 1974), pp. 65-80.

Stucker, James P. "Transport Improvements, Commuting Costs, and Residential Location," *Journal of Urban Economics* 2 (April 1975), pp. 123-43.

Thompson, Wilbur R. *A Preface to Urban Economics* (Baltimore: The Johns Hopkins University Press, for Resources for the Future, 1965).

Tolley, George S. "The Welfare Economics of City Bigness," *Journal of Urban Economics* 1 (July 1974), pp. 324-45.

Waldo, Robert D. "Urban Land: Values and Accessibility," *Land Economics* 50 (May 1974), pp. 196-201.

Westaway, J. "The Spatial Hierarchy of Business Organizations and its Implications for the British Urban System," *Regional Studies* 8 (August 1974), pp. 145-55.

Wheat, Leonard F. *Regional Growth and Industrial Location: An Empirical Viewpoint* (Lexington, Mass.: Lexington Books, D.C. Heath and Co., 1973).

Wingo, Lowdon, Jr. *Transportation and Urban Land* (Baltimore: The Johns Hopkins University Press, for Resources for the Future, 1961).

Wilson, A.G. *Entropy in Urban and Regional Modelling* (London: Pion Press, 1971).

Zaharia, Thabet. "Urban Transportation Accessibility Measures: Modifications and Uses," *Traffic Quarterly* 28 (July 1974), pp. 467-79.

Part IV: The Intercity Passenger Sector

19 Amtrak and Intercity Rail Passenger Service in the Eastern United States

With few exceptions, rail passenger service within the Northeast and Midwest regions is provided by the National Railroad Passenger Corporation (Amtrak).[1] These combined regions reflect a very significant part of Amtrak's total market; for example, in federal fiscal year 1974 Amtrak routes that operated totally within the two regions accounted for 1.7 billion passenger miles, or about 40 percent of Amtrak's total. If those routes that were only partially within these two regions are considered as well, the passenger miles were almost 4 billion or 90 percent of the Amtrak total.

The Northeast and Midwest regions include 17 states with a population of nearly 100 million, or almost 50 percent of the total population of the United States. However, the regions' area contains only 12 percent of the nation's total land. If rail passenger service requires a high-density population to survive, then it must succeed in this region. Unfortunately, over 90 percent of Amtrak's system-wide operating deficit was sustained by routes serving this area; of these losses, $74 million, or 45 percent of the total Amtrak deficit related to routes wholly within the area, and another $87 million or 50 percent of the total, related to routes that serve the area but extend beyond it.

Intercity travel in the United States, by all modes of transportation, has been growing at a faster rate than the population and even faster than the gross national product. At the same time, rail passenger travel had been declining steadily until recently. It is interesting to note that the turnaround occurred even before the gasoline shortage in the autumn-winter of 1973-74. The overall decline in rail passenger service can be related to competing modes of intercity travel. In the markets defined as travel by for-hire carrier, the rail service share fell from 55.8 percent in 1947 to 4.4 percent in 1970; at the same time, the certificated air passenger service share grew from 10.3 percent of the market to 77.7 percent (see Table 19-1). In addition to this shift in for-hire carriage, private automobile passenger miles increased 49.8 percent and gained almost 5 percentage points in market share (see Table 19-2).[2]

1. The exceptions are the routes served by the Southern Railway and the Chicago, Rock Island and Pacific Railroad (presently bankrupt).

2. Although the above discussion indicates that intercity rail passenger service has declined markedly over the last 30 years, a considerable volume of service remains. The 14 railroads that operate trains in the Northeast and Midwest regions under contract to Amtrak are Atchison, Topeka and Santa Fe; Boston & Maine; Burlington Northern; Central Vermont; Chessie System; Chicago, Rock Island and Pacific; Delaware and Hudson; Illinois Central Gulf; Louisville and Nashville; Milwaukee Road; Penn Central; Richmond, Fredricksburg and Potomac; Seaboard Coast Line; and Southern. It is generally recognized that transcon-

Table 19-1
Intercity Travel by For-hire Carrier

Carrier	1947	1958	1965	1970
		Billions of Passenger Miles		
Rail	40.8	18.8	13.5	6.2
Bus	24.8	20.8	23.8	25.4
Certificated air	7.5	27.9	57.9	110.2
Total	73.1	67.5	95.2	141.8
		Percentage Distribution		
Rail	55.8	27.9	14.2	4.4
Bus	33.9	30.8	25.0	17.9
Certificated air	10.3	41.3	60.8	77.7
Total	100.0	100.0	100.0	100.0

Source: U.S. Department of Transportation, *1972 National Transportation Report* (Washington, D.C.: 1973), p. 75.

The decline in intercity rail travel has also been accompanied by a decline in railroad passenger capacity. Class I railroads owned 39,000 passenger train cars in 1949, 28,000 in 1960, and 11,000 in 1970.[3] Thus, within the decade from 1960 to 1970, the number of cars declined 60 percent. While rail passenger seat miles declined from 71,409,000 in 1960 to 33,829,000 in 1969, airline capacity grew rapidly. Total seat miles available on class I intercity air carriers increased from 52,220,000 in 1960 to 194,448,000 in 1969. The rapid shrinkage in rail capacity accounts for an increase in rail load factors from 24.6 in 1950 to 35.9 in 1969. At the same time, air load factors were sinking due to tremendous jumps in capacity, as Table 19-3 indicates.

Intercity rail transportation route mileage had been decreasing since World War II and additional service cuts made at the time of the creation of Amtrak worsened the situation. On top of this decline in service, the creation of Amtrak by the Railroad Passenger Service Act (RPSA) of 1970[4] meant that, pursuant to the statutory plan and the basic system design, approximately 50 percent of the intercity passenger train mileage was discontinued on April 30, 1971.

Associated with the recent upsurge in intercity rail travel, Amtrak statistics

tinental and long-distance passenger trains represent a tourist or leisure type of service, suggesting that truly viable rail passenger activity will only occur in the high density corridors of the Northeast and Midwest regions.

3. The data presented in this paragraph were extracted from U.S. Department of Transportation, *1972 National Transportation Report* (Washington, D.C.: 1973), pp. 74-75.

4. PL 91-518, enacted October 30, 1970 and amended by PL 92-316, June 22, 1972.

Table 19-2
Intercity Travel by Mode

Mode	1947	1958	1965	1970	Percent Change, 1958-70
		Billions of Passenger Miles			
Motor vehicle					
Automobile	347.8	684.9	817.7	1,026.0	+49.8
Bus	24.8	20.8	23.8	25.4	+22.1
Rail	40.8	18.8	13.5	6.2	−67.0
Air					
Certificated air carriers	7.5	27.9	57.9	110.2	+295.0
General aviation	0.6	2.1	4.4	10.0	+376.2
Total	421.5	754.5	917.3	1,177.8	+56.1
		Percent Distribution			
Motor vehicle					
Automobile	82.5	90.8	89.1	87.1	
Bus	5.9	2.8	2.6	2.2	
Rail	9.7	2.5	1.5	0.5	
Air					
Certificated air carriers	1.8	3.7	6.3	9.4	
General aviation	0.1	0.3	0.5	0.8	
Total	100.0	100.0	100.0	100.0	

Source: U.S. Department of Transportation, *1972 National Transportation Report* (Washington, D.C.: 1973), p. 75.

for fiscal year 1974 also display a substantial growth in rail passenger service over fiscal year 1973. In the Northeast and Midwest regions, passenger trains are still serving most of the major markets; in some cases there has been little decline in service: For example, in 1949, 560 seats were available between New York and Chicago each way daily,[5] whereas in 1974, 490 seats were available on that same route. Nevertheless, outside of the Northeast Corridor no more than two round trips daily are available on any route. Some trips are available only two or three times per week. In spite of many hopeful signs in terms of the number of passenger railroads, passenger miles, route miles, capacity, and frequency of service, the current level of rail passenger service in the United States is dramatically lower than it was 30 years ago.

Another standard of comparison for United States rail passenger service is

5. *Business Week* (December 3, 1949), p. 20.

Table 19-3
Operating Characteristics of Intercity Passenger Carriers for Selected Years

Mode	1950	1955	1960	1965	1970
		Average Revenue per Passenger Mile (in Current Cents)			
Class I rail	2.74	2.70	3.03	3.14	4.02
Class I motor carriers	1.89	2.05	2.71	2.88	3.60
Scheduled domestic airlines					
Coach	4.11	4.32	5.01	5.52	5.42
First class	5.79	5.90	7.06	7.33	8.27
Average coach and first class	5.56	5.36	6.09	6.06	5.96
		Average Length of Haul (in Miles)			
Rail	128	129	139	125	79
Bus	52	65	78	94	106
Air	461	519	583	614	673
		Average Load Factors			
Rail	24.6	27.0	29.8	34.1	35.9
Bus	50.7	47.1	45.3	48.2	46.7
Air	61.2	63.3	58.6	54.7	48.9

Source: U.S. Department of Transportation, *1972 National Transportation Report* (Washington, D.C.: 1973), p. 75.

the level of service in other nations. Table 19-4 is a comparison of passenger kilometers per capita in selected major countries; in each of the countries considered, the current level of rail activity per capita exceeds that in the United States. Furthermore, most countries are planning to expand their high-speed rail service over the next 15 years.[6]

According to the Interstate Commerce Commission in its findings entitled *Adequacy of Intercity Rail Passenger Service*:

The decade preceding passage of the RPSA of 1970 saw a deterioration of the quality of passenger train service. Hundreds of complaints were received by the Commission telling of dirty washrooms, late trains, attendants unwilling to give aid or information, unattended and dingy stations, and mechanical malfunctions.

When Amtrak took over the surviving passenger train system on May 1, 1971,

6. For statistical evidence relating the importance of speed to the quantity demanded for intercity rail service, see James Sloss and James T. Kneafsey, "The Demand for Intercity Rail Travel: A Comparison of the British and American Experiences," *Journal of Transport Economics and Policy* (forthcoming).

Table 19-4
Levels of Rail Activity for Selected Countries in 1970

Country	Population (Millions)	Square Miles (Millions)	Passenger Kilometers (Millions)	Number of Trips (Millions)	Passenger Kilometers per Capita
United Kingdom	55.5	0.24	30.4	823.9	0.55
Canada	21.1	9.98	2.7	13.3	0.13
France	51.5	0.54	40.8	605.6	0.79
West Germany	61.5	0.25	37.3	979.9	0.61
Japan	105.0	0.37	189.7	6,534.5	1.81
United States	203.8	3.54	17.3	284.0	0.09

Source: International Union of Railways, *International Railway Statistics* (Paris: 1970).

service and the attendant conditions improved somewhat. Nevertheless, complaints have continued to be filed with the Commission reporting that unsatisfactory pre-Amtrak conditions have persisted.[7]

Whereas intercity trains could at one time maintain reasonable speeds, ICC testimony indicates that carriers are scheduling service at a slower pace: This "may reflect many years of deferred maintenance, particularly on the lines of the railroad in reorganization in the northeast, which necessitates slower speeds than were possible several years ago."[8] In spite of this unfortunate slowdown in average speed, when one considers the total trip time from origin to destination, rail compares favorably with bus and auto and in some cases even approaches air. Although the line-haul speed of trains is slower than that of airplanes, access and egress time can result in a roughly equivalent total trip time for passengers whose destinations are near to rail terminals. Rail's greatest door-to-door travel time advantage accrues to persons traveling from one central business district to another, for access and egress time are minimized. Rail's ability to compete in terms of speed could be enhanced in the future if certain improvements in equipment and track are implemented. In the Northeast Corridor, for example, the proposed improved high-speed rail system calls for smoother and better maintained track surfaces, increased banking on curves, more gradual transition from straight track to curved, modern electrification, and new electric-traction powered cars. This system is expected to reduce current travel times between Boston and New York (currently three hours and 45 minutes) and between New York and Washington, D.C. (two hours and 55 minutes) by approximately 30 percent.[9]

7. *Ex parte* No. 277 (Sub-No. 1), 344 ICC 758, 759 (1973).
8. Ibid at 778.
9. See Table 19-5 for passenger trip data for the period 1970-73.

Table 19-5
Northeast Corridor City-Pair Rail Passenger Traffic, 1969-73

	Metroliner Train Passengers					Conventional Train Passengers					Total Train Passengers				
	1973	1972	1971	1970	1969	1973	1972	1971	1970	1969	1973	1972	1971	1970	1969
	(in Thousands)					(in Thousands)					(in Thousands)				
NYP-PHL	638	584	383	286	99	1,472	1,518	1,636	1,853	2,377	2,110	2,102	2,019	2,139	2,476
NYP-TRE	12	13	15	14	7	987	963	997	1,016	1,013	999	976	1,012	1,030	1,020
NYP-WAS	520	492	410	357	239	356	269	230	291	492	876	761	640	648	731
PHL-WAS	368	326	237	165	69	143	145	181	248	391	511	471	418	413	460
NYP-BAL	223	208	176	152	72	143	128	121	168	289	366	336	297	320	361
NWK-TRE	--	--	2	1	--	360	363	386	358	337	360	363	388	359	337
NWK-PHL	45	40	29	20	7	263	285	305	319	349	308	325	334	339	356
NYP-WIL	152	142	106	79	31	88	88	100	128	191	240	230	206	207	222
TRE-PHL	2	2	3	2	1	208	236	287	317	367	210	238	290	319	368
PHL-BAL	107	99	70	48	18	92	101	122	164	224	199	200	192	212	242
BAL-WAS	44	35	19	12	6	102	110	137	187	240	146	145	156	199	246
PHL-WIL	14	13	7	3	1	97	105	143	193	252	111	118	150	196	253
NWK-WAS	65	55	42	31	16	39	38	38	47	65	104	93	80	78	81
WIL-WAS	63	56	39	22	11	27	27	37	52	74	90	83	76	74	85
TRE-WAS	37	36	40	29	14	40	40	38	49	67	77	76	78	78	81
NWK-BAL	30	24	22	15	6	19	20	21	28	39	49	44	43	43	45
WIL-BAL	11	10	7	4	2	17	20	25	35	48	28	30	32	39	50
TRE-BAL	7	7	8	6	3	19	22	20	25	28	26	29	28	31	31
NWK-WIL	13	9	8	5	2	11	11	13	16	20	24	20	21	21	22
TRE-WIL	2	3	2	1	1	9	10	11	13	15	11	13	13	14	16
Total	2,353	2,153	1,625	1,252	605	4,492	4,499	4,848	5,507	6,878	6,845	6,652	6,473	6,759	7,843

Source: U.S. Department of Transportation, Federal Railroad Administration, *Rail Passenger Statistics 1973* (Washington, D.C.: July 1971), p. 10.

The rail passenger mode has difficulty, however, in providing reliable and consistently attractive passenger service. Amtrak has experienced numerous problems related to its antiquated rolling stock, conflicts with freight operations, and so on. Nevertheless, passenger trains do have the potential for providing reliable service since, among other reasons, they are not normally so severely affected by inclement weather conditions as are other modes. Also, there was the experience and historical precedent of punctual rail service from the pre-World War II years. In terms of convenience associated with general availability of services to the consumer, rail passenger service is considered presently inferior to other modes in terms of such factors as: information and reservation services, access to terminals, parking availability, range of payment methods (for example, use of credit cards and financing), and baggage handling. However, Amtrak is in the process of improving all these elements of convenience and might eventually achieve parity with other modes.

At the present time rail passenger service offers riding comfort that is in some respects superior to that of the other modes. For example, trains are roomy and offer passengers the opportunity to walk around, view scenery, eat in different locations, sleep, and so forth. Although many routes are currently plagued with difficulties, rail service potentially has the ability to exceed all other modes in terms of rider comfort, as well as to meet or surpass their standards of cleanliness and ancillary services that include extensive menus, entertainment, telephone, and secretarial services, and land-ferry services for personal automobiles. Few of these options are currently available, and there is a question as to their potential profitability. But if the market were favorable for such services, Amtrak should be able to supply them efficiently.

Amtrak's task in providing better levels of service is certainly not insurmountable. With the assistance of subsidies, other countries have generated superior conditions for intercity rail passenger service. To quote a few excerpts from a recent optimistic publication:

In Great Britain, home of the famous crack trains such as *The Flying Scotsman*, 100-mph trains are becoming common, and as a result there was a 60-percent increase in passengers between 1966 and 1969, while airline travel dropped 20 percent in the same period. . . . Britain has 1,000 daily intercity trains (in addition to 15,000 commuter trains), and most are handsome, relaxing to ride, and punctual. . . .

Canadians view their Turbo Train as only a preliminary to their newest high-speed rail train, the LRC—"Light, Rapid, Comfortable". . . . [it will] operate over "existing rail routes at substantially higher speeds." . . .

It is debatable which European train is number one, but it is probably France's *Mistral*. . . .

Although their current rail service is fast and efficient, the West Germans are planning still faster service. . . .

If everyone in America could take a ride on Japan's New Tokaido Line . . . between Tokyo and Osaka, it might set American railroading ahead twenty years. . . .[10]

The ICC claimed that certain high-density rail markets represent commuter services rather than intercity rail passenger service. In particular, it has argued that:

. . . train Nos. 200 through 298, between Philadelphia, Pa., and New York, N.Y., do not constitute "intercity rail passenger services" within the meaning of Section 102(5) of the Rail Passenger Service Act of 1970, but are "commuter and other short-haul service" . . . within the exemption thereof.[11]

In spite of this ruling, Amtrak has continued to provide intercity passenger service between New York and Philadelphia, the nation's highest density market. During 1973 a total of 2,110,000 persons (including 638,000 passengers on Metroliners) were origin/destination travelers between these two cities. While the future of both commuter rail service and intercity rail passenger service is in financial jeopardy, one fact does remain clear: Increased patronage has occurred following improvements in the level of service, an observation that has been most salient in the Northeast Corridor with the introduction of Metroliner service. If rail passenger service is ever to be viable, it can only become profitable if the level of service (especially train speed) continues to improve.

10. Thomas C. Southerland, Jr. and William McCleery, *The Way to Go: The Coming Revival of U.S. Rail Passenger Service* (New York: Simon and Schuster, 1973), pp. 23-47.

11. U.S. Interstate Commerce Commission, *Finance Docket No. 26634*, Penn Central Transportation Company (Debtor). Status of Certain Passenger Service (July 26, 1971), p. 24.

20 Demand for Intercity Passenger Transportation

Although numerous manuscripts and articles have been written on the demand for passenger transportation, the results have been far less than conclusive. The most difficult and interesting area for demand analysis appears to be in the short-haul markets. This interest is especially true in the railroad industry since forecasting demand for rail service has not been highly refined. Just the same, short-haul travel demand models for all modes have been developed and estimated, and can reveal some very basic characteristics about the markets for short-haul and long-haul service.

These demand models can be loosely classified into two basic categories: first, aggregate models, which attempt to predict aggregate demand in a given corridor on the basis of such variables as fares, frequency, travel time, and populations of the modal cities; and second, individual choice models, which focus on the behavior of individual travelers, and attempt to estimate the probability of a given choice on the basis of the characteristics of the modes involved. The latter type of model is frequently used to estimate the value of travel time for various consumer groups. The aggregate demand models can again be divided into "specific mode" and "abstract mode" models. The former models estimate separate demand functions for each mode; although the different modes may be, and usually are, considered substitutes, a trip by auto in these models is considered to be a different good than a trip by plane. The "abstract mode" model, on the other hand, treats each mode as no more than a bundle of characteristics (principally speed, fare, and frequency) so that a single demand function may be used to estimate the demand for all modes. The following discussion considers first specific mode models, then abstract mode models, and finally individual choice models.

One of the earliest empirical studies on transportation demand was provided by F.M. Fisher, who estimated a demand function for rail passenger traffic in the Boston-New York corridor.[1] Using postwar time series data through 1956, he generated a price demand elasticity of −1.3 for rail service. In another study at the CAB, Sam Brown used a similar procedure to estimate the demand for air transportation in the Los Angeles-San Francisco market and also found a demand elasticity of −1.3 for air transport.[2] Each of these studies considered

1. F.M. Fisher, *A priori Information and Time Series Analysis* (Amsterdam: The North Holland Press, 1960), p. 142.

2. Sam Brown, "Measuring the Elasticities of Air Travel," *Proceedings of the Business and Economics Statistics Section of the American Statistical Association* (1965) pp. 278-85.

only the demand for one mode (although Fisher incorporated bus fares and auto ownership into his rail demand function).

The first study to estimate demand relationships for all modes was the Systems Analysis and Research Corporation model developed in 1963 by Gerald Kraft.[3] In this model separate demand functions were estimated for rail, auto, bus, and air travel in the Northeast Corridor, using 1960 cross-sectional data. Total travel by a given mode between a city pair was a function of travel time, fare, fares of other modes, times of other modes, populations, and incomes. The variables were estimated in logarithms so that the resulting coefficients were elasticities.[4] Separate demand functions were estimated for business and personal travel. The estimated price elasticities of demand for each mode were less than one (greater than −1) for all but personal rail travel, for which the price elasticity was estimated to be −3. While the SARC model estimated reasonable elasticities of fare and travel time, the cross elasticities and income elasticities were somewhat less plausible. For example, although the elasticity of rail travel with respect to the bus fare was 2.3, the elasticity of bus travel with respect to the train fare was zero. The income elasticities of demand are even less plausible: The highest estimated income elasticity of demand was for personal bus travel, 2.54, compared with only 1.91 for air travel. The implausible estimates of the SARC model are probably due to combination poor data, misspecification, and simultaneous equations bias.

The "abstract mode" approach, developed by William J. Baumol and Richard E. Quandt at Mathematica, treats each mode as a bundle of characteristics and hence allows use of a single equation to predict the demand for different modes.[5] The simplest Baumol-Quandt specification of the demand function is as follows:

$$V_{ijk} = A(T^b_{ij})^{a_1}(T^r_{ij})^{a_2}(C^b_{ij})^{a_3}(C^r_{ij})^{a_4}(F^b_{ij})^{a_5}(F^r_{ij})^{a_6} \cdot (P_iP_j)^{a_7}(T_iY_j)^{a_8}(M_iM_j)^{a_9} \qquad (20.1)$$

where V_{ijk} is travel volume by mode k between nodes i and j; T^b_{ij} is best (fastest travel time by any mode between nodes i and j; T^b_{ijk} is travel time by mode k divided by travel time by the fastest mode between i and j; C^r_{ijk} is the cost by

3. Systems Analysis and Research Corporation, *Demand for Intercity Passenger Travel in the Washington-Boston Corridor* (Boston: 1963). See also Chapter 7, *supra.*

4. Estimates of elasticities with respect to fares and travel times were constrained to have the signs predicted by economic theory; for example, the elasticity of demand for rail service with respect to the train fare was constrained to be less than or equal to zero, while the elasticity of demand for rail service with respect to the bus fare was constrained to be greater than or equal to zero.

5. William J. Baumol and Richard E. Quandt, "The Demand for Abstract Transportation Modes: Theory and Measurement," *Journal of Regional Science* 6 (May 1966), pp. 13-26.

mode k divided by the cost of the cheapest mode; F^b_{ij} is the best (most frequent) departure frequency of any mode between i and j; F^r_{ijk} is the departure frequency of mode k divided by the departure frequency of the most frequent mode between i and j (the auto is assumed to be the most frequent with a hypothetical departure every 15 minutes; so this variable is generally omitted); P_i is population at node i; Y_i is per capita income at node i; and M_i is any one of a number of characteristics of the nodes relevant to travel demand (for example, service-oriented cities generate more traffic than manufacturing cities). Note that in this model, direct substitution can occur only between a given mode and the best (fastest, cheapest) modes. This was presumably deemed a necessary simplification but there is no empirical reason to expect that it is true. Quandt and Young in 1969 estimated this model (with numerous variants) using 1960 cross-sectional data for both the Northeast Corridor and California intrastate markets.[6] Although all specifications of the model yield good overall fits, the results appear very sensitive to the model specification and to the selected sample data. Nevertheless, some important generalizations can be drawn from the results of the Baumol-Quandt model. For practically every one of the specifications, the relative price elasticity estimate [a_4 in equation (20.1)] exceeded 1.6 (less than −1.6). This implies that in general, every mode is a good substitute for the cheapest mode (presumably the bus). On the other hand, the price elasticity for the cheapest mode is sometimes positive and never significant; this implies that while the modes are good substitutes, the overall amount of travel in a corridor is not sensitive to the fare of the cheapest mode. For travel time the elasticities for both best and relative time were consistently estimated to be negative and generally significant.

What do the Baumol-Quandt model results imply about the trade-off between speed and frequency? These results could be of great importance in determining the market potential for the intercity passenger train, but, unfortunately, the statistical results on this count are ambiguous. For some specifications and data samples, the elasticity of demand for a mode with respect to frequency was only 0.2 and insignificant; yet, with other specifications and data samples, the elasticity exceeded one and was significant. There is a suspicion about a travel demand function whose frequency elasticity is at least one over its entire range, which implies that regardless of the number of scheduled departures a carrier may have at a given station, then it can keep adding departures and expect to keep the load factor constant. This is almost the result found by Quandt and Young for some of their equations. On the other hand, a frequency elasticity of

6. R.E. Quandt and K.H. Young, "Cross-Sectional Travel Demand Models: Estimates and Tests," *Journal of Regional Science* 9 (August 1969), pp. 201-14. More recently, Quandt and Goldfeld have estimated the same model, again using data for the California intrastate markets, with an estimation process employing both additive and multiplicative errors. The results were very similar to the ones discussed here. See "The Estimation of Cobb-Douglas-Type Functions with Multiplicative and Additive Errors," *International Economic Review* 11 (June 1970), pp. 251-57.

zero (consistent with some other Quandt-Young results) does not make sense either; surely individuals desire some choice as to when they travel. It would appear that the elasticity of demand for a mode with respect to its frequency is not constant, but this makes any predictions from a constant elasticity demand function a difficult task indeed.

Although the abstract mode model can estimate the effects of various modal characteristics on demand, it has the inherent disadvantage that it cannot account for certain nonquantifiable but very real characteristics of each mode. Some travelers, for example, simply do not like trains, while to others, buses are anathema; some people are fearful of air travel. To test for this effect, Quandt and Young incorporated dummy variables into their model for bus and auto travel. For the Northeast Corridor data, the dummy variables for both bus and auto travel were negative and significant, implying that bus and auto travel are inferior goods by Quandt and Young's interpretations.

The overall conclusions from the results of these aggregative demand models indicate that demand for a mode is generally quite sensitive to both its fare and its speed. For air and bus transportation the results on price elasticities appear to differ: The SARC model estimates elasticities less than unity; yet the abstract mode model implies that for any mode more expensive than the cheapest, the price elasticity should be high. Again, it might be that price elasticities are not constant. A reduction in the bus fare below its existing level may not generate any new traffic; yet, if the fare is increased to the point where it approaches the air fare, the bus firms would probably lose substantial business. Similarly, demand for air travel is probably inelastic for business executives, but elastic for much personal travel. Extrapolation of a constant elasticity demand function could again lead to misleading results. For rail travel, however, the picture is perhaps somewhat clearer. Practically all models have found a demand elasticity greater than unity for rail travel, at least within the existing range of railfares (between bus and air fares).[7] The only result inconsistent with elastic demand for rail travel is the SARC estimate of an elasticity less than one for business rail travel in the Northeast Corridor. But this is probably offset by the same model's estimate of the elasticity for personal rail travel, which was −3, since personal travel is more than half of the total rail travel in the Northeast Corridor.[8]

The transport demand models based on individual choice used surveys of large numbers of individual travelers. The methodology of this procedure is fairly complicated, including not only regression analysis, but often of binary choice, which entails the use of probit, logit, and discriminant analysis.[9] One of

7. See Ronald Francis, "The Demand for Rail Service: A Comparative Analysis," M.S. Thesis, Department of Civil Engineering, M.I.T., 1973.

8. U.S. Department of Transportation, *Rail Passenger Statistics in the Northeast Corridor* (Washington, D.C.: U.S. Government Printing Office, 1969), table 9.

9. This is not the appropriate place to discuss in detail these varying methodologies. A good discussion of binary choice models may be found in Rodney Plourde, "Development of a Behavioral Model of Travel Mode Choice," Ph.D. diss., Department of Civil Engineering, M.I.T., 1971.

the primary benefits of the individual choice approach is that it allows estimation of the value of travel time for individual travelers. This is often accomplished by estimating the amount that certain travelers are willing to pay in fares for a given increment in speed, and relating this extra amount to the income of the travelers involved; it is generally agreed that the value of time is related to hourly income, although the estimates vary quite sharply depending on the nature of the numerous studies. Studies of short urban trips have indicated a time value of zero to one-third of the wage rate. On the other hand, studies of longer, suburban trips (8-20 miles) indicate a time value of 40 to 70 percent of the wage rate.[10]

Although most of the individual decision-type models have been estimated for commuter transportation, one study by Reuben Gronau has focused on intercity travel.[11] The most plausible of Gronau's results show that for trips of 175 to 500 miles, airline business travelers place a value on their travel time of about 55 to 65 percent of the wage rate.[12] For trips over 500 miles, the number would appear to be about 70 to 75 percent of the wage rate. For personal travel, on the other hand, Gronau finds a time value of zero, which on the surface seems peculiar, because if air travelers had a zero time value, one might ask why would they be flying? The hypothesis that the value of time increases with trip length is only mildly supported by Gronau's results.

10. Plourde, "Behavioral Model," chaps. 2, 5.

11. Reuben Gronau, *The Value of Time in Passenger Transportation: The Demand for Air Travel* (New York, Columbia University Press, 1970), table 9.

12. This result is based on the assumption that the typical air traveler earns the average male professional wage. Gronau presents results for other assumptions about the wage rate but argues that since the vast majority of business air travelers are business and professional people, and 91 percent of them are men, the most accurate available wage rate is for business and professional men. See Ibid., p. 44.

21 Domestic Airline Issues

In transportation it is relatively easier to develop a set of industry definitions.[1] The industry boundaries are usually determined by regulatory statute. In the transportation literature, especially in the area of transportation planning, three terms receive substantial usage: goals, objectives, and policies.[2] The determination of regional or statewide goals, objectives, and policies in transportation planning is achieved throughout the planning process and itself is one of the important features of the process. Likewise in the theory of the firm, these three terms are significant ingredients in the observation of corporate and business firm behavior.

The best way to make projections about economic variables is to examine the fundamental factors underlying the explanations of economic growth. The primary determinants of the trends that these variables will follow are embedded in the structural and institutional elements of the economy. Some of these variables are known over long periods with virtual certainty: for example, the increase in the population over 16 years of age for the next 10 years (barring unforeseen catastrophe). Others depend to a greater extent on cyclical fluctuations in the economy, on the level of existing capital stock, and on institutional patterns like the average length of schooling and age of retirement. A thorough understanding of these variables, their interactions, and the data bases from which these values are extracted are necessary for the transportation and economic research to develop useful models of cost estimation and demand forecasting in each of the principal modes.

Although the demand for air transportation services has been a thoroughly researched topic, the state of the art in demand forecasting still remains relatively poor. In some cases erroneous projections led analysts to question the specifications of the demand models. In other cases inadequate information or data of dubious quality hindered the task of model testing. Still in other cases the inabilities of model structures to forecast longer range developments have been frustrating to researchers.

The basic problem in applying econometric and mathematical programming

1. See Chapter 2, supra.

2. In general, a goal is the end toward which an effort is directed, but not necessarily attained: It is to be sought and not necessarily achieved; an objective is an end of an action: a point to be reached, capable of both measurement and attainment (objectives are successive levels of attainment in pursuing a goal); and a policy is a definite course of action selected among alternatives (usually constrained) to guide and determine decisions (present and future) on developing later transportation programs.

methods as an operational tool for regulatory agencies or for modern transportation firms is that corporate managers face multiple objective problems that are difficult to reduce to profit maximization or to any other single objective function. Although executives presumably do maximize their own utility functions, no one in practice as yet has ever quantified the objective function of a single living manager. Perhaps a better way to analyze the type of problems actually confronted by management is to develop corporate simulation models. These are large-scale "what if" models that attempt to link the financial, marketing, production, and various other sectors of actual business firms to produce a longer range tool for corporate planning. Among the large American firms presently using corporate simulation models are Monsanto, Exxon, A.T.& T., Texas Instruments, Xerox, and Westinghouse Electric.

The use of econometric and advanced statistical methods by the regulatory agencies is deplorable. Either no methods are used at all or naive models are presented as evidence in regulation cases. In those situations when modeling efforts are attempted, the credibility of the models usually are effectively demolished by expert witnesses for the industrial or company defendants.[3] Why then do the agencies develop (usually from scratch) and present models that are so easily discredited given their general lack of manpower depth in economic and statistical expertise? Partial answers might be that they are misguided attempts to save dollars for the taxpayers, or simple ignorance, or budgeting constraints with the agencies, or something more.

On the other hand, it may be unrealistic to expect any regulatory commission to undertake profit regulation or complex planning:

> . . . the present institution embodies the worst of both possible worlds—monopoly without effective control, private enterprise without incentive or stimulus, governmental supervision without the possibility of effective initiative in the public interest.[4]

This phenomenon does not appear to be limited to the transportation industries, as a recent study on the Federal Power Commission indicates.[5]

A good example of the lack of advancement in the state of the art in estimating the demand for railroad freight services is illustrated in a recent article by Dennis P. Tihansky.[6] There have been numerous studies of trade patterns for particular commodities, but the unreliability of historical data and other constraints have retarded the necessary analytical research.

---

3. See Joe L. Steele, *The Use of Econometric Models by Federal Regulatory Agencies* (Lexington, Mass.: Lexington Books, D.C. Heath and Co., 1972).

4. Alfred E. Kahn, *The Economies of Regulation: Principles and Institutions, Volume II* (New York: John Wiley and Sons, 1971), p. 328.

5. Stephen G. Breyer and Paul W. MacAvoy, *Energy Regulation by the Federal Power Commission* (Washington, D.C.: The Brookings Institution, 1974).

6. See Dennis P. Tihansky, "Trends in Rail Freight," *Traffic Quarterly* 28 (January 1974), pp. 101-18.

Intercity Air Service

Between 1950 and 1965 air traffic in the free world grew at an annual average rate of 14 percent. With such rosy statistics in the background and with the dawn of the wide-body jet lying ahead, forecasters in the late 1960s were prone to overestimate the future growth of both international and domestic air transportation. Part of the explanation for the errors in the forecasts was due to deficiencies in forecasting methods (see Chapter 8); but part also was due to unexpected and drastic changes in economic conditions in the mid-1970s.

One issue that the airline companies must face in the near future concerns the ways in which each company might increase its profitability. Not all companies will increase profitability at the same rate (or even survive for that matter) because each firm represents a different type of carrier within the industry. On the basis of the data presented above in Chapter 10, the structure of the industry is dominated by the trunks, although there exist nine other types of carriers as segmented by the CAB (and as indicated in Table 21-1). Improving the revenue side (demand) of these operations is a possible way for the airlines to improve their profitability. Tables 21-2 and 21-3 provide a synopsis of the leading financial and operating indicators for the major firms in the airline industry. Given that rates are fixed and that some 58,000 links (called city-pairs) are served in the domestic air transportation network, most airlines practice the various forms of nonprice competition that is not unlike the behavior of most

Table 21-1
The Structure of the United States Airline Industry, 1975

Type of Carrier	Number of Firms
Domestic trunk lines[a]	11
Local service[b]	9
Intre Hawaiian and Intre Alaskan	6
Helicopter	3
All cargo	3
International and territorial	1 (plus 9 domestic trunk lines)
Other	4
Intrastate	(mainly California, Texas, Florida)
Supplemental	
Passengers and/or cargo	9
Fixed base operators	3
Third-level operators	1,605 (including 180 commuter airlines)

[a]Including Pan American World Airways.

[b]Including Air-New England.

Source: Civil Aeronautics Board, mimeograph (January 1975).

Table 21-2

Rate of Return on Adjusted Investment, Certificated Route Air Carriers, Calendar Years 1965-72

Carrier	Year (Including Investment Tax Credit) 1965	1966	1967	1968	1969	1970	1971	1972
Total certificated Route air carriers	14.07	13.03	9.85	6.15	4.16	1.02	3.57	5.28
Pan American	13.41	15.56	10.53	–0.17	–0.17	–0.57	–2.58	–2.84
Domestic operations of the Big Four								
American	10.51	19.09	7.93	5.98	6.64	–1.23	3.17	2.76
Eastern	11.54	6.01	6.46	0.77	2.99	3.65	5.39	7.24
TWA	11.01	7.65	4.45	1.72	1.45	–8.32	2.03	6.47
United	9.96	7.46	9.18	5.03	5.99	–1.13	2.42	5.28
Domestic operations of the other trunks								
Braniff	16.15	16.03	2.20	5.28	6.22	1.79	5.97	6.07
Continental	19.82	21.84	14.47	5.72	4.73	5.43	6.76	6.11
Delta	24.63	29.86	19.97	15.97	14.16	13.26	8.00	14.19
National	20.01	16.31	17.94	13.61	9.96	–0.53	6.42	8.22
Northeast	--	3.73	–15.47	1.11	–66.85	–57.08	–76.26	2.83
Northwest	21.05	16.60	15.00	11.23	8.96	–7.95	2.10	3.26
Western	15.43	16.69	11.51	7.25	–0.24	3.96	4.41	5.62

Local service carriers[a]								
Allegheny	10.18	7.38	4.36	2.97	2.85	6.74	5.21	10.77
Frontier	12.70	11.83	4.60	−3.34	−11.53	−0.70	2.72	21.77
Mohawk	15.97	4.39	3.61	−2.24	0.18	−9.39	5.26	−15.86
North Central	12.02	10.36	8.49	5.15	2.95	8.26	6.86	12.67
Ozark	11.17	10.99	8.20	4.55	−0.03	2.59	12.47	6.58
Piedmont	15.01	8.01	10.68	5.11	4.15	3.21	6.64	9.91
Southern	15.27	10.95	2.43	3.50	3.20	7.21	2.75	12.11
Texas International	14.00	9.41	4.56	1.89	−5.75	−13.22	−3.87	5.11

[a]Excludes Hughes Air West and Air New England.

Source: Civil Aeronautics Board, *Handbook of Airline Statistics*, 1971 and 1973 editions.

Table 21-3
Selected Operating Statistics for the Largest Airline Firms, 1973[a]

	Overall Revenues Ton-Miles[b]	Freight Ton-Miles[b]	Mail Ton-Miles[b]	Freight Revenues[c]	Operating Revenues[c]	Passenger Revenues[c]	Revenue Passenger Miles[d]	Passengers Enplaned[e]
1. United	3,747	645	164	$135	$1,940	$1,654	27,029	30,250
2. Pan American	3,561	860	229	188	1,424	1,049	19,518	10,409
3. TWA	2,918	475	158	98	1,452	1,054	20,440	14,148
4. American	2,836	529	98	114	1,475	1,296	20,654	21,163
5. Eastern	2,023	207	59	56	1,259	1,130	16,875	26,201
6. Delta	1,761	176	68	56	1,122	1,021	15,022	24,604
7. Northwest	1,254	246	86	52	584	474	8,007	7,987
8. Flying Tiger	976	681	151	120	174	--	--	--
9. Continental	750	144	22	29	387	340	5,661	6,449
10. Western	724	51	22	15	414	379	6,357	7,908
11. Braniff	713	83	33	24	428	370	5,488	7,553
12. National	687	75	18	20	413	382	5,900	6,862
13. Seaboard	471	359	37	53	74	--	--	--
14. Allegheny	375	26	15	14	329	294	3,290	10,833
15. Airlift	224	102	1	16	37	--	--	--
16. Frontier	146	9	4	5	124	104	1,308	3,375
17. Hughes Airwest	136	5	2	3	130	108	1,259	3,625
18. North Central	114	9	3	6	126	102	955	4,194
19. Piedmont	110	6	2	4	107	90	994	3,526
20. Southern	89	5	2	3	83	64	721	2,494

[a]All data are for systems operations.
[b]Ton-mile data are in millions.
[c]Revenue data are in millions of dollars.
[d]Passenger mile data are in millions.
[e]Passenger data are in thousands.

Source: Air Transport Association of America, *Air Transport 1974* (Washington, D.C.: 1974), pp. 5-7.

oligopolistic industries. These practices also fall under the general heading of "service" competition and quite often are stressed through the use of advertising expenditures by the companies. The expectation by the airline firms in the use of selling expenditures (including advertising) is that advertising expenditures induce additional patronage and thereby increase revenues. The extent to which revenues are increased by advertising was the subject of an empirical study by Gerald Kraft, who argued that

> . . . If these are any economies of scale and if there is some positive response of demand to advertising, the possibility is open that more output could be generated at reduced prices while maintaining normal returns.[7]

Kraft has postulated an interesting model that attempts to relate output and total cost, including a fair rate of return or capital. In his graphical analysis Kraft compared the revenue function of the industry without any advertising with its revenue function net of advertising, as Figure 21-1 suggests:

> Curve *ON* shows a total revenue curve assuming no expenditures for advertising. If such expenditures are incurred, the total revenue relationship can be expected to shift upward, indicating that purchasers of air travel are willing to purchase larger quantities at each price, or pay higher prices for the same quantity. This upward shift of the total revenue curve corresponds to a shift of the demand

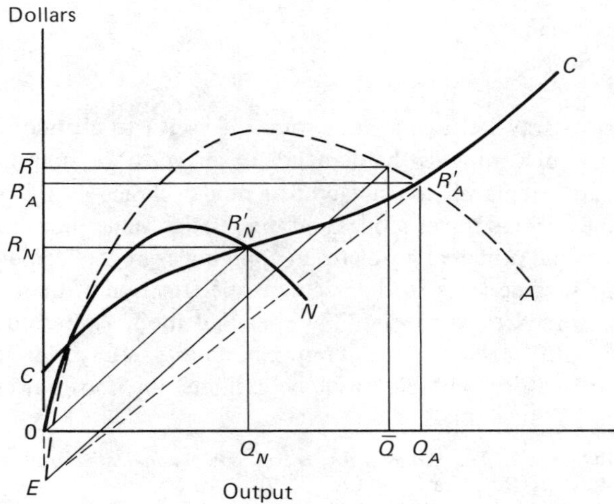

Figure 21-1. The Relationships Among Advertising, Fares, and Revenues in the Airline Industry.

7. Gerald Kraft, "The Role of Advertising Costs in the Airline Industry," in *Transportation Economics* (New York: National Bureau of Economic Research, 1965), p. 106.

curve upward and to the right. In the illustration, it is assumed that an amount EO is expended on advertising, and that the resulting total revenue curve is shifted downward by distance EO to construct a total revenue net of advertising, curve EA. . . . In the absence of advertising, total cost and total revenue are equated for an output of OQ_N. This output will be produced if the price is set equal to OR_N/OQ_N, i.e., equal to the slope of the line from the origin to the point of intersection of the total cost curve with the total revenue curve, R'_N. The line OR'_N represents the total revenue curve when the price is fixed at OR_N/OQ_N.

When an advertising expenditure of EO is incurred, an output OQ_A, greater than OQ_N, will equate total revenue with total cost (advertising expense having been deducted from total revenue). The line ER'_A has a smaller value of slope than the original line, indicating that a lower price will equate total revenue and total cost under a system with advertising than one without.[8]

The interesting inference from this analysis is that it is possible that airline companies can increase output (patronage), increase advertising expenditures, *lower* fares, and even increase profitability. Of course, this experiment might be difficult in practice even if the CAB were willing to allow for some minor variations on fares by individual companies. As conditions appear now, the trunk airlines could reap some temporary benefits from curtailed flight schedules, high load factors, and higher rates, even though patronage is down.

Measuring the Demand for Transportation Service

Recent studies of travel demand have found it useful to abandon the concept that there is any such thing as the demand for air, auto, or train travel as such, and have instead attempted to characterize modal choice as a function of the attributes of the various travel modes and the relative value the consumer places on each.[9] One of the principal problems in applying aggregate demand models to transportation issues pertains to the accurate specification of the model.[10] This problem is reinforced once the initially specified model is tested and various statistical problems arise. In the context of this study, multicollinearity among the explanatory variables usually exhibits the most intransigent dif-

8. Ibid., pp. 104-6.

9. Richard E. Quandt, ed., *The Demand for Travel: Theory and Measurement* (Lexington, Mass.: Lexington Books, D.C. Heath and Co., 1970).

10. For an attempt to examine the recursive and simultaneous nature of the much larger class of industrial organization models, see J. Fred Weston and Michael Intrilligator, "An Econometric Approach to Industrial Organization," paper presented at the Winter Meetings of the Econometric Society, Toronto, Ontario (December, 1972).

ficulty.[11] Another perennial issue in single equation regression models is that no allowance is made for feedback between the dependent variable and the explanatory variables. In fact, the empirical tests of most models suggest that the price variable is the most significant among all possible candidates in explaining variation in the number of trips by any mode. This finding, of course, is consistent with the predictions of microeconomic theory: that quantity is a function of price. An important issue remains, however, pertaining to the situation when fare is included as an independent variable in explaining variations for one particular type of train journey in the United States following the introduction of Metroliners and Turbotrains on the New York-Washington and New York-Boston segments of the Northeast Corridor.[12] This circumstance has provided two completely different levels of fare, speed and convenience for Metroliner and conventional rail service. Each service is interdependent to the extent that the traveler's selection of one involves rejection of the other as well as competing modes.

Quality of Service

Not only does the question of quality of service apply to existing transportation systems, it also is important in analyzing the demand for commodities themselves. For durable commodities like automobiles or farm equipment, quality differences can arise in both new and used markets. For many such commodities the users can select from a variety of new items or from used items that have deteriorated to a lower quality. In the cases of housing and of housing location, especially, the quality distributions of homes, new housing units, and the rental prices at given quality levels may be important issues of the public interest.[13]

In an important study of international airline operations, Mahlon R. Strasz-

11. Multicollinearity is a phenomenon that occurs in a single equation regression when two or more independent variables are so highly correlated with one another that it is impossible to isolate their respective effects on the dependent variable. In the regressions with severe multicollinearity, three remedies are usually attempted to alleviate the problem: either (1) the less important variable of the collinear pair is jettisoned, or (2) one of the collinear variables is changed to a ratio variable, or (3) the collinear variables are combined themselves into a single variable.

12. Even though fares have been raised sharply on these "higher" classes of service, the number of passengers demanding the service has also increased.

13. For example, a study arguing that the prices of low quality housing units are high relative to the prices of higher quality dwellings is Richard F. Muth, *Cities and Housing* (Chicago: University of Chicago Press, 1969). Not necessarily agreeing with Muth, but developing an extended theory of differentiable commodities, is the study by James L. Sweeney, "Quality, Commodity Hierarchies, and Housing Markets," *Econometrica* 42 (January 1974), pp. 147-67.

heim evaluates performance by an economic efficiency criterion.[14] His static model relates estimated firms' cost to its route system, factor prices, and scheduling ability. He finds substantial variation in relative efficiency among a 32-firm sample. Attributing this variation to "excess" seat-mile costs, he concludes that:

> . . . Elimination of this excess could convert an industry which is just breaking even into one with reasonable profits. Profit-maximizing firms in a competitive market could not long exist with cost disadvantages of this magnitude.[15]

The international airlines, in particular, are realizing that the freight portion of their business can contribute substantially to revenues and that increased utilization of equipment, facilities, and workers in the freight sector can yield additional profits. To achieve these targets, air freight has been considered practically as a separate service and given individualized attention.[16] General Motors Corporation alone has an annual freight bill of $1.3 billion and constantly is searching for opportunities to minimize this outlay. Included in this search is the possibility of using air service on a wider scale if such service were less costly.[17]

Airline Costs

On the cost side there are three general areas of aeronautical technology that keep improving over time and which thereby allow newer aircraft to be superior.[18] These three areas are the following:[19]

14. Mahlon R. Straszheim, *The International Airline Industry* (Washington, D.C.: The Brookings Institution, 1969), Chapter 9.

15. Ibid., p. 170.

16. Boeing Commercial Airplane Company, *Potential Air Commodity Identification: A Suggested Methodology* (Renton, Washington, D.C.: The Boeing Company, 1974).

17. Boeing Company has been evaluating the design for a new jet cargo aircraft with a capacity of 29,000 cubic feet of containerized space (compared with a capacity of 22,000 cubic feet in the U.S. Air Force C 5-A aircraft, heretofore the largest). A fleet of these planes would be the principal asset of an ambitious firm that would use converted military airports as freight terminals. Given that the firm's board of directors includes several well-known executives of major corporations, its long-run goal of capturing 15 percent of the global freight-hauling business may not be so far fetched. See "Revolutionary Air Freight Firm," *Wall Street Journal*, November 27, 1973, p. 12.

18. Between 1963 and 1973, domestic airline fares increased by only 4 percent whereas the consumer price index exhibited a 54 percent increase. This approximately constant level of fares was due largely to a reduction in operating costs *per passenger* as a result of the introduction and diffusion of the jet-engine technology and of larger capacity aircraft.

19. For a thorough discussion of these areas, see Robert W. Simpson, "Technology for Design of Transport Aircraft," NASA/MIT Summer Workshop on Air Transportation (Waterville Valley, N.H.: July 1972).

Areas of Technology	Measure of Technology Level		
1. Aerodynamics	$V(L/D)$	=	speed x (lift/drag ratio in cruise)
2. Structures	W_E/W_G	=	empty weight fraction
		=	(operating empty weight/ gross weight)
3. Propulsion	SFC	=	cruise specific fuel consumption (lbs. of fuel per hour/lbs. of thrust)

Using data from these three inputs along with other information on load factors and payload ranges, a "profitable load diagram"[20] can be constructed to show the points where a given airline can earn a profit by carrying given loads over specific distances. These ranges of profitability are shown in Figure 21-2. The shaded areas represent points where a profit can be made using a general type of aircraft to carry a given load over this trip distance. If the areas overlap, it is preferable to choose an aircraft where the point lies close to the upper boundary

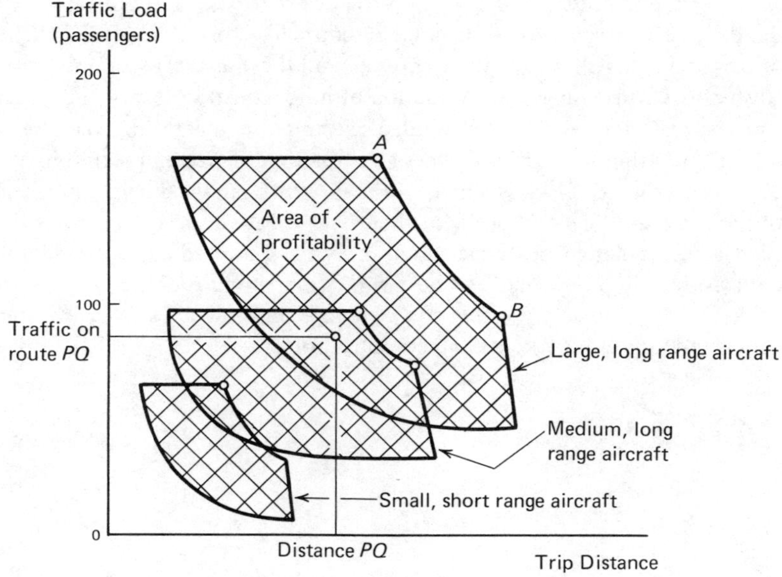

Figure 21-2. Feasible Operating Ranges for Aircraft.

20. Ibid.

of payload-range limits since it is more profitable (that is, choose the medium range aircraft for point *PQ* in Figure 21-2). Notice that the profitable load diagram cannot be uniquely associated with a particular aircraft because of its assumptions, but rather with an airline and a set of routes since the indirect costs are specific to the airline and the yield values are specific to a set of routes or city pairs. Notice also that the hyperbolic form of the break-even load curve is due to the differing slopes of the yield and total cost curves with trip distance. If yields, or fares were proportional to cost over distance, then the break-even load would be constant with trip distance.

The usual measures of performance for a transport aircraft are the following:

Cruise Performance	– Payload (passengers) versus Range (Statute miles)
Cost Performance	– (\$/block hour, \$/available seat mile)
Runway Performance	– takeoff and landing distance (feet)
Speed Performance	– max. cruise speed
Noise Performance	– noise footprint size, or peak noise (*PNdb*)

For a long range transport aircraft, the aircraft designer wishes to maximize cruise and cost performance subject to constraints specified for takeoff and landing, speed, and noise performance. If the designer wishes to optimize takeoff and landing performance for shortrange aircraft, like for *STOL* or *VTOL*, then cruise performance will be less than optimal, and these aircraft will only perform well over short cruise ranges. Introduction of noise constraints into the design of transport aircraft requires the knowledge of the noise generation characteristics of engines and other propulsive devices as a function of size and technology, and thereby also will cause less than optimal cruise and takeoff and landing performance. The designer's problem then is to create an aircraft design that is matched to some design objective stated in terms of desired or required levels of these measures of performance. The airline company's problem is to operate each aircraft at the lowest possible cost, which is difficult to estimate because of system or network requirements and complications.

Selected Bibliography: The Intercity Passenger Sector[a]

Allen, W. Bruce. "A Current View of a Portion of the Eastern U.S. Transport Market," *Journal of Transport Economics and Policy* 9 (January 1975), pp. 50-61.

Carlson, R.J., and Norton, H.S., "Is Amtrak the Answer?" *Transportation Journal* 11 (Fall 1971), pp. 52-59.

Cover, Virgil D., "The Rise of Third Level Air Carriers," *Transportation Journal* 11 (Fall 1971), pp. 41-51.

Douglas, George W., and James C. Miller III. *Economic Regulation of Domestic Air Transport: Theory and Policy* (Washington: The Brookings Institution, 1974).

Eads, George, *The Local Service Airline Experiment* (Washington: The Brookings Institution, 1972).

Elle, Bjorn J. *Issues and Prospects in Interurban Air Transport* (Stockholm: Almquist and Wiksell, 1968).

Fair, Marvin L., and Ernest W. Williams, Jr. *Economics of Transportation and Logistics* (Dallas: Business Publications, Inc., 1975).

Friedlaender, Ann F. *The Interstate Highway System* (Amsterdam: North Holland Press, 1965).

Gronau, Reuben. *The Demand for Intercity Air Transportation* (New York: National Bureau of Economic Research, 1970).

Howard, George P., ed. *Airport Economic Planning* (Cambridge, Mass.: M.I.T. Press, 1974).

Ruppenthal, Karl M., ed. *Issues in Transportation Economics* (Columbus: Charles E. Merrill Books, Inc., 1965).

Straszheim, Mahlon R. "The Determination of Airline Fares and Load Factors: Some Oligopoly Models," *Journal of Transport Economics and Policy* 8 (September 1974), pp. 260-73.

Turvey, Ralph. "A Simple Analysis of Optimal Fares on Scheduled Transport Services," *The Economic Journal* 85 (March 1975), pp. 1-9.

---

[a]For additional references, see the selected bibliography at the end of Part II.

Part V:
The Commodity (Freight) Sector

22 Intercity Rail-Truck Competition

One of the most perplexing problems in transportation economics is the determination of traffic (passenger or freight) diversion. This problem arises in the context of the modal split issue, especially in the analysis of competition among alternative modes. In the urban passenger world, metropolitan planning agencies need to know the impacts that would occur on the existing network of roads if their commuter rail operations were to cease. In a similar vein, regional planners would like to know the impacts on the highway and airline networks if Amtrak were to terminate certain short-haul passenger service. Even more important as a topic of current interest is the impact on the residual freight carrying network and the regions presently served if railroad freight operations in the Northeast were to suddenly cease.

This chapter addresses certain costs likely to be incurred from a diversion to alternative modes of traffic carried by the bankrupt railroads that were being reorganized by the United States Railway Association in 1975.[1] The principal classes of costs are those directly borne by the shipper and a wide range of social costs such as the impact on highways from additional trucks, congestion, energy consumption, and adverse environmental impacts. Direct costs to the shipper include not only the charges paid for the movement of freight but also the entire set of costs associated with a firm's production and distribution operations. General trends in carrier revenues per ton-mile as a measure of direct transport costs to the shipper are first considered, followed by a discussion of these costs in the context of the full range of distribution costs necessary to evaluate the economic cost of diverting rail traffic to alternative modes.

Direct Costs to Shippers

In Table 22-1 is a comparison of the average cost to shippers measured in carrier freight revenues per ton-mile as incurred on shipments by rail with those on shipments by other modes for the period 1964 to 1972. Both air freight and contract motor carrier rates have declined slightly as multiples of the rail rate, while the common motor carrier rate as a multiple of the rail rate has fluctuated

1. These railroads include the Penn Central, Ann Arbor, Central of New Jersey, Erie Lackawanna, Lehigh Valley, Reading, and the Lehigh and Hudson River. As of March 1975 these companies had petitioned to join the eventual Consolidated Railroad Corporation. Another Northeast railroad in the process of reorganization is the Boston & Maine, which has chosen to remain outside ConRail.

Table 22-1
Alternative Modal Rates Relative to Railroad Freight Rates, 1964-72[a]

	Rail Freight Revenue per Ton-Mile (¢)	Ratio of Mode Rate to Rail Rate				
			Class I Motor Carriers			
		Air	Common	Contract	Pipe-lines	Water Carriers
1964	1.28	16.38	5.20	6.13	0.23	0.35
1965	1.27	16.11	5.09	6.03	.22	.35
1966	1.26	16.04	5.03	5.80	.21	.34
1967	1.27	15.67	5.24	5.80	.20	.30
1968	1.31	15.24	5.29	5.52	.20	.31
1969	1.35	15.58	5.34	5.44	.20	.30
1970	1.43	15.32	5.22	4.79	.19	.30
1971	1.59	14.22	4.94	4.53	.18	.30
1972	1.62	14.04	4.94	4.33	0.18	0.29

[a]These figures are not homogeneous since they represent different traffic mixes of commodity characteristics and lengths of haul.

Source: Derived from U.S. Department of Transportation, *Summary of National Transportation Statistics* (Washington, D.C.: November 1973).

considerably. Pipeline and water carrier rates as a fraction of rail rates have become smaller. All surface rates relate to class I carriers or the equivalent and therefore do not encompass the entire spectrum of modal alternatives.

Several studies have claimed that ICC regulatory policies have been responsible for market distortions in domestic freight transportation.[2] According to the claimants, one of the most preciously preserved policies of the ICC and the carriers is the "value-of-service" rate structure, which sustains rates for both rail and truck transportation of manufactured commodities above the long-run marginal costs of transporting these commodities by rail.[3] The primary effect of this policy appears to have been the diversion of some traffic away from rail to motor carriers, which historically have provided better and more reliable service even though their costs are higher than rail transportation. The claimants also argue that if the railroads were allowed to reduce the rates on their high- and medium-valued commodities to marginal costs, they would increase their market

2. A recent summary of these studies may be found in George W. Hilton, "The Costs of the Interstate Commmerce Commission," in U.S. Congress, Joint Economic Committee, *The Economics of Federal Subsidy Programs: Part 6–Transportation Subsidies* (Washington, D.C.: U.S. Government Printing Office, 1973), pp. 707-33.

3. For a detailed discussion of this value of service pricing, see Ann F. Friedlaender, *The Dilemma of Freight Transport Regulation* (Washington, D.C.: The Brookings Institution, 1969), chaps. 2-4.

share by some amount.[4] The studies do disagree, however, on the magnitude of the resulting market share differential.

In a 1969 study Robert W. Harbeson argued that if rail rates were lowered to approach marginal costs, the railroads would capture all but a small fraction of the traffic now carried by trucks on hauls exceeding 100 to 200 miles.[5] He derived these results from a transport-inventory cost model developed a decade earlier in the Meyer, Peck, Stenason, and Zwick study.[6] On the basis of these results, Harbeson estimated the total social cost of ICC rate regulation for manufactured commodities to be in the range of one to $3 billion in 1963.[7] Also in 1969, Ann F. Friedlaender arrived at the same conclusions regarding the impact of regulation on modal shares, although she calculated the welfare loss of regulatory policies in a different way.[8] George W. Hilton, on the other hand, argued that the Friedlaender-Harbeson calculations excluded the costs of damaged merchandise and schedule unreliability incurred in railroad transportation. If these costs were counted in the calculations, he claimed a reverse result—that no feasible railroad rate reductions could divert significant amounts of traffic from the motor carriers.[9]

For estimates of the relative marginal costs of rail and truck transport in the United States, the two most accepted studies are those of the Meyer et al. study and of Ann F. Friedlaender's book. In a more recent volume, John R. Meyer and Mahlon Straszheim have updated the Meyer et al. study's earlier results to a 1960 base.[10] Since Friedlaender's estimates are for 1963, the results of the two studies should be roughly comparable and are presented in Table 22-2. Although the results do differ somewhat (except for the cost of rail carload shipments of bulk commodities), the numbers are of a similar order of magnitude. Averaging Meyer-Straszheim estimates of rail carload or piggyback cost of 9 mills per ton-mile for such commodities with Friedlaender's equivalent figure of 11.4 yields a figure in the range of 1.0 cent per ton-mile. Similarly, averaging the Meyer-Straszheim truck cost of 25 mills per ton-mile with Friedlaender's figure

4. Of course, the recent evidence indicates that railroads have been seeking rate increases during inflationary periods.

5. Robert W. Harbeson, "Toward Better Resource Allocation in Transport," *Journal of Law and Economics* 12 (October 1969), pp. 321-38.

6. John R. Meyer, Merton J. Peck, John Stenason, and Charles Zwick, *The Economics of Competition in the Transportation Industries* (Cambridge, Mass.: Harvard University Press, 1959), pp. 192-93.

7. Harbeson, "Better Resource Allocation," pp. 321-38.

8. Friedlaender, *Dilemma*, pp. 36-43.

9. Hilton, "Costs of the Interstate Commerce Commission," pp. 728-31.

10. John R. Meyer and Mahlon Straszheim, *Techniques of Transport Planning, Volume I: Pricing and Project Evaluation* (Washington, D.C.: The Brookings Institution, 1971), pp. 171-73.

Table 22-2
Comparative Costs of Rail and Truck Transport in the United States

Mode (Source)	Long-run Marginal Cost (Mills per Ton-Mile)
Meyer & Straszhein (for the year 1960)[a]	
Rail carload	
Bulk commodities	7.0
Manufactured commodities	9.0
Rail piggyback	9.0
Truck	25.0
Friedlaender (for the year 1963)[b]	
Rail carload	7.0
Bulk commodities	7.0
Rail piggyback	11.4
Truck	21.7

[a]From John R. Meyer and Mahlon Straszheim, *Techniques of Transport Planning, Vol. I: Pricing and Project Evaluation* (Washington, D.C.: The Brookings Institution, 1971), p. 172.
[b]From Ann F. Friedlaender, *The Dilemma of Freight Transport Regulation* (Washington, D.C.: The Brookings Institution, 1969), p. 51.

of 21.7 mills yields an average truck cost of 2.3 cents per ton-mile. Thus, the ratio of truck to rail costs should be in the range of 2.0 to 2.5.

For more recent evidence on this issue, Table 22-3 compares freight revenues per ton-mile for shipments over the rail, water, and intercity trucking modes by the industries that produce the bulk of the tonnage on the railroads in the ConRail Region, as derived from *Transportation Projections.* (It should be noted that these amounts paid by industry for freight services do not necessarily cover comparable hauls and loading weights.) The data in this table are more recent in quality and reflect 1970 figures (in constant 1965 cents). In general, the main inferences from this table are, first, that substantial variations exist in the relative rates (and presumably in relative costs), and, second, that the ratio of truck to rail rates may exceed those of the above cost studies. Indeed, for some commodities the ratio of truck to rail marginal costs may approach 3.0 for carload and truckload hauls. If LTL traffic is included in the calculation, the ratio is even higher. On the other hand, as will be seen later in the chapter, some very recent evidence suggests that this ratio (or truck/rail cost differential) may be very small. In summary, the answer to which value of this ratio is best depends on the commodity mix and the type of trucking carriage included in the determination of cost. Clearly, this is an important empirical issue on which future research is warranted.

Table 22-3
Selected Modal Rates by Selected Commodities, United States, 1970 (in Constant 1965 Cents)

Commodity	Rail	Water	Total	Intercity Trucking For-hire	Intercity Trucking Private
Agricultural	1.44¢	0.24¢	4.20¢	3.14¢	6.71¢
Iron ores	1.31	0.19	7.14	10.79	4.88
Coal	0.90	0.18	7.30	8.05	4.88
Sand, etc.	1.09	0.35	4.72	4.63	4.88
Food products	1.59	0.64	4.44	4.32	4.83
Pulp & paper	1.47	1.00	6.49	6.72	4.83
Chemicals	1.41	0.38	3.85	3.45	4.83
Stone, clay, etc.	1.57	2.52	3.54	2.97	4.83
Steel mill products	1.69	0.66	3.07	2.97	4.83
Motor vehicle & parts	3.34	2.37	5.50	5.55	4.83
	Ratio of Mode Rate to Rail Rate				
Agricultural	base	0.17	2.91	2.18	4.66
Iron ores		0.15	5.45	8.24	3.73
Coal		0.20	8.11	8.94	5.42
Sand, etc.		0.32	4.33	4.24	4.48
Food products		0.40	2.79	2.72	3.04
Pulp & paper		0.68	4.41	4.57	3.29
Chemicals		0.27	2.73	2.47	3.43
Stone, clay, etc.		1.61	2.25	1.89	3.08
Steel mill products		0.39	1.81	1.76	2.86
Motor vehicle & parts		0.71	1.65	1.66	1.45

Source: Wilbur Smith and Associates, "Rail System Alternatives," report prepared for the United States Railway Association, Washington, D.C., October 1974.

The Role of Distribution Costs

Two acknowledged features of freight transport markets are that each mode possesses different inherent capabilities for performing diverse transport missions and that shippers of different commodities simultaneously require differentiated services from the carriers. As a result, there is a virtual "substitutability continuum" whereby the different modal types satisfy shippers requirements in varying degrees. While the notion of such a continuum is plausible, it might be more analytically useful to think in terms of substitutional categories.

In general terms, three traffic categories are particularly meaningful for purposes of this alternative mode analysis: (1) railbound freight, (2) truckbound freight, and (3) shipments that can be attracted to alternative modes where they are reasonably close substitutes in meeting shipper requirements. Ultimately the three categories have a common base in cost. In the first case, the rail mode has an overwhelming cost advantage, truck similarly dominates in the second, but in the third there are sufficient qualitative and cost similarities to induce substantial numbers of shippers to use each of the alternatives, indicating a high degree of substitutability.

The considerations that underly these substitutional relationships are highly complex and sorting them out both conceptually and empirically (insofar as data permit) is a difficult task. One must distinguish first between carrier incurred costs and the service prices or rates charged that are paid by shipppers. The question here is the extent to which substitutability is governed by particular rate-cost relationships that might be subject to alteration by managerial or regulatory fiat. Another important distinction is between the prices paid to carriers by shippers for movement services (freight carriage) and those that arise from the performance of other but closely related functions that represent other elements of the distribution process. These two elements are closely related and are defined into the distribution process essentially because they are influenced by the modal choice in the movement process and provide trade-off opportunities for different system configurations. As elaborated below, these outlays associated with nonmovement functions but that are influenced by modal selection are labeled "nontransport costs."

Intermodal Substitutability

Consideration of intermodal substitutability raises two highly distinguishable questions. The first concerns the modal selection criteria and processes employed by shippers and their ultimate choices. The second involves the potential cost, or degree of sacrifice that may be involved, if the movement mode is switched to an alternative. Both aspects involve a consideration of the two types of shipper incurred costs previously mentioned, the rates paid for carrier services, and the associated nontransport costs. The former must be further associated with carrier-incurred costs in order to evaluate in economic terms the rates and ultimately questions of intermodal substitutability.

Transport costs, and ultimately rates, are dictated essentially by technical factors and relationships and in particular situations are determined substantially by attributes of the commodity being moved and the haul over which it is carried. These relationships are portrayed below in generalized terms for the rail and truck technologies that are most relevant for alternative mode considerations. The primary variables to be portrayed are the length of haul and the loading density of the commodity.

The left-hand side (A) of Figure 22-1 shows rail-truck cost relations over different distances assuming the same loading for all lengths of haul. In this

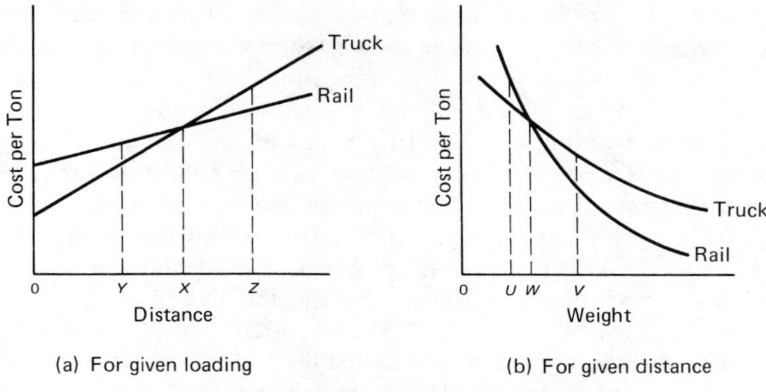

Figure 22-1. Truck-Rail Cost Relations.

standard portrayal, terminal costs are lower and line haul costs per mile are higher for truck than for rail. Accordingly, there is a breakeven distance (denoted *X*), with truck costs lower for shorter hauls and rail costs lower for longer hauls. Traffic clustering in the break-even zone may be considered competitive since rate-cost relationships are subject to sufficient adjustment to swing some shippers and the transport cost (and associated rates) relationships are sufficiently close to give broad significance to nontransport cost elements. Beyond *Y* and *Z*, however, these relationships do not obtain and intermodal substitution is limited. The right-hand portion (B) of Figure 22-1 indicates that, as a general case, rail costs are less affected by loading weight than truck costs and thus closely approach a rectangular hyperbola. Being more affected, truck costs decline less rapidly with loading and another breakeven point and competitive zone arise. This chart also portrays situations of very light and very heavy loadings that are the effective province of the two modes.

In addition to haul length and commodity weights, substitutability is influenced by the character of the distribution requirements of particular commodities or of particular suppliers. One significant distinction involves measures of the relative importance of the shipper's transport costs (movement rates) and the nontransport or logistical costs in the total complex. It is apparent the rail-truck cost relations and associated rate relations will significantly depend on loading and haul lengths. This dependency requires that direct comparisons between the two modes and assessments of the potential impacts of substituting trucks for rail services must insure functional comparability. With the terminal factor as a constant, costs and rates per mile (revenue per ton-mile) decline with distance, a feature that is reinforced by the typical taper in rates that creates a "hump" in the short-haul area. A bias is accordingly created when the revenue yield of alternative modes are compared for hauls of different lengths. Strict accuracy requires, in fact, that comparisons be confined to the *same* movements.

For commodities where the two are competitive, truck and rail rates are often about the same. A comparison of overall ton-mile revenues gives a different picture, however, with rail averaging 1.62 cents and class I motor carriers from 4.33 to 4.94 cents in 1972.[11] This is because there are some very high-value and low-density commodities bearing high rates without rail competition; similarly, railroads carry low-value bulk commodities at low yields that truckers seldom carry. For manufactured commodities, in general, the rate differentials between rail and truck service are frequently quite modest. One formulation of this relationship is stated by Alexander L. Morton in ratios between rail and truck revenues per ton-mile for the same commodities and hauls.[12] These ratios are based on truck revenue data for 1965, especially supplied to the U.S. Department of Transportation, and more recent figures on a broad scale are unavailable. It is generally understood, however, that truck and rail rates have moved rather closely together in recent years and that the ratios developed remain valid, at least as to general order of magnitude. Most of the ratios are substantially below 2.0. While the ratios are generally modest, it should be emphasized that they are limited to shipment sizes up to 25 tons and to manufactures.

Another more recent study conducted by the Association of American Railroads further reveals the potential for close rail-truck price competition.[13] This comparison is couched in terms of rail rates and the calculated costs of specialized carriers dealing exclusively in truckload lots. Since the costs are inclusive, covering all items including overhead, they are regarded as a reasonable surrogate for actual or at least attainable rates and competitive potential. The commodities covered in Table 22-4 are grain, coal, canned goods, and steel, with truck costs differentiated by empty backhaul percentages. With a 25 percent empty return the truck cost for grain shipments was lower than rail rate range for both the short- and long-distance blocks of 200 to 400 and 400 to 1,200 miles. At 100 percent empty return trucks are closely competitive for the 200 to 400 mile range, but rose to 3.3 cents compared with rail's 2.5 to 2.7 cents for the longer range. It should be noted, however, that grain is an exempt commodity for truckers and frequently serves as a backhaul "filler," so that the lower empty return may be more realistic, offering the prospect of highly competitive truck services for grain as well as other relatively heavy loading and low value unmanufactured products of agriculture.

The truck showing is similarly favorable for canned goods when the empty backhaul is kept to 25 percent, beating the rail rates for all mileage blocks shown. In fact, truck costs would be attractive even with somewhat higher

11. Transportation Association of America, *Transportation Facts and Trends, 1972.*

12. Alexander L. Morton, "Truck-Rail Competition for Traffic in Manufactures," *Proceedings of the Transportation Research Forum (1971)*, p. 162.

13. Association of American Railroads, AAR Staff Studies Group (June 21, 1974).

Table 22-4
Selected Rail Rates vs. Truck Costs (Cents per Ton-Mile)

	Distance (Miles)	Rail Rates	Truck Costs	
			(Empty-Backhaul)	
			25%	100%
Grain	200- 400	3.2-3.5	2.0	3.3
	400-1200	2.5-2.7		
			(Empty-Backhaul)	
			100%	
Coal	200- 300	2.2-2.9		
	500- 600	1.6-1.8	3.3	
			(Empty-Backhaul)	
Canned Goods	200- 300	4.0-4.4	0%	25%
	500- 700	3.2-3.5		
	1100-1500	2.6-2.7	1.9	2.4
			(Empty-Backhaul)	
Steel	175- 225	4.4-5.5	25%	75%
	400- 550	2.9-4.9		
	900-1050	2.8-3.1	2.3	3.2

Source: Derived from Association of American Railroads, AAR Staff Studies Group, *Truck-Rail Competition and the Effect of Increased Truck Weights*, Staff Memorandum, 74-9 (1974).

empty returns for distances up to 700 miles, which would generally cover any movements within the USRA region. The truck costs for steel movement are also generally favorable, running lower for all blocks shown with a 25 percent empty return and being highly competitive up to 550 miles even with a 75 percent empty backhaul. Only for coal do the rail rates better the truck costs for all distance blocks.

It is evident from available data that substantial volumes of traffic move by truck, even with the rate premiums that have been described for many shipments.[14] In numerous circumstances the traffic in a commodity will be split between the truck and rail alternatives, with each carrying a significant share. This proposition is amply illustrated by data from the *1967 Census of Transportation* for manufactures as compiled by Alexander L. Morton.[15] Although it is an arbitrary dividing line in view of the substitutability continuum

14. See Brian C. Kullman, "A Model of Intercity Rail Truck Competition," Ph.D. diss., Department of Civil Engineering, M.I.T., Cambridge, Mass., 1973.

15. Morton, "Truck-Rail Competition," pp. 161-64.

that was mentioned earlier, this analysis accepts a minimum or 10 percent participation as indicating a competitive situation, entailing significant substitutability. The census recognizes 84 shipper classes, excluding producers of petroleum products. The truck share exceeds 10 percent in all cases. Of less significance but still of relevance is that the rail share exceeds 10 percent in all but 16 cases which account for only 2.9 percent of total tonnage.

The Dynamics of Intermodal Competition

The following section is a brief review of the literature describing the latent demand for rail traffic and the dynamics of intermodal competition. A short annotation of each source is included.

1972 National Transportation Report

Perhaps the most general study of recent vintage was the rail traffic sensitivity analysis incorporated into the Department of Transportation's (DOT's) *1972 National Transportation Report.*[16] This study estimated the impact of significant structural changes in the intermodal price and service cross elasticities. The DOT study concluded that railroad traffic in the aggregate was relatively insensitive to substantial improvements in the rail system or increases in the cost of waterway transportation.

Woods and Domencich

In a 1971 TRF paper, Douglas W. Woods and Thomas A. Domencich analyzed the economic benefits associated with a possible shift in intercity freight traffic from the highway to the rail system.[17] The study estimated the long-run marginal costs of highway versus rail transportation and took into consideration rail and truck operating costs as well as the extra inventory costs that a rail shipper assumes because of heavier loads, longer lead times, poorer reliability, and greater loss and damage. The study concluded that the competitive break-even point for truck and rail shipments was on hauls between 100 and 200 miles. The authors estimated total trucking tonnage moving over 200 miles by assuming that the truck shipments sampled in the 1967 Census of Transporta-

16. U.S. Department of Transportation, *1972 National Transportation Report* (Washington, D.C.: July 1972).

17. Douglas W. Woods and Thomas A. Domencich, "Competition Between Rail & Truck in Intercity Freight Transportation," *Proceedings of Transportation Research Forum* (November 1971), pp. 257-88.

tion were representative of all truck shipments. The census had reported that 41 percent of common carrier manufactured truck tonnage and 20 percent of manufactured tonnage shipped by private carriage moved over 200 miles. When these mileage percentages were applied to estimates of total common carrier and private carriage tonnage, the result indicated that 24.2 percent of the truck tonnage could have moved more economically by rail. Depending on assumptions as to the magnitude of non-ICC regulated trucking included in the 24.2 percent estimate, this amount of diversion would have increased national railroad traffic 15 percent to 30 percent. It is possible that this methodology may have overstated the amount of potential diversion, for although size of shipment was included as a factor in determining break-even mileage, it was assumed that the railroads might be able to divert all shipments moving more than 200 miles regardless of shipment size.

Morton

Alexander L. Morton's studies also focused primarily on rail and motor carrier traffic through analyses of the 1967 Census of Transportation and the waybill file of the Middle Atlantic Motor Carrier Conference.[18] Among his more important findings are:

> If shipment size would be readily altered, approximately 59 per cent of all Census of Transportation tonnage would be rail-truck competitive with competition defined as rail and truck each having at least a 10 per cent share of a given commodity mileage block. . . .
>
> But, if plant location and shipment economics meant that shipment sizes could not readily be altered, the competitive tonnage on the basis of weight-mileage blocks dropped to 24 per cent. . . .
>
> Within the same weight-distance block, shipppers paid on the average 18 per cent more to ship a given commodity by truck than by rail.[19]

While his data implied that there was a significant amount of tonnage that might be diverted to rail, Morton did not attempt to forecast how much tonnage in fact would be shifted. In general, Morton's work has proven to be a valuable input to recent estimates of future latent rail demand.

Kullman

Brian C. Kullman's study of rail-truck competition contained an excellent analysis of the Census of Transportation data, concentrated on both weight and

18. Morton, "Truck-Rail Competition," pp. 155-72.

19. Ibid., pp. 160, 167.

mileage blocks (in contrast to Woods and Domencich), and estimated the magnitude of revenue generated by rail competitive truck traffic.[20] He then proceeded to derive a model of rail-truck competitive analysis using logit and discriminant analysis. His principal findings of interest are: The competitive portion of the inter-city truck market was approximately 16 percent of the total dollars spent for U.S. truck transportation in 1968; if all of this traffic had been diverted and had moved at rail rates, the increased rail revenue would have been 22 percent to 34 percent; the apparently large truck market, when stratified to eliminate that traffic which can be considered non-rail competitive under present methods of operation, is much smaller than had been anticipated; and the demand for rail service "would appear to be less than unit elastic to rate changes"; that is, a 25 percent decrease in rates would produce less than a 25 percent increase in traffic.[21]

Kullman also concluded that the railroads' share of the rail-truck competitive market depended on the value of the commodity, the annual tonnage shipped by a firm, and mileage. He claimed that railroads could not compete effectively for medium value ($800/ton) commodities at distances under 600 miles unless there was substantial annual tonnage. Kullman's research supported the contention that the railroads' natural traffic consists of regular heavy shipments moving relatively long distances. His data also suggested that the railroads would have great difficulty regaining the medium-high value, infrequent, short-medium haul shipments from the motor carriers.

Staff Reports of the Association of American Railroads

During the spring and summer of 1974 the Association of American Railroads released a series of staff reports that focused on rail-truck competition.[22] These reports are of particular interest since they questioned the accuracy of some of the traditional economic comments on the railroad industry. A summary of the principal findings is the following:

1. The major truck competitor to the railroads is not regulated common carriage since these carriers tend to specialize in less than truckload (LTL) shipments between 600-10,000 pounds.
2. The major competitor is the owner-operator.

20. Brian C. Kullman, A Model of Rail/Truck Competition in the Intercity Freight Market, Ph.D. diss., Department of Civil Engineering, M.I.T., June 1973.

21. Ibid.

22. Association of American Railroads, AAR Staff Studies Group, *Truck-Rail Competition and the Effect of Increased Truck Weights*, Staff Memorandum 74-9 (1974); and Daryl Wyckoff, *A Summary of the Marketing and Policy Implications of the Structure of the Motor-Carrier Industry*, Consultants Report 74-1 (1974).

3. It was estimated that there were approximately 250,000 owner-operators accounting for 25 percent to 40 percent of the total intercity truck tonnage.
4. Owner-operators have costs well below those of the large common carrier motor carriers and increases in highway user charges would not have any major effect on these costs.
5. If increased size and weight legislation were passed, owner-operator costs (including normal empty return ratios) would be significantly below rail rates even in so-called "natural" rail markets, as Table 22-5 suggests.

The general tenor of these reports is that no longer should anyone take comfort in the historic notion that the railroads are inevitably the low-cost mode of intercity freight transportation for long distance hauls and heavy loadings.

Hartwig and Linton

In a master's thesis subsequently reprinted as a research report by Northwestern University's Transportation Center, James C. Hartwig and William E. Linton developed a model of shipper behavior on rail-truck modal choice, using actual data from a large shipper.[23] Their model was designed to predict whether a given shipment would move by truck or rail on the basis of data such as freight cost, transit time, carrier reliability, and value of the commodity. They argued that the proportion of shipments moving by truck or rail is more sensitive to modal cost changes than to changes in modal time or reliability, and that the proportion or market share of truck is more heavily influenced by the value of

Table 22-5
Selected Rail Rates and Owner-Operator Costs

Commodity	Distance (Miles)	Rail Rates (¢/Ton-Mile)	Owner-Operator Costs at 90,000 lbs. Gross Truck Weight (¢/Ton-Mile)	Empty Backhaul (%)
Grain	400-1,200	2.5-2.7	2.7	75
Canned goods	500-1,500	2.7-3.5	2.6	50
Steel	400-550	2.9-4.9	2.3	25

Source: Association of American Railroads, AAR Staff Studies Group, *Truck-Rail Competition and the Effect of Increased Truck Weights*, Staff Memorandum 74-9 (1974), table 1.

23. James C. Hartwig and William E. Linton, *Disaggregate Mode Choice Models of Intercity Freight Movement*, Northwestern University Transportation Center Research Report (1973).

the commodity than by freight cost, time, or reliability.[24] Of course, it must be remembered that their findings explained the behavior of only one shipper.

Miller

In another Transportation Research Forum paper Edward Miller analyzed railroad waybill data for 1964 and 1969 to determine the impact of rate changes on rail traffic. His statistical regressions defined changes in tons as the dependent variable and changes in rail rates and national production as the independent variables. With the exception of iron ore-beneficiating, iron ore concentrates, ordnance, and miscellaneous coal or petroleum products, Miller found that the best estimate for the elasticity of tons carried by rail was "–1.2 with a 95 per cent confidence limit that it lies somewhere between –0.4 and –1.9."[25] Needless to say, much additional research needs to be pursued on the estimating of various elasticities of demand for commodities hauled by rail and by motor trucking.

Concluding Comments

It is apparent that substantial research has been undertaken in the past five years relating to the question of rail-truck modal choice. The results of this research can be summarized as inconclusive in that there is little agreement within the research community concerning the latent demand for rail service, the values of the coefficients in the various demand models constructed, and the amount of additional traffic above and beyond normal forecasts that the railroads could reasonably expect to capture.

The pessimists suggest that the opportunity for additional traffic is relatively poor—perhaps an additional 2 or 3 percent increase in tonnage. The optimists talk in terms of a 15 percent to 35 percent increase in rail tonnage or revenue, but only if *all* motor truck traffic exceeding specific distance and/or weight distance blocks are captured. Yet, the staff of the Association of American Railroads (AAR) questions whether railroads can hold on to existing traffic, much less divert additional tonnage, if owner-operator costs are less than rail rates. As of early 1975 the pessimists seem to be more accurate, especially in view of the situation in the railroad industry in the Midwest and Northeast regions of the country. The research question then becomes, ironically, how much additional traffic will be diverted *to* trucking? This question is especially important in the ConRail region where the diverted tonnage could be substantial.[26]

---

24. Ibid., p. 98.

25. Edward Miller, "Effects of Rates on the Demand for Railroad Services," *Proceedings of the Transportation Research Forum* (Denver: 1972), p. 300.

26. See Temple, Barker and Sloane, Inc., *Macroeconomic Impacts of Truck Diversion*, report prepared for the United States Railway Association (Washington, D.C.: February 1975).

23 State of the Art in Commodity Transportation

In traditional transportation planning procedures, commodity movements have been equated with truck movements. Methodologies were developed on the basis of estimating future truck movements and then adding these truck movements to the estimated future total vehicle streams to determine capacity requirements. There was very little concern with the movements of commodities and with facilities that did not involve truck movements. To a great extent this focus on trucks is understandable. The overwhelming proportion of intraurban movements of goods are by truck and utilize existing streets and highways. However, both in the context of short-run and long-run transportation planning, a broader approach to planning for commodity movements now needs to be taken.

In the short-run context two issues are of particular significance to planning for commodity movements in metropolitan areas. These are issues of costs and of impacts. Transportation cost is an element in the cost of all goods and services and, in the case of a great many goods and services, it is a significant component of final cost. For example, one recent general study has estimated that approximately 4.5 percent of the cost of food to the consumer is transportation cost.[1] In the aggregate, a very large amount of money is involved. Furthermore, the cost of urban goods movement reflects in a very real sense, the level of service that is provided in an urban context. If congestion is great, if parking, standing, and access facilities are inadequate, and if other factors detrimental to service are operative, the cost of commodity transportation increases very rapidly. Along these lines, a study done some years ago indicated that the cost of urban goods movements in New York City is approximately twice the cost of similar movements in Louisville, Kentucky.[2] The second factor significant to commodity movements is that of their impact. A variety of impacts must be distinguished. There are generally in highly localized areas major impacts on the general traffic stream, with such movements and their vehicle characteristics adding extraordinarily to congestion. The lack of adequate off-street loading or unloading facilities in all but the newest sections of urban areas is another factor that tends to impact on urban traffic streams. Since, in many instances, commodity transporting vehicles tend to use and be concentrated on a limited number of roadway facilities, there is in the vicinity of such facilities a market

1. "Waste in Marketing Lifts Grocery Costs," *New York Times*, (September 13, 1974) sec. 3, pp. 1ff.

2. Wilbur Smith and Associates, *Motor Trucks in the Metropolis* (Washington, D.C.: August 1969).

impact on air and noise pollution levels. All of these are problem areas that have not in the past been adequately handled by the urban transportation planner.

Over the longer term, the concern of the transportation planner with commodity flows must focus essentially on planning to provide for transportation facilities of all kinds that will be consistent with and adequate to the forecast economic development of the metropolitan region. This means that, in long-range planning, the planner must base his work on sound and comprehensive economic analyses and forecasts at the metropolitan level and for such subareas of the metropolitan area as may be considered significant. He must also be concerned with aspects of transportation for which decisions on investment in facilities and vehicles falls generally into the private rather than the public sector.

The brief preceding discussion should have indicated that little work has characteristically been done in transportation planning dealing with the issues reviewed above. Clearly, the economic significance of commodity transportation is enormous. Drawing on recent U.S. Department of Agriculture statistics for 1973, the total national transportation bill for food products alone is \$6.1 billion annually, much of which is accrued under inefficient conditions.[3] Thus, an objective of commodity transportation planning could be stated as being the achievement of increases in efficiency and productivity of commodity transportation, particularly in urban areas. Another objective would be achieving the greatest unit cost reductions in commodity transportation that can be sought. Yet, this simultaneously can only be done within the constraints imposed of keeping environmental and other impacts as moderate as possible. These objectives cannot be achieved simply through planning and implementation undertaken in the public sector, for much of the relevant decision making falls into the private sector. The achievement of the broad objective that has been stated is as much in the interest of the private sector as it is in the interest of the public sector, and, hopefully, the two interests will develop instrumentalities for the closest possible cooperation along these lines. Accomplishing effective commodity transportation planning is not a simple process. For solving both short-range and long-range problems, a viable data base containing information about the metropolitan economy and its historic pattern of development as well as forecasts of the likely future evolution of the local economy is required. In addition, comprehensive data are required concerning transportation facilities and vehicle fleets utilized in commodity transportation. A further requirement is an inventory of proposed plans for the future development for such facilities.

One of the principal problems of commodity transportation planning is that the demand side (that is, economic development and change) and the supply side (that is, the transportation facilities and vehicle fleets) do not often change in a coordinated fashion. Those individuals making decisions concerning capital investments in transportation facilities generally try to base their decisions on

3. *New York Times*, sec. 3, pp. 1ff.

estimates of future demand. Quite often such estimates are faulty and information to improve them is difficult to obtain. Those making decisions concerning growth and change in various sectors of the economy generally make the assumption that transportation for the commodities and services generated will be available. Thus, one ordinarily finds a situation in which there are leads and lags, and in which the demand and supply sides are not in a state of equilibrium. Consequently, one of the functions of commodity transportation planning is to try to reduce the differentials between the demand and supply sides to the extent that it is possible to do so.

State of the Art in Commodity Flow Analysis

This brief overview of the principal concerns of commodity transportation planning does not do justice to the very real complexity of the subject matter. In a full-scale commodity transportation study many issues would have to be addressed. As indicated, though, the absolutely critical factor in beginning is a thorough understanding of the metropolitan economy and of the major commodity flows that come into, and go out of, or pass through the metropolitan area. Within the metropolitan economy as a whole, usually there are major and distinct industries that are of particular significance to that area. These industries may be critical because they are a major factor in providing employment, or because the value of goods generated by them is large, or for a number of other reasons. For transportation planning purposes, these industries and their transportation requirements should be investigated separately.

In some ways an analysis of commodity flows offers greater scope for quantitative and substantive inquiry than does a study of demand for passenger travel. Whereas the selection of a mode of transportation by a passenger is inevitably a psychological matter of consumer choice in which economic analysis can only make limited inferences about the preferences of passengers, the choice of a carrier or transportation firm for hauling commodities, on the other hand, does not in and of itself generate pleasure. This difference suggests that modal choice issues in commodity transportation are more likely to be based on economic considerations and thereby should be amenable to formal economic analysis.

It is paradoxical, though, that the state of the art in passenger demand modeling is more advanced than that in commodity flow analysis. This situation may very well change during the next year or two, especially in view of the current attention being focused on intercity commodity flows and urban goods movement, occasioned principally by the impacts of the recent oil embargoes and by a wide range of environmental concerns with vehicles and vehicle movements.

Quantitative methods for predicting passenger demand and modal choice have advanced very rapidly over the past few years. The state of the art has advanced a long way since the invention of the gravity model. New methods, employing less data collection and more efficient utilization, have been developed during this period. Among the more promising of the available techniques are disaggregate behavioral models and small-scale simultaneous equation econometric models.[4] These approaches appear to be equally attractive for commodity modal choice models. In fact, they have already been employed on a trial basis and have proven to be both workable and encouraging. These new modeling approaches are likely to have considerably more impact than the original abstract-mode models developed during the Northeast Corridor studies in the mid-1960s. These pioneer efforts were designed to be illustrative but they have demonstrated not to be very practical for prediction purposes.

Two specific problems currently exist with research on commodity flows performed to the present time: First, an adequate data base does not currently exist, so that the current commodity models using this approach are calibrated with data that are basically inadequate. And second, methods of handling a variety of commodities are needed. Presently existing models clearly suffer from both these deficiencies. With respect to the lack of data, it would appear that this has been a constraint long enough. For the development of disaggregate modeling especially, the data requirements are not so complicated as they would have been formerly and it is entirely practical to procure the necessary data. With econometric models, a combination of publicly available data (selected carefully) and private source information (which is reliable and can be sustained) would be an immense step forward. Hopefully this step alone will result from some current research efforts in analyzing commodity flows.[5] The development of usable commodity demand models simply should no longer be prevented due to the lack of data.

The prospect of preparing a commodity flow model also is no longer a mystery.[6] It will not be necessary to calibrate a new model for each commodity, but one generic model can be specified, estimated, and calibrated to serve generally. It may or may not be possible to rely on a single model overall, but one for each general *class* of commodities can be easily developed. Furthermore,

4. See especially the articles in John F. Kain and John R. Meyer, eds., *Essays in Regional Economics* (Cambridge, Mass.: Harvard University Press, 1971), by J.W. Milliman, "Large-Scale Models for Forecasting Regional Economic Activity," pp. 309-51, and James C. Burrows and Charles E. Metcalf, "The Determinants of Industrial Growth at the County Level: An Econometric Analysis," pp. 352-401.

5. The reader is referred to a series of reports on commodity flow analysis prepared by M.I.T.'s Urban System Laboratory in 1974 for the California Department of Transportation in Sacramento and the Southern California Association of Governments in Los Angeles.

6. For a recent article suggesting that even the gravity model still best describes the patterns of commodity shipments under the special case of a price discriminating spatial commodity, see John H. Niedercorn and Josef D. Moorehead, "The Commodity Flow Gravity Model: A Theoretical Reassessment," *Regional and Urban Economics* 4 (June 1974), pp. 69-75.

it is clear that this impetus for promoting and funding this type of research must come from the state or regional level, especially if the scope of the analysis is regional in origin. Since it frequently occurs in comprehensive and detailed empirical studies, there may be no way to escape the need to adopt some simplifying and perhaps even bold assumptions at the beginning of a commodity flow analysis, especially for a regional economy.

In the heavily populated and industrialized areas of most regions, people are dependent on intricate systems of transportation that, more often than not, are financially unprofitable. In addition, obsolete facilities and growing demands have created seemingly insoluble difficulties in the movement of both commodities and passengers, and the current methods of dealing with these difficulties have yielded only small prospects of relief. In recent years metropolitan areas have borne most of the impact of the domestic population growth that, together with rising incomes, have aggravated the strain on transportation facilities. As urbanization and economic growth continue, it is clear that major revisions and shifts in public policy will be necessary if transportation problems like traffic congestion, efficient land development, occupational access, and distributional needs are to be relieved. These problems cannot be solved merely by providing additional transportation capacity. The fundamental requirement, then, is a comprehensive approach that considers an examination both of past developments and the complex issues in public finance, urban government, urban planning, and applied microeconomic analysis.

Urban, metropolitan, and regional events have received wide attention in the literature during the past two decades. The inherent complexity of modeling or simulating the characteristics of land use also has been widely recognized.[7] As one might expect, applying quantitative analysis to such complex phenomena incurred some eloquent criticism from the beginning, partially on the premise that such effects clashed "with the humanist,"[8] and partially because it opposed other methods of planning.[9] In recent years different forms of criticism have been levied against modeling and simulation, with some suggesting that the approach is vacuous.[10] Undoubtedly many researchers have been frustrated and

7. The National Bureau of Economic Research has been regarded as the prime source of empirical economic research for many years. One of its major programs recently has been the Urban Simulation Model, which was intended to develop a model of urban land use and to calibrate it on several, selected metropolitan areas. Some of the results are reported in two volumes: H. James Brown et al. *Empirical Models of Urban Land Use* (New York: National Bureau of Economic Research, 1972); and Gregory K. Ingram et al., *The Detroit Prototype of the NBER Urban Simulation Model* (New York: National Bureau of Economic Research, 1972).

8. William Weismantel, "Dante's Inferno: The First Land Use Model," *Journal of the American Institute of Planners* 25 (November 1959), pp. 215-25.

9. George Raymond, "Simulation vs. Reality," in Ernest Erger, ed., *Urban Planning in Transition* (New York: Grossman Publishers, 1970).

10. Douglas B. Lee, Jr., "Requiem for Large Scale Models," *Journal of the American Institute of Planners* 39 (May 1973), pp. 47-55.

disillusioned by the disproportionate amount of person-days associated with heretofore limited payoffs.

The Underlying Importance of Grain Shipments

Grain shipments generated in the mid-continent United States are transported to consumption points within the country and to overseas destinations. Since transportation charges on bulk commodities like corn are high relative to their value, shippers usually seek the lowest cost way to transport grain, assuming that time is not a factor. If it is assumed economically rational behavior of this kind is followed consistently by all merchants in the grain trades, then the constrained linear programming transportation model can be used as a pattern of flows that minimize the total cost of shipping all projected grain tonnages from points of origin to both domestic and foreign destinations.[11] Agricultural exports have become a more important element in the nation's balance of trade (and balance of payments), especially in view of the $18 billion increase in foreign oil imports between 1973 and 1974. The value of agricultural exports in 1974 was to $21.9 billion while the value of agricultural imports was $10.9 billion.

An increasing awareness of the complexity of the interactions between the agricultural and nonagricultural sectors in product and factor markets has led to an interest in agricultural sectoral analysis. The transportation analyst should be concerned with the indirect effects of agricultural policies and trends on the nonagricultural sectors, especially the rail and trucking portions of the transport sector. For example, agricultural policies for increasing foreign exchange through Third World trade subsidies may have favorable effects on the agricultural economy in the short-run (with increased revenues), but through increases in wholesale (and retail) food price and in agricultural investment many have a high opportunity cost in the nonagricultural sectors, eventually leading to increases in transportation rates.[12] On a larger scale, multisectoral planning models in recent years have become accepted by economists as useful devices for the analysis of resource allocation in general and the determination of investment opportunities in particular.[13] The majority of these models have been constructed within the framework of mathematical programming, especially of the linear programming

11. See John M. Jordan, "Economic Rationality in Commodity Flows: The Case of the United States Corn Trade in 1964," Ph.D. diss., Purdue University (West Lafayette, Ind., 1970).

12. See Derek Byerlee and A.N. Halter, "A Macro-Economic Model for Agricultural Sector Analysis," *American Journal of Agricultural Economics* 56 (August 1974), pp. 520-33.

13. See Robert S. Pindyck, *Optimal Planning for Economic Stabilization* (Amsterdam: North Holland Publishing Company, 1973).

type.[14] Still, the current state of the art in commodity flow analysis reflects only bare beginnings.

---

14. For a thorough overview of multisectoral planning models, see Alan S. Manne, "Multi-Sector Models for Development Planning: A Survey," *Journal of Development Economics* 1 (June 1974), pp. 43-69.

24 Identification of Data Sources for the Analysis of Commodity Flows

Primary on-site data and information for commodity and freight movements can be collected through interviews with executives, operators, and other knowledgeable personnel of commercial banks, carrier firms, large shippers, terminal companies, and government agencies. Most primary information can be collected through an informal and personnel questionnaire pertaining to the classes and types of commodities hauled. Questions can be selective, depending on the nature of the participating individuals interviewed. The participants can be asked to describe commodity flows about which they are informed or over which they are responsible.

In addition, voluminous data published by a number of agencies of the federal government are available. Since the data for commodity flows are related to industrial activities, the public domain data provided by the U.S. Bureau of the Census and by other agencies have represented a good starting point for determining the availability and comprehensiveness of existing information. For many industrial categories, the data are categorized at the national, state and often county levels.

A key factor relevant in the analysis of commodity flows is the availability of secondary (or public) data. For most regions the important sources of secondary data stem from the federal censuses, including the Censuses of Manufactures, Business, Transportation, Selected Services, and Trades. These censuses are taken (or planned to be taken) every five years or so. For example, there was a Census of Transportation in 1963, another in 1967. Taken decennially in the first year of each decade are the Censuses of Population and Housing, both of which are widely used in socioeconomic and transport studies.

A detailed discussion of these secondary sources of information and of their underlying methodologies is presented in the following section. Selected commodities and industries from secondary sources are a useful foundation on which state and regional planning agencies should continue their efforts to explore current and future research programs. These sources are deemed instrumental in providing the necessary foundations on which to develop an eventual comprehensive commodity flow modeling capability for the agencies. At this point the purpose of the private source data should be only to supplement this broad set of published information, providing for the agencies a unique and desirable summary of the region's critical industries.

At the statewide level, various censuses may be conducted. For example, both the Commonwealths of Massachusetts and Pennsylvania take an annual industrial census. In most states the best sources of industrial and economic data are the State Departments of Finance, Transportation, Agriculture, Commerce, and Employment Development. To a large extent the formats of the data sets in the state departments hinge on the structure of data bases in their national counterparts.

In addition, major studies emanating from special projects may be important sources of information. These projects might include such items as publications of the University of Michigan Consumer Research Center; national consumer surveys of the Bureau of Labor Statistics; data from the Penn Jersey Transportation Study; OBERS projections; consulting firm forecasts; and the vehicles files of the state Public Utilities Commissions. The key determinants of the appropriate sources of data are the quantity and quality of data and their relevance to the specific needs of a particular study.

Selected Sources of Secondary (Public) Information on Commodity Flows

Census of Transportation

The Census of Transportation was undertaken for the first time on a national basis in 1963 by the U.S. Bureau of the Census. It was repeated in 1967 and 1972, with the publication of the 1972 data scheduled for publication in early 1975. The 1967 census consisted of three independent surveys–National Travel, Truck Inventory and Use, and Commodity Transportation.

The National Travel Survey is concerned with the volume and characteristics of travel by residents of the United States. The survey consists of a nationwide probability sample of about 18,000 households who responded by mail to a questionnaire each quarter. The data show the estimated number of households from which someone took one or more trips, persons who took at least one trip, person-trips, person-nights, and person-miles. The data reflect travel characteristics like means of transport, purpose of trip, duration of trip, distance, size of party, type of lodging, origin and destination regions, and by such household characteristics as family income level, occupation and education of household head, and age of traveler.

The Truck Inventory and Use Survey presents data on the nation's truck resources, other than vehicles owned by federal, state, and local government agencies. The survey consists of a probability sample of motor truck licenses in each of the 50 states and the District of Columbia. The data shows the number of trucks and tractor-trailer combinations, truck-miles, and average miles per truck, by major use, body type, body size, class, year model, type of fuel, range of operations, vehicle type and axle arrangement, products carried, and maintenance.

The Commodity Transportation Survey presents data on the intercity transportation of commodities shipped by the industrial sector of the United States. A probability sample of about 1.4 million bills of lading or other shipping documents was selected from the files of approximately 13,000 manufacturers throughout the country, representing the universe of about 100,000 plants with total employment of 20 or more employees. The data are classified by shipper groups and shipper classes; geographic areas, such as production areas, geographic divisions, and selected states; and commodity groups. Data are shown for tons and ton-miles by means of transport, length of haul, commodity, weight, origin and destination areas, size of plant, and availability of transport facilities. Percentage distributions of shipments by means of transport, distance shipped, and availability of transport facilities are also presented for smaller manufacturing establishments. In spite of some limitations, this survey is the richest source of information on commodity movements presently in existence.

Census of Construction Industries

The 1967 Census of Construction Industries covered all establishments primarily engaged in contract construction (general contractors or special trade contractors) or in construction for sale on their own account (operative builders) or in subdividing real property into lots (subdividers and developers, except cemeteries) as defined in the 1967 edition of the Standard Industrial Classification (SIC) Manual. Construction firms were divided into employers (those firms with payroll) and nonemployers (those firms with no payroll). For the employer firms a basic mailing list was obtained from the Internal Revenue Service (IRS) and the Social Security Administration (SSA). A sample of 125,000 employer establishments was selected from a universe of about 400,000 single-establishment employer firms and 3,000 multiestablishment companies, all single-establishment companies with the equivalent of ten or more employees and a sample of single-establishment companies with fewer than 10 employees. Statistics for the nonemployer firms were obtained from administrative records of the federal government. The Census of Construction Industries provides data on number of establishments, number of proprietors and working partners, total employees and total receipts for individual industries or industry groups. Data are available for each state, the District of Columbia, and the total United States.

Census of Manufactures

The Census of Manufactures is another economic census conducted by the U.S. Bureau of the Census. The census includes general statistics (for example, total employment, payroll, production-worker employment, man-hours, wages, cost of materials, value of shipments, inventories, capital expenditures, and value added by manufacture) by industry, by geographic area, by employment size of establishment, by degree of product specialization within plant, and by type of ownership. Information is supplied on the detailed industrial characteristics of each state and the largest standard metropolitan statistical areas (SMSAs); also overall measures of manufacturing activity are shown at the county and individual city level down to cities of 10,000 or more population. The compilation entitled "Location of Manufacturing Plants" displays for each of the 3,100 counties in the United States the number of manufacturing plants, by size, for each of 420 industries. The basic industry and production classification system employed is the Standard Industrial Classification (SIC) code. The basic mailing lists for the Census of Manufactures were obtained from Internal Revenue Service (IRS) and Social Security Administration (SSA) records, supplemented by the Annual Survey of Manufactures (ASM) list of 60,000 establishments.

Census of Business

The Census of Business is one of the economic censuses required by law. The Census of Business consists of firms engaged in retail trade, wholesale trade, and selected services which operate in the United States. In addition, it covers public warehouses, dental labs, law firms, architectural and engineering firms, travel agencies, and truck and bus carriers not subject to economic regulation by the Interstate Commerce Commission. The kinds of businesses covered are defined in the Standard Industrial Classification (SIC) Manual. Most data are available for the United States, each state, District of Columbia, Guam, and the Virgin Islands; data also are provided by kinds of business for counties, SMSAs, and some other selected cities.

County and City Data Book

The *County and City Data Book* is a statistical abstract supplement published by the U.S. Bureau of the Census. Most statistics in this book were derived from the latest censuses of population, housing, governments, manufactures, business, mineral industries, and agriculture. In addition, statistics from many other governmental and private agencies are included. The data available include the following: area, population, birth and death rates, education, labor force, families and income, social security, public assistance, housing, presidential vote, local government finances, government employment, banking, manufactures, retail trade, wholesale trade, selected services, mineral industries, farm population, and agriculture. Information is available for the United States, states, census divisions and regions, SMSAs, counties, cities, urbanized areas, and unincorporated areas.

County Business Patterns

County Business Patterns was first published in 1946 by the Social and Economic Statistics Administration, U.S. Bureau of the Census. These statistics provide information on reporting units, payroll, and employment by industry classification and county location. Industry classifications are based on the 1967 edition of the Standard Industrial Classification (SIC) Manual. Summary data by industry are also provided for the United States, for the 50 states, and the District of Columbia, and for Puerto Rico, the Virgin Islands, American Samoa, and Guam. Summary totals for all SMSAs outside of New England and for metropolitan state economic areas (MSEAs) in New England that are whole-county equivalents of SMSAs are available in table 3 of the U.S. Summary. The data contained in the *County Business Patterns* are derived from employment and payroll information reported on Treasury Form 941, Schedule A.

OBERS Projections

The OBERS projections are a major output of a program of economic data collection, analysis, and projection conducted by the Bureau of Economic Analysis (BEA),[1] the U.S. Department of Commerce, Economic Research Service (ERS), and the U.S. Department of Agriculture with assistance from the Forest Service. The reports include projections of economic activity for the nation, functional economic areas, water resource regions and subareas, and the 50 states by 10-year intervals from 1980 to 2020. Included are projections of population, personal income, output, and employment earnings, with the last three items shown by industry. Also included are projections of land use by broad categories for the same period. The projections were derived from historical information of essentially the same geographic and industrial detail. Some supplemental materials also are available upon request, including the disaggregate data and projections for SMSAs and for non-SMSA counties.

The OBERS projections are based on long-run or secular trends, and thus ignore the cyclical fluctuations that characterize the short-run path of the economy. The general assumptions underlying the projections are the following: (1) population growth will be conditioned by a decline of fertility rates from those of the 1962-65 period; (2) reasonably full employment at the national level, represented by a 4 percent unemployment rate, will prevail at the points for which projections are made; as in the past, unemployment will be dispropor-

1. Formerly the Office of Business Economics (OBE).

tionately distributed regionally, but the extent of disproportionality will diminish; (3) no foreign conflicts are assumed to occur at the projection dates; (4) continued technological progress and capital accumulation will support a growth in private output per man-hour of 3 percent annually; (5) new products to appear in the future will be accommodated within the existing industrial classification system; and (6) growth in output can be achieved without ecological disaster or serious deterioration.

Faucett Associates Reports

Transportation Projections to 1980 and 1990, by Jack Faucett Associates, Inc., is based on the U.S. Department of Transportation (DOT) Input/Output Model to make the projections. The projections encompass all modes of transportation, passenger, and freight, and are presented for both commercial carriers and private operations. These projections include the following items: gross national product and industry output; commercial passenger travel; private passenger travel; freight transportation, including the breakdown by type of freight, estimation of freight revenues, physical measures and other distributions of output; miscellaneous transportation expenditures, gross product originating in transportation sectors, and employment in transportation and related industries.

Survey of Current Business

The *Survey of Current Business* is published monthly by the Bureau of Economic Analysis. The information includes the national business situation, national income and product tables, current business statistics, and other business and economics related articles and data. Current business statistics provide information for nearly 2,500 statistical series dealing with gross national product, industrial production, advertising, finance, commodity prices, industry statistics, labor force, employment, hours and earnings, trade, construction, and real estate. Historical and summary statistics are published biennially in *Business Statistics*, a supplement to the *Survey of Current Business.*

25 Modeling in Commodity Transportation

It is very important to understand the fundamental role played by models in the commodity transportation planning process. Since planning is an operation based upon faith in one's future perceptions, the quantitative understanding of the possible range of outcomes provided by the use of models is invaluable to state and regional planning agencies. The most powerful models are those that are generalizations of basic transportation processes. While a number of such basic transportation processes can be identified with the present menu of analytic tools, we continually should be seeking to identify and understand others. The development of such basic processes then should be an important ingredient of any fundamental research program to be undertaken by federal, state, or regional agencies whose principal interests and responsibilities lie in the transportation planning arena.

One of the most important forms of modeling needed for commodity flow analysis is the ability to work with industry trade flows. Such a form of interindustry trade model is the input/output system developed by Wassily Leontief more than two decades ago.[1] A variety of refinements and embellishments of the input/output technique have occurred over the years and these will undoubtedly be useful in the modeling process. In particular, one use is that a multiregional input/output analysis allows trade flows in which the influence of monetary and fiscal policies as well as capital investment policy can be traced. Dynamic versions of these models, which must utilize time series data, are particularly instrumental in analyzing the impacts of differential investment programs or other time-dependent effects. The dynamic models do not, however, possess the industry detail of an input/output model.

Another form of useful model is one that replicates commodity distribution between points of production and points of consumption. While very little research has been done in this area, the concepts have been established in the economic and regional science literatures. A basic problem, though, still appears to be the huge number of commodities and the consequent difficulty in obtaining adequate data for the calibration and use of separate models for each commodity. As an attempt to overcome some of this difficulty, research on the use of commodity attributes rather than commodities themselves is an alternative approach that appears likely to yield useful results.

Another area for the research and development of models is that of

1. Wassily Leontief, *Structure of American Industry* (Cambridge: Harvard University Press, 1951).

behavioral modal choice models for commodity flow demand. The continuing development of urban passenger demand models suggest that substantial elements in methodologies can be transferred from this already fairly well developed field.[2] The modal choice decisions for individual shipments can be captured in the parameters of the model by careful econometric modeling.

The development of useful operational cost-performance models for existing modes in the United States still needs to be undertaken. These models should use variable factor inputs and should be sensitive to a wide variety of variables in the traffic level and should be able to link physical characteristics of the system. Work conducted for developing countries might be extended to the United States relatively easily, with the appropriate modifications.[3]

An area that has received a great deal of emphasis recently, yet in which much remains to be done, is that of models for predicting the impact of air pollution, noise, vibration, and adverse effects caused by transport facilities. These models must be sensitive to selective government controls so that the various control models for each of the modes, developed from the viewpoint of the carrier (firm) is desirable. Only by understanding the carrier's objectives and building models that optimize its objective function can the planning and regulatory agencies hope to understand the carrier's response to specific government actions.

A clear understanding of such complex phenomena as commodity flows is difficult to achieve. Nevertheless, it is apparent that the development of data and their careful analysis is fundamental to the process of understanding these flows. Massive amounts of data are not necessary; actually they may retard rather than aid the learning process. While some data observation and gathering must typically be undertaken prior to model formulation and calibration, detailed data collection for use in calibration should be left until after model formulation is completed. Successive iterations of superior data and extensive model-building

2. During the last decade various empirical investigations into the modal choice decisions of travelers have estimated the values that individuals placed on time spent on travel. In these studies the individual modal choice is influenced by the cost and time characteristics (attributes) under consideration. Many of the choice models in the literature consider only the ticket cost and the time spent on a particular mode. If the total costs were included in the estimation from origin to destination (rather than just terminal to terminal), then the total time parameter would be the sum of the time spent on the mode, access and egress time, and the average waiting time at the origin for the scheduled arrival of the mode. Also, in most models, the probability choice was binary, particularly in urban cases, in that the individual's choice was between his automobile and some other form of transit. A multimodal model is certainly more stringent and therefore estimation is more difficult. Many of these points apply equally to commodity flow modeling as well as to passenger demand modeling. See, for example, Peter L. Watson, *The Value of Time-Behavioral Models of Modal Choice* (Lexington, Mass.: Lexington Books, D.C. Heath and Co., 1974).

3. Examples of this extension might include the Harvard/Brookings model of Colombia and the Engineering Computer International, Inc. model of Venezuela. Also, see Alan A. Walters, "An Inquiry into Interregional Economic Modeling," *Papers and Proceedings of the American Economic Association* 78 (May 1969), pp. 00-00.

then represent the ideal process by which to develop an effective modeling capability.

The Value of Regional Economic Analysis for Commodity Transportation

The development of regional economic analysis has sparked an increasing interest in the design and measurement of the term "gross state product" (GSP).[4] One of the difficulties in using the term is that no federally collected data currently exist for GSP. The fundamental gap between personal income by state, available at the state level, and GSP is on state business income. Similar difficulties arise in the calculation of "gross regional product"; yet, the latter concept needs refinement as an ingredient to a practical regional analysis of commodity flows.

One advantage of an econometric model at the statewide level is the prediction of performance for the state economy. At the regional level the identical argument is applicable, although the data requirements are more stringent since the level of analysis becomes more disaggregate. An alternative way to denote performance in the regional economy is to construct regional activity indices, which can be designed to interpret the weighted impact resulting from fluctuations to production sectors of relative (or critical) importance to the region. The index then can serve as a gauge for the state economy by reflecting weighted growth, consistency, productivity, or stagnation of diverse production sectors of the regional economy.[5] In the food industry, for example, transportation costs accounted for approximately 5 percent of the total retail dollar spent nationally on $132 billion worth of food by consumers in 1973.[6] Since almost half of the motor trucks engaged in food transportation are empty at any one moment because of ICC backhaul constraints, and since railroad cars hauling food products were moving only 12 percent of the time, the inefficiency costs resulting from these sources are staggering.[7] The extent to which these inefficiency costs are distributed regionally remains an unresolved issue.

If one views the distribution of manufacturing activities as a dynamic phenomenon within a region like New England or the San Francisco Bay Area,

4. See W.L. L'Esperance and Daniel Fromm, "A Note on Estimating Gross State Product," *Growth and Change* 5 (April 1974), pp. 46-47. This term refers to the goods and services produced at the *state* level, and it is not to be confused with the newer federal term "gross domestic product," developed by the U.S. Department of Commerce.

5. For an illustration of this method, see D.R. Epley, "A Test of Base Theory Using Income Indexes Constructed from a State Input-Output Table," *Review of Regional Studies* 3 (Spring 1972-73), pp. 1-12.

6. "Waste in Marketing Lifts Grocery Costs," *New York Times* September 15, 1974, sec. 3, pp. 1ff.

7. Ibid., p. 4.

then there exists a compelling challenge to record and interpret change and ultimately to forecast the rate and direction of manufacturing growth. The importance of this kind of change has generally not been acknowledged, although a recent study has explored the possibilities of developing an industrial location theory based on the growth of the firm.[8] It depicts two specific stages of the firm's growth: The first is where a firm has fixed scale and location but strives to operate more efficiently in order to lower unit costs; the other involves the application of William Alonso's model of urban land use to the case where a firm can change both its scale and the location.[9] In any particular region the effects of general economic growth also will be conditioned by local aspects such as its land and infrastructural resources. The local comparative advantages and industrial mix are likewise important. As a statistical fact, strong growth in most regions has placed stress on the land resource, raised the price of land, and pushed a proportion of new or relocating firms into suboptimal locations. The implications of these firms' uses and requirements for transportation rights-of-way and facilities at present and in future years should be the ultimate goal of the underlying research into commodity flows. In order to pursue this line of inquiry successfully, certain data on inputs and outputs are required, as will be indicated.

Manufacturing firms located within urban areas often occupy sizeable areas of land and represent substantial investments in buildings and equipment. Historically, then, there have been strong forces of inertia associated with industrial location in urban areas. Coupled with a tendency by firms to cluster in a few concentrated industrial zones, the attractiveness to study industrial growth within the cities has been lacking. In fact, the study of firm distributions within urban areas has been relatively ignored when compared with the numerous analyses of residential and retailing location.

In regional areas most firms experience some form of economic growth characteristics. It is generally believed that firms are consistently operating between 80 and 95 percent of their maximum capacity, so that an increase in demand can be handled temporarily by utilizing excess and existing capacity. One label for the additional costs associated with employing full use of resources (overtime, etc.) is "stretching" costs.[10] At a later stage in growth, sustained demand might lend to an increased investment in plant, or facilities and to additional workers being hired. These additional costs might be called "frictional."[11] Finally, when an existing facility can no longer accommodate growth,

8. M.T. Daly and M.J. Webber, "The Growth of the Firm Within the City," *Urban Studies* 10 (October 1973), pp. 303-17.

9. William Alonso, *Location and Land Use* (Cambridge, Mass.: Harvard University Press, 1964); Daly and Webber, "Growth of the Firm," pp. 303-17.

10. T.Y. Shen, "Cyclical Behaviour of Manufacturing Plants," *Journal of Industrial Economics* 16 (April 1968), pp. 106-25. If the firm selects external means in which to grow, it then may pursue a program of diversification and incurs "shift" costs.

11. Ibid.

a change in scenery is required, resulting in additional location costs. The impacts of these three types of growth related costs on transportation requirements in a region are illustrated in Figure 25-1. Assuming temporarily that firms in the region do pursue a profit maximizing objective, this growth related cost analysis can be linked with Alonso's well known model of land use to provide a more comprehensive treatment of the roles of industrial firms in regional economic growth.

The use of economic theory in commodity flow analysis should provide a partial hint as to how complex systems might behave and also some understanding of the inferential links of the systems: "Simplifying assumptions are not an excrescence on model building; they are its essence."[12] Among the major difficulties in the long debate on the objectives of the firm in economic theory are its imprecision and its inability to produce a viable alternative approach. The theory of the firm, based on profit maximization, has provided a foundation for the superstructure of other theories, such as location theory. In the criticism of the theory of the firm, organizational theory most frequently is proposed as a rival. Its proponents claim that by focusing on how a firm actually operates,

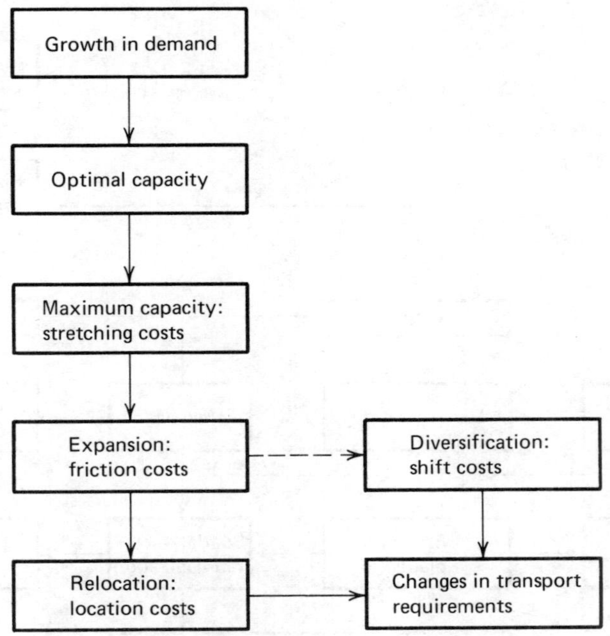

Figure 25-1. Stages in the Growth of Industrial Firms in Regional Areas.

12. Robert M. Solow, "Rejoinder to Richardson-I" *Urban Studies* 10 (June 1973), p. 267.

rather than on how it ought to operate, a better understanding is gained of such problems as the location of the firm. In the context of urban areas, it also has been claimed that more understanding is gained from considering how a firm grows, rather than how it operates.[13] Along this avenue of inquiry, Figure 25-2 shows the leading interrelationships among economic development, regional industrial growth and transportation requirements.

A Limited Regional Data Set

With data of the above classifications it should be possible to develop a modeling capability for regional economic analysis. Such an approach might suggest a

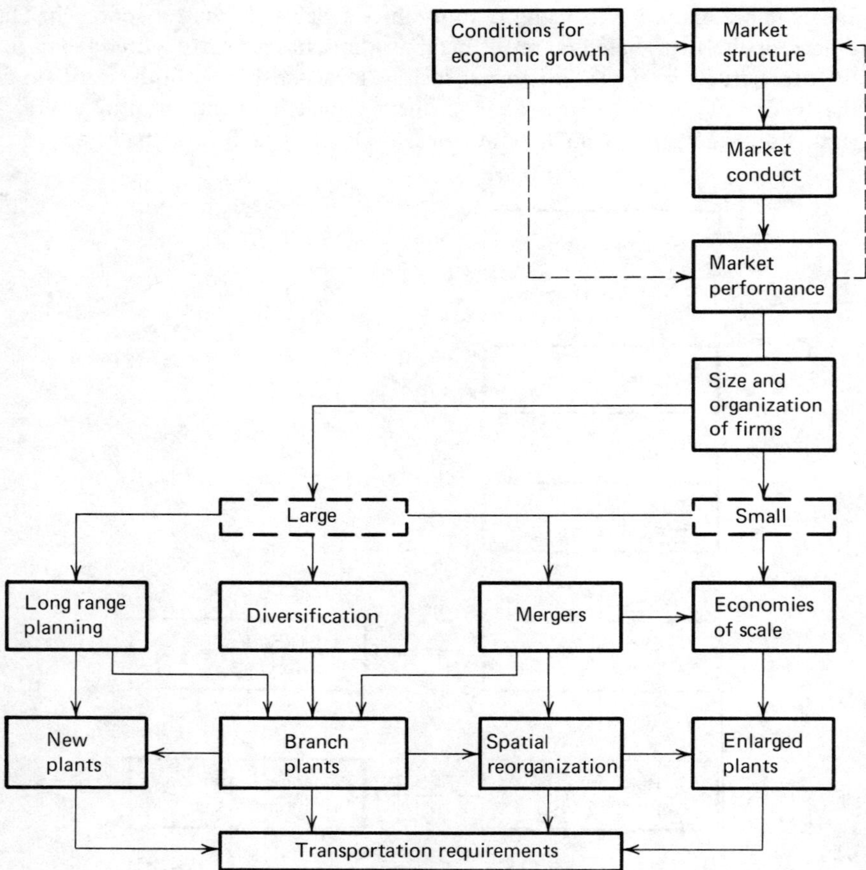

Figure 25-2. Effects of Economic Development on Regional Industrial Growth and Transportation Requirements.

13. Daly and Webber, "Growth of the Firm," pp. 303-17.

synthesis of methodological and empirical requirements between the extremes of a theoretically simple economic base study and a very complex regional econometric forecasting model. The immediate disadvantage of this synthesis would be some loss of detail from that which is obtained in a typical forecasting model. Sufficient detail should be retained with this synthesis to allow inferences of the interrelationships between activities of certain critical industries and overall regional economic growth. Furthermore, observations on fewer economic and transport variables are required to implement this approach than are needed to estimate forecasting models.

Planning agencies contemplating the construction of small-scale regional econometric models should be prepared to face a severe shortage of useful data. Although employment figures are generally available for most SMSAs,[14] various other important series (such as output, wages, and receipts) must often be constructed from fragmentary information. Even if observations are available for each variable in a particular analysis, statistical problems are likely to occur. The most prominent problem is that, since regional models must at this point in the state of the art be estimated by annual data, there will be relatively few observations and therefore few statistical degrees of freedom.[15] The principal outcome of this problem is to suggest that substantial amounts of future research be generated for exploring the impacts of selected commodity flows with quarterly data and for examining other forms of transportation activities so that the transport sectors can be linked with other subsectors in existing larger scale models.

Concluding Comments

The survey of data sources on commodity flows and economic variables discussed above should be regarded as a prelude to a more comprehensive economic analysis of the industry structures and commodity flows for states and economic regions. At the present time the ultimate objective of such a comprehensive commodity flow analysis for both the state and regional planning agencies should be to determine the most appropriate position that the planning agencies should adopt regarding the longer range transportation requirements resulting from future commodity flows. In order to reach this determination the planning agencies must optimize their positions within the constraints of their operating budgets. With a given amount of available funding, planning agencies appear to have at least four options in analyzing commodity flows: (1) to ignore them; (2) to develop *new forms of models* that would be tested with existing data; (3) to develop more *systematic sources of data* with which existing models

14. For example, see the California Base Data of the Economic Sciences Corporation, Berkeley (1974).

15. For extended discussions of econometric methods and applications, see Carl F. Christ, *Econometric Models and Methods* (New York: John Wiley and Sons, Inc., 1966), or A.S. Goldberger, *Econometric Theory* (New York: John Wiley and Sons, Inc., 1964).

could be tested; and (4) to develop some combination of options (2) and (3). Option (1) does not deal with the problem; option (2) is a high-risk venture that easily could result in no positive payoff; option (3) could be another number-collecting exercise; thus option (4) appears to be the most practical approach for planning agencies to pursue, given limited budgets, and it is the general approach on which the above comments are based. Option (4), the development of more systematic and reliable sources of information combined with some initial attempts at modeling commodity flows, also requires an infrastructure of continuous financial support and an adequate base of manpower resources—individuals who are trained in and/or dedicated to commodity transportation. Clearly, this is an appropriate long run goal.

In recent years most state and regional planning agencies have been involved in the development of procedures for the consideration of system environmental factors in transportation planning. In the process of developing these procedures, two general problems have arisen. First, in many portions of their work, the regional agencies have tended to duplicating each other's efforts. The mechanism for coordinating these procedures and disseminating ideas among regions has yet to be developed, and remains a critical need, especially in the area of commodity flows. Second, for the smaller regions who lack the manpower and resources to undertake activities for the development of sophisticated analyses, this coordination and dissemination is particularly crucial. For those regions where states are coordinating the jurisdictional activities the efficient management of these factors will be instrumental to the credibility and viability of the planning process. In addition, for these smaller regions and for other ones as well, a particular agency's contributions on commodity flow analysis can be disseminated quite effectively. This framework could be the first step toward a comprehensive regional transportation planning tool for planning agencies on the freight side of the joint commodity-passenger transportation scenario. After this first step has been taken, the planning tool for the state should be capable of incorporating planning decisions and forecasting their impacts on all the regions under its jurisdiction. The present state of the art does not suggest a series of forecasting models, but rather it provides a set of guidelines and sources of information as a potential foundation for the model development and eventual model implementation that could be crucially needed two or three years hence.[16]

16. For an integrated model system that analyzes alternative regional multimodal freight transportation infrastructures, see M.S. Bronzini et al., "A Transportation-Sensitive Model of a Regional Economy," *Transportation Research* 8 (February 1974), pp. 45-62.

26 Growth and Change in a Regional Economy: The Concept of the Critical Industry

A useful way to assess commodity flows throughout a state or within a region is to focus the analysis on the economic contributions of important industries. This kind of analysis potentially can capture the economic attributes of the leading or critical industries that require, produce, or haul commodities throughout the state or region. Ideally, one would desire data on the flow of commodities among principal origin-destination (O/D) points or between zonal pairs, but these data are rarely available. Consequently, county-to-county data can only be used to generate a regional aggregation of commodity flows. At some point in the future, though, one would hope that a series of specific O/D information be developed for commodity flows on a city-pair basis. This series would be monitored by the staff members of state and regional planning agencies and would be designed to conform with other statewide or regional data sets that are currently available.

The starting point for any survey of the field is to determine the availability and the structure of presently existing data sets. In the case of selecting critical industries, the key measures should depend on the variety of outputs and inputs that are relevant to each industry. This is not so simple a task, however, since much controversy surrounds the calculation of the optimal measures of output and input. With this lack of agreement on the dimensions in mind, an appropriate approach might involve several output measures that could then provide the basis for an initial overview of the selected industries.

The selection of the critical industries associated with commodity flows will depend on the relative "contribution" of each industry to the state's economy or to the region's economy. Clearly, the industries deemed critical should be those that contribute the most. This criterion of contribution should reflect the dollar magnitude or value of each commodity that is transported (not necessarily produced) throughout the state or region. Since these data are not yet available, one must rely on measures of dollar sales or receipts as indicators of economic contribution for specific classes of commodities.

Another criterion pertains to insuring compatibility of the data for the different industries. This criterion is intricate because the productive processes vary for each industry, quite often resulting in different units of measurement. Moreover, the intense difficulties of making interindustry comparisons are sufficiently known and documented so as to preclude a precise mapping or exact duplications of the measures for multiindustry data. One advantage of the revenue measure discussed above is that it avoids these comparative difficulties.

A final criterion is that the industries selected should be generally transport intensive. Since the ultimate objective of a commodity flow analysis is to assess long range transportation requirements, it follows that the focus should be limited to those industries that either utilize transport quite heavily (like agriculture and manufacturing) or require moderate amounts of transport for hauling relatively high-value commodities (like livestock). This criterion is especially important in view of the planning agency's need to forecast future developments in its area by transferring commodity flow data into vehicle information and finally into transportation requirements.

In order to illustrate the concept of "critical industry" in its application to the freight transportation problems of a regional economy, a case study of the regional economy encompassing six counties in southern California is presented. The remainder of this chapter discusses the general features of this regional economy and selected properties of each critical industry for the region.

Critical Industries Affecting Commodity Transportation in the Southern California Region: A Case Study

On the basis of a set of initial interviews and investigations of economic and transportation data in California, a list of fairly aggregate (similar to two-digit level SIC codes) industries was developed to reflect the most significant production of goods and services within the southern California region, hereafter referred to as the SC region.[1] This region consists of six counties, including Los Angeles, Orange, San Bernardino, Riverside, Ventura, and Imperial. Its definition as a region is consistent with the boundaries prescribed by the regional planning agency, The Southern California Association of Governments.[2]

Although the southern California (SC) region is merely a regional economy within the state of California, its "gross *regional* product" in 1974 was probably surpassed by only a few nations. In fact, the current gross *state* product of California is surpassed by only five nations (excluding the United States): U.S.S.R., West Germany, Great Britain, France, and Japan.[3] The internal structure of the SC economy is as complex as most national economies; nevertheless, several important differences stand out; first, since the region's residents are taxpayers and beneficiaries of both the state and federal govern-

1. The following discussion is based on a series of reports prepared by H.W. Bruck, James T. Kneafsey, Paul O. Roberts et al. on *Commodity Flow Analysis* for the California Department of Transportation (Sacramento) and the Southern California Association of Governments (Los Angeles) in 1974. The author gratefully acknowledges the permission to use some material from these reports to the two agencies.

2. Note that the region as defined by the Southern California Association of Governments excludes San Diego, which is considered a separate political and socioeconomic area.

3. *Statistical Report*, Statistical Office of the United Nations, 1973.

ments, the rapidly growing governmental sectors in the region must be regarded conceptually as an external sector;[4] second, its boundaries are not neatly defined as with other government units; and third, it does not exercise a particular trade policy as nations do because the region's commerce with other regions and states is barrier-free.

Twenty years ago large segments of the SC counties were heavily dependent on agriculture. While agriculture is still an important industry in several SC counties, its relative importance has been declining during the last two decades. Especially during the 1960s sharp changes have occurred in the composition of industries in the SC region, particularly in Orange, San Bernardino, and Riverside Counties. Shifts in the current composition of industries in all six counties have important land usage implications for both planning and analytic purposes; the forecasts of future changes in the industrial composition and the economic base of each SC county are important ingredients to a future comprehensive commodity flow analysis.

In recent years the most rapid growth in employment and overall economic activity in the state of California has occurred in Orange County.[5] In 1973, for example, increases in employment for that county were approximately twice the rate of increase for the whole state. As a result of this pronounced growth, the extent to which differential growth rates occur in the future in the SC counties is a topic worthy of significant economic research. Clearly the long-run transportation requirements on both rights-of-way and terminals/facilities will be affected by differential growth rates and by changes in the composition of the critical industries. Also, the industrial composition of manufacturing activity in the SC region is expected to change noticeably in the years ahead. The prominence of the aerospace industry should decline, continuing the trend that commenced around 1967. In Orange County, attempts to broaden employment in the light of manufacturing industries should diminish that county's traditional reliance on aerospace activities and alleviate the periodic economic instability that is characteristic of such dependence. In fact, while manufacturing and aerospace employment should continue to grow in the near future, the strongest growth sectors are likely to be government, services, and the trade industries. Since these latter industries may be less transport intensive than heavy manufacturing, they may require lower levels of transportation facilities or even different forms of transportation equipment.

In the 1967 report on California's economic growth, Ivan M. Lee claimed that economic forecasts ". . . require the imposition of realistic conditions and

4. This is because of the constraints imposed by a modeling of the region's economic activities. It is not possible to capture that portion of the region's flow of funds stemming from local and municipal government activities, even though in the *SC* region the magnitude is substantial.

5. See the public documents on annual averages of civilian employment in the state, published by the California Department of Human Resources.

constraints, and the development of such conditions itself would present a substantial forecasting problem."[6] In that study he specified the input-output relations (that is, the flow, stock, and primary resource coefficients) and the income-consumption relations for the state. A more comprehensive forecast for the state was provided by Pinkas Zusman's study in 1971.[7] Zusman's quantitative study explored the relationships between the state's economic development and its patterns of production and trade and between structural changes and their effects on state economic development. Such an inquiry at the SC regional level should prove fruitful, especially with the assistance of the San Francisco Federal Reserve District Bank data. However, such an effort should only be undertaken after a careful examination of the availability and appropriateness of economic information from this important source and from other forecasting groups, like the Business and Economic Research unit at U.C.L.A. To a large extent, these sources can generate county or SMSA projections on business and economic conditions, but they also possess the best sources of data on structural change in the industrial and agricultural sectors of the region.

The 1974 population of the six SC counties is estimated at approximately 10.3 million people, with the largest number residing in Los Angeles County. Demographic and economic data are available from the regional planning agencies. The current transportation and transport-related data are collected and maintained by the LARTS personnel at the State Department of Transportation (CALTRANS). The primary sources of data for passenger travel are the 1970 Census of Population and the 1967 LARTS O/D travel survey. An easy linkage to these data sets should be made for commodity flow data, especially in view of the wide range of existing censuses and private sources of information.

With the assistance of these sources of data and with the use of the above criteria to determine the selection of industries, a list was composed that included those industries deemed critical. As a first stage of a commodity flow analysis, the list is not necessarily exhaustive of critical industries but merely identifies a sufficiently large number of candidates. The critical industries selected are retail trade, wholesale trade, selected services, light manufacturing, heavy manufacturing, minerals and the extractive industries, construction, transportation, agriculture, livestock and livestock products, banking, aerospace and aircraft, petroleum, foreign trade, tourism, and government.

Each of these industries was examined from the point of view of the private sector to determine data availability and its utilization of transportation in general. In addition, public source data are documented from the perspective of the nation, state, and the six SC counties.

---

6. Ivan M. Lee, "Conditional Projections of California Economic Growth," (Berkeley: University of California, Giannini Foundation Monograph November 19, 1967), p. 1.

7. Pinkas Zusman, "California Growth and Trade, 1954-1963: An Inter-Industry Analysis Emphasizing Agriculture and Water Resource Development" (Berkeley: University of California, Giannini Foundation monograph Number 27, 1971).

For the purpose of the initial survey and interviews, an attempt was made to collect as much data, information, and suggestions as possible on commodity flows. From the published sources were tabulated the relevant and publicly available data; from interviews in the private sector some additional sources of information were indicated. The following section, then, is a summary of the data tabulations and interviews. The data and these commentaries are combined from both public sources and private source reports.

Intraregional Commerce

Commerce and business activity in the SC counties represents one of the most important categories on which to collect information. The level of business activity is greatest, of course, in Los Angeles County (more than one-half of the region's employment is centered there). Since this category is quite heterogeneous, it is desirable to separate business activity into three workable categories: wholesale trade, retail trade, and a cluster called "selected services." Each of these three categories involves a substantial amount of transportation support, mostly motor trucking. Although the majority of the activity is urban in orientation (that is, local or short-distance movements), the magnitude of business activity is quite substantial in the region.

Fuel price and availability qualify as important factors in affecting the future flows of commodities in the region, especially in regard to motor trucking. The cost to the region (and to the economy) of not having available fuel in sufficient quantity and at sufficiently low price is likely to be very large. The availability of fuel is one of the most fundamental of the transport needs because, if fuel is not available, the transport process itself will change its economics drastically. If the fuel price hikes are passed on to consumers in higher retail prices, the quantities of commodities demanded will change and the transport industries could undergo radical change as well. Likewise, if fuel prices change, there are other ramifications to the economy, in particular, the levels of wholesale trade, retail trade, and other commercial services could experience sharp declines with cutbacks in supply of materials resulting from any prolonged fuel shortages.

The most useful available information on commerce and business activity are secondary data. The best source is the 1967 Census of Business, which provides data on the number of establishments and the annual dollar sales by establishment by type of business. Industries at the two-digit level can be segmented into retail, wholesale, and other "selected" categories. While the data are available for the nation and the state, they do not exist at the county and SMSA levels.

Manufacturing

The 1967 Census of Manufactures contains more detailed data (three-digit SIC level and beyond) and is the primary source on which the Census of

Business is based. The Census of Manufactures is one of the most comprehensive data files available.

Manufacturing industries represent a very heterogeneous group of activities. From the above discussion, census data are collected for a wide range of manufacturing inputs and outputs from the two-digit to seven-digit levels. The most desirable general dichotomy for the SC region appears to be between light and heavy manufacturing. Included in the former category would be appliances, most food and grocery stores, electronics parts, household goods, and the like. In the heavy manufacturing category would be aerospace production, heavy equipment, oil refining equipment and machinery, construction equipment, and so on. Unfortunately, there are too many overlaps in the census categories to make this dichotomy useful with existing data sets. Even in the area of private sources, too much ambiguity in the various manufacturing categories precludes any precise tabulation of data. However, if there are sufficient questions about a particular manufacturing industry, private sources are superior ways to generate information.

Mineral and Extractive

Most of the nonmetallic mineral activity in the SC region occurs in Los Angeles County although scattered production occurs in the other counties as well. More important, though, are the firms extracting oil and gas. Practically all of this type of extraction is done in Los Angeles, Orange, and Ventura Counties. The data for these industries are fragmented, but, in view of the likelihood of their increasing critical features, more attention should be focused on collecting compatible information.

Construction

The construction industries are very substantial users of transportation equipment and rolling stock in the SC region. These industries would include general building construction, heavy construction operators, special truck contractors, and developers and operative builders. While new housing starts declined during 1974 and with the term structure of interest rates reflecting a rising trend, shorter range construction outlooks are often unclear. Nevertheless, the longer run prospects suggest that the construction industries, returns will be correlated with the economic growth of the region. Consequently, this section will probably continue to be a heavy user of transportation. Aggregate information on this sector can be gathered from the 1967 Census of Construction. More detailed, although sketchy, regional or SMSA data are available in the 1971 California Statistical Abstract.

Transportation

Transportation data with standard two- and three-digit SIC industry information are available from the 1967 Census of Transportation.[8] These data are segmented in four general ways:

1. By scope: national, state of California, and production area (25 in the USA)
2. By commodity class[9]
3. By mode
4. By distance shipped

This census is one of the richest sources of information in existence on the movement of commodities. Its only drawback, insofar as the SC region is concerned, is that county data are not available; but production area data are available, and in California two such areas are defined: the San Francisco production area and the Los Angeles production area.[10]

These data represent an excellent starting point for any comprehensive commodity flow analysis. The estimates of tonnage and ton-miles are based on reports collected from a sample of manufacturing establishments (firms) located in California.[11] The total tons and ton-miles represent the total intercity commodity movements by essentially all manufacturing firms in the state, except for plants with less than 20 employees. Still needed are more disaggregate flows with different forms of cross-tabulation, at county and metropolitan levels. Nevertheless, the 1967 (and 1972) Census of Transportation data tapes should be acquired by any planning agency contemplating current research in this area.

Agriculture

With the spectacular increases in the prices of many farm crops since the summer of 1973, the agricultural industry has become again a very critical industry, both at the national and state levels. This is especially true in California and in the SC

8. The 1972 Census of Transportation was not yet available for inclusion in this writing; it should be published in early 1975.

9. Only selected two-digit industries 20 through 39 are presented as being illustrative of transport intensiveness. Other industries could be added easily as conditions warrant.

10. The Los Angeles production area (#25) consists of three Standard Metropolitan Statistical Areas (SMSA): Los Angeles-Long Beach; Anaheim-Santa Ana-Garden Grove; and San Bernardino-Riverside-Ontario.

11. The estimates of tons and ton-miles in the Los Angeles production area are based on reports from a sample of shipments in 1967 by approximately 771 manufacturing establishments located in this production area. See the discussion on U.S. Bureau of Census, 1967 *Census of Transportation*, vol. III, p. 516.

region, where the values of many crops are reaching historic highs. The implications of the new trends developing in the statewide agricultural sector have widespread extensions to the future supply considerations and demand conditions for the industry. If the drought and frost conditions in the rest of the country are as serious as some agronomists suspect, the demand for many California (and SC) farm commodities could rise sharply, and eventually in future years increased supplies might be forthcoming (which, of course would require additional transport features).

In any event, this industry may be the best empirically documented of any. Numerous data are available at the *county* level, with most of the information being coordinated by the State Department of Agriculture. Also, the data available at the statewide level provide an excellent basis on which to estimate vehicle and facility requirements for this industry. Secondary data are available from the U.S. Department of Agriculture in the 1969 Census of Agriculture. These data include the number of farms, acreage, and value of commodities sold during 1969 at the national, state, and county levels; the SC region accounts for about 30 percent of all the agriculture crops produced in California, with Imperial and Riverside counties the prime growing areas.

Livestock

In terms of value of sales, the livestock industry (including poultry) in the SC region is approximately one-half the size of the agricultural industry. For the whole state, these two industries produced in 1973 a volume of $7.6 billion, which as a point of comparison exceeded the state of Michigan value of production in the automobile industry by a half a billion dollars. For the SC region, agriculture and livestock industries account for approximately $2.4 billion in sales in 1973, again with most of the activity occurring in Imperial and Riverside counties. Table 26-1 displays the values of the most important livestock and agricultural information for each SC county during 1973.

California Banking Industry

The structure of the statewide commercial banking industry in California experienced significant changes during the past decade. From a peak level of 200 banks in 1964, the number of competing banks declined primarily because of mergers and acquisitions to 144 in 1970. Since that time the number of banks has risen to 174 in 1974, with most of the growth occurring in the smaller and even newly formed banks.

The commercial banking industry in the state of California is dominated by five large banks. From the total of 174 banks chartered and in business

Table 26-1
Critical Crops and Livestock Information in the SC Counties for 1973[a]

1. Los Angeles County	
Agriculture	
Vegetables	$11,853,100
Field crops	11,850,000
Alfalfa hay	8,035,000
Livestock, Poultry, and Dairy	
Milk	$18,711,000
Turkeys	7,920,000
Eggs	5,674,000
Fed steers and heifers	5,445,000
2. Riverside County	
Agriculture	
Grapefruit	$20,388,000
Alfalfa	19,666,000
Valencia oranges	19,140,000
Grapes	18,582,000
Navel oranges	15,712,000
Lettuce	12,267,000
Carrots	11,324,000
Potatoes	10,400,000
Dates	8,894,000
Cereal grains	7,975,000
Cotton	6,755,000
Lemons	5,212,000
Livestock, Poultry, and Dairy	
Eggs	67,878,000
Milk	63,061,800
Beef	41,081,600
Turkeys	5,600,000
3. Imperial County	
Agriculture	
Lettuce	$73,200,000
Hay, alfalfa	53,424,000

Table 26-1 (cont.)

Sugar beets	31,936,000
Cotton lint	30,160,000
Wheat	26,000,000
Cantaloupes	12,504,000
Sorghum	8,280,000
Livestock	
Cattle	186,461,000

4. San Bernardino County

Agriculture	
Navel oranges	$ 8,659,200
Grapes	7,133,000
Lemons	6,009,500
Valencia oranges	5,843,300
Alfalfa hay	5,042,000

Livestock, Poultry, and Dairy	
Milk	$112,305,000
Eggs	60,172,000
Cattle and calves	21,466,000
Turkeys	9,123,000

5. Ventura County

Agriculture	
Lemons, fresh	$72,629,900
Valencia oranges, fresh	24,482,500
Celery	22,089,000
Strawberries, fresh	16,488,900
Lemons, proc	12,148,100
Lettuce	10,837,900
Miscellaneous vegetables	7,776,000
Avocados	7,638,400
Green lima beans proc	5,082,100
Beans	5,065,300

Table 26-1 (cont.)

Livestock, Poultry, and Dairy	
Chicken eggs	$15,246,900
Poultry	9,695,600
Cattle and sheep	5,181,800
6. Orange County	
Agriculture	
Strawberries	$16,452,800
Valencia oranges	11,201,700
Tomatoes	6,694,300
Livestock	
Chicken eggs	$18,012,300

[a]Includes all items with volumes exceeding $5 million during 1973.
Source: California Department of Agriculture, 1974.

throughout the state, there were 3,566 branch offices available for customers to use as of July, 1974. More than two-thirds of these offices belong to the five largest, distributed as shown in Table 26-2. Three SC area counties house the first, second, and eighth largest number of branch offices, as the distribution in Table 26-3 shows.

The five large commercial banks in California are important sources of information, data, and assistance on the production of the leading commodities. Most of the data are available on a county basis and in some cases on regional and subcounty levels. Most large banks finance the capital spending programs of the largest (and even some small) companies in the leading industries of the state. In some industries (like agriculture) virtually all the financing for new investment is through the commercial bank medium. In these industries certain kinds of data are maintained by the banks as a basis for making projections and short range forecasts. Even in the partially financed industries, the banks need to keep comprehensive information on all phases of activity so that they can be reasonably accurate about the growth of the programs that they are forecasting. While some of this information is indeed proprietary, the commercial banking data are extremely important in extending the latitude of useful information on current commodity flows throughout the state. If particular pieces of information, like annual forecasts of commodity revenues or shipments by county, are deemed necessary to add to the public information file, one possible way of

Table 26-2
California's Largest Banks

Commercial Bank	Number of Branch Offices (July 1974)
1. Bank of America	1,019
2. Security Pacific National	465
3. Crocker Citizens	362
4. Wells Fargo	300
5. United California Bank	254

Table 26-3
Distribution of California Banking Branch Offices by County

County	Number of Offices
1. Los Angeles County	1,075
2. Orange County	261
3. San Diego County	229
4. San Francisco County	206
5. Santa Clara County	184
6. Alameda County	182
7. San Mateo County	109
8. San Bernardino County	107

estimating these data is to piece together disparate bank source projections (or sufficiently aggregate counts in order to avoid disclosure) on certain types of commodity flows.

Perhaps a more important source of data, especially since it is a public agency, is the Federal Reserve District Bank of San Francisco. At this institution one can find annual data on the income and product accounts of the 12th Federal Reserve District, in which California activities are dominant. Both quarterly and monthly data on business activity can be generated by the bank's economics department. If a working arrangement between the bank and regional or state planning agencies could be set up, county estimates of different levels of business activity (akin to the critical industries) should be available.

Aerospace and Aircraft

Federal government expenditures on research and development in the aerospace and aircraft industries during the last 20 years have contributed a substantial portion to the economic growth of the SC region. In recent years, however, a general trend has been apparent of a diversification in the employment base away from aerospace and aircraft production toward light manufacturing firms, financial companies, and headquarters facilities. To a large extent the original growth of aerospace and aircraft-related firms stemmed from United States military prime contract awards. An interesting question for economic analysis to resolve is: If California could maintain a constant share of the total Department of Defense contract awards, what effects would this have on the state and regional economy?[12]

Petroleum

With the economic impacts of recent events in the energy areas creating unforeseen disorders, the importance of oil refining, natural gas exploration, and petroleum production is an unquestioned fact. Until recently data in this area were not widely scrutinized. Even now, very little data on the actual movements of petroleum products by mode of transportation are available in the SC region. The best source seems to be the U.S. Department of Interior, Bureau of Land Management (L.A. office). Other possible sources include the American Petroleum Institute (Washington), U.S. Department of the Interior, Bureau of Mines (Arlington, Virginia), Federal Highway Administration, and the California Trucking Association. Without question, this is an area in which significant, additional empirical work must be forthcoming.

Foreign Trade

The California economy can be described as a "subnational 'open' economy—a compartment in a spatially partitioned national economy—affected by federal law and administrative actions and by developments in markets outside California."[13] Nowhere are these external factors more apparent than in the foreign trade sector, which includes all exports and imports through the ports in California. Quite extensive data on foreign trade movements are maintained by the U.S. Army Corps of Engineers, by the U.S. Department of Commerce Maritime Administration, and by the State of California Department of Commerce.

In California there are three U.S. Customs Districts: San Francisco, Los

12. See W.L. L'Esperence, G. Nestel, and D. Fromm, "Gross State Product and an Econometric Model of a State," *Journal of the American Statistical Association* 29 (September 1969), pp. 798-800.

13. See B.F. Roberts, Gail Wittels, and M.H. Jorgenson, "The CEFP/CAL 4 Econometric Model of California," Working Paper, California Economic Forecasting Project, University of California, Berkeley, November, 1972, p. 1.

Angeles, and San Diego. Within each district are several ports, one of which is the headquarters port of that district. For example, in the SC region, the classification of ports in the Los Angeles Customs District (for purposes of computing United States foreign trade statistics) is shown in Table 26-4. Five-digit data on movements through the customs districts are available, although the surface modes by which these commodities are hauled are lacking. Nevertheless, the data are sufficiently broad to allow projection of movements to be made by the Army Corps of Engineers' staff members (San Francisco).

The best way to identify exports and imports of a region (or state) is to collect data directly from firms and establishments by interview.[14] Each firm can be asked to provide data on both its sales disaggregated by type of commodity and by source or origin. Obviously, this would be an enormous task in terms of energies, manpower, and costs, although it does represent an appealing path for a more comprehensive analysis on commodity flows, especially in a large region like southern California.

Tourism

According to the Chambers of Commerce in both Los Angeles County and the city of Los Angeles, tourism is the *state's* third largest industry with expenditures in the SC region alone approximating $2 billion in 1973. Data are rather fragmentary for the tourist industry, however, largely because of the multiple facets of what "tourism" means. Also, the industry's use of commodities (and

Table 26-4
The Los Angeles Customs District

Code Number	Port
04	Los Angeles (headquarters)
07	Port San Luis (including San Luis Obispo)
09	Long Beach (including Huntington Beach, Newport Bay)
11	El Segunda
12	Ventura
13	Port Hueneme
15	Capitan
19	Morro (including Estero Bay)
20	Los Angeles International Airport

14. This is especially true in the case of surface commodity flows across the Mexican border. Calexico, in Imperial County, for example, is an important exchange point for imports and exports in the SC region.

their resulting transportation requirements) is very substantial, but it is quite cumbersome to measure. Nevertheless, the Southern California Visitors Council has been able to estimate the *number* of tourists to southern California for the last six years:

1968–7,882,000
1969–8,185,000
1970–8,248,000
1971–7,599,000
1972–8,144,000
1973–8,444,000

Forecasting the future numbers of tourists and their impacts on the existing transportation system is an exercise independent of commodity flow analysis. However, because of the industry's relative importance in the SC economy, and because of the spillover effects on the commodities and services necessary to support this industry, its impacts on overall transportation requirements should not be overlooked.

Government

While the government sector (federal, state, and municipal) is not necessarily heavily involved in commodity flows, it nonetheless is a huge and growing sector of the region's economy. In fact, in most private forecasts of the region's economy, this sector is expected to be the most rapidly growing over the next 10 to 15 years, especially in Orange and Los Angeles counties.[15]

Transportation Planning Implications

One of the most intriguing fields of study in transportation planning is the analysis of modal choice. When this analysis is extended to the area of commodity flows, the interest becomes greater. Why do shippers choose one mode of transport instead of another? What levels of service do they demand? And how do they value them? If the precise answers to these questions were readily known, then the state of the art in transportation would be improved immensely. At one time the common practice was to assume that shippers always chose the lowest cost form of transportation available. This view slowly became refined to indicate minimum transport cost by minimum total distribution cost. This latter cost is a more complex concept that broadens transport costs beyond simple freight charges to include the marginal costs of insurance,

15. See Bank of America's "Focus on Orange County," San Francisco, June 1974.

loss and damage, warehousing, and interest. Regardless of which cost concept is appropriate, however, it behooves the planning agencies to develop the capability to assess the impacts of the interactions of the shippers, carriers, and users of commodities in the future.

A useful analysis of commodity flows in regions like southern California has important transportation planning implications for state and regional planning agencies. With a changing funding program in prospect during the next 10 years and with the need for the continually judicious allocation of expenditures by the federal government and by state and local planning agencies, the selection of specific programs to finance becomes a crucial issue. Regional planning agencies naturally have quite limited budgets so that a focus on only the most significant transportation issues in the next decade becomes all the more compelling.

Among the primary concerns in transportation system planning are the predictions of passenger and vehicle movements and the provision of the facilities necessary to support these movements. In order to predict these movements accurately, separate estimates of passenger and commodity demands are necessary. These demands can then be transformed into vehicle demands that then affect the rights-of-way and terminals/facilities necessary to support them. Consequently, the answers to the really important question: "What are the forecasts for a region's (or a state's) transportation requirements over the next 5 to 20 years?" can be solved through the process of derived demand. In other words, the facility requirements depend on the demand for and supply of vehicles and their attributes, which in turn depend on the demand for travel by passengers and the wholesale and retail demands for commodities. It is only this latter area of inquiry that has been the subject of the above short case study. In any event, no derived demand study is possible (crude or otherwise) without adequate data, thus explaining the empirical focus of the discussion. Furthermore, only after determining the suitability of the data available on commodity flows by the truck, water, rail, and air modes should the planning agencies embark on a formal modeling research program.

27 Transportation and Logistics

The general commodity common carrier (for-hire) trucking firm is engaged primarily in less-than-truckload (LTL) shipments. The profitability range for such firms is in hauling shipments between 500 and 10,000 lbs. with the average shipment in the order of 1,500 lbs. Because of the generally small size shipments of general commodities, most trucking firms may not be competing with the railroads that carry large amounts of carload traffic.

A more significant competitor to the railroad industry is not the motor common carrier firm, but the large group of owner-operators, most of whom own only a single tractor and trailer.[1] A precise estimate of their numbers is difficult, but a safe guess is in the range of 250,000. These owner-operators are principally interested in the truckload (TL) business rather than the LTL traffic of the general commodity common carriers.[2] These owner-operators are estimated to produce in the range of 100 to 180 billion ton-miles annually, or perhaps two-fifths of the total motor trucking intercity ton-miles.[3] Since much of this traffic is exempt commodity TL tonnage with reduced rates (comparable to rail rates), most of the owner-operator's business appears to be cost competitive with the railroads rather than service competitive with the regulated motor trucking firms.

Another 40 percent of the total motor trucking intercity ton-mile market is estimated to be handled by private carriers. These are firms that haul their own goods through internally owned corporate subsidiaries. In many cases these carriers attempt to balance their loads by seeking exempt commodity traffic for backhauls that would otherwise be deadhead movements. Much of the traffic gains by private carriers have resulted from the diversion of tonnage from the railroads, and further shifts in modal shares can be expected if railroad branch line abandonments and trackage shrinkage continue.

1. See D. Daryl Wyckoff and David H. Maister, *Owner-Operators in the Motor Carrier Industry* (Lexington, Mass.: Lexington Books, D.C. Heath and Co., 1975).

2. The owner-operators fall into three general classes: the independents who haul TL traffic exempt from regulation; those who contract with common carriers for specified periods; and those on long-term leasing arrangements with specialized carriers that haul large amounts of single commodities like steel, motor vehicles, refrigerated items, and petroleum products.

3. Ibid.

The Case of Agriculture

The current transportation of agricultural commodities is an extremely important issue of both macro and microeconomic policy. The advancements in grain production, stemming largely from the development of wider agricultural export markets, have required a reappraisal of various features of the transport of these commodities from the farm through the distribution channels.

Accompanying the rise in agricultural acreage and production are the advances in harvesting techniques that have enabled farmers to move large quantities of grain and livestock to nearby markets. The traditional method of grain movements was to a local elevator that was usually located on a rail branch line. If the elevator operator was faced with too much grain, the spillover was either stored outside or transported to a larger "terminal" elevator. For many years the problems of rail transportation from the local to terminal elevators has been compounded by the shortage of boxcars (and often the inadequacy of existing cars). Further accentuating the change in grain marketing practices has been the more extensive use of motor trucking and barge transportation as competitors with railroad movements. A more recent complication from new export business has been the congestion occurring in the transfer of grain movements from domestic carriage to ships at certain major ports around the country. These substantial (yet basically simple) transportation problems need to be resolved, especially in view of the critical importance of United States agricultural export revenues that are necessary to partially offset current petroleum imports.

The current outlook in the agricultural industry appears quite favorable for United States' farmers as recently passed legislation becomes effective.[4] The Agriculture and Consumer Protection Act of 1973, signed into law on August 10, 1973 provides a "target price" support plan for grains and cotton for the four years of 1974 to 1977 inclusive. While the new plan maintains average allotment and price support loans, it is significantly different from the previous system of price supports and cash payments for diverting crop land from production. The new farm law represents an historic turning point in agricultural program philosophy. It now will focus on expanding output after years of curtailment and shrinking of the agricultural plant. With shortages rather than surpluses dominating the early 1970s, a huge expansion in grain production (both nationally and internationally) may be in prospect during the next three to five years.[5] If this prospect is realized, even partially, significant increases in the util-

4. Of course, demand factors (both domestic and international) and supply conditions (largely dependent on weather events) ultimately determine the final wholesale price of each commodity.

5. Nevertheless, the 1973 legislation does provide for restrictions on output that would be imposed in the event of real or threatened surpluses. The most important feature of this legislation is that the farmer will sell his crops in the free market for existing prices. If his average prices fall short of the legally established targets (which currently are well below

ization of transportation equipment will be required. The fundamental questions, however, are: What will the modal split of the traffic be and how efficient can the carriers move this traffic?

Part of the solution may be derived from merely analyzing the process of freight car movements (especially for agricultural products). A measure of relative inefficiency of railroad industry practices thus can be illustrated by the utilization pattern of freight cars. Figure 27-1 portrays a typical freight car utilization example: From a national average car cycle (in 1974) totalling 25.6 days, only 14 percent of the average car's time is involved in the line haul portion of its operation of which 33 percent is spent in intermediate operations; 29 percent is occupied at a railroad's terminal operations at points of origin/destination and 23 percent is used at the shipper's siding. The length of time which a freight car spends in switching yards at both terminal and intermediate points is far in excess of the physical time actually required in performing the switching and classification operation.[6] Surely this is a major source of both "excess capacity" and network unreliability in the industry.[7]

During the period 1975-79 a unique program of providing 60,000 additional box cars to be built for the railroad industry was established. These standard 50-foot box cars are the result of the so-called RAILBOX plan to alleviate some

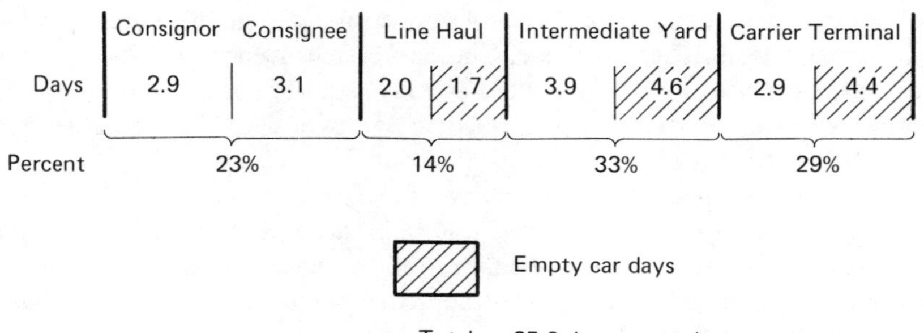

Figure 27-1. A Typical Freight Car Cycle, 1974. Source: U.S. Department of Transportation, "Rail Service in the Midwest and Northeast Region," Federal Register 39, no. 30 (February 12, 1974), p. 5403.

market prices; for example, the target price for corn is $1.38 per bushel while the December 1974 cash corn price was $3.80 per bushel, and the February 1975 cash corn price was $3.05 per bushel), the U.S. Department of Agriculture will pay him the difference, with the total cash payment being limited to $20,000 per farmer.

6. The time required is a function of the yard characteristics, but normally terminal switching (or classification) requires less than 30 minutes per car and intermediate switching and classification less than 10 minutes per car.

7. See the M.I.T. *Studies in Railroad Operations and Economics*, vols. 1-15.

of the perennial shortages of viable rolling stock equipment that has plagued the industry for many years, particularly the western portion of the country, and particularly in the grain belts.

Logistics

The economic trends that have occasioned a drift from railroads to highway transportation, a national phenomenon particularly pronounced in the Northeast, have been reviewed elsewhere.[8] Aside from the dislocations imposed by energy constraints and business cycles, the prospects are strong that these trends will be sustained and possibly even accelerate. Among these factors the most important are the increased processing of goods and a shift from lower to higher value commodities. It is quite probable that the more actively growing sectors of the past and forseeable future create marginal rail transport demand. Furthermore, as the structures of cities have changed with the growth of peripheral areas, railroad terminals have been left in congested and undesirable areas while motor trucking has shown to be much more flexible in its terminal location decisions.

While the total cost concept of logistics has grown rapidly in recent years as inventory and other distribution costs mounted, it is by no means generally applied. In other words many firms and shippers are still shipping these products with incomplete logistical analyses. The basic repetitiveness of these allocative decisions, without benefit of the logistics audit required for distributions system redesign when appropriate, is well documented by a decision process study of several large Pittsburgh firms.[9]

Transportation market developments in recent years have been largely attributable to exogenous forces that lead to predictable modal shifts. However, there are other dynamics that may be foreseen by which shippers could adjust to endogenously imposed changes. One approach is the redesign of distribution systems (rather than straight rail-to-truck transfers), which would in many cases ameliorate the adverse effects of any switch of modes. Such redesign might incorporate an increased number of distribution warehouses, with long interregional hauls by rail and further distribution within the region by truck. Other accommodations might result in plant relocations. The relatively greater efficiency of truck transport for shorter hauls of finished products might dictate as a longer run accommodation, a stronger market orientation, and a corresponding diffusion of manufacturing. For the Northeast, for example, this approach could

8. See Richard J. Barber, "The American Railroads: Posture, Problems, and Prospects," in *The Penn Central and Other Railroads*, Committee on Commerce, U.S. Senate, 92nd Cong., 2nd Sess. (Washington, D.C.: U.S. Government Printing Office), pp. 224-34.

9. Merrill J. Roberts and Associates. *Intermodal Freight Transportation Coordination: Problems and Potential* (University of Pittsburgh: 1966).

create a system of interregional rail transportation of raw and semifinished materials and the intraregional truck delivery of finished products. The production reorientation envisaged for the longer run would generally be geared to gain maximum locational advantage from trucking capabilities. Such relocation is not a drastic development but occurs regularly throughout the economy and in response to many forces other than transportation.

Each transportation mode varies widely in important qualitative attributes of its service outputs as measured by such dimensions as elapsed time of a shipment, required packaging outlays, completeness of the service (door-to-door), schedule frequency, and schedule reliability. Transportation provides the movement components of distribution systems and is thus integrated with the other components that include production scheduling, inventory control, packaging, customer servicing standards, and storage. The most efficient transport component optimizes the system as a whole by achieving the lowest overall total distribution costs to minimize the sum of the transport charges and the associated nontransport expenses. Since this objective is not necessarily achieved by the lowest cost transportation, this is the consideration that frequently warrants the payment of premiums for truck service.

An abstract example of the application of the total cost principal can be advanced by reference to two such highly differentiated products as computing equipment and crude oil, with their hypothetical logistics configurations portrayed in Figure 27-2: In both of these situations, in spite of the great differences in the relationship between the logistic element costs, the indicated switch is to a configuration that involves a higher expenditure for improved transportation and a more than proportionate drop in inventory costs.

There are a number of technologically based ways in which overall distribution cost savings can potentially be affected by the use of truck instead of rail services. Except for rare cases of the shipment of unusually large items that cannot be accommodated by trucking there are apt to be few circumstances where the nonmovement components of distribution systems would be adversely affected. Accordingly, the maximum unfavorable impact is likely to be the difference in transport charges that evidence demonstrates to be modest in many cases. It is even more likely that for many shipments the cost premium would be more than offset or at least ameliorated by other distribution cost advantages. Furthermore, the major contemporary problem of railroad industry rationalization and its possible elimination of rail service could result in structural changes in production, distribution, and motor trucking operations that would further ameliorate the impact.

Car Utilization

Free interchange of freight cars throughout the United States is a key factor in the ability of railroads to produce efficient transportation. In no other industry

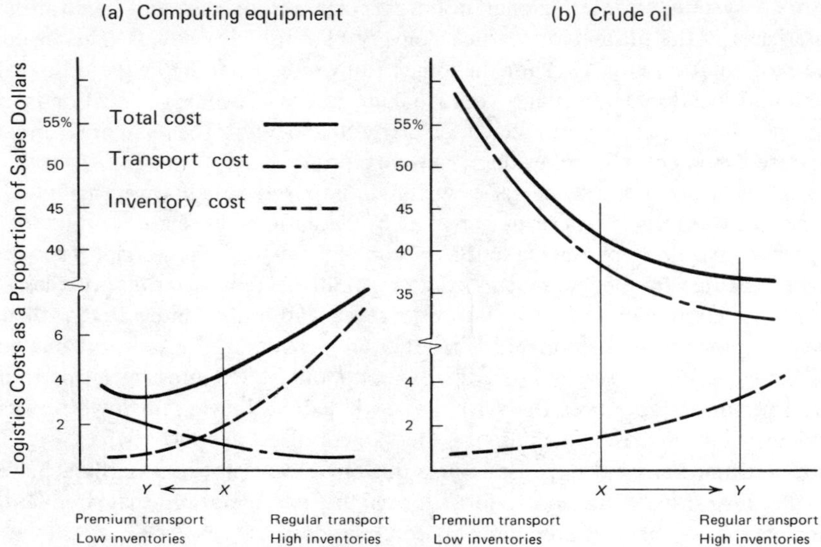

The relative costs (hypothetical) of various transportation and inventory alternatives for the distribution of computing equipment (a) and crude oil (b).

Figure 27-2. Alternative Transportation-Inventory Configurations. Source; James L. Heskett, Nicholas A. Glaskowsky, Jr., and Robert M. Ivie, *Business Logistics–Physical Distribution and Materials Management*, 2nd ed., p. 48. Copyright © 1973 The Ronald Press Company, New York.

are the production tools and capital investment so freely exchanged with competitors since most freight cars are completely compatible on any line on almost any train. However, there are some specialized cars with characteristics that exceed the certain basic restrictions that have been placed on car designs. These limiting dimensions of a freely interchangeable car have been specified by the Association of American Railroads as:

Maximum height: 15'6" above the rail
Maximum width: 10'8"
Minimum clearance of truck, brake rigging, and car body:
2 1/2" above the rail (effective January 1, 1980, the minimum clearance is increased to 2 3/4" above the rail)[10]

Many railroad personnel rue the advent of the specialized car and long for the

10. Association of American Railroads, *Interchange Rules*, Rules 88-A-1 and 88-B-1.

return of the general-purpose car. Container cars, for example, can be general-purpose cars, to be used in captive, "fixed-consist" service with high load factors. Many commodities, furthermore, are hauled more efficiently in containers than in conventional railroad cars. An improved car service must begin with a timetable and involve minimum intermediate handling. Quite often, though, a shipper with some clout can convince the railroad to hold a train for his load or can procure some other service. The result is that the supply of gondolas or other cars farther down the line suddenly becomes short. For any particular railroad on any given day, there always seems to be a shortage of cars. This perennial car shortage has had an interesting and complex impact on the resale market for used cars—namely, that the prices of rebuilt equipment have not been significantly different from the prices of new equipment. Table 27-1 shows a variety of uses and features for several major classes of railroad cars. An example of equipment costs is presented in Table 27-2.

The proportion of loaded to total car-miles hauled annually by railroads has been declining during the last three decades.[11] While the reasons for this decline are various, the observed increase in coal and mineral shipments is not a sufficient explanation. Rather, a better reason appears to be the continual shift from general-purpose equipment, such as standard box cars and open hoppers, to these special-purpose box cars, covered hoppers, rack cars, and refrigerator vehicles.[12] This process of investment in specialized equipment has continued at an accelerating rate at the expense of the fleet of general-purpose rolling stock that has borne an increasingly aged condition. Since these specialized vehicles are designed to carry some type of traffic for which the chances of return loading are slim, the ratio of loaded to total car-miles is bound to decrease. Aside from the shift of attention away from the general-purpose rolling stock, additional dangers loom for the industry if the lack of balance between outward and return flows of freight is not reflected in the rate structure, as it is in ocean transportation. In addition, the absence of official data on modern developments such as containerization complicates the task of analyzing these trends in the detail that they warrant.

In any case, the pure logistics (or physical distribution management) problem boils down to the interactions among consumers, shippers, and carriers. The focus of logistics is on the supply-demand paradigm faced by the shipper for maximizing his profit. Such an equilibrium set of variables is illustrated in Figure 27-3.

---

11. This ratio has fallen from 0.67 in 1946 to 0.56 in 1973 for the industry as a whole. For individual companies the variation has been greater; in fact, some companies in 1973 even experienced ratios less than 0.50.

12. See Roger D.H. Jones, "Another Nail in the Railroad Coffin," *Transportation Research* 7 (December 1973), pp. 413-19.

Table 27-1
Markets for Used Railroad Cars

Type of Freight Car	Resale of Operable Equipment: Primary Buyers (Railroads)	Resale of Operable Equipment: Secondary Buyers – Industrial	Secondary Buyers – Others	Sale of Scrap Equipment: Salvage	Sale of Scrap Equipment: Scrap
Box Cars	U.S. railroads; Private car companies (North American Car and General American Car); Canadian and Mexican Railroads.	Industries with their own car fleet (lumber and food industries); automotive industry for transportation of parts interstate and intraplant.	Small number for use as storage sheds, garages, etc.	Wheels & trucks, air brake equip., draft gear & couplers; cushion underframes.	Cast steel, structural steel, plate steel.
Gondolas	U.S. railroads (steel and steel products carriers); captive steel railroads (Union Railroad, Birmingham Southern, B. & L.E.).	Large heavy industry for in-plant service (steel, motor, and paper companies); large scrap dealers for in-plant service.	Small number for storage bins and bulk material containers.	Same as above.	Same as above.
Flat Cars	Other class I railroads (carriers of extra dimensions and heavy machinery); Private car companies for refurbishing and resale or lease to other railroads.	Heavy industry for intra and inter plant service (General Electric, Westinghouse, American Bridge).	Small number for ramps and platforms of various kinds.	Same as above.	Cast steel, structural steel.
Hoppers	U.S. railroads–primarily handlers of coal, ore, sand, and gravel; captive steel railroads for revenue and non-revenue service.	Coal producers, light and power companies who have their own fleets of cars (Consolidation Coal Company, Commonwealth Edison).	None	Same as above.	Cast steel, structural steel, plate steel.

Covered Hoppers	U.S. railroads–very much in demand for transportation of grain, flour, sugar, lime, cement, etc.; private car companies.	Large grain, food, and cement industries with their own car fleets; steel industry for intra plant use.	These cars are so much in demand they would never get to an "other" use.	Same as above.	Same as above.
Auto Rack Cars (Bi and Tri Level)	U.S. railroads–automobile carriers; private car companies for refurbishing and lease or resale to other railroads; Canadian National and Canadian Pacific Railways.	Manufacturers of racks; for resale or lease to other railroads; trailer train company.	None.	Wheels & trucks, same as above except: cushion underframes (on cars only).	Cast steel, structural steel (on the
Cabooses	U.S. railroads; limited sale of modern cabooses.	None.	Wooden Caboose is popular for cabanas, guest houses, and restaurants.	Wheels & trucks, air brake equip., draft gear & couplers; cushion underframes; stoves; cushions, communication equipment.	Cast steel, structural steel, plate steel.
Refrigerator Cars	U.S. railroads; mechanical type only. Private car companies.	Large food companies (Campbell Soup, General Foods, Kelloggs, etc.). Probably would only buy the insulated box type.	None.	Same as above.	Same as above.
Tank Cars	Private car companies for few remaining in railroad ownership.	Industries using tank cars (chemical, oil companies).	Storage tanks either under or on top of ground.	Same as above.	Same as above.
Stock Cars	Private car companies for few remaining in railroad ownership.	Some kosher meat packers own a few cars or lease them (Cross Brothers).	Occasional sale to circuses for animal transport.	Same as above.	Same as above.

Source: Compiled from data collected by Simpson and Curtin, Inc. and by Temple, Barker and Sloane, Inc. (February 1975).

Table 27-2
Selected Railroad Equipment Costs, 1975

	1975 Cost	Estimator
Boxcar (50 foot, 70 ton, class A)	$23,000	Norfolk & Western
Flatcar (60 foot, 100 ton, general service)	21,000	Norfolk & Western
Track evaluation car (diesel, self-propelled)	350,000	Union Pacific
Metroliner car (produced by Budd Co., Inc.)	410,000	Amtrak[a]
PATH subway car	250,000	PATH

[a]See also Association of American Railroads, Information Letter No. 2145 (November 6, 1974).

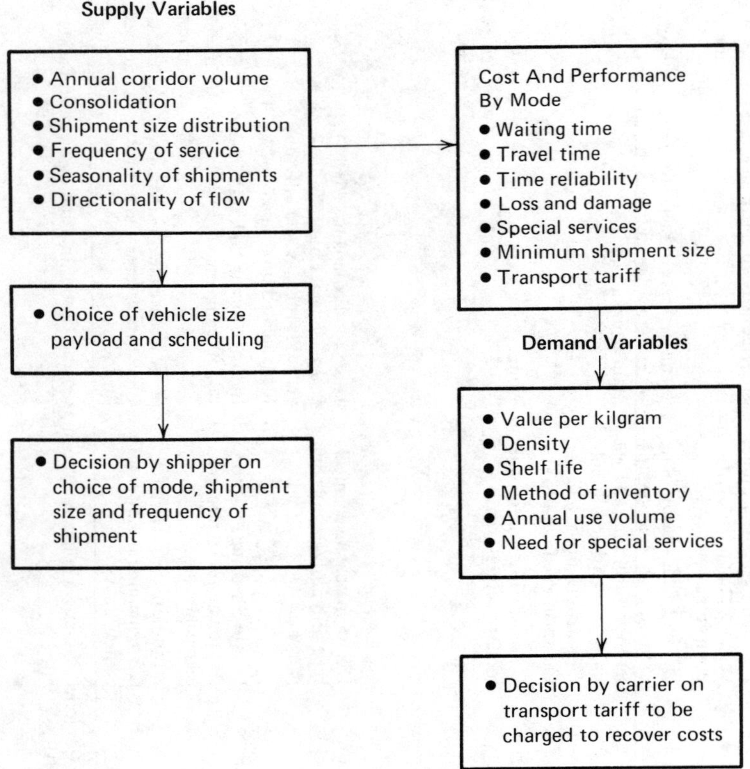

Figure 27-3. Supply-Demand Equilibrium for Freight Transportation.

Selected Bibliography: The Commodity (Freight) Sector

Chisholm M. and P. O'Sullivan. *Freight Flows and Spatial Aspects of the British Economy* (Cambridge, England: Cambridge University Press, 1973).

Highway Research Board. *Urban Commodity Flow*, Special Report 120, 1971.

Hille, Stanley J. "Urban Goods Movement Research—A Proposed Approach," *Traffic Quarterly* 21 (January 1971), pp. 25-38.

McQue, Robert. "Cargo Vehicle Productivity," *Management Science* 18 (October 1971), pp. 836-51.

Milkius, Walter. "Estimating Freight Traffic of Competing Transportation Modes: An Application of the Linear Discriminant Function," *Land Economics* 45 (May 1969), pp. 267-73.

O'Sullivan, P. and B. Ralston. "Forecasting Intercity Commodity Transport in the U.S.A." *Regional Studies* 8 (August 1974), pp. 191-95.

U.S. Bureau of the Census, Census of Transportation 1963, vol. 3. *Commodity Transportation Survey*, pts 3 and 4 (Washington, D.C.: U.S. Government Printing Office, 1966).

U.S. Bureau of the Census, Census of Transportation 1967, vol. 3. *Commodity Transportation Survey* pt 2 (Washington, D.C.: U.S. Government Printing Office, 1970).

U.S. Department of Commerce, Maritime Administration. *Domestic Waterbourne Shipping Market Analysis: Executive Summary* (Chicago: Kearney-Management Consultants, February 1974).

Walters, A.A. *Integration in Freight Transport* (London: The Institute of Economic Affairs, 1968).

Walter, C.K. "Measuring Pick-Up and Delivery Cost for Small Shipments," *Transportation Journal* 14 (Fall 1974), pp. 51-56.

Watson, Peter L., James C. Hartwig, and William E. Linton. "Factors Influencing Shipping Mode Choice for Intercity Freight: A Disaggregate Approach," *Proceedings of the Transportation Research Forum* 15 (October 1974), pp. 139-44.

Part VI: Microeconomic and Econometric Applications to Transportation

28 The Estimation of Cost Functions in Railroad Operations

The dominant characteristic of a railroad's operations is its multiple-service function. Included in these multiple services are freight and passenger service, yard and line-haul service, bulk and less-than-carload commodities, perishable and merchandise traffic and terminal services. In many studies of railroad costing, the extent of joint operations and fixed cost has involved a heavy reliance on statistical estimates of railroad cost.[1]

As we have seen from earlier discussions, one of the primary difficulties specifying a production function for railroad operations is to separate out the freely individual from the joint effects. Once the appropriate level of specification is determined in the production function then plausible and accurate estimates of cost can be made.

Numerous costing methods have been used at various times and for various purposes by transportation analysts. In fact, in very few other industries have different techniques of costing been experimented and pioneered. This is largely due to the inherent difficulties of costing the joint service operations that so abound in the transportation industries.

The traditional method for estimating a long-run cost function is to fit the following relationship over a cross section of firms:

$$TC = \alpha + \beta Z \tag{28.1}$$

where TC is a vector of total cost observations, Z is a vector of output observations (such equations sometimes contain more than one output variable), and α and β are the intercept and slope, respectively. These equations usually are assumed to be linear, but sometimes they are log-linear or have a squared output term. For this procedure to yield a long-run cost function, it is necessary to assume that each firm in the sample adjusts all its inputs so as to minimize costs. In the case of the railroad industry, there is reason to doubt that this is being done, simply because of the indivisibility of the railroad plant, and because of the lags in the regulatory process in the adjudication of proposed track

1. For a synopsis that shows the inaccuracies of the ICC's costing formulae, see Zvi Griliches "Cost Allocation in Railroad Regulation" *Bell Journal of Economics and Management Science* 3 (Spring 1972), pp. 26-41.

abandonments.[2] As a result, the railroad plant is in many cases likely to be overbuilt, with a cumulative cost of excess capacity. Nevertheless, there does exist the possibility of differentials in track quality, especially when railroads suffer declines in tonnage.

Production function analysis in the railroad industry is complicated not only by the fixity and indivisibility of the physical plant but also by the variety of services provided using that plant. A study of railroad costs must recognize this multiple-product (service) nature of the railroad firm.[3]

In this chapter, two separate types of output are specified for the analysis: gross ton-miles of freight service and gross car-miles of passenger service. More output variables are desirable and can be incorporated but some simplification is necessary to make estimation feasible as a first attempt. In general, it can be argued that passenger and freight services are provided according to separate production functions, but they have one very important element in common: both use the same physical plant, which is fixed. If the amount of physical plant available to a railroad firm can be measured in terms of track mileage, then two separate production functions can be specified relating each type of output to inputs unique to it and to the track services allocated to it. With fixed trackage, this yields a joint short-run cost function for both types of output (passenger and freight).

To derive such a short-run cost function, assume a modified Cobb-Douglas production function, with no restriction on returns to scale. The production functions for freight and passenger services can then be written, respectively, in the following deterministic forms:

$$Z_f = AT_f^{\alpha_1} R_f^{\alpha_2} F_f^{\alpha_3} L_f^{\alpha_4} \tag{28.2}$$

and

$$Z_p = \beta T_p^{\beta_1} R_p^{\beta_2} F_p^{\beta_3} L_p^{\beta_4} \tag{28.3}$$

where Z_f and Z_p represent gross ton-miles of freight and passenger services, respectively, L represents labor input, F represents fuel input, R represents rolling stock input, T represents plant input (track and related structures), and the subscripts f and p refer to factor inputs allocated to freight and passenger

2. One of the problems in using data collected from the proceedings of abandonment proceedings is that the railroad companies tend to overestimate the costs of the services that they are proposing to abandon.

3. For this reason, microeconomic theory texts that deal with the characteristics of multiproduct forms are better references than the more traditional ones. For example, see Thomas Naylor and John Vernon, *Microeconomics and Decision Models of the Firm* (New York: Harcourt, Brace & World, Inc., 1969).

service, respectively.[4] The short-run problem for a railroad firm is to adjust fuel, rolling stock, and labor to each service in order to minimize costs for any output level and to allocate the services of the fixed factor, trackage, between the two outputs to minimize costs. Since the railroads are regulated common carriers, they must carry all traffic at existing regulated rates; hence it is feasible that they treat output as exogenous and attempt to minimize costs. Mathematically, the problem is as follows: Minimize

$$TC = r_1(T_f + T_p) + r_2(R_f + R_p) + r_3(F_f + F_p) + r_4(L_f + L_p) \tag{28.4}$$

subject to equations (28.2) and (28.3) as constraints, plus the additional constraint that

$$T = T_f + T_p \tag{28.5}$$

where the r's represent rentals on the various factors and T is the fixed amount of trackage for a given railroad. The solution to this minimization problem can be derived through one grand Lagrangean expression. While the mathematics are presented elsewhere, suffice it to say that the procedure involves the separate derivations of short-run cost functions for freight and passenger service, assuming given allocations of trackage, and then a joint derivation of a short-run cost function from these two separate ones. The long-run cost function for each service can be derived from the short-run cost functions by differentiating short-run costs with respect to both outputs, by applying first order conditions, and solving for Z_f and/or Z_p.

A more condensed version of this specification is to treat capital as the fixed input with fuel and labor as the variable ones. Assuming that the empirical difficulties of imputing an appropriate measure to capital are not burdensome, the condensed forms of the production functions would be

$$Z_f = AK_f^{\alpha_1} F_f^{\alpha_2} L_f^{\alpha_3} \tag{28.6}$$

and

$$Z_p = BK_p^{\beta_1} F_p^{\beta_2} L_p^{\beta_3} \tag{28.7}$$

4. This adaptation is treated in Theodore E. Keeler, "Railroad Costs, Return to Scale, and Excess Capacity: A Neoclassical Analysis," Working Paper No. 35, Department of Economics, University of California, Berkeley (April 1973); and his more recent "Railroad Costs, Returns to Scale, and Excess Capacity," *Review of Economics and Statistics* 56 (May 1974), pp. 201-8.

where Z is an output measure, and K, F, and L represent the inputs of capital, fuel and labor, respectively. The subscripts f and p indicate the portions of output and inputs related to freight and passenger operations. Since railroad managements have treated passenger service as a different function from freight operations, the assumption that there are separate production functions for these services again appears reasonable.

The short-run objective for any railroad company then is to adjust fuel usage and labor utilization to each service in order to minimize costs for any output level and to allocate the fixed factor, capital, between the two outputs so as to minimize costs. So as to minimize costs subject to equations (28.6), (28.7), and

$$K = K_f + K_p, \tag{28.8}$$

the objective is to minimize

$$TC = r_1 (K_p + K_p) + r_2 (F_p + F_p) + r_3 (L_p + L_p) \tag{28.9}$$

By setting up the augmented functions for the two sectors f and p:

$$G_f = r_1 K_f + r_2 F_f + r_3 L_f + \lambda_1 (Q_p - AK_f^{\alpha_1} F_f^{\alpha_2} L_f^{\alpha_3}) \tag{28.10}$$

$$G_p = r_1 K_p + r_2 F_p + r_3 L_p + \lambda_2 (Q_p - BK_p^{\beta_1} F_p^{\beta_2} L_p^{\beta_3}) \tag{28.11}$$

find

$$\frac{\partial Z_f}{\partial F_f}, \frac{\partial Z_f}{\partial L_f}, \frac{\partial Z_f}{\partial \lambda_1}$$

Solve for optimal F and L:

$$F_f^* = C_1 Q_f^{1/e} K_f^{-\alpha_1/e} \frac{r_1}{r_2}^{\alpha_2/e} \frac{r_3}{r_2}^{\alpha_3/e} \tag{28.12}$$

$$L_f^* = C_2 Q_f^{1/e} K_f^{-\alpha_1/e} \frac{r_2}{r_3}^{\alpha_2/e} \frac{r_2}{r_1}^{\alpha_3/e} \tag{28.13}$$

where

$$C_1 = \left[A \frac{\alpha_1}{\alpha_2}^{\alpha_1} \frac{\alpha_3}{\alpha_2}^{\alpha_3} \right]^{-1/e}$$

$$C_2 = \left[A \left(\frac{\alpha_2}{\alpha_3}\right)^{\alpha_2} \left(\frac{\alpha_1}{\alpha_3}\right)^{\alpha_3} \right]^{-1/e}$$

and

$$e = \alpha_2 + \alpha_3$$

Now, since

$$SRTC_f = r_1 K_f + (C_1 + C_2) r_2^{(\alpha_2/e)} r_3^{(\alpha_3/e)} Z_f^{(1/e)} K_f^{-(\alpha_1/e)} \tag{28.14}$$

set $\dfrac{\partial SRTC_f}{\partial K_f} = 0$ and solve for K_f

substitute K_f into $SRTC_f$, yielding:

$$LRTC = d_1 Z_f^{(\alpha/\beta)} \tag{28.15}$$

where

$$\alpha = 1/e = 1/(\alpha_2 + \alpha_3)$$

$$\beta = k/e = \frac{(\alpha_1 + \alpha_2 + \alpha_3)}{(\alpha_2 + \alpha_3)}$$

Equation (28.15) then is the long-run total cost function that expresses cost as a (non)linear function of output. This particular specification ignores the influence of passenger operations even though they appeared in the earlier steps of the derivation. If passenger operations were regarded significant, then a joint function would result from the combination of equation (28.14) and its passenger counterpart. Also, in this specification the fixed factor is capital, which can be allocated more reasonably between freight and passenger sectors than can trackage, if instead the model was represented by equations (28.2) and (28.3).

User Costs

Variable costs include "any sacrifice of future value or any future realization of higher costs that are causally attributable to present production."[5] This latter

5. See Alfred E. Kahn, *The Economics of Regulation: Principles and Institutions*, vol. 1 (New York: John Wiley & Sons, Inc., 1970), p. 71.

portion of variable cost is labeled "user cost," which is the loss in the net value of a firm's assets to its participation in production in lieu of not participating in production during any given time period. It may be measured as the discounted, present value of the additional expected yield that could be obtained from the productive facilities if they were not used now.[6]

Summary

In recent years the increased interest in economic analysis applications has brought about improvements in the specifications of industry production functions. These developments have contributed to better explanations of industrial behavior and simultaneously have provided a necessary basis on which to estimate cost relationships, particularly in the railroad industry. Put simply: A cost function is only meaningful if something is known about its linkage to the underlying production function. This linkage will be discussed more thoroughly in the next chapter.

---

6. For the classic statement of user cost, see John Maynard Keynes, *The General Theory of Employment, Interest and Money* (New York: Harcourt, Brace & Co., 1936), pp. 52-55 and 66-73.

29 The Use of Production Function Analysis

Productivity and performance are key variables on which regulatory commissions and governmental agencies should have a large impact of a change in the supply side of transportation operations.[1] The general problems associated with productivity measurement, interpretation, and explanation are the subject of an extensive literature. The wide-ranging works of W.E.G. Salter[2] and John W. Kendrick[3] in the early 1960s have provided a foundation for analyzing and developing improved productivity and performance measures. The usual approach in the analysis of performance measures and productivity change has been to focus on the time-honored but "partial" (Kendrick's term) productivity ratio of output per unit of labor input (in person-years or person-hours). At a later stage of his analysis, Kendrick used the more general ratio of output per unit of total factor input (combined labor and capital input). Either ratio can be useful in measuring the saving in inputs over time due to all causes, but it cannot measure the total change in productive efficiency. Such change is affected by shifts in the composition of total factor input as factors are substituted for each other when relative factor prices and the techniques of production change over time.

Using an aggregate production function approach, Edwin Mansfield in 1965 estimated the annual productivity increase in the railroad industry at 3 percent.[4] In a more recent series of studies, Paul H. Banner and his associates at the Southern Railway have investigated the problems of measuring productivity in the railroad industry.[5] They reexamined the specification of input and output

1. On November 26, 1974 the ICC sponsored a "Productivity Measurement Conference" in Washington. The focus of this conference was on measuring rail and motor carrier productivity and developing the appropriate data sources to measure such productivity. While the policy results of the conference were disappointing, it was an important event in terms of regulatory history since it signified for the first time a comprehensive approach to the economic analysis of the *sources* of productivity change in transportation.

2. Salter, W.E.G., *Productivity and Technical Change* (Cambridge, England: Cambridge University Press, 1960).

3. Kendrick, John W., *Productivity Trends in the United States* (Princeton: Princeton University Press, 1961).

4. Mansfield, Edwin, "Technical Change in the Railroad Industry," *Transportation Economics* (New York: National Bureau of Economic Research, 1965).

5. Paul H. Banner, "Utilization of Capital and Labor in the Railway Industry," Transportation Engineering Conference, AMSE (Washington, D.C.: 1968); his "Output per Manhour in the Railway Industry," presented at the Transportation Research Forum (Denver: November 1972); and his "The Measurement of Productivity in Rail Transportation," presented at the Annual Meeting, ASME (Denver: September 1973).

measures in the railroad industry and generated some new ones that essentially represented composite measures of output like weighted car miles, carloadings, and train miles. In all cases the notion of an underlying production function process was implicit.

These considerations lead naturally to the perception that the production function underlies each meaningful analysis of productivity change. In spite of formidable difficulties that are simultaneously conceptual, theoretical, and practical, and that stem from the currently incomplete state of both the theory of production and of the knowledge of input and output flows, it is considered essential to suggest an interpretive treatment of productivity flows in transportation operations. This treatment would include the fitting of a set of production functions to existing data for each of the transportation industries. An interpretive treatment of shifts in productive efficiency would not, however, be fully explanatory of such movements in the railroad industry. Rather, it would be a first stage analysis providing estimates in quantitative terms of the distribution of the several sources of a given amount of movement of unproductive efficiency. Beneath these sources lie the fundamental causes that also can be subject to explanatory analyses and to empirical testing.

Inasmuch as any transportation system consists of a number of subsystems or parts that have some common objectives and functions operating effectively, a system's efficiency can be measured by its technology and its cost, time, and responsiveness to particular needs. The most important fact underlying this technology is that productivity change reflects the major source of industrial, and particularly railroad, economic growth.[6] The basic method employed in reaching this conclusion is to compare the rate of growth of output with a weighted average of growth of inputs. The difference, or residual, is customarily assumed to be the rate of productivity (or technical) change.

Performance measures in the historical sense (using time series, cross-sectional, or pooled data) typically have provided a basis only for making crude comparisons among different sets of operators (industries or firms, generally). They do not in and of themselves reflect any measurement of causality, either in the sense of how a set of inputs affects output within the same industry or in the sense of how operating practices of one transportation enterprise affect the performance of other contiguous ones. They do, however, provide a critical foundation on which causality can be imputed through the linkage of a set of production and cost functions.

The crucial linkages among outputs, inputs, and their performance are illustrated in Figure 29-1, which is a flow chart depicting the theoretically

6. Early works suggesting this result in the aggregate include: Moses Abramovitz, "Resource and Output Trends in the United States Since 1870," *American Economic Review Papers and Proceedings* 4 (May 1956), pp. 5-23; Robert M. Solow, "Technical Change and the Aggregate Production Function," *Review of Economics and Statistics* 34 (August 1957), pp. 312-20; Kendrick, *Productivity Trends*; and Edward F. Denison, *Why Growth Rates Differ* (Washington, D.C.: The Brookings Institution, 1967).

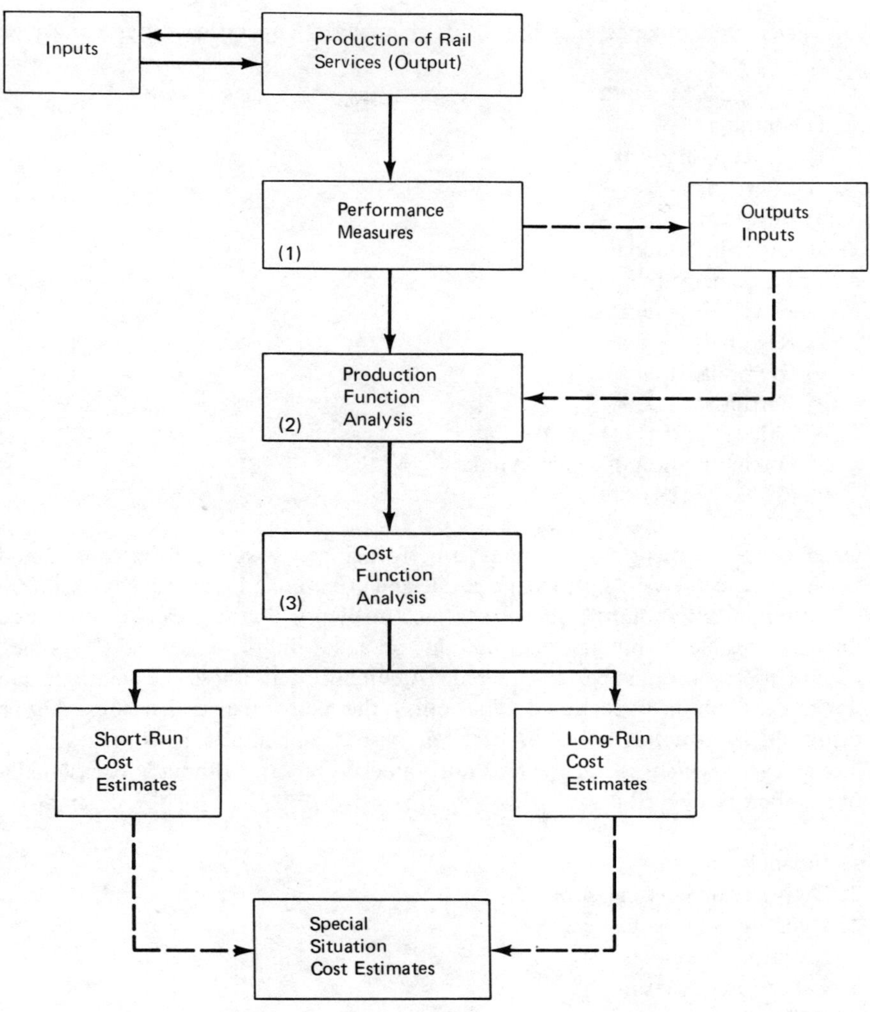

Figure 29-1. Linkages Among Inputs, Outputs, Production, and Cost.

correct way to estimate costs in railroad operations. Cost functions usually depict cost as a function of output, whereas performance measures merely are ratios of outputs to inputs. The production function, however, is necessary to specify the behavioral relationship between these outputs and inputs; it is the crucial linkage relationship and is discussed in the following section.

A fairly broad coverage of literature has been devoted to various aspects of performance measures, particularly in the railroad industry. In order that any given performance measure be usable, several operating criteria must be determined:

1. The industry
2. The level of analysis
   a) Interfirm
   b) Intrafirm
3. Modal or intermodal
4. The time period
5. The level of aggregation
   a) Regional
   b) Divisional
   c) Corridor
   d) Link-specific (O-D pair)
      (1) Summation of selected links
      (2) Network-specific

Once these specifications are made, a performance measure can be constructed by selecting a relevant output and input and combining them (usually as a ratio of output to input) into a single measure. In theory this step can be conducted on all possible combinations, but in practice only the set of "feasible" combinations should be considered. Assuming that these calculations are undertaken on cross-sectional data only, the performance measures can be displayed as a matrix of ratios between output and inputs, as is suggested by Table 29-1, which is segmented into nine different (although occasionally overlapping) categories:

1. Financial measures
2. Disaggregate cost measures
3. Operations measures
4. Inventory measures
5. Labor force measures
6. Reliability measures
7. Energy measures
8. Environmental measures
9. Accessibility measures

These items are discussed in detail elsewhere but are presented here merely to be suggestive of the direction in which an analysis of improved performance measures could lead.[7]

These major measures represent the following dimensions of activities: finance, disaggregate expense, operations, inventory, labor force, reliability,

7. For the most recent evidence on this topic, see H.W. Bruck and James T. Kneafsey, "Toward a Generalized Structure of Transportation Service Measures," *Papers and Proceedings of the Transportation Research Forum*, 15 (October 1974).

Table 29-1
Selected Transportation Performance Measures

Financial Measures: Operational	Inventory Measures
Total operating revenue	Number of power units
Total operating expenses	Vintage of power units
Total operating income	Number of transport units
Net operating income	Vintage of transport units
Working capital	Number of terminals/yards
Operating ratio	Vintage of terminals/yards
Financial Measures: Consolidated	Number of new units purchased
Total revenue	Number of refurbished units
Total expenses	Number of inoperative units
Total income	Percentage of equipment leased
Net income	Reliability Measures
Rate or return on investment	Variance of unit arrivals
Rate of return on stockholders' equity	Variance of unit departures
Cash flow	Variance of running time
Disaggregate Cost Measures	Number of misconnections
Investment in fixed plant and equipment	Delay minutes
Terminal expense by category	Frequency of delay
Yard expense by category	Loss and damage payments
Line haul expense by category	Energy Measures
System expense by category	Total amount of fuel consumed
Operational Measures	Total cost of fuel consumed
Total revenue tons (passengers)	Total BTUs consumed
Total revenue ton-miles (passenger-miles)	Environmental Measures
Unit miles	Pollutant emissions per unit mile
Unit hours	Noise levels per unit
Average length of haul	Accessibility Measures
Average speed per unit	Number of SMSAs served
Unit loadings (loading and unloading efficiency)	Percent of SMSAs served
Labor Force Measures	Total population of SMSAs served
Number of employees by type	Capacity of parking facilities available
Man-hours worked	Public transportation available
Man-hours paid for	

energy, environment, and accessibility. Each category or measure can be subdivided into more detailed components and then into its basic elements. The following discussion highlights these major measures and some selected components and elements of major importance to the specification and understanding of the flow chart that appears in Figure 29-1.

Financial Measures. These measures represent the managerial and monetary performances of firms and enterprises providing transportation services. The measures reflect the traditional balance sheet and income statement entries as prescribed by standard business firm accounting practices. Financial measures suggest a specific dimension of performance (and ultimately of service) by focusing on the basic incentive of all business enterprises: profit.

The measures can be divided into two components: operational and consolidated. Operational financial measures pertain to only those areas of the enterprise that relate to strictly transportation operations, like operating revenues and operating expenses. Consolidated financial measures are more comprehensive since they cover all phases of the agency, including noncarrier investments. Items like rate of return and cash flow are extremely important measures of performance, but their uses must be treated with caution: for example, rates of return can be sharply different depending on their respective denominators.

In the operational financial measures, two widely used entries are working capital and the operating ratio. Working capital is a standard term, representing the difference between current assets and current liabilities, and is comparable across modes. Operating ratio, however, is more modal specific. It is the ratio of operating expenses to operating revenues and is reported as such in the trucking industry; it also can be calculated easily for the other modes.

Disaggregate Cost Measures. In a certain sense, these measures are subsets of the expense measures discussed above (operational or consolidated). Yet, these measures appear sufficiently important to justify a separate analysis. Annual investment expenditures reflect an extremely valuable measure by itself. The other measures are disaggregated into the four principal levels of transportation activities: terminal, yard, road (or line-haul), and system. The purpose of this categorization is to focus on particular sectors of the transportation system as a method of isolating problems and as a basis for deriving alternative statistical constructs.

Operational Measures. These measures depict the strict operations of the transportation system. For example, in Table 29-1, total revenue ton-miles (the second line item under Operational Measures) could be calculated for any mode and could be split between common and contract carrier movements. In the case of passenger volumes, total revenue passenger miles would be the sum of the number of X revenue passengers transported Y miles by rail, bus, or air modes (and auto, if it were included). In general, these measures refer to the physical activities of the transportation system and are to be distinguished from purely financial and economic (cost) measures.

Inventory Measures. These measures are related to the stock of capital that transportation companies and enterprises own or lease in order to offer their transportation services to shippers and to the public. The measures simply pertain to the quantity of units and to their average age or vintage. Their purpose is to focus on the amount of power available and the degree of obsolescence of the equipment—a logical source of productivity and quality of service.

Labor Force Measures. These measures indicate the number and types of employees available to transportation firms and enterprises. A general division can be made between management and union workers or between operating and nonoperating employees. An important distinction is between person-hours worked and person-hours paid for; the former is useful as an input to the amount of time actually worked (as an input to productivity), whereas person-hours paid for includes fringe benefits, work rule practices and other nonwork time which contractually represents an expense to the firm. With the exception of rail data collected by the ICC data for these two person-hour measures do not appear to be available yet for the other modes.

Reliability Measures. Reliability might be the most significant variable affecting shippers' choice (and possibly passengers' choice in commuter and urban travel) as suggested by several shipper surveys. Unfortunately, very little data are available on the variable, except from company sources.

Energy and Environmental Measures. These measures are published for all common carrier modes and represent the amount of energy consumed, its cost, and its by-products. A need for data relating these measures to the automobile mode is a task of the Department of Transportation or the Federal Energy Administration.

Accessibility Measures. A necessary requirement for future empirical information on improved performance measures is the acquisition of accessibility measures. A thorough investigation of SMSA, SEA, county, and regional frameworks is required in order to assess the best estimates of accessibility measures. Most of these data are readily available. Any presently unavailable or newly required data might be generated through existing institutions like the Federal Reserve District Banks, real estate development associations, railroad terminal companies, private nonprofit research groups, and industrial development agencies of state governments.

The Estimation of Production Functions

The production function is one of the basic tools in the modern theory of economic growth. In recent years the increased interest in this subject has brought forth improvements in the specifications of industry production functions that have contributed to a better explanation of industrial behavior and simultaneously have provided a necessary basis for estimating long-run costs relationships. Since the efficient long-range development of operational measures in each transportation industry requires reliable forecasts of future production and cost patterns, current research should provide the best methodological basis on which these forecasts can be made. Recently, a wide variety of methods ranging in sophistication from simple linear models to more elaborate multiplicative functions have been developed and tested by a M.I.T. research team to estimate productivity and costs in the railroad industry.[8]

The estimation of production functions is becoming a frequently used procedure for identifying the growth component attributable to progress in all industries, including transportation.[9] A production function describes the maximum quantity of output obtainable from any quantitative combination of the physical inputs that are included in the function. If Q represents output, L stands for labor input, K for capital input, and E for an energy input, then a production function may be written as $Q = f(L,K,E)$. Quite obviously, this measure requires estimates of both inputs and outputs and of the behavioral linkage between the two in the form of the coefficients of the production function.

There are at least three principal reasons for suggesting a production function approach. The first is the general desirability for accuracy, precision, and clarity to facilitate scientific analysis. A second and related reason concerns a particular objective: if it is known a priori why performance in transportation operations should be measured, then it is easy to decide what kinds of measures of inputs and outputs are appropriate. Statistical testing then becomes the means by which this appropriateness is determined. A third reason for being concerned with the production function approach relates to the infrastructure of general cost analysis and to the estimation of cost functions.[10] The statistical estimation of cost functions has been in the strict sense an empirically evasive effort in spite of the literature being replete with different sorts of estimation attempts. The chief reason for a paucity of meaningful estimates is that rarely are the cost functions related to the behavioral properties of the productions from which the cost functions can be derived. In past studies researchers, in their haste to relate costs to output, ignored the theoretical and practical linkages between production functions and output and between production functions and costs.

Conventional microeconomic theory describes the importance and requirements of specifying production functions prior to the estimation of costs. Expressed simply, it is essential that the appropriate form of a production function for each industry or firm (that is, the behavioral and statistical relationship between output and input) be specified before any meaningful costs can be estimated. In other words, accurate cost functions can be derived only when each underlying production function is specified and when certain assumptions (such as cost minimization) are maintained. As an example, the

8. James T. Kneafsey, "Costing in Railroad Operations: A Proposed Methodology," M.I.T./F.R.A. Studies in Railroad Operations and Economics, vol. 13, March 1975.

9. See for example M.L. Adenson and A.J. Stoga, "Returns to Scale in the U.S. Trucking Industry," *Southern Economic Journal* 40 (January 1974), pp. 390-96.

10. See again the excellent article by Zvi Griliches, "Cost Allocation in Railroad Regulation," *The Bell Journal of Economics and Management Science* 3 (Spring 1972), pp. 26-41.

M.I.T. study investigated the specification and empirical testing of six alternative forms of production functions for railroad operations at the interfirm level of analysis in which published ICC and AAR data were used.[11] The deterministic versions (that is, excluding error terms) of these production functions are the following:

Linear	$Z = A + a_1K + a_2L + a_3E$
Log-linear	$Z = AK^{a_1}L^{a_2}E^{a_3}$
Cobb-Douglas	$Z = AK^{a_1}L^{a_2}E^{a_3}$ where $a_1 + a_2 + a_3 = 1$
Constant elasticity of substitution	$Z = A\,[\delta K^{-\rho} + (1 - \delta)L^{-\rho}]^{-\nu/\rho}$
Embodied technical change	$Z = A(e^{\lambda}K^{a_1})L^{a_2}E^{a_3}$
Disembodied technical change	$Z = Ae^{\lambda}(K^{a_1}L^{a_2}E^{a_3})$

where

Z = output measure

A = intercept term (efficiency measure)

K = capital input

L = labor output

E = energy input

λ = rate of technological change

δ = distribution parameter

ρ = substitution parameter

ν = homogeneity parameter

a_1, a_2, a_3 = elasticities of output with respect to the respective inputs.

The analysis was conducted on particular input/output measures for, first, class I railroads in the southern region (southern district) as published by the Interstate Commerce Commission in *Transport Statistics in the United States: Part I, Railroads* for the years 1962 and 1972, and second, for specific internal data provided by one railroad in that district. Separate statistical procedures were employed for road-haul and yard operations on the assumption that production and cost functions underlying these respective activities manifest differing characteristics. As a starting point, ton-miles-revenue freight-road service was selected as the measure of output. Inputs for the road and yard analyses were chosen on the basis of two criteria—the availability of data that could be

11. Kneafsey, "Costing in Railroad Operations."

differentiated between these respective functions and a capability to allocate the data among capital, labor, and energy.

Relationship Between Short-run and Long-run Cost Functions

The most popular form of production function model has been the Cobb-Douglas function, which is a special case of the CES form.[12] Using isoquant analysis, the relation between the long-run and short-run cost functions can be shown graphically.[13] In order to derive these functions for the Cobb-Douglas production function form, one can consider a single-product, two-input competitive model, as depicted in Figure 29-2, which illustrates the derivation of the expansion path *OP* for this model. The expansion path in Figure 29-2 is nonlinear to indicate the general case; yet, if the production function is homogeneous, the expansion path must be a straight line.

The path *OP* is a long-run expansion path. In considering the analogous function in the short run, that is, a "short-run expansion path," the quantity of factor K (capital) is held to be fixed at $\bar{K}$ and the horizontal line $\bar{K}S$ then defines the short-run expansion path. To increase output in the short run, the firm can only increase the quantity of L (labor) since K is fixed at $\bar{K}$.

Long-run and short-run cost functions may be derived by an examination of the long-run and short-run expansion paths. The long-run expansion path *OP* in Figure 29-2 provides the information for the long-run cost function as does the short-run path $\bar{K}S$ for the short-run cost function. For example, one point on *OP* is the tangency between isoquant Z_2 and isocost line C_2 that is plotted in Figure 29-3 when total cost is measured vertically and total output horizontally. Plotting all other points on the long-run expansion path *OP* results in the long-run cost function *LRTC*.

The same procedure may be performed for the short-run function: that is, transfer the cost-output values defined by each point on $\bar{K}S$ in Figure 29-2 to Figure 29-3. The result is the short-run cost function *SRTC*. In Figure 29-2 the two expansion paths have one point in common; that is, the intersection point that corresponds to an output of Z and a cost of C_2. In Figure 29-3 this same

12. Since its introduction in 1928, no single form has been more widely used. The reasons for this are several: It is simple to explain; it is a plausible form in that it displays constant returns to scale (which happens also to be the dominant empirical observation in transportation) and diminishing returns to an input; it is relatively easy to handle in connection with questions of aggregation; and it is easily estimated by standard regression techniques.

13. A good reference on this topic is James M. Henderson and Richard E. Quandt, *Microeconomic Theory* (New York: McGraw Hill, 1958), which has been one of the more definitive works in microeconomics during the last decade. Also, a text that I have used in teaching is Thomas H. Naylor and John M. Vernon, *Microeconomics and Decision Models of the Firm* (New York: Harcourt, Brace & World, Inc., 1969).

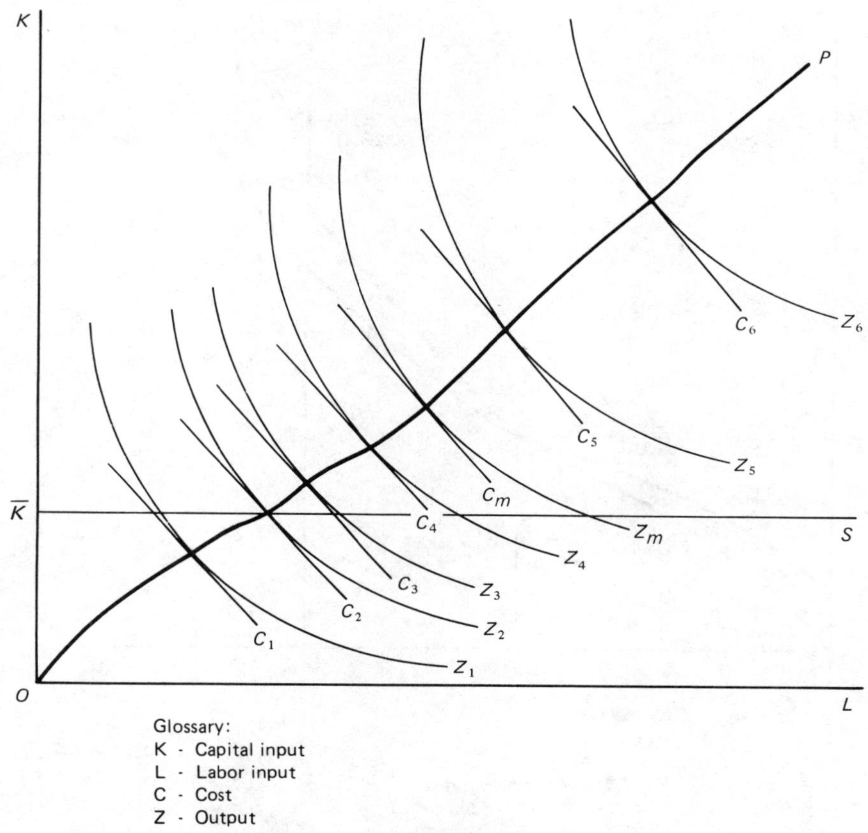

Figure 29-2. The Derivation of the Expansion Path *OP*.

point is the tangency point between *SRTC* and *LRTC*. At all other output levels *SRTC* exceeds *LRTC* since in the long run all inputs are variable with each level of output produced at minimum possible cost. In short run, however, the firm does not have perfect flexibility, and is constrained by the invariability of input *K*.

Several properties of Figure 29-3 are interesting. The short-run cost function has a positive intercept on the *C* axis, while the long-run function begins at zero. This reflects the fact that fixed costs exist only in the short run. Also, *SRTC* becomes vertical at an output level of *Zm*, while *LRTC* begins to increase. The explanations for these two phenomena are quite different. The *SRTC* function rises because of the law of diminishing returns, that is, with the application of more and more *L* to the fixed quantity of the other factor $\overline{K}$, whereas the *LRTC* function rises because of the assumption that decreasing returns to scale occur at relatively high output levels.

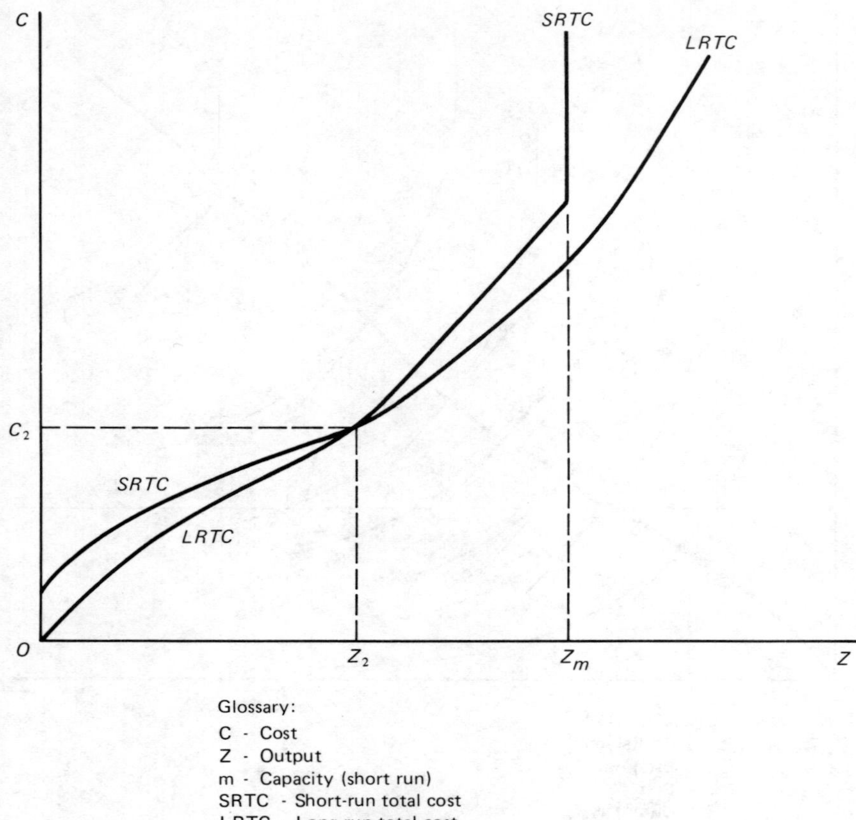

Figure 29-3. Cost Equilibrium.

Concluding Comments

Statistical cost and production function estimates of transportation operations must be interpreted and used with caution. Limitations on publicly available data restrict empirical cost estimates to applications only for generalized situations. While it is extremely difficult to obtain cost estimates for specific operations, it is important to obtain average or typical cost figures that may be used for the broad purpose of managerial regulatory policies.

The cost coefficients in some statistical studies in the railroad industry, in particular, represent estimates of railroad cost characteristics for operations conducted under average operating conditions and may directly affect regulatory problems and costing. The influence of variables excluded from any analysis will be consequential if the factors have a systematic effect on the costs. Even should such systematic, nonrandom factors modify the results, the influence may be accommodated by making slight procedural adaptations or by including additional information about the cost structure in order to transform averages into estimates better suited to special situations. Rough adjustments for the systematic influence of omitted variables can be made by observing any consistent tendency in the statistical errors of estimate. Also, if something is known about the form of the production function and about the approximate ordinal magnitude of cost differences for separate output or fixed capital input categories that have been aggregated into one variable in the cost analysis, then deviations from the norms can be accounted for by recomputing the values of the outputs or the inputs. Regardless of the data available for a particular study, it is anticipated that the methodology employed in this chapter by linking the features of productivity, production functions, and cost functions should provide a better rationale once a more effective set of guidelines for the empirical investigator of transportation operations. At minimum, one's appreciation for the actual meaning (and difficulties of) production and cost should be enhanced.

30 Economies of Scale in the Railroad Industry

The railroad industry has fallen into the doldrums not because the need was filled by competing modes, but because it was not filled by the railroad companies themselves. In case after case the railroads allowed traffic that they could have maintained to slip away to other modes, partially because the managerial philosophy in the industry focused on a strictly railroad orientation theme rather than on transportation service. A fundamental question prevails concerning the extent to which railroad managements are to blame for the limitations placed on the railroad companies to expand freely into other modes of transportation by the Interstate Commerce Commission's interpretations of existing transport legislation.[1] Research studies in recent years generally support the concept, originally introduced in the famous *Doyle Report*,[2] of allowing more intermodal mergers and combinations on a provisional basis.[3] Yet, these recommendations are not based on any empirically strong evidence that would suggest larger enterprises being more efficient (and thereby more profitable). In fact, insufficient research has been devoted to the impacts of changes in market structure on efficiency in the principal transportation modes. Neither the industrial firms nor the regulatory agencies have developed a framework for determining whether each of transportation industries is operating under a position of economies of scale or diseconomies of scale. This topic is very important because of both its empirical fascination and its policy implications.[4]

Fundamental to any analysis of the structure of the American transportation industries is this issue of economies of scale. During the past two decades the economics literature has been replete with controversy over how to measure industrial economies of scale (and not only in transportation). There seem to be two basic problems: first, what the precise meaning of scale economies is[5]—whether it should apply to the industry, to the firm, or to the plant (or

1. A thorough analysis of the federal government policy toward intermodal ownership appears in Robert C. Lieb, *Freight Transportation: A Study of Federal Intermodal Ownership Policy* (New York: Praeger Publishers, 1972).

2. *National Transportation Policy*, U.S. Senate Report 445, 87th Cong., 1st Sess. (1961).

3. Lieb, *Freight Transportation*.

4. The traditional policy implications for decreasing cost industries (that is, economies of scale) have been the justification for subsidies and the demands for marginal cost pricing.

5. The conventional interpretation of "scale economy" refers to the points to the left of the minimal position of the long-run average cost function, whereas "returns to scale" refers to the reaction in percentage terms of a change in output to a proportionate change in *all* corresponding imports simultaneously. The latter term implies an underlying production function methodology of stricter terms than that of economies of scale.

subdivision of the firm); and second, how to impute the various sources of scale economies within the industry, firm, or plant to internal factors such as line-haul operations, management, hierarchical levels of organization, and technological diffusion. Various empirical attempts in the literature have dealt with the first problem reasonably well,[6] but refinements on the second problem are still lacking.

The pioneering study for measuring scale economies in the railroad industry has been provided by Kent J. Healy[7] who used correlation analysis to relate the size of the railroad firms and its rate of return. More specifically, he considered five different size groups (large to small) and three different measures of size[8] to infer a positive relationship between smaller size firms and a higher rate of return; that is, the higher the rate of return for a given railroad, the more likely it would be in a smaller size group. Furthermore, he argued that any sized railroad exceeding 10,000 employees was likely to experience diseconomies of scale.

Other studies in that era concentrated on the estimation of cost functions for specific rail operations. Most noteworthy are those by George H. Borts[9] and John R. Meyer's group at Harvard.[10] More recent analysis of rail cost functions have been developed by Robert E. Gallamore,[11] Thomas G. Moore[12] and Zvi Griliches.[13] Other cost studies that rely on underlying production function theory have been presented by Theodore E. Keeler[14] and James T. Kneafsey.[15] The general conclusions emanating from these studies is either that most of the evidence suggests constant returns to scale in the railroad industry, or that there is no significant evidence indicating strongly positive scale economies. The only exceptions are certain economies for individual railroad firms, for certain

6. See Kent T. Healy, *The Effects of Scale in the Railroad Industry*, (New Haven, Conn.: Yale University Press, 1961); Theodore E. Keeler, "Railroad Costs, Returns to Scale, and Excess Capacity," *Review of Economics and Statistics* 56 (May 1974), pp. 201-8; and John R. Meyer, Merton J. Peck, John Stenason, and Charles Zwick, *The Economics of Competition in the Transportation Industries* (Cambridge, Mass.: Harvard University Press, 1959).

7. Healy, *Effects of Scale.*

8. Assets, number of employees, and operating revenues.

9. George H. Borts, "The Estimation of Rail Cost Functions," *Econometrics* 28 (January 1960), pp. 108-31.

10. Meyer et al., *Economics of Competition.*

11. Robert E. Gallemore, "Railroad Mergers: Costs, Competition, and the Future Organization of the American Railroad Industry," Ph.D. diss., Department of Economics, Harvard University, 1968.

12. Thomas G. Moore, *Freight Transportation Regulation* (Washington, D.C.: The American Enterprise Institute for Public Policy Research, 1972).

13. Zvi Griliches, "Cost Allocation in Railroad Regulation," *The Bell Journal of Economics and Management Science* 3 (Spring 1972), pp. 26-41.

14. Keeler, "Railroad Costs."

15. James T. Kneafsey, "Costing in Railroad Operations: A Proposed Methodology" M.I.T./F.R.A. Studies in Railroad Operations and Economics, vol. 13, March 1975.

line-haul and terminal operations, and even perhaps for regional operations (although no adequate empirical tests are yet available).[16] It is anticipated that some additional light will be shed on this matter in the future with the linkage of cost and production function methodologies, especially on those suggested in the recently completed studies mentioned above.

If the "aggregate" production function for the railroad industry is homogeneous of the first degree, this does not imply that each company views *its* production function as the same kind of function. Each railroad is concerned only with those factor inputs, or other conditions affecting costs, over which it can exercise control; and it can regard its production function as being obtained from the underlying more aggregate production function by assigning constant values to the variables over which it has no control in given situations. Hence, it is possible to consider rising long-run cost curves for individual railroads and therefore to argue the existence of limits to the size of rail companies.

Most of the empirical studies of the average and marginal cost curves of individual firms that have appeared in the literature have used cross-sectional contemporaneous-accounting data for different firms or plants with the intention of demonstrating information on economies of scale. Some of these studies have suggested that the cost curves are horizontal over the usual range of output. Limited advances have occurred as a result of these applications, partly because the nonexistence of single, homogeneous product lines causes the observed phenomena to be inconsistent with the theoretical constructs, and partly because the theory itself does not present a strong reason to expect that cross-sectional data will yield the relevant cost curves.[17] But this does not imply that cross-sectional studies necessarily will yield results inconsistent with what the theory purports.

Admittedly, cross-sectional analyses may provide at best a weak verification of scale effects, but they clearly provide useful information on other problems of interest. It is essential to remember why information is wanted with respect to economies of scale. If we wonder what size rail company has minimum costs (and define minimum costs in a way where it is required that the company achieve it), the answer would be: companies of existing size. A strong case can be stated that in any industry, in which the resources used cannot be regarded as unspecialized, there will tend to be firms of different size. So what may be sought is not an "optimum size of firm," but an "optimum distribution of firms by size." Some companies clearly have lower unit costs than others. The purpose here is to suggest a possible way to determine the minimum point of the long run average cost curve for the industry.

16. James T. Kneafsey, "Mergers, Technical Change, and Returns to Scale in the Railroad Industry," *Proceedings of the Transportation Research Forum* 13 (November 1972), pp. 439-58.

17. Milton Friedman argues that the problem is that the proper questions have not been asked of the data on the costs of firms of different sizes. See his *Price Theory* (Chicago: Aldine Publishing Co., 1962), pp. 139-44.

The statistical method employed to approximate the net relationship between railroad size (scale) and per employee cost would naturally be multiple regression. The data would be cross-sectional, based on selected class I railroads. The regression equation would include the following variables:

X_1 = operating expenditures per employee
X_2 = number of employees (middle of the month count)
X_3 = tractive effort (thousands of kilograms)
X_4 = ton-miles
X_5 = percentage of locomotive fleet and car fleet built or new since 1957.
X_6 = bad order ratio
X_7 = change (percentage) in number of employees between any five year period

such that

$$X_1 = a_0 + (b_{11}X_2^2 - b_{12}X_2) + cX_3 + (d_{11}X_4^2 + d_{12}X_4) + (-eX_5)$$
$$+ fX_6 + gX_7 + u \qquad (30.1)$$

including expected signs.

Parabolic relationships between per employee cost and size and between cost and ton-miles are assumed. The relations between cost and the other independent variables are all assumed to be linear. Solving for minimums

$$\frac{\partial X_1}{\partial X_2}, \quad \frac{\partial X_1}{\partial X_4}$$

and setting their values equal to zero yields a measure of scale effects.

Returns to Scale

The response in output (ton-miles) to a proportionate increase of all inputs has been described by the term, "returns to scale." If output increases by the same percentage as the change in inputs, returns to scale are labeled constant for the range of input combinations under consideration at any time. They are increasing if output increases by a greater proportion and decreasing if output increases by a smaller proportion. A single production function may exhibit all three types of returns with the type of returns depending on the range at which inputs are being changed.[18] In some cases a production function may exhibit increasing returns for small amounts of inputs, then pass through a stage of constant returns, and ultimately exhibit decreasing returns to scale as the amounts of inputs added become larger and larger.

Since homogeneous production functions display most easily the concept of returns to scale, the general form of modified Cobb-Douglas production function (that is, with unconstrained returns to scale) is widely used throughout the literature. As long as the production function is homogeneous of any degree, the expansion path (which is the locus of tangency points between isoquants and their corresponding isocost constraints) will be a straight line.[19]

A production function homogeneous of degree one also generates a linear long-run total cost function.[20] Let $(\bar{K},\bar{L})$ be the optimum input combination[21] for the production of one unit of Z. The corresponding production cost is $r_1\bar{K} + r_2\bar{L}$ and $c = aA$ where $a = r_1\bar{K} + r_2\bar{L}$. Marginal and average cost are both equal to the constant a.

The total cost function for the Cobb-Douglas production function can be derived more easily in the conventional manner. Writing out the production function, cost equation, and expansion path function[22] respectively,

$$Z = AK^{\alpha}L^{1-\alpha} \tag{30.2}$$

$$C = r_1K + r_2L \tag{30.3}$$

$$(1 - \alpha)r_1K - \alpha r_2L = 0 \tag{30.4}$$

Solving for capital and labor yields

$$K = \alpha C/r_1 \tag{30.5}$$

18. A production function is homogeneous of degree k if $f(tx_1,tx_2) = t^kf(x_1,x_2)$ where k is a constant, t is any positive real number, and x_1, x_2 are inputs. Returns to scale are constant if $k > 1$, constant if $k = 1$, and decreasing if $k < 1$. A function that is homogeneous of degree one is said to be linearly homogeneous, but this does not imply that the production function itself is linear.

19. A straight line expansion path, however, does not necessarily imply a homogeneous production function; for example, the sixth degree production function

$$Z = Ax_1^2x_2^2 - Bs_1^3x_2^3$$

possesses a linear expansion path, but it is not homogeneous.

20. A good reference on this topic is James M. Henderson and Richard E. Quandt, *Microeconomic Theory*, New York: McGraw Hill, 1958, one of the more definitive works in microeconomics during the last decade.

21. In relation to our earlier production functions, K is capital and L is labor.

22. The expansion path equation represents the growth of the optimal input combinations over time as the railroad produces higher output.

$$L = (1 - \alpha)C/r_2 \tag{30.6}$$

and substituting these values into the production function gives

$$Z = \frac{\alpha C^{\alpha}}{r_1} \left[\frac{(1 - \alpha)C^{1-\alpha}}{r_2} \right] \tag{30.7}$$

The solving for C in terms of Z and the parameters, the total cost function is now

$$C = aZ \tag{30.8}$$

where

$$a = \frac{r_1^{\alpha} r_2^{1-\alpha}}{A\alpha^{\alpha}(1 - \alpha)^{(1-\alpha)}}$$

For the cases when the production function is nonhomogeneous, the resulting total cost function will be nonlinear. In general, though, the long run cost function can be solved in a similar fashion as long as the required ingredients are present, namely, the expansion path equation (30.5), the production function (30.3), and the general form of the cost function (30.8).

Kent J. Healy in his pioneering study used simple correlation techniques to measure scale effects and concluded that there was a sharp absence of any scale economies for railroads beyond the size of 10,000 employees. His models were crude and a retesting of his hypotheses seems in order. Consider the following two equations:

$$OW/OR = f(D, S) \tag{30.9}$$

and

$$RR = f(D, S) \tag{30.10}$$

where

D = density (thousands of dollars revenue per mile)

S = scale (thousands of employees)

OW = operating wages

OR = operating revenue

RR = rate of return (that is, net operating income after taxes but before interest divided by sum of stock, surplus, and long term debt averaged as of beginning and end of year).

The total operating costs of a railroad during a one-year period are dependent upon the tonnage of commodities transported and the number of miles each ton is carried. The average relationship between total costs (*TC*), total tonnage (*T*), and miles per revenue ton (*M*), can provide the basis for an estimate of costs per ton (*TC*)/*T* on commodities transported between selected pairs of points. The statistics can be separated for "large" railroads and "small" railroads[23] on the basis that the latter railroads have both technical conditions and input factor price conditions that are different from those of the large railroads, but that conditions in one large railroad were quite similar to those in another large railroad. This stratification of observations by size avoids the downward bias in the estimated relationship from fuller utilization of equipment in larger railroads that generates user costs which are not reported.[24]

Cost functions of this type can be fitted first between six pairs of points for any two premerged railroads for a time period set of data, and then on a cross-sectional basis for one year for both equivalent long hauls and short hauls of selected merged and unmerged companies.

The basic cost function would seem to be multiplicative since increases in tonnage to any location would increase cost by amounts that vary directly with mileage (and perhaps interchanges, which are ignored here). The general form would be

$$C = aM^b T^c X^d \tag{30.11}$$

where

T = tonnage of a bulk commodity (say coal)

X = tonnage of other products

M = mileage between a pair of points

a, b, c, d = parameters.

For a given railroad's time series data, the complete multiplicative equation is

$$C/T_1 = (aM^b T_1^{c-1})(X_2^{d2} X_3^{d3} X_4^{d4})(e_i D_i) \tag{30.12}$$

where

T_1 = tonnage of the leading commodity hauled, say coal

23. In general, "large" railroads must have averaged more than 175 miles per revenue ton and more than 50 million tons transported, say in 1960.

24. This is the point made by George H. Borts in "The Estimation of Rail Cost Functions," *Econometrica* 28 (January 1960), p. 118.

X_2, X_3, X_4 = tonnage of agricultural products, animal products, and automotive components, respectively—the three next largest commodities transported

$e_i D_i$ = time variables.

The $e_i D_i$ takes the value "0" for all cost items not incurred in the base year, "1" for all base year items; similarly, D_2 has the value "1" for all of the next year's items and "0" otherwise. This is a "shift" variable that attempts to allow for the effect of increasing input factor prices on C/T.

The cross-section data will be fitted by the following (similar) function:

$$C/T_1 = aM^b \, T_1^{c-1} \, X^d \tag{30.13}$$

where

T_1 = tonnage of bulk commodity that is the largest transported and

X = tonnage of all other products.

Clearly, nonhomogeneity of T could be a problem.

The probability that a railroad will introduce a new technique is an increasing function of the proportion of railroads already using it and the profitability of doing so, but a decreasing function of the size of the investment required. The equation may be stated as:

$$G_i = a + b\pi_i + cS_i + u_i \tag{30.14}$$

where

G_i = rate of diffusion (the number of years that elapsed between the time when 10% of the railroads had introduced the ith innovation and the time when 90% had done so)

π_i = relative profitability of the ith innovation (average payout period in general divided by average payout period for the investment in the ith innovation)

S_i = size of required investment (the average initial investment in the innovation as a percent of the average total current assets of the firms).

The pioneering work in this area is by Edwin Mansfield[25] who found that practically all of the variation among the rate of "imitation" in four selected

25. For a thorough development of this concept, see Edwin Mansfield, "Intrafirm Rates of Diffusion of an Innovation," *Review of Economics and Statistics* 54 (November 1963), pp. 379-88.

industries was explained by his model. Thus, a hypothesis can be formulated that significant innovations have occurred at a higher rate in railroads that have merged than in those that have not. In order to test this hypothesis, we must examine the influence of various factors on the interfirm rate of diffusion,[26] the rate at which railroads introduce a new technique and begin to substitute it for older methods. Some types of railroads tend to be relatively quick to begin using new techniques (possibly merger-minded ones) and others are relatively slow. By holding π_i and S_i constant, a comparison can be made with respect to the average rates of diffusion between the merged and unmerged roads on data from twelve or more major innovations.

Economies of Scale: A Case Study

Most merger or control cases intend to demonstrate as major benefits the elimination of duplicate services and facilities, but the Chesapeake and Ohio/ Baltimore and Ohio (C&O/B&O) control case of 1963 is a classic success. It focused primarily on the financial resuscitation of a potentially bankrupt railroad by another with a strong working capital position.

For years the C&O was stymied in its efforts to investigate new areas for profit. It had been a major carrier of coal and metallurgical items from Appalachian mines to Newport News, Virginia for export, or to the Middle West for domestic steel mills. It also handled a satisfactory merchandise business on the northern and western end of the railroad. During the late fifties the C&O upgraded its equipment, maintenance of way, and car fleet, which jointly generated a large amount of cash through earnings and depreciation write-offs. The difficulty was that no real opportunities for growth and glamour existed.

By contrast, the B&O was experiencing serious financial problems. In its fiscal year 1961 B&O sustained an operating loss of more than $31 million. Bankruptcy seemed imminent for the road also suffered from heavy fixed debt, critical car shortages, and a large percentage of bad order rolling stock. In addition, its vital artery between the eastern seaboard and the southwestern gateways lacked sufficient clearances for the newer, larger piggyback and auto-rack cars, an important and potentially very lucrative source of revenue.

The C&O has demonstrated that a strong railroad initially need not endanger its financial strength in assuming control over an inept one. By a purchase of the weaker carrier's stock issue, the stronger road becomes authorized to lease new cars to that carrier, improve its physical plant, and assist in overhauling its managerial and sales techniques. Inasmuch as the B&O was experiencing serious financial and managerial problems, the C&O in 1963 selected the consolidation path as being preferable to an outright merger. Thus a trial period was provided to determine whether an eventual merger would suit the best interests of each

26. Ibid.

carrier. Since that time the C&O has expanded into a conglomerate firm, known as the Chessie System, which has become one of the country's few innovative and profitable railroad firms.

31 Economies of Scale in the Motor Trucking Industry

In its strictest sense, economies of scale must be defined in terms of the production function of the firm. As discussed previously, the production function defines the technological relationship between any given assortment of inputs and the maximum output that they can produce. As such, this function gives no consideration to prices and cannot determine by itself the optimal, or least cost, set of inputs for a given output. It does describe all contributions of inputs that, when used in the technologically most efficient process, can be used to produce any given level of output. In mathematical form, the production function is generally written as $Z = f(K,L,F, \ldots)$ where Z is maximum output and K, L, and F are the amounts of various inputs, results representing capital, labor, and fuel, respectively.

Given any initial set of inputs, *returns to scale* refers to the effect on maximum output of a proportionate increase in all factors of production. If output rises in the same proportion, then constant returns to scale are claimed to exist.[1] In such a case larger firms have no advantage over small firms in terms of physical productivity, and vice versa. If output rises less than proportionately to an equiproportionate increase in all inputs, then decreasing returns to scale exist. In this situation, smaller firms own an advantage in physical productivity. In the case of increasing returns to scale, maximum output rises more than in proportion to an equiproportionate increase in all inputs, and larger firms are hence more efficient. Clearly, then, the efficiency of an industry that faces increasing returns to scale, given the size of existing firms, can be increased through mergers and consolidations, and it is in this context that serious consideration should be given by policy makers to such reorganizations.

If new empirical tests suggested the existence of scale economies in any of the transportation industries, the atmosphere for renewed merger and consolidation activities may be enhanced. Conventional economic theory would predict that the financially sound carriers would be interested in acquiring other less profitable carriers provided that the marginal returns were satisfactory and compatible with the sound carriers' portfolios of other investments. As a matter of public policy, the financially sound carriers might also be encouraged to acquire carriers on the border of bankruptcy, or portions of them, through various incentives such as tax write-offs and accruals. One form of consolidation that has been recently popular in the railroad industry is the abandonment of unnecessary or unprofitable lines. Prior to 1974 very little attention had been

1. This possibility occurs in the case of the linear homogeneous production function.

given to effective national policy on the rail abandonment issue. Part of the problem stemmed from the difficulties associated with measuring the externalities from the retention of certain rail lines. On the other hand, mandated retentions of these lines by the large railroad firms without government subsidy, through the historically tested practices of cross-subsidization of weak routes by profitable ones, appear to have been both uneconomic and self-destructive.[2] Viewed in this fashion, the ICC's policies may have been too restrictive, since the regulatory agency, lacking any viable alternative, has required continued cross-subsidization on some routes. Furthermore, without any adequate understanding of the returns to scale issue, the ICC has been forced to adjudicate on the basis of incomplete information and analysis. This situation has been no less true in the motor trucking industry than in the railroad industry.

Mergers can provide the opportunity for cost savings and increased profits but, if unimpeded, can result in an increase in concentration to an extent adverse to competition in the industry. From either viewpoint, mergers (especially in transportation) should be studied to determine their future effects and trends on the individual firms and the industry as a whole.

The motor carrier industry is one of the most active in the merger movement. Each year over 200 applications for unification are filed before the ICC, which grants a large proportion of them. Considering the amount of merger activity and the importance of a sound motor carrier industry to the health of American industry in general, it is surprising that so little research has been performed by the ICC on the effects of motor carrier mergers. In the academic literature a number of economists have used the results of their cost studies of the motor carrier industry to suggest that increased size does not produce economies of scale. Others have viewed with some disapproval the apparent increase in concentration. The following section of this chapter reviews the more significant studies pertaining to scale effects in the motor trucking industry.

Scale Effects in the Motor Trucking Industry

Although returns to scale are strictly defined in terms of the production function, it has been more convenient to examine the cost functions faced by a firm in a given industry. If input prices are assumed to be constant at all times, then increasing returns to scale can be expected to result in declining average costs. This assumption is generally justifiable since the range of production of a single firm is generally insufficient to affect the market price for inputs. In the case of the railroad and motor trucking industries, this assumption is further bolstered by the fact that a merger within either industry is unlikely to affect significantly the total industry demand for a factor, and hence its price. Suffice

2. See Robert B. Carson, *Main Line to Oblivion–The Disintegration of the New York Railroads in the Twentieth Century* (Port Washington, N.Y.: Kennikot Press, 1971).

it to say that in the case of falling marginal costs, and more generally in the case of falling average costs, consolidation of small firms could yield substantial public benefits.[3]

The interpretation of returns to scale as referring to changes of all inputs in equal proportion (that is, movement along a vector) has remained a standard one for many years.[4] A general relationship has been derived in the literature between returns to scale (along the vector) and the shape of the average cost curve measured in the normal fashion along the expansion path, which need not be a vector.[5] Even as early as 1911, F.Y. Edgeworth perceived that returns to scale ought to be measured along the expansion path the firm actually uses, which need not be a vector.[6]

All theory, and economics is no exception, is an abstraction from reality designed to sharpen understanding of the most essential conceptual insights. As such, theoretical concepts are often difficult to apply directly to the analysis of a particular industry such as motor trucking. At the outset, two important complications must be faced. One is the identification of output and the other is the distinction between system "size" and traffic density.

Output is difficult to identify simply because it consists of many different components. Motor trucking firms provide freight services that consist of a number of different elements. In particular, characteristics of freight service include but are not limited to ton-miles, vehicle-miles, and a number of methods of loadings.[7] Hence, it is impossible to measure output in units that are above any reproach. In general, however, previous research has adopted ton-miles of revenue freight as the best available measure.[8]

Perhaps the earliest major study of motor carrier mergers was conducted by Walter Adams and John Hendry.[9] It was a special study for the Select

---

3. Declining marginal costs imply declining average costs, but the reverse does not necessarily hold.

4. See Lowell Bassett, "Returns to Scale and Cost Curves," *Southern Economic Journal* 36 (October 1969), pp. 189-90.

5. See A. Sandma, "Returns to Scale and the Average Cost Curve," *Swedish Journal of Economics* 73 (1971), pp. 261-62; and J. Kirker Stephens, "Returns to Scale and the Average Cost Curve: Comment," *Swedish Journal of Economics* 75 (March 1973), pp. 110-11.

6. F.Y. Edgeworth, "Contributions to the Theory of Railway Rates," *Economic Journal* 21 (1911), pp. 346-70.

7. The difficulty of measuring output is more pronounced in the railroad industry where there exist the additional factors of passenger service, train-miles, and numerous switchings, interchanges, and loadings.

8. See George W. Wilson, "On the Output Unit in Transportation," *Land Economics* 35 (August 1959), pp. 266-76; also his *Essays on Some Unsettled Questions on the Economics of Transportation* (Bloomington, Ind.: Foundation for Economic and Business Studies, Indiana University, 1962); T.M. Whitin, "Output Dimensions and Their Implications for Cost and Price Analyses," *Journal of Business* 45 (April 1972), pp. 305-15; Charles E. Olson and Terence A. Brown, "The Output Unit in Transportation Revisited," *Land Economics* 48 (August 1972), pp. 380-82; and my *The Economics of the Transportation Firm* (Lexington, Mass.: Lexington Books, D.C. Heath and Co., 1974), chap. 3.

9. See W. Adams and J. Hendry, *Trucking Mergers, Concentration and Small Business: An Analysis of Interstate Commerce Commission Policy, 1950-1956* (Washington, D.C.: Select Committee on Small Business, United States Senate, 1956).

Committee on Small Business of the United States Senate and its purpose was to

> . . . assemble, systematize, and evaluate factual data so as to gain some insight into the Commission's administration of section 5 of the Interstate Commerce Act and to discover if, as a result of mergers and acquisitions, there were any discernible trends toward concentration in the trucking industry or discriminations against small carriers and shippers.[10]

They concluded that concentration of the industry was increasing through mergers, that little consistency could be found in the approaches or decisions of the ICC, that large and small carriers were being treated differently with the large carriers being favored in merger decisions, and that increasing concentration cannot be justified on a cost basis.[11] This conclusion was based on a number of cost studies, primarily those of Merrill J. Roberts[12] and Robert A. Nelson,[13] which indicated that mergers could not be justified on the grounds that larger size led to greater efficiency and lower transportation costs. Instead, it appears from these studies that increased efficiency was related primarily to better route utilization. The reference to the findings of these two studies was included in the Adams and Hendry report mainly to show that in assuming that increased size leads to greater efficiency, the commission was "unaware and ignorant of the true sources of operating efficiency" in its policy toward mergers.[14]

The Roberts' study investigated the influence of firm size on costs in order to determine the relationship between efficiency and financial health. Centering his study on the class I carriers of general commodities in the central territory (to obtain some homogeneity of data), he found that as firm size increased, costs fell.[15] While this would appear to indicate economies of scale, further investigation showed that larger firms had more favorable operating characteristics than the small firms and that route utilization and average haul therefore were the more likely determinants of cost, rather than firm size. An interesting result of Roberts' important study was the interaction (cross-product) of route utilization and average haul in determining costs: "The evidence adduced for the firms studied establishes the absence of economies of scale in this industry."[16] On mergers he concluded that "the evidence indicates that firm expansion *per se* is not an avenue to greater efficiency as measured by unit capacity costs."[17]

10. Ibid., p. 2.

11. Ibid., pp. 3-6.

12. Merrill J. Roberts, "Some Aspects of Motor Carrier Costs: Firm Size, Efficiency and Financial Health," *Land Economics* 32 (August 1956), pp. 228-38.

13. Robert A. Nelson, *Motor Freight Transport in New England, A Report to the New England Governors Council* (Boston: 1956).

14. Adams and Hendry, *Trucking Mergers.*

15. Roberts, "Motor Carrier Costs."

16. Ibid., p. 238.

17. Ibid., p. 236.

John R. Meyer, Merton J. Peck, John Stenason, and Charles Zwick prepared a classic study on the economics of competition in the transportation industries.[18] Part of their study was to determine the costs of the various modes in each industry. An estimate of the costs of motor trucking was provided by the following equation:

$$C = 192.5 + 42.6 \log S + (336 - 0.041 \log S) H$$

where

C = costs of shipment in cents per hundredweight

S = size of shipment in hundredweight, and

H = distance shipped in miles.

The inference of this equation is that motor carrier costs vary markedly with size of shipment and distance of shipment.[19] Total unit costs decline with distance because of the distribution of terminal expense over a higher number of ton-miles.[20] Intuitively, scale is not the only influence on costs. It is possible that while a strong relationship seems to exist as exhibited by a long-run cost curve, the correlation may be spurious. From the Meyer et al. study,

> The ICC has consistently reported that line-haul costs decline with distance shipped. However this is largely a spurious correlation reflecting the fact that size of shipment and length of haul are correlated.[21]

More recent studies in the motor trucking industry, however, have suggested the possibility of increasing returns to scale.[22] In particular are the studies by P.W. Emery,[23] Stanley J. Warner,[24] Gary N. Dicer,[25] and Rajindar K.

18. John R. Meyer, Merton J. Peck, John Stenason, and Charles Zwick, *The Economics of Competition in the Transportation Industries* (Cambridge, Mass.: Harvard University Press, 1959).

19. Ibid., p. 94.

20. Ibid.

21. Ibid., p. 93.

22. The major exception is E.M. Patton, "Implications of Motor Carrier Growth and Size," *Transportation Journal* (Fall 1970), pp. 34-52.

23. P.W. Emery, "An Empirical Approach to the Motor Carrier Scale Economics Controversy," *Land Economics* 41 (August 1965), pp. 285-89.

24. Stanley J. Warner, "Cost Models, Measurement Errors, and Economies of Scale in Trucking," in M.L. Burnstein et al., *The Cost of Trucking: Econometric Analysis* (Dubuque, Iowa: William S. Brown Publishers, 1965), pp. 1-46.

25. Gary N. Dicer, "Economics of Scale and Motor Carrier Optimum Size," Quarterly Review of Economics and Business (Spring 1971), pp. 31-37.

Koshal.[26] The two most recent studies of importance also depict increasing returns to scale: first, an article using production function analysis by Mark L. Ladenson and Alan J. Stoga,[27] and a book on trucking mergers by James C. Johnson.[28] The recent evidence notwithstanding, future answers on this issue will depend on more accurate portrayals of cost and production function analyses applied to motor carrier data.

26. Rajindar K. Koshal, "The Cost of Trucking: Econometric Analysis," *Journal of Transport Economics and Policy* 12 (May 1972), pp. 147-51.

27. Mark L. Ladenson and Alan J. Stoga, "Return to Scale in the U.S. Trucking Industry," *Southern Economic Journal* 44 (January 1974), pp. 390-96.

28. James C. Johnson, *Trucking Mergers* (Lexington, Mass.: Lexington Books, D.C. Heath and Co., 1973).

32 The Function of the Independent Regulatory Commission: A Proposed Method for Evaluating Mergers in the Railroad Industry

The general problem of regulation in the railroad industry by the Interstate Commerce Commission (ICC) is that of establishing or maintaining the necessary conditions for the efficient utilization of economic resources under a system of private enterprise. In some cases this might imply that a single firm provides the total service in a particular environment: For many markets in the past, it was normally efficient for several railroads to serve a given town or community since a substantial fraction of total rail costs was indivisible and invariant with traffic. As a result, one railroad often could handle the traffic at a total cost that was considerably lower than the aggregate costs of several railroad firms with their separate facilities.

Exactly the same argument has been applied to the case of the public utilities: On account of economies of scale of their systems, a single network ordinarily is cheapest. Yet, the application of the "natural monopoly" argument to railroads is rather strained, for railroads generally have neither a monopoly nor a "substantial" portion of the total traffic of all modes, and even if they did, it would not necessarily follow that regulation was the best method of amending the effects of monopolistic behavior. In fact, many writers have contended that, historically, government regulation has contributed to the demise of railroad rates of profitability. If this hypothesis is in fact true, then an important issue can be raised concerning the methods of the regulatory commission in performing its functions.

An important observation is that railroad mergers and consolidations are adjudicated according to different standards and by a different regulatory agency than mergers in other industries are decided. It has been alleged that the actual affirmation of a merger by the ICC tends to refurbish the status quo aspects of its continued regulation in a postmerger situation. However, a sufficient treatment of this topic is beyond the scope of this text, so it is assumed in this discussion that existing levels of regulatory involvement by the ICC will prevail.

On the basis of this assumption, the mechanism of "merger" in the railroad industry becomes partially a responsibility of government and is not left entirely to the market system. What matters are the impacts of mergers, both short and long run. For the impacts to be evaluated effectively, the analysis must be approached along the following two lines: First, it must be focused on some of the loose ends that have served as criteria in the past for adjudicating mergers, and second, it must demonstrate that mergers induce efficiencies and benefits that in the absence of merger, would not occur. This is not to say that all mergers must have been good ones, but it does require that a significantly large number must have yielded efficient impacts.

A major reason for the dilemmas in merger cases is the diversity of the interests involved: the railroad companies, the users and shippers, the governmental agency, and the general public. To satisfy all parties is ideal but unlikely; thus, the objective should be to develop criteria that are consistent with the welfare of the major participating groups with the anticipation that a near-optimal solution be attained. If two railroads intend to merge, the ICC should wish to know, first, how the performance of the merged structure would compare with the premerged configurations for given rail services, and, second, how the performance of the merged structure would shift over time as the levels of service change. These will become the conditions by which a *dynamic* model can describe and evaluate merger generated changes in the structure of the railroad industry. In light of the crucial importance of the necessity for an evaluation method for mergers and rationalization in the railroad industry, it is suggested that an optimal control theory approach to this issue will represent a close approximation to what the ICC can utilize for adjudication after it assimilates the required data into the overall industry framework.

The Need for Mergers in the Railroad Industry

In recent years only a few railroad companies have shown a consistent record of earnings and growth. The direction and degree of internal expansion plans by the railroads are unclear and diversification efforts are sporadic and seem to be pursued without strong objectives. Antiquated work rules inhibit the implementation of certain technological advances, and in many cases the needs of shippers and passengers, in terms of equipment and service, are not being fulfilled. Consequently, serious issues regarding the public interest have arisen such that a choice must be made that will determine the extent to which the railroad industry is to survive as a vital component of the free enterprise system.

In the future it is anticipated that the railroad industry will face the requirements of increased speeds, improved signaling systems, superior yard facilities, better communications, transformed interchanges, and a number of other property and operational advances. In order to meet these needs the mechanism of merger could provide the desired impetus in the following ways: first, by allowing the combined railroads to realize the benefits of economies of scale attributable to larger size; second, by inducing cost savings through consolidation of duplicate or extra facilities; third, by insuring that the postmerger competition, both intermodal as well as intramodal, will contribute to the public interest by generating improved service to rail users and by stimulating technological improvements; and fourth, by demanding that new procedures, different standards, aggressive marketing, and fresh philosophies of conducting business be established by the companies involved.

The basis for merger has two facets: one, short term, and the other, long term. In the short run the impacts of mergers are realized in terms of a railroad company's operating efficiency in the small where cost minimization is the pursued operating policy. Over the longer term the impacts are visible in terms of its operating efficiency in a larger context (or what is called allocative efficiency). This suggests that a certain level of competition might imply a different industrial organization than efficiency in the small, and efficiency in the small might imply a different organization than efficiency in the large. The essential point is that different merger policies might yield different consequences.[1] If larger size railroads are required for viability reasons, then the process of how the increased size is brought about is crucial in terms of public policy considerations.

The allocative efficiency consequences of any merger that increases both efficiency and market power can be evaluated only by net effects, insofar as all the relevant effects can be determined. The consideration of both immediate and eventual effects will ordinarily require the consideration of industry as well as local impacts. The implementation of a merged system thus would involve the expected monopoly power consequences of a merger being allowed in comparison with those that would result if the economies instead were realized by internal expansion.[2] A decision with respect to the timing tends to be affected by the rate of growth of market demand for rail services, that is, ceteris paribus the greater the rate of growth of market demand, the easier it is to achieve the requisite expansion by internal means and the less compelling is the case for merger.[3] If the expected rate of growth of rail services for the companies tended to be low, particularly for the smaller railroads, the stronger would be the conditions for merger.

The Process of Adjudicating Mergers

The process of merger can be treated as an innovation, or the implementation over time of a new idea or structure. If the managerial goal of railroad companies

1. An end-to-end merger normally will induce substantially different impacts than a merger of parallel lines. For one of the better narrative treatments (and recommendation) of end-to-end mergers, see *Improving Railroad Productivity*, Final Report of the Task Force on Railroad Productivity to the National Commission on Productivity and the Council of Economic Advisers (Washington, D.C.: November 1973).

2. See Oliver E. Williamson, "Economies as an Antitrust Defense: The Welfare Tradeoffs," *American Economic Review* 58 (March 1968), pp. 18-63.

3. This inference is based on the assumption that changes in market structure, once introduced, tend to persist.

were to maximize profits, mergers would occur only when they produce some increase in market power, when they produce a technological or managerial economy of scale, or when the managers of the acquiring railroad possess some special insight into the opportunities for profit in the acquired railroad which neither its managers nor stockholders possess. It has been the modus operandi of competitive economics that suggests that firms tend to select the most efficient of the available means of production. The absence from view over time of less efficient processes creates the illusion that either no alternatives exist or any alternative is massively difficult to implement. This illusion is heightened by the feeling that mergers contain an optimal set of institutional arrangements, appurtenances, structure, and personnel. Furthermore, the industry adjusts to any given merger that allows it to become more ingrained such that the merging railroads' survival depends upon the speed and effectiveness with which they adopt these supplementary arrangements and adjust to the new conditions. Thus, the accessories of the process of merger become the conditions under which the mechanism of merger operates and through which it imparts its contribution and significance to the growth of the merged railroad and the industry.

The Basic Model

The Interstate Commerce Commission is an organization that has the statutory responsibility of supervising and regulating the affairs of the railroad industry.[4] If the ICC intends to function as an optimal agency, then it will be dealing with complex systems that would include:

1. Dynamic-optimal service processes, such as the quality and frequency of rail service between various city-pairs
2. Decision-making elements (called controllers), who would adjudicate issues in the areas of company mergers, rates, abandonments, diversification efforts, and complaints
3. Transmission lines that link the controllers and processes in a form of a hierarchical structure.

The higher level controllers (the commission members) send information to the subsystems that would be lower levels of the hierarchical structure. The lower level controllers would be responsible for the less important issues of railroad operations, such as handling local rate and tariff changes, operating violations, maintenance deficiencies, and so on. The global result produced by these subsystems is reduced considerably in the case of either nonoptimal

4. The affairs of the other transport modes regulated by the ICC under statutory requirement also should be included within the scope of its jurisdiction.

organization or poor transmission. Therefore the problem of a synthesis of organization structures that are optimal represents a certain theoretical and practical interest. In order that this problem be solved, it is necessary to introduce a measure of the quality of organizational structure, from which an optimum structure can be selected.

Assume that the ICC consists of controlled dynamic processes, ($P_1, P_2, \ldots, P_n$), local level controllers ($C_1, C_2, \ldots, C_n$), the overall controller (C), the commission, transmission lines (L_i for $L = 1, 2, \ldots, n$), which link C with the n local level controllers and transmission lines (L_j for $j = 1, 2, \ldots, m$) which link the local level controllers with the class I railroad companies ($R_1, R_2, \ldots, R_m$).

The behavior of the controllers can be specified by given objective functionals, which together with the process and constraint equations can be used for the derivation of optimal control algorithms.[5] Since the organizational composition of the ICC is the principal interest in this chapter, attention will be devoted to the computation of the performance characteristics of the optimum regulatory process, which are essential for the evaluation of organizational quality. The term OPC (optimum performance characteristics) will be used to denote this quality index and relatively little attention will be given to the derivation of the algorithms.

In that context the ICC regulatory activities can be considered as a dynamic process, which is described by a given operator A:

$$y = A(x) \text{ for } y, x \in X \tag{32.1}$$

Consider a case when the ICC requests that a railroad with zero current profits improve its efficiency in a given time period T with minimum resource utilization. For simplicity, assume that the railroad's only area of business is to ship goods in one direction over a given distance D. Also assume that capital inputs are fixed and that the amount of goods shipped depends solely on the labor input (x) such that

$$x(t) \xi L^2 [0, T] \tag{32.2}$$

denoting the number of shipments as S, assume that a process equation to explain this activity is

$$S(d^2 D/dt^2) - kx(t) = 0 \tag{32.3}$$

where k is a coefficient of labor productivity. The solution to this input-output relationship then can be expressed as the integral operator in $L^2 [0,T]$

5. See Kelvin Lancaster, *Mathematical Economics* (New York: The Macmillan Company, 1968), especially pp. 376-84 and for other references.

$$y(t) = y(0) + k/S \, {}_0\!\int^t (t - \alpha) x(\alpha) d\alpha \tag{32.4}$$

The optimization problem consists in finding such a function $x(t) \xi L^2 [0,T]$ that minimizes utilization cost, proportional to

$$F(x) = {}_0\!\int^T [x(t)]^2 dt, \tag{32.5}$$

subject to two constraints:

$$H(x) = y(T) - y(0) = k/S \int (T - \alpha) x(\alpha) d\alpha = Y \tag{32.6}$$

and

$$W(x) = dy(t)/dt \mid_{t=T} = k/S \, {}_0\!\int^T x(\alpha) d\alpha = 0 \tag{32.7}$$

Equation (32.7) requires that the adjudication of the efficiency of the process occur at $dt(t = T)$.

Calculus of variations methods can be used to solve this problem such that the necessary condition for optimality requires that the strong gradient of the functional $\overline{F}(x) = F(x) + \lambda H(x) + \lambda_2 W(x)$ is equal to zero (where λ_1 and λ_2 are Lagrangian-type multipliers),[6] or that

$$\nabla \overline{F}(\overline{x}) = 0 \tag{32.8}$$

and

$$|| \nabla H(\overline{x}) || > 0, \; || \nabla W(\overline{x}) || > 0.$$

From this optimality condition is obtained:

$$2\overline{x}(t) + \lambda k/S(t - \alpha) + \lambda 2 \;\; k/S = 0.$$

from which the *OPC* can be derived[7] as

$$A = F(x) = (3/4) \, Y^2 S^2 / K^2 T^3 \tag{32.9}$$

Since A is a monotonic function of Y and T it can be shown that the same form of OPC is obtained when the equality constraint in equation (32.6) is replaced by $H(x) \geqslant Y$. In the control theory literature, many types of dynamic

6. These conditions follow from Ljusternik's theorem. See M.D. Canon, C.D. Cullum, Jr., and E. Polak, *Theory of Optimal Control and Mathematical Programming* (New York: McGraw-Hill, Inc., 1970), pp. 204-5.

7. From Equations (32.6) and (32.7): $\overline{x}(t) = [3Y(T/2 - t)] / (kT^3/S)$ and from Equation (32.5), $A = F(x)$ can be derived.

optimal processes have been derived,[8] and in most cases they assume a simple analytic form:

$$A^{\alpha}, B^{\beta}, \ldots, Y^{\psi}, Z^{\omega} = (k)^{q}, \tag{32.10}$$

where

$$q = \alpha + \beta + \ldots + \omega$$

and where

$$A, B, \ldots, Y, Z,$$

α, β, k are positive numbers and $\omega, \psi, \ldots$, negative numbers.[9] Since the properties of the optimal process are better as k is smaller, k can be used as a quality index (for example, in the case of equation (32.9), which could be written as $AT^3Y^{-2} = (3/4a)^2$ where $a = k/S$.

It should be observed that when the OPC are described by a function like equation (32.14), the aggregation and optimization processes can be applied to multilevel structures yielding at each stage the same form of OPC with quality indices that can be derived by fairly simple relations. In other words, the amount of variables or information that comes into account at each control level is strictly limited. It is also possible to evaluate qualities of different organizational structures, and it is in this context that the impact of mergers on structural arrangements in the railroad industry can be assessed. Assume, for example, that three different processes, described by equation (32.10), with performance levels k_1, k_2, k_3 and three different types of possible structural arrangements are given. The corresponding quality indices can be derived as follows:[10]

$$k_a = \lambda_i k_i + \lambda_2 k_2 + \lambda_3 k_3,$$

$$k_b = \lambda_i k_i + \lambda_{23}\lambda_2 k_2 + \lambda_{23}\lambda_3 k_3,$$

$$k_c = \lambda_{12}\lambda_1 k_1 + \lambda_{12}\lambda_2 k_2 + \lambda_3 k_3,$$

---

8. For example, see: M.R. Hestenes, *Calculus of Variations and Optimal Control Theory* (New York: John Wiley & Sons, Inc., 1966); R.V. Gamkreledze, "On Some Extremal Problems in the Theory of Differential Equations with Applications to the Theory of Optimal Control," *Journal of SIAM*, Series A, Control, III (1965), pp. 106-28; and R. Kulikowski, "Optimum Control and Synthesis of Organizational Structure of Large Scale Systems," in H.W. Kuhn and G.P. Szego, eds., *Lecture Note in Operations Research and Mathematical Economics* (New York: Springer-Verlag, 1969), pp. 441-56.

9. The Cobb-Douglas model is a special case of this form; See Kulikowski, "Optimum Control," p. 444.

10. See Hestenes, *Calculus of Variations*, Chap. 8.

where $\lambda_1, \lambda_2, \lambda_3, \lambda_{12}, \lambda_{23}$, represents losses introduced by transmission links which connect the respective controllers. The subscripts *a, b*, and *c* reflect three alternative structures as depicted in Figure 32-1.

Many different configurations of regulatory structure in the railroad industry can be considered in view of a particular merger or consolidation proceeding. The ICC can insist that a number of criteria be met and decide itself how to supervise the affairs of the particular railroad company. The configurations are deterministic, independent dynamic systems that depict alternative ways in which different performance (or efficiency) measures can be evaluated. For example, in Figure (32-1A) the commission itself could deal directly with the railroad firm's management who would be performing various processes (in this case, P_1, P_2, and P_3); or, as in Figures 32-1B and 32-1C, a lower level ICC official or examiner could deal with some of the activities of the railroad, while others would be the direct responsibility of the commission itself. Alternatively, one can view the configurations as those of separate railroads and compare each

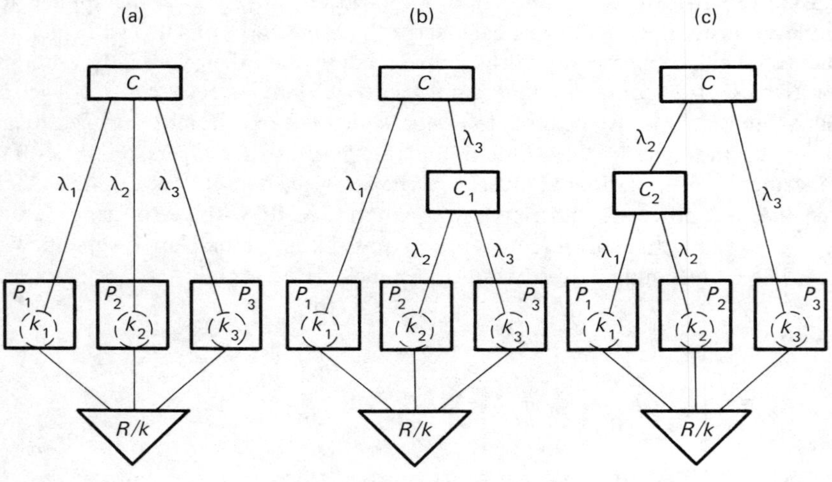

where

R — Railroad after merger (or as an autonomous operation)

λ — Transmission links

C — The ICC

C_1, C_2 — Lower level controllers in the ICC

P — Processes

k — Performance levels (that is, the OPC of a process, which could be the overall operation)

Figure 32-1. Three Possible Alternative Configurations of Regulatory Structure in the Railroad Industry.

one on the basis of separate operations versus a merged operation. The intrinsic value of this method is that in each case an OPC can be determined, regardless of whether the comparison is among different structures within the same company, whether it is among different structures on an interfirm basis, or whether it is between merged firms and premerged firms.

These results provide the conditions on which merger or restructuring cases resulting in different structural configurations might be evaluated in the future. The merger phenomenon in the railroad industry is treated as one part of the overall regulatory process. Insofar as all relevant impacts after a merger can be imputed to the merger per se, the performance characteristics of the resulting structure can be compared with the ex ante merger situation. It is in this context that the preceding analysis has been attempted. In light of the crucial importance of the necessity for an evaluative method for mergers and restructuring in the railroad industry, it has been suggested that an optimal control theory approach to this issue will represent reasonable methodology for the Interstate Commerce Commission to utilize for adjudication after it assimilates the required data into the overall industry framework.

Regardless of the magnitude of the impacts, and how they are estimated, the ICC will continue to be ultimately responsible for the adjudication decision. The evidence from this discussion suggests that in most instances the amount to be gained in overall efficiency terms from dragging out cases is small, while the amount to be gained from expediting the case proceedings, and by transferring regulatory resources toward increased control in situations like the Penn Central, is frequently significant.

Policy Applications

In its first annual report to the President and to the Congress, the United States Railway Association (USRA) in November of 1974 claimed that it could "substantially improve" the financial status of the bankrupt railroads in the northeastern United States.[11] In this report the USRA promised to examine 10,000 miles of the 61,000 miles of track in the area for potential abandonment. In an earlier report on the northeast rail situation, the U.S. Department of Transportation labeled 15,575 miles of track of the same network as being "potentially excess." The whole question of abandonment is subject to close scrutiny. Are there significant cost savings or is it:

> . . . gigantic, economic nonsense—a hoax that trains can become profitable by massive cutting of service to hundreds of thousands of shippers, communities and passengers.[12]

11. United States Railway Association, *Preliminary System Plan* (Washington, D.C.: February 26, 1975).

12. "USRA Sees Need for Subsidies Even If Bankrupt Roads are Reorganized," *Traffic World* (November 18, 1974), p. 23.

For the 50-year period prior to 1970 railroad abandonments were piecemeal decisions where each one averaged about 15 miles of track. With the imminent pressures on the Northeast railroads following the Penn Central bankruptcy proceedings in 1970, abandonment proceedings began to raise the dockets of the ICC. With the passage of the Regional Rail Reorganization Act of 1973 and with the advent of ConRail, the issues of abandonments, mergers and industry restructuring takes on added importance. In spite of the new legislation, merger proceedings still are a cumbersome process (that is, the regulatory lag is inefficiently long). For example, in November of 1974 the ICC approved the merger of the Chicago, Rock Island & Pacific Railroad (RI) into the Union Pacific Railroad (UP). This case has been on the dockets for 10 years and represents the most complicated railroad merger case in the country. Under the conditions of the merger, the UP must sell the lines of the RI south of Kansas City to the Southern Pacific (SP) and the Atchison, Topeka & Santa Fe railroads (AT&SF), and also sell the RI lines from Denver to Omaha to the Denver & Rio Grande Western Railroad (D&RGW). Further conditions require the inclusion of the Missouri-Kansas-Texas Railroad (MKT) in the SF system and indemnification procedures for adverse impacts to the Chicago & Northwestern, Kansas City Southern, Milwaukee, Frisco and MKT railroads. In March 1975, however, the Rock Island filed for bankruptcy under Chapter 77 proceedings so that the fate of the railroad at the time of the writing is undecided.

Perhaps the only solution is a grand scheme that examines the national railroad network and not just a case-by-case approach. Of course, this approach has been suggested (and attempted) before. One possible scheme, however, has been suggested by Henry Livingston and is illustrated in Figure 32-2. Regardless of the restructuring effort involved, the crucial indicator and measure of economic performance will be the expected rate-of-return. This measure clearly has to experience an increase for the firms in the railroad industry if survival is realistically expected.

Rate of return on net investment historically has been regarded as one of the leading measures of the financial condition of firms in the railroad industry. Table 32-1 shows the most recent data on individual firm's rates of return, as calculated by present ICC accounting standards. The rate base at the present time includes all transportation property less depreciation and amortization, plus cash, materials, and supplies. The denominator, "Net Railway Operating Income," or NROI as it is frequently labeled then includes the net revenues from railway operations less railway tax accruals, plus rents. The rate of return is simply the ratio of these two figures. As Table 32-1 indicates, 1973 was a year of slight improvement, but the overall performance is still miserable in comparison with other industries, as it has been for most of the past 45 years. It is apparent that restructuring indeed is warranted.

The best type of railroad organization would appear to be aligned with long-haul operations. Yet, the *conventional* railroad company organization on

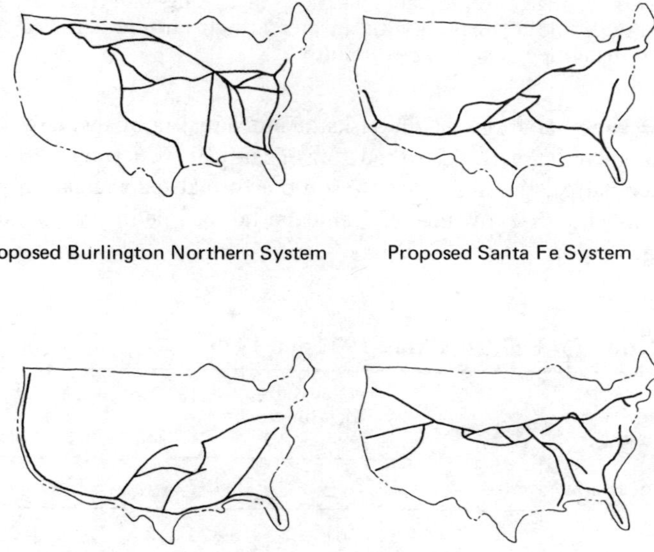

Figure 32-2. The Livingston Railroad Plan. Source: James Blaze, "Towards a National Policy of Super Railroads," *Proceedings of the Fifteenth Annual Meeting, Transportation Research Forum* (San Francisco: October 1974), p. 28. Original data taken from: Nancy Ford, "A Plan for Tomorrow," *Modern Railroads*, September 1973 (an interview with Henry Livingston, v.-p., Clark, Dodge & Co. Other Railroad Restructuring Proposals can be found in: U.S. Department of Transportation, *Western Railroad Mergers*, 1969; Herb Bixler, "Two Rival U.S. Rail Systems Seen Preferable to One AT&T-Type Setup," *Traffic World*, October 16, 1972; and Herbert Whitten, "Key to Railroad Economics–A Rail Common Market," *Handling & Shipping*, December 1973.

short-haul railroads tends to become more inefficient as the number of interchanges and other transactions grow more complex with increasing geographic dispersion by the companies. On account of this problem, D. Daryl Wyckoff has argued for the re-evaluation of:

. . . the desirability of an implied national transportation policy that continues to merge weak small railroads together to form larger weaker railroads. Unless such mergers change the merger partners into long-haul carriers, or a new organization capable of dealing with an increasingly different management task is adopted, this policy is doomed to failure.[13]

In spite of large variations in the tasks of individual railroads, large and small, there is a great similarity in their organizational structures. With such an observed similarity, the argument for a more formalized evaluation procedure, especially in the case of the ICC and the railroad industry, becomes quite compelling.

Table 32-1
Rates of Return for Railroad Firms, 1972 and 1973

	Net Railway Operating Income (000)		Rate of Return (Percent)	
Railroad Firm	1973	1972	1973	1972
Total U.S.	$ 849,361	$ 822,862	3.04	2.97
East	50,154	38,638	0.49	0.37
Railroads in Reorganization				
AA	*d* 1,867	*d* 1,105	*d*	*d*
B&M	*d* 4,492	*d* 5,504	*d*	*d*
CNJ	*d* 5,609	*d* 6,329	*d*	*d*
EL	*d* 6,977	*d* 7,744	*d*	*d*
LV	*d* 7,924	*d* 8,942	*d*	*d*
PC	*d* 92,664	*d* 105,238	*d*	*d*
RDG	*d* 8,677	*d* 12,126	*d*	*d*
(Total)	$*d* 128,210	$*d* 146,988	*d*	*d*
ACY	1,314	550	7.16	2.92
B&O	40,231	36,510	4.10	3.72
BAR	2,257	2,744	3.81	4.31
B&LE	6,742	5,045	9.04	6.60
CPLM	*d* 781	*d* 511	*d*	*d*
CV	329	1,185	1.46	5.38
C&O	48,333	52,412	5.69	5.96
C&EI	6,175	3,340	6.32	4.47
D&H	1,904	1,241	2.29	1.49
DT&S	962	878	6.74	5.99

13. D. Daryl Wyckoff, "Realigning U.S. Railroad Organizations to Cope with Changed Management Tasks," Working Papers HBS 75-12, Graduate School of Business Administration, Harvard University (April 7, 1975), p. 2.

Table 32-1 (cont.)

Railroad Firm	Net Railway Operating Income (000)		Rate of Return (Percent)	
	1973	1972	1973	1972
DT&I	364	3,998	0.52	5.57
EJ&E	7,468	4,609	11.86	7.39
GTW	*d* 6,804	*d* 13,944	*d*	*d*
IT	1,519	1,313	5.60	5.81
LI	*d* 78,915	*d* 65,987	*d*	*d*
MEC	2,131	1,029	3.45	1.68
MI	3,392	3,152	8.17	7.25
MGA	1,452	1,920	3.25	4.07
N&W	120,843	130,275	6.03	6.45
PRSL	*d* 4,783	*d* 5,065	*d*	*d*
P&LE	11,363	10,661	5.24	4.87
RF&P	6,073	5,512	9.77	9.34
WM	6,795	4,759	4.69	3.16
South	$ 269,760	$ 253,943	5.37	5.22
AGS	9,195	9,002	7.37	7.41
CGA	16,714	12,809	10.75	8.67
CNTP	20,375	19,329	10.31	10.54
CLIN	9,394	10,816	8.11	9.12
FEC	5,925	5,470	7.51	7.00
GA	*d* 977	197	*d*	0.95
GSF	4,380	3,933	11.43	12.30
ICG	42,757	22,623	4.26	2.33
L&N	50,401	46,578	4.85	4.40
NS	128	567	0.35	1.56
SCL	39,543	49,801	3.40	4.55
SOU	71,925	72,818	6.87	7.24
West	$ 529,447	$ 530,281	4.17	4.26
ATSF	81,408	86,764	4.78	5.28
BN	43,482	48,200	1.81	2.07
C&NW	22,117	18,855	6.97	6.51
MILW	2,001	*d* 6,783	0.36	*d*
CRI&P	*d* 18,185	*d* 5,503	*d*	*d*
C&S	3,961	5,562	5.00	6.45
DRGW	16,773	17,910	6.34	6.84
DMIR	7,713	4,836	8.60	5.41
DW&P	4,281	2,257	42.50	22.04

Table 32-1 (cont.)

Railroad Firm	Net Railway Operating Income (000)		Rate of Return (Percent)	
	1973	1972	1973	1972
FW&D	*d* 231	1,585	*d*	*d*
GB&W	246	8	1.37	*d*
KCS	4,845	10,423	2.28	5.09
LS&I	234	75	1.23	*d*
MKT	*d* 2,015	969	*d*	*d*
MP	40,438	38,681	4.68	4.42
NWP	143	1,845	0.46	6.10
OE	91	98	0.66	0.79
SLSF	17,859	22,589	3.99	5.06
SLSW	38,424	30,180	10.53	9.32
SOO	19,883	13,809	7.31	5.48
SP	77,805	93,119	3.76	4.51
T&P	10,961	11,894	4.45	4.72
TP&W	334	619	2.73	4.94
UP	151,342	132,085	7.83	7.00
WP	5,244	5,678	3.38	3.59

d = deficit.

Source: Interstate Commerce Commission, *Transport Economics* 1, no. 4 (1974), pp. 10-11.

33 Industrial Organization Applications

In a strictly economic sense the transportation industries should behave similarly to other industries and the firms that comprise the transportation industries should perform similarly to other firms on the nonregulated industries. All are competing for the same investment sources in the various money (short-term) and capital (long-term) markets. From the production side, different industries and their firms have different technological characteristics and therefore may require different production functions to portray their behavior accurately. Recent evidence in the growing interest of the appropriate theoretical and empirical specifications of particular production functions suggests that the answer depends on the industry under observation. Alternative parametric forms have been derived, analyzed, and tested on various bodies of data (both time series and cross-sectional). The general conclusions to be drawn from these statistical tests are that certain industries specified by the Cobb-Douglas (*CD*) form exhibit greater explanatory powers, others by the constant-elasticity-of-substitution (*CES*) form, and still others by the variable-elasticity-of-substitution form.[1] These specifications should be no less true for firms in the transportation industries.

The application of industrial organization analysis to transportation should be a worthwhile exercise.[2] Lessons can be learned by considering the market structure and economic performance standards of the transportation industries. In this arena the student will find a large number of firms, well-defined industry boundaries, and large sets of data (hopefully improving in quality), each an important ingredient to using industrial organization tools. This chapter examines a selected number of issues in transportation that might be handled more effectively within an industrial organization framework.

Competition and Monopoly

The Antitrust Division of the U.S. Department of Justice has been actively interested in recent years in certain cases involving changes in the market structure of the transportation industries, especially in the airline and railroad

1. See C.A.K. Lovell, "CES and VES Production Functions in a Cross-Section Context," *Journal of Political Economics* 81 (May/June 1973), pp. 705-20.

2. See my *The Economics of the Transportation Firm* (Lexington, Mass.: Lexington Books, D.C. Heath and Co., 1974).

merger cases. In some cases the Justice Department has actually intervened when it considered the regulatory commission to be deficient in its evaluations of the evidence. The carriers generally have acted as if they are immune from antitrust proceedings—they presumably would rely on the authority of their regulatory agency to be decisive.[3] The whole issue of the relevance of antitrust violations rests on the characterization of whether transportation markets are competitive or monopolistic.

A substantial amount of the enforcement of the Antitrust statutes is based on a concern with exclusion of competing firms in markets. Examples of exclusionary practices in the eyes of the antitrust advocates are tying arrangements, vertical mergers, exclusive dealerships, predatory pricing, and group boycotts. These practices are challenged as thwarting competition on grounds independent of the efficiency of the firm or firms charged with the excluding. The remainder of the practices with which antitrust law should be concerned falls into the category of "collusive" practices, whereby competing firms voluntarily eliminate competition among themselves in order to restrict output and raise prices.[4] The best examples of collusive practices are cartelization and horizontal mergers, and it is these that are observed most frequently in the transportation industries.

A recent phenomenon in transportation has been the conglomerate merger. The term "conglomerate merger" means those mergers including both transactions involving the purchasing of all the assets of one company by another and also transactions in which the stock of one company is exchanged for that of the stock of another company in order to form one consolidated company.[5]

Transportation firms can by-pass the ICC and its inherent delays in adjudication by reorganizing and spawning a parent holding company. This process can be pursued without the approval of the ICC. During the middle and late 1960s, many class I railroads selected this path for growth: Illinois Central, Santa Fe, Missouri-Kansas-Texas, Union Pacific, Boston and Maine, and Chicago and North Western, to name a few. In fact, the Chicago and North Western Railroad, which was modeled after the Bangor and Aroostook Railroad structure, provides an interesting study of this process of growth: It experienced success, growth, failure, and decline over a span of only three years, from 1966 through 1968.[6]

---

3. Prior to 1904 railroads were immune from the Sherman Act provisions and were free to consolidate at will. In 1904 the Northern Securities Company case brought merger cases in the railroad industry under the antitrust statute umbrella (*United States vs. Northern Securities Co.*, 193 U.S. 197, 337-38 (1904)). Beginning with the Transportation Act of 1920, Congress directed the ICC to formulate plans for consolidating the railroads in a limited number of systems; since that time the responsibility for insuring competition in the railroad industry has rested with the ICC, especially in view of specific criteria stated in Section 5(2) of the Transportation Act of 1940.

4. See Richard A. Posner, "Exclusionary Practices and the Antitrust Laws," *University of Chicago Law Review* 41 (Spring 1974), pp. 506-35.

5. See U.S. Federal Trade Commission, Bureau of Economics, *Statistical Report on Large Mergers in Manufacturing and Mining, 1948-1967* (Washington, D.C.: 1968).

6. For a discussion of these events, see Conway L. Lackman, "Implication of Conglomerates for Transportation in the 1970's," *Transportation Journal* 14 (Fall 1974), pp. 36 ff; and Robert C. Higgins and Lawrence D. Schall, "Corporate Bankruptcy and Conglomerate Mergers," *Journal of Finance* 30 (March 1975), pp. 93-113.

Transportation firms are limited in revenues and growth by the nature of their business. They do not directly contribute to the production of other commodities (aside from goods used in transportation), so that most tonnage generated by a carrier is "diverted" from another carrier or another producing area. Yet, many carriers represent attractive investment opportunities to other nontransport firms, partially because the carriers on the whole generate a fairly steady cash flow and partially because many carriers own extremely valuable nontransportation resources, like real estate and land. In some cases, transportation firms that have joined the conglomerate category have witnessed a redistribution of their assets and the use of leverage to their disadvantage. One classic case of such abuse was the way in which Jay Gould redistributed the assets of the Katy Railroad many decades ago.[7] A more recent case involved the plight of Greyhound Lines, a subsidiary of the Greyhound Corporation, which in 1962 initiated an aggressive program of diversification into food products, meat processing, and competitive software, using the bus company's assets as a catapult.[8]

While recent evidence suggests a decline in rampant conglomeration, the dilemma of the transportation companies remains. Expressed simply, both the revenues and earnings of the transportation firms must improve continually as a means of attracting, sustaining, and deepening the investment capital necessary for the modernization of equipment, plant, and facilities, for the upgrading of the levels of service, and for the development of advanced technologies. On the other hand, the firms must be protected, as one author expressed, "from financial predators and from the dotage, impedimentation, and paternalism of the ICC."[9]

Although economists generally salute competitive market structures, they often disagree over whether a particular market is in fact competitive—usually because there are different interpretations of what competition is. Even when there is agreement on the meaning of competition, there are difficulties in procuring the required data. Where adequate data have existed, various studies have attempted to justify the use of the concentration ratio as a measure of competition by relating the concentration rate to rate of return. Typically these studies suggest either a weak positive correlation between various measures of concentration and rates of return as a reflection of efficiency (performance) rather than monopoly.[10] Nevertheless, the popular notion prevails that concentration ratios are an indicator of competition, especially in cases of conglomerate mergers.[11]

---

7. See V.V. Masterson, *The Katy Railroad and the Last Frontier* (Norman, Okla.: University of Oklahoma Press, 1952), especially pp. 200-242.

8. 366 ICC 575 and ICC Finance Docket 25982 (April 6, 1970).

9. Lackman, "Conglomerates," p. 42.

10. See Harold Demsetz, *Concentration and Rates of Return*, mimeo, University of Chicago, 1971.

11. For an interesting empirical analysis that rejects the allegation that conglomerate mergers induce harmful effects on competition, see Lawrence G. Goldberg, "The Effect of Conglomerate Mergers on Competition," *The Journal of Law and Economics* 16 (April 1973), pp. 137-58.

Concentration

Since World War II most economists felt that increased concentration created an atmosphere in which oligopolists were more likely to conduct collusive practices.[12] This view that successful collusion, either by tacit or by explicit means, was more likely in concentrated industries reached a culmination in the recommendations of the 1969 White House Antitrust Task Force that deconcentration legislation be added to the antitrust arsenal.[13] These recommendations were based on a statement claiming "a close association between high levels of concentration and persistently high rates of return."[14] The statement was based on a selected number of studies by Joe S. Bain, H. Michael Mann, and George J. Stigler showing a correlation between concentration and profitability.[15] To point out a dilemma in such studies, Yale Brozen recently argued that none of these research efforts had examined the "persistence" of high rates of return in concentrated industries[16]—and the argument goes on.

If there is a growing conglomeration of American industries with its potential for crystalizing existing market structure, industrial concentration may increase. If this event happens the future performance of these industries is in danger. From a public policy point of view, deconcentration alone of these industries probably would not accomplish desired goals: "Relief must go to the heart of the problem: the extent and methods of advertising."[17] In a recent article, Willard F. Mueller and Larry G. Harmon suggest that different underlying economic factors influence concentration trends in various industries.[18] To identify and quantify the significance of these factors, they develop the following model:

---

12. See Leonard Weiss, "Quantitative Studies in Industrial Organization," in Michael D. Intritigator, *Frontiers of Quantitative Economics* (Amsterdam: North-Holland Press, 1971), p. 363. An exception to this prevailing view was presented in Paul W. MacAvoy, *The Economic Effects of Regulation: The Trunk-Line Railroad Cartels and the Interstate Commerce Commission before 1900* (Cambridge, Mass.: M.I.T. Press, 1965). In this book, MacAvoy argued that the observed behavior of a few railroads in the upper mid-West did not suggest effective collusion, even though freight rates were explicitly agreed upon by the participants. The cartel simply proved unstable.

13. "White House Task Force on Antitrust Policy," Report 1, in *Trade Regulation Reports*, Supplement to No. 415 (Washington, D.C.: May 26, 1969).

14. Ibid., p. 1-8.

15. Joe S. Bain, "Relation of Profit Rate to Industry Concentration: American Manufacturing, 1936-1940," *Quarterly Journal of Economics* 65 (August 1951), pp. 213-324; H. Michael Mann, "Seller Concentration, Barriers to Entry, and Rates of Return in Thirty Industries, 1950-1960," *Review of Economics and Statistics* 48 (August 1966), pp. 296-307; and George J. Stigler, "Theory of Olyopoly," *Journal of Political Economy* 44 (February 1964), pp. 26-52.

16. Yale Brozen, "Concentration and Profits: Does Concentration Matter?" *Antitrust Bulletin* 19 (Summer 1974), pp. 381-99.

17. Willard F. Mueller and Larry G. Harmon, "Trends in Industrial Market Concentration, 1947 to 1970," *Review of Economics and Statistics* 56 (November 1974), p. 519.

18. Ibid.

$$\Delta CR = a + b_1 B + b_2 G + b_3 S + b_4 E + b_5 L + b_6 M + b_7 H$$

where

ΔCR = change in concentration
B = beginning level of concentration
G = industry growth
S = size of industry
E = net firm entry
L,M,H = low, medium, and high (respectively) measures of product differentiation in the industry.

and where the expected signs of the coefficients are:

S – negative
B – negative
G – negative
E – negative
L – not clear
M – positive
H – positive

The best results are for the four firm concentration rates for the period 1947-70 with a sample of 15 firms:

$$\Delta CR-4 = \underset{(4.96)^{\dagger\dagger}}{9.54} \; \underset{(-5.51)^{\dagger\dagger}}{-0.19B} \; \underset{(-1.52)}{-0.003G} \; \underset{(-1.00)}{-0.001S} \; \underset{(-2.10)^{\dagger}}{-0.02E}$$

$$+ \underset{(5.18)^{\dagger}}{14.75H} \; \underset{(2.39)^{\dagger\dagger}}{+4.74M} \; \underset{(-0.81)}{-1.97L}$$

$$R^2 = 0.36$$

† t-value is significantly different than zero at 5% level using a one-tail test
†† ditto at 1% level

They concluded that:

. . . High market concentration pervades much of American manufacturing. Some may quibble over the precise level and trend of concentration. But the indisputable fact of life is that in many industries productivity is concentrated in a few hands, has been concentrated in a few hands for many decades, and will in all probability remain so unless some explicit public policy initiatives are taken to change things.[19]

The classical, competitive view of industry structure suggests that any rapid changes in concentration would be induced by shifts in cost conditions and not by alteration in the barriers to entry. Since changes in costs can be transferred to changes in profits, industries experiencing increases in concentration should exhibit greater disparities between large and small rates of return. The monopoly view of concentration, however, does not imply this disparity, for if an industry is able to sustain collective practices there is no reason to suppose that the difference between large and small firm profit rates should widen. Harold Demsetz, in a recent article, presented an empirical explanation of industry structure and profitability, and concluded that the data are more consistent with the competitive view.[20] While his results are very tentative, the conclusion is important since it questions the beneficial effects of an active deconcentration or antimerger policy. There remains the serious need to produce more analysis and data to evaluate such policies, which might produce more inefficiency than they eliminate.

Profitability

Industrial performance is a multidimensional concept, which includes allocative efficiency, technological progress, profitability, and redistributive equity among its characteristics. Beneath these dimensions lie issues of subjective judgment. For example, how much profitability is "desirable" or "excessive" for an industry? Or, how much advertising expenditures might not be regarded as "wasteful" for an industry?[21]

In empirical studies of industrial organization, it has been hypothesized that differences in monopoly power and economies of scale are among the more important explanations of differential interfirm profitability rates. The argument is that firms operating in situations of monopoly power or economies of scale will tend to earn higher profit rates. In addition, it has been hypothesized that monopoly power and economies of scale variables are positively correlated with several other attributes of the firm, like size, market share, recent economic growth, and the firm's volume of advertising

19. Ibid., pp. 519-20.

20. See Harold Demsetz, "Industry Structure, Market Rivalry and Public Policy," *The Journal of Law and Economics* 16 (April 1973), pp. 1-9.

21. For an empirical test of industrial performance focusing on subjective choice, see Steven R. Cox, "An Industrial Performance Evaluation Experiment," *Journal of Industrial Economics* 22 (March 1974), pp. 199-214.

expenditures.[22] On the other hand, it has been argued that evidence of these positive correlations can neither confirm nor deny the hypothesis that the above firm attributes can be linked with either monopoly power or economies of scale.[23]

Under a number of strong assumptions, it has been shown in the economy literature that a profit-maximizing monopolist should produce durable commodities of exactly identical desirability as a competitive industry with the same cost structure.[24] In a recent article, however, Richard Schmalensee showed that the desirability of a commodity is not independent of market structure when the item is sold rather than leased or rented.[25] The automobile industry is an obvious example of a case where several firms with substantial market power sell durable goods rather than rent them. Schmalensee's analysis suggests that these firms chose to sell a durable good on which maintenance can be productively performed, but do so at a level that is not at minimum cost. In efficiency terms, he would argue that these firms should always prefer to rent.

Innovation

In virtually every study of industrial research and development (R&D), authors have posited some type of relationship between R&D expenditures and profits.[26] While a large firm may expend greater funds on R&D to make available additional technological opportunities, it may also suppress and

22. See Marshall Hall and Leonard Weiss, "Firm Size and Profitability," *Review of Economy and Statistics* 49 (August 1967), pp. 319-30; W.S. Comanor and T.A. Wilson, "Advertising, Market Structure and Performance," *Review of Economics and Statistics* 49 (November 1967), pp. 423-40; N.R. Collins and L.E. Preston, *Concentration and Price Cost Margins in Manufacturing Industries* (Berkeley: University of California Press, 1968); William G. Shepherd, "The Elements of Market Structure," *Review of Economics and Statistics* 54 (February 1972), pp. 25-37; and B.T. Gale, "Market Structure and Rate of Return," *Review of Economics and Statistics* 54 (November 1972), pp. 412-23.

23. See Richard B. Mancke, "Causes of Interfirm Profitability Differences: A New Interpretation of the Evidence," *Quarterly Journal of Economics* 88 (May 1974), pp. 181-93.

24. See: Peter L. Swan, "Durability of Consumption Goods," *American Economic Review* 60 (December 1970), pp. 884-94; Peter L. Swan, "The Durability of Goods and Regulation of Monopoly," *The Bell Journal of Economics and Management Science* 2 (Spring 1971), pp. 347-57; and E. Sieper and P.L. Swan, "Monopoly and Competition in the Market for Durable Goods," *Review of Economic Studies* 40 (July 1973), pp. 333-51.

25. See Richard Schmalensee, "Market Structure, Durability, and Maintenance Effort," *Review of Economic Studies* 41 (April 1974), pp. 277-87.

26. See: Joseph A. Schumpeter, *Capitalism, Socialism, and Democracy* (New York: Harper & Row, Inc., 1959); Frederic M. Scherer, "Corporate Inventive Output, Profit and Growth," *Journal of Political Economy* 73 (June 1965), pp. 290-97; Henry G. Grabowski, "The Determinants of Industrial Research and Development: A Study of the Chemical, Drug, and Petroleum Industries," *Journal of Political Economy* 76 (March/April 1968), pp. 292-306; and Ben Branch, "Research and Development Activity and Profitability: A Distributed Lag Analysis," *Journal of Political Economy* 82 (September/October 1974), pp. 999-1011.

frustrate innovative ingenuity. This happens because "the organization man" replaces "the innovative entrepreneur" in the large firm, even though increasing amounts of technology may prevail.[27] In Joseph A. Schumpeter's terms, the important factor was the quality (and newness) of innovative entrepreneurship and that the firm was merely a secondary element.[28]

Quite often some empirical tests purporting to demonstrate some facet of the Schumpeter-Galbraith-Schmookler hypotheses are ambiguous and perhaps unappropriate for drawing certain inferences relating to firms' research and development (R&D) experiences.[29] It is important to distinguish between studies relating the elasticity of the value of R&D output to firm size (Schumpeter's hypothesis is that this elasticity with respect to firm size exceeds one) and investigations of the elasticity of R&D inputs with respect to firm size (the focus of some empirical studies).[30] As an indication of varying results, William Comanor, in a study examining three relationships among firm size, R&D inputs, and technical change, concluded that there were substantial diseconomies of scale in R&D associated with large firm size.[31] For a later time series in the same industry, however, John M. Vernon and Peter Gusen reached the opposite conclusion: namely, that the elasticity of technical change with respect to firm size increases with size.[32]

One small-sample empirical study on both research and development projects revealed that the work orientation of a project, either research or development, can have a significant influence on project outputs while the degree of autonomy and influence over technical work matters on a project may be unrelated to output levels.[33] These results and their implications are generally in accord with the overall conventional wisdom in management practices.

In a recent article, Morton I. Kamien and Nancy L. Schwartz presented a comprehensive model of firm inventive activity that incorporates for the first time the realistic assumption that rivalry for patents among firms exists.[34] The diffusion of technology refers in a literal sense to the adoption of a new

---

27. See P.J. McNulty, "On Firm Size and Innovation in the Schumpeterian System," *Journal of Economic Issues* 8 (September 1974), pp. 627-32.

28. Joseph A. ·Schumpeter, *Capitalism, Socialism and Democracy* (New York: Harper & Row, 1950), p. 101.

29. See F.M. Fisher and Peter Temin, "Returns-to-Scale in Research and Development: What Does the Schumpeterian Hypothesis Imply?" *Journal of Political Economy* 81 (January/February 1973), pp. 56-70.

30. For example, William S. Comanor, "Research and Technical Change in the Pharmaceutical Industry," *Review of Economics and Statistics* 47 (May 1965), pp. 187-99.

31. Ibid., p. 190.

32. John M. Vernon and Peter Gusen, "Technical Change and Firm Size: The Pharmaceutical Industry," *Review of Economics and Statistics* 56 (August 1974), pp. 294-302.

33. See William E. Souder, "Autonomy, Gratification and R&D Outputs: A Small-Sample Field Study," *Management Science* 20 (April 1974), pp. 1147-56.

34. See Morton I. Kamien and Nancy L. Schwartz, "Patent Life and R&D Rivalry," *American Economic Review* 64 (March 1974), pp. 183-87.

technique or invention by the firms in an industry once the technique has been introduced. Professor Edwin Mansfield in particular has presented impressive empirical evidence that the diffusion of a major innovation is a well-defined process.[35] Typically the number of users of an innovation grows slowly at the beginning, then accelerates, and then exhibits a decreased rate of growth as full equilibrium demand is approached.

Allocative Efficiency

Harvey Leibenstein's "Theory of Inert Areas" is a valuable concept that allows the problems of inducing change within firms to be incorporated into a theoretical model.[36] While some later disagreement has arisen over the precise definition of X-efficiency, Leibenstein states that the degree of X-efficiency is

> . . . the degree to which actual output is less than maximum output (for given inputs) . . . (and) a central notion is that firms do not produce on the outer bounds of their production possibility surface.[37]

K.J. Blois has modified this definition to be "the rate of the actual cost per unit of output to the theoretical minimum cost of attaining that output.[38] The difference between this latter definition and Leibenstein's original one can be illustrated by considering a firm operating with two or more inputs. If that firm is operating with no X-inefficiency (or at the theoretical minimum cost for that level of output) and a change in relative input prices occurs, then if the firm does not adjust its use of inputs while maintaining its current level of output (a likely short-run event) it is no longer operating at minimum cost–*but* it is still operating on the outer bound of its production possibility surface.[39]

A Concluding Point

Very little research has focused on developing theories to explain the results of behavior (optimizing or otherwise) on the part of individual firms. Also the idea

35. Edwin Mansfield, *The Economics of Technological Change* (New York: W.W. Norton and Co., 1968). Also, T.Y. Shen examines the possible explanation for changes in outputs and inputs of a temporal sample of manufacturing plants and concludes that a diffusion model modified to incorporate X-efficiency improvements yields the most satisfactory results. See his "Technology Diffusion, Substitution, and X-Efficiency," *Econometrica* 41 (March 1973), pp. 263-84.

36. Harvey Leibenstein, "Allocative Efficiency vs. 'X-Efficiency'," *American Economic Review* 56 (June 1966), pp. 392-415; and "Organizational or Frictional Equilibria, X-Efficiency, and the Rate of Innovation," *Quarterly Journal of Economics* 83 (November 1969), pp. 600-623.

37. Liebenstein, "Organizational or Frictional Equilibria," p. 600.

38. K.J. Blois, "Some Comments on the Theory of Inert Areas and the Definition of X-Efficiency," *Quarterly Journal of Economics* 88 (November 1974), p. 686.

39. Ibid.; By Leibenstein's original definition, this would not be a case of X-inefficiency.

that firm behavior with respect to "risk taking" varies systematically with market structure has received little attention.[40] Just as Richard E. Caves used findings from several industrial organization studies to propel his own theory of risk avoidance, so too should transportation analysts search more deeply into transportation firm data with the anticipation of understanding more fully the intricacies of the relationship between market structure and firm performance.[41] Such theories are needed as a prerequisite to meaningful analyses of firm behavior[42] in any industry and especially in the transportation modes.

---

40. See F.R. Edwards and A.A. Heggestad, "Uncertainty, Market Structure, and Performance: The Galbraith-Caves Hypothesis and Managerial Motives in Banking," *Quarterly Journal of Economics* 87 (August 1973), pp. 455-73.

41. Richard E. Caves' contribution appears in "Uncertainty, Market Structure and Performance: Galbraith as Conventional Wisdom," in Jesse W. Markham and Gustav F. Papanek, eds., *Industrial Organization and Economic Development: In Honor of E.S. Mason* (Boston: Houghton Mifflin Company, 1970), pp. 283-304.

42. Even in the more heavily researched banking industry, very little attention has been given to this issue, with the exception of Michael A. Klein, "A Theory of the Banking Firm," *Journal of Money, Credit, and Banking* 3 pt. 1 (May 1971), pp. 205-18. See also "A Comment: A Theory of the Banking Firm," by John J. Pringle, *Journal of Money, Credit, and Banking* 5 (November 1973), pp. 990-96.

34 Selected Statistical Issues

The analysis of any transportation system or project always should involve some form of statistical or econometric technique. The choice of the appropriate technique or method depends on a variety of factors and constraints facing the agencies or groups that are sponsoring the analysis. The following discussion briefly describes some of the basic problems associated with the use of a few selected techniques of statistical analyses.

Cost-benefit analysis, simulation methods, and the linear programming model represent popular approaches of mathematical programming to handle special kinds of transportation problems. The theory of optimizing in mathematical programming methods can be split into two parts: first, one that deals with the requirements of the internal consistency of a program or system, as a whole, that is, the assurance of the full coordination of the many interdependent decisions that must be fulfilled if a program is to be realized; and second, the other that covers the problems relating to selecting the best solution from among the broadest range of choices. The application of optimizing techniques to transportation systems for project development and implementation, as well as to quality management problems, is well grounded. To a greater extent, however, the techniques have been applied to particular projects or systems without regard for the integrated relationship which the project(s) may have to the economy of a region as a whole, or for the phasing of various investments relating to the particular pattern of growth that might be anticipated.

Within such a conceptual framework the critical sectoral interdependencies and bottlenecks or capacity considerations are minimized. In fact, the transportation sector may be, or may become, a critical bottleneck in the economy that must be relieved on a time schedule basis if the other sectors are to be enabled to deliver their outputs to sustain socially desirable growth rates. Taken as a bottleneck problem to be solved on a time basis, the question of budget constraints or no budget constraints is then really reduced to one of—do we have a consistent program of development in which public priorities have been properly specified and all our resources for the given period have been allocated optimally? In general, the statistical complex of planning problems can be decomposed into the following states:

1. How much to invest in an aggregate manner over a number of years
2. How to distribute the total investment among the different public sectors
3. How to select the best, or most efficient, method of using the resources allocated to a given transportation sector

These questions pertain to the whole range of regional and national econometric models. They also apply to the inventory of input-output models that have been used in numerous regional and statewide analyses.

Both Data Resources, Inc. (of Lexington, Mass.) and Chase Econometric Associates, Inc. (of Bala Cynwyd, Pa.), a subsidiary of the Chase Manhattan Bank, N.A., have developed over the past few years macroeconomic forecasting models that have been among the more significant contributions to the arenas of economic modeling and of business-economic forecasting as mentioned in Chapter 8. These quarterly models forecast a broad range of macroeconomic variables and are marketed on a fee basis to a large number of business, professional, and governmental clients. Although the models are continuously updated, most clients are only interested in the values of the forecasts and in the commentaries attached to these values. Clients ordinarily do not question the underlying statistical assumptions and foundations. While these models are large-scale systems (like the Wharton, FRB-MIT-Penn, and other large macro-models), each equation is usually estimated using the ordinary least squares method. Each equation is uniquely specified, tested, and calibrated in accordance with standard econometric practices.[1] The major problems of interpretation pertain to those normally associated with single equation, multiple regression estimates. The two principal problems are: specification and multicollinearity.

Specification refers to the appropriate selection of the independent variables in the equation. The theory of the single equation model is that changes in each of the independent variables cause or "explain" changes in the dependent variable (which is the variable to be forecast). There are two general ways to conduct a model specification: The first is to intuitively consider those variables that should influence the dependent variable, postulate the way in which they are related (linear or nonlinear), and then test the specification with actual data collected from a sufficiently large sample of observations to (hopefully) confirm the model. This approach is theoretically more appealing but quite often results in statistically problematical outcomes, usually traceable to poor data of perhaps dubious quality. The other way to conduct a specification is to employ computer application iterations to a set of "possible" independent variables (including lagged variables and various transformations). The outcome of these iterations reflects the "best" statistical results with a given set of data. The main drawbacks of this approach are that the model is only as good as the data are and that an intuitively "correct" independent variable might be affected if its observations did not yield statistically consistent results with the other variables.

Multicollinearity refers to the degree of intercorrelation between each pair of independent variables. It is essential for each pair of independent variables to

---

1. A better approach, at least on theoretical grounds, would be to specify a simultaneous equation system in order to capture the interactions of causality and then to use simultaneous equation methods to test the "true" model. Unfortunately, this approach can be more intricate and expensive and forecasters usually are forced to back off to use single equation methods.

have low intercorrelations or else they are not truly independent of one another.[2] If it is very high then values of the two coefficients of the independent variables that are intercorrelated are questionable and any resulting forecasts are then based on statistically suspicious (perhaps even wrong) coefficients.[3] This problem of multicollinearity becomes more serious as additional independent variables are placed in a single equation specification. The three general methods to handle multicollinearity are: (1) to use first differences of the independent variables; (2) to use lagged variables; or (3) to jettison one of the intercorrelated variables.

Another major problem in statistical analysis is *autocorrelation.* As is well known, there are three major consequences of autocorrelated errors in regression analysis: (1) Estimates of the coefficients are inefficient; (2) forecasts based on the equations are suboptimal; and (3) the usual significance tests in the coefficients are invalid.[4] If one finds the residual series in a regression estimate is strongly autocorrelated, then it is difficult to interpret the coefficients of the equation. In spite of the explicit warnings on the dangers of autocorrelated errors in virtually every econometric textbook, it is common to observe in many applied studies time-series regression equations with an apparently high degree of fit (denoted by the coefficient of multiple correlation, R^2) but with an extremely low value for the Durbin-Watson (*D-W*) statistic. If such a regression result is experienced in practice, especially one when the *D-W* statistic is low, the only conclusion that can be reached is that the equation is misspecified, regardless of the R^2 value.[5] Ordinarily, equation misspecification is considered to result from a combination of omitted relevant variables, included irrelevant variables, or autocorrelated residuals. The usual recommendations for alleviation are to either incorporate a lagged dependent variable, or to take first differences of the variables in the equation, or to assume a simple first-order autoregressive form for the residual of the equation.[6]

---

2. Most multiple regression computer programs exhibit a matrix of partial correlation coefficients for all the variables. The closer the partial correlation coefficient (ρ) is to zero, the lower the degree of intercorrelation. Perfect correlation is reflected by a value of 1.0 (or −1.0 for negative perfect correlation).

3. Suppose that an equation for forecasting the price of highway trailers is estimated as $HT = 16.84 + 102.5\ ULCM + 42.5\ PIPE$ where

HT = Wholesale price index for highway trailers
$ULCM$ = Unit labor costs, manufacturing
$PIPE$ = Implicit price deflator, fixed business investment in equipment

This specification claims that variations in *ULCM* and *PIPE* (ignoring its interpretation) *independently* influence variations in *HT.* By inserting forecasted values of *ULCM* and *PIPE*, one can then determine the forecasted values of *HT.* But, if *ULCM* and *PIPE* are highly intercorrelated (which they are, for $\rho = +0.99$), then the coefficients of *ULCM* and *PIPE* (102.5 and 42.5, respectively) could really have other values (like 22.0 and 300.5) so that the independent contributions of these variables are obfuscated.

4. See C.W.J. Granger and P. Newbold, "Spurious Regressions in Econometrics," *Journal of Econometrics* 2 (July 1974), pp. 111-20.

5. Ibid., p. 117.

6. See E. Malinvaud, *Statistical Methods of Econometrics* (Amsterdam: North-Holland Publishing Co., 1966).

In summary, then, a good statistical analysis is one when all the tests of measurement and significance are met. In particular, an analyst would like to specify a single equation model appropriately and then subject the specification to an empirical test with a sufficiently large number of observations (more precisely, sufficiently large degrees of freedom). The "best" results for a single equation estimate then would yield the following: high R^2, low multicollinearity, no autocorrelation, high t-ratios, high F-statistic, and intuitively meaningful coefficient values. For simultaneous equation systems, additional tests must be conducted.[7]

Economic aggregation theory provides an excellent general structure that can be applied to the specific case of any transportation network aggregation. With this approach the network aggregation can be characterized as the application of an *aggregation function* to a micronetwork (a detailed representation of a transportation system) to provide a macronetwork (a smaller, less complex, version of the micronetwork). This is represented in Figure 34-1.

The basic issue of concern in aggregation problems is the extent to which the behavior of the micronetwork can be diagnosed on an observation of the behavior of the macronetwork. In the ideal case, total consistency is said to exist between the networks, and everything about the micronetwork can be known by studying the macronetwork. As Yugi Ijiri points out, however, the conditions necessary to achieve this consistency for aggregation problems in general are very stringent.[8] Moreover, in many situations only partial consistency is necessary in transportation network analysis. The results of network analyses typically become inputs to decision-making processes of one form or another, and these processes sometimes only require a part of the information available from the micronetwork. If this essential information is preserved and available from analyses of the macronetwork, then this represents sufficient consistency between the two networks; decisions then can be made on the basis of partial information. In other situations, only the relative rankings of various network analysis output measures, for a set of network alternatives, are important to the decision-making process.

Once the goal of total consistency has been abandoned in any aggregation

Figure 34-1. The Aggregation Function.

7. Still perhaps the best single source of statistical problems is J. Johnston, *Econometric Methods,* rev. ed. (New York: McGraw-Hill, Inc., 1972).

8. Yugi Ijiri, "Fundamental Queries in Aggregation Theory," *Journal of the American Statistical Association* 66 (December 1971), pp. 766-82.

problem, the determination of the *errors and biases* inherent in the partially consistent approach becomes a critical task. In most studies, two different approaches to determining errors and biases can be taken: first, an analytic approach, in which rigorously formulated aggregation functions are analyzed mathematically to reach conclusions as to their errors; and second, an empirical approach, in which the proposed aggregation functions are applied to micro or detailed networks to obtain macro or aggregate networks. (Models can then be applied to both scales of network and the results can be compared.) Both of these approaches to determining errors require a careful definition of the elements of the micronetwork to be preserved in the macronetwork; or, phrased differently, the type of consistency to be maintained by the aggregation structure must be determined. This requires, of course, a clear definition of the intended uses to be made of the outputs of network models.

To exemplify this discussion, we can apply the conceptual structure to a given transportation network application area, for example, the prediction of highway travel. Experience in the highway network application area indicates that at least two classes of intended users have been identified and separate aggregation approaches have been developed in response to the particular needs of each. The first class is represented by highway design engineers, who desire to obtain detailed information about individual links on a network. An aggregation approach, which can be termed "windowing" because it preserves detail in only a small area, has been developed to serve their needs. The second class, represented by system planners, wish to answer broader questions about alternative systems, such as total user cost, average delays per trip, and total trips generated. An aggregation approach that has been developed to serve their needs can be termed "sketch planning" because it generally covers a whole area, providing a constant reduced level of detail. These two classes of intended users are representative of similar classes present in a number of transportation application areas.[9]

The theory of economic aggregation relevant to the network problem in transportation has two principal aspects: first, aggregation and its effects in estimating macroparameters and hence on policy formation; and second, aggregation and its implications for prediction. Although these two problems can be studied separately, they are neither truly independent nor incompatible with one another and consequently can be regarded as aspects of the same problem.[10] In order to examine the implications of aggregation for these two aspects, consider a simple linear micro model to be specified by:

9. For additional information on these issues, see Marvin L. Manheim, Richard E. Nestle, and Uzi Landau, Working Papers, Department of Civil Engineering, M.I.T. (1974).

10. See K.L. Gupta, *Aggregation in Economics* (Rotterdam: Rotterdam University Press, 1969).

$$y_{it} = b_i x_{it} + c_i z_{it} \quad \text{for } i = 1, \ldots, n \text{ and } t = 1, \ldots, T \tag{34.1}$$

from which the corresponding macro level would be

$$Y_t = bX_t + cZ_t \tag{34.2}$$

where

$$Y_t = \sum_i y_{it} \quad X_t = \sum_i x_{it} \quad Z_t = \sum_i z_{it} \tag{34.3}$$

In order to integrate the expression of the macrorelations in terms of the micro parameters, one can form a set of auxiliary equations:[11]

$$x_{it} = B_i X_t + C_i Z_t \tag{34.4}$$

$$z_{it} = D_i X_t + E_i Z_t \tag{34.5}$$

from which can be derived

$$b = \frac{1}{n} \sum_i b_i + n\,[\mathrm{Cov}(b_i, B_i) + \mathrm{Cov}(c_i, D_i)] \tag{34.6}$$

$$c = \frac{1}{n} \sum_i c_i + n\,[\mathrm{Cov}(b_i, C_i) + \mathrm{Cov}(c_i, E_i)] \tag{34.7}$$

The terms in the square brackets of equations (34.6) and (34.7) can be measured as the aggregation bias. This definition and estimation of aggregation bias is the heart of aggregation theory, because the primary concern amounts to knowing the conditions under which the aggregation bias will vanish.

The importance of aggregation bias for parameter estimation is twofold: first, the stability of the macrorelations depends not only on the corresponding microrelations but also on the coefficients of the auxiliary equations that can be altered either by autonomous factors (such as shifts in population) or by government public policy; and second, any sources of instability can be broken down into two parts: the bias due to the corresponding microparameters and the bias due to the noncorresponding microparameters, both of which are subject to estimation and measurement.[12] The importance of this latter distinction is

11. Henri Theil, *Linear Aggregation of Economic Relations* (Amsterdam: North Holland Publishing Company, 1954), pp. 12 ff.

12. Ijiri, "Fundamental Queries," pp. 766-82; and my "Costing in Railroad Operations: A Proposed Methodology," *M.I.T. Studies in Railroad Operations and Economics*, vol. 13 (1974), Appendix C.

demonstrated by the fact that if one is interested in the stability of the macrorelations (for a transportation network) and if the bias due to the noncorresponding microparameters is insignificant, then the major concern shifts to analyzing the temporal behavior of the distribution of the corresponding macrovariables alone.[13] If this was not the case, however, the larger the number of explanatory variables, the greater would be the difficulty in insuring the stability of the macrocoefficients and hence the macrorelations.

Historical studies in the theory of economic aggregation have focused on the recommendations of specific procedures to the econometric investigator. The theory usually has been applied to basic types of economic problems: reduced forms of simultaneous equation systems,[14] an input-output matrix,[15] a linear programming problem,[16] prediction models,[17] and a step-wise clustering algorithm.[18] Each of these statistical techniques have been used in analyzed transportation problems. In the broadest sense, aggregation theory can be applied to any situation whereby a portion of the information available for the solution of a problem is sacrificed in exchange for facilitating the solution of the problem. Given the initial judgment of the investigator regarding this trade-off, then the statistical conditions can be derived accordingly.

13. H.A.J. Green, *Aggregation in Economic Analysis* (Princeton, N.J.: Princeton University Press, 1964), chap. 9.

14. Theil, *Linear Aggregation*, pp. 12 ff.

15. Green, *Aggregation*, chap. 9; and W.D. Fisher, *Clustering and Aggregation in Economics* (Baltimore: The Johns Hopkins Press, 1969), chap. 3.

16. Green, *Aggregation*, chap. 9.

17. Gupta, *Aggregation in Economics.*

18. Fisher, *Clustering and Aggregation*, chap. 3.

35 Energy Consumption in Freight Transportation

The general usage of energy in the United States during the past two decades has doubled and currently is divided approximately in the following way: Industrial use accounts for 42 percent; residential and commercial use, 33 percent; and transportation, 25 percent. The separation of the transportation end use of energy is intercity passenger, 6 percent; urban passenger, 9 percent; intercity freight, 4 percent; and urban freight, 6 percent.[1] A significant point of interest from the figures is that the vast freight tonnages that move on an intercity basis use less energy than any of the other categories. It is estimated that about 54 percent of our petroleum fuels are used to produce transportation.[2] From an energy point of view there are high degrees of interfuel substitutability in the electric generation, residential, commercial, and industrial sectors. Transportation, however, relies almost entirely on petroleum liquids. While there is a potential for large efficiency improvements in all sectors, a special effort must be made to minimize wasteful activities in transportation where the conversion efficiencies are notably poor.[3]

There are various aspects to an analysis of the energy problem as it relates to transportation. One aspect is the energy intensiveness of each mode of transportation. Energy intensiveness is defined as the inverse of energy efficiency: the more energy intensive a mode of transport is, the less efficient its use of energy. This approach is one in which the BTUs per ton-mile are used to determine the energy intensiveness for freight transportation (see Table 35-1). As developed by this method, the most efficient modes are pipelines and waterways; railroads are not very efficient, trucks are even less efficient than rail, and aircraft have the lowest efficiency. A careful refinement of the different facets of fuel efficiency by mode of transport, however, suggests that energy intensiveness as expressed in BTUs per ton-mile, ignores the fact that the services performed (or the unit of output) by each of the modes are not strictly comparable. Another facet is that the circuitry factor is much greater between origins and destinations for some modes of transportation than for others. Still another facet is that, for the many

1. See Eric Hirst, "Transportation Energy Conservation: Opportunities and Policy Issues," *Transportation Journal* 13 (Spring 1974), p. 43.

2. U.S. Department of Transportation, Transportation Systems Center, *Transportation Energy in the United States, 1972-1985* (Washington, D.C.: Report for *Project Independence*, 1975).

3. See Lawrence Livermore Laboratory, *An Assessment of U.S. Energy Options for Project Independence*, prepared for the U.S. Atomic Energy Commission, Report UCRL-51638 (Washington, D.C.: September 1974).

Table 35-1
Rail and Truck Fuel Consumption (BTUs)[a]

	All Rail Traffic				
	Total	Coal	Oil	Electricity	Trucks–All Highways
1950	2,045	1,453	568	24	1,460
1955	825	291	511	22	1,805
1960	501	--	483	18	2,153
1965	524	--	508	16	2,655
1970	524	--	510	14	3,426
1971	523	--	509	14	3,608

[a]Figures are in trillions of BTUs.
Source: U.S. Department of Transportation, *Summary of National Transportation Statistics 1973.*

short hauls and the light density traffic that characterize the state of affairs on many rail lines currently proposed for abandonment, motor carriers are less energy intensive than the railroads. Since the rail data include passenger traffic, a rough approximation of the fuel consumed in the movement of freight can be developed from the following data on annual locomotive miles in millions by type of traffic for the selected years since 1960, as reported in Table 35-2. By interpolation in that table, it is estimated that freight shipments involved the consumption of 70.0 and 69.5 percent of total BTU equivalents used by rail in 1950 and 1955, respectively.

In order to determine the energy use of intercity motor carriers, it is necessary to eliminate fuel consumed in local freight transportation. Using estimates of the energy use by intercity freight trucking developed by Oak

Table 35-2
Annual Locomotive Mileage[a]

	Total	Passenger	Freight	Percent Freight
1960	611	189	422	69.1
1965	1,060	211	849	76.0
1970	1,421	143	1,278	89.9
1971	1,335	57	1,278	95.7

[a]Mileage figures are in millions.
Source: U.S. Department of Transportation, *Summary of National Transportation Statistics 1973.*

Ridge National Laboratories for 1950, 1960, and 1970,[4] and interpolating for 1955, 1965, and 1971 on the basis of the trends in the percentage of rural vehicle miles traveled (VMT) of total truck VMT as reported in the annual editions of *Highway Statistics* of the U.S. Federal Highway Administration, estimates of intercity freight movements by trucks were used as a basis for calculating the percentages of motor carrier consumption of fuels in BTU equivalents, as reported in Table 35-3.

Applying the rail freight percentages and the intercity truck percentages to the respective total BTU fuel-equivalent consumption by the two modes produces an estimate of total intercity commodity energy use for the rail and trucking modes (see Table 35-4). Applied to the rail and truck freight ton-miles reported for the selected years in the *Statistical Abstract*, these fuel use totals can be used to calculate the BTU-equivalent fuel consumption per ton-mile (see Table 35-5). The BTU use per ton-mile is 4 percent below that reported in the cited *Industrial Energy Studies for Ground Freight Transportation* for rail freight movements in 1971, but 44 percent greater than the intercity truck estimate; and the truck estimate above is only 3 percent below the "general" truck consumption reported in that study. It is not possible to identify the source of the discrepancy but these estimates derived over time by the same method serve at least to establish relative trends that appear reasonably comparable. The drastic reduction in rail consumption of fuel per unit of freight movement was due to the conversion from coal to diesel oil in the early 1950s. Both rail and truck appear to have achieved their greatest fuel efficiencies a decade later; since 1965, however, the trend estimates above indicate that rail

Table 35-3
Intercity Truck Fuel Use

	Truck Fuel Consumption (Intercity)
1950	44.2%
1955	48.1
1960	52.1
1965	54.8
1970	57.5
1971	58.2

Source: Derived from U.S. Department of Transportation, *Summary of National Transportation Statistics 1973.*

4. *As reported in Industrial Energy Studies of Ground Freight Transporation*, Peat, Marwick, Mitchell & Company, and Jack Faucett Associates, Inc. (Washington, D.C.: July 1974).

Table 35-4
Intercity Freight Shipment Fuel Use[a]

	Rail	Truck
1950	1,432	413
1955	573	595
1960	346	816
1965	398	921
1970	471	1,120
1971	501	1,176

[a]In trillions of BTUs.
Source: Derived from U.S. Department of Transportation, *Summary of National Transportation Statistics 1973.*

Table 35-5
Intercity Freight Ton-Mile Energy Use

	Annual Ton-Miles (Billions)		BTU Use per Ton-Mile	
	Rail	Truck	Rail	Truck
1950	628	173	2,280	2,388
1955	655	223	875	2,671
1960	595	285	582	2,863
1965	721	359	552	2,566
1970	771	412	611	2,719
1971	746	430	672	2,735

Source: Derived from U.S. Department of Transportation, *Summary of National Transportation Statistics 1973.*

fuel consumption per ton-mile in BTU equivalents has increased 21.7 percent while truck consumption has increased only 6.6 percent. Regardless of the measure used in any study, the research analyst has to be careful to specify the terms and boundaries of his analyses.

A relative measure of the cost of energy used in the transport of freight by rail and trucking carriers can be developed from data on fuel costs for the same set of selected years. In Table 35-6 is an application of the unit costs to the fuel consumption data derived above for freight movements by the rail and truck modes. These unit costs then can be used to derive the total costs of energy use by these two modes and the cost per ton-mile. The conversion from coal to diesel fuel appears to have resulted in a marked reduction in the fuel cost per ton-mile of freight shipped by rail for the 1950-60 period (about 46 percent) but

Table 35-6
Estimated Energy Cost of Intercity Rail and Truck Shipments

	Production Value of Coal (Dollars/Ton)	Rail (Cents/Gal.)	Truck (Cents/Gal.)	Electricity Revenues (Kilowatt-Hour)	Energy Costs (Millions of Dollars)		Energy Costs per Ton-Mile	
					Rail	Truck	Rail	Truck
1950	4.84	8.30¢	15.10¢	1.52¢	450.8	451.5	0.72¢	2.61¢
1955	4.72	10.10	16.18	1.68	326.3	710.6	0.50	3.19
1960	4.69	9.50	16.08	1.84	254.6	967.9	0.43	3.40
1965	N.A.	9.00	15.38	1.71	280.8	1,063.9	0.39	2.96
1970	N.A.	10.80	17.68	1.63	389.4	1,480.2	0.51	3.59
1971	N.A.	11.60	18.11	1.72	445.9	1,599.1	0.60	3.72

N.A. = not available.

Source: U.S. Bureau of the Census, *1973 Statistical Abstract* (Washington, D.C.: 1974).

since then, these costs have increased 54 percent. The fuel cost per ton-mile for freight shipped by trucks (except for a decline around 1965) have generally increased throughout this period. The overall increase in truck fuel costs per ton-mile for the 1960-71 period amount to 43 percent whereas the overall decline in rail fuel cost per ton-mile for the same period was 17 percent.

Table 35-7 compares recent (1972) energy efficiency levels for the major transport modes in both passenger and commodity movements and also projects 1980 and 1985 levels based on an assumed imported crude oil price of $7.00 per barrel.[5] For the passenger modes, energy efficiency is expressed in passenger-

Table 35-7
Energy Efficiency of Transportation Modes, 1972-85[a]

	1972	1980	1985
Passenger Modes (Passenger-miles/gallon)[b]			
Urban passenger			
Auto	23	25	28
Bus	79	90	90
Rail	42	47	48
Intercity passenger			
Auto	48	53	60
Bus	118	120	120
Rail	36	43	45
Air	15	16	17
Freight Modes (Ton-miles/gallon)			
Urban freight			
Truck	19	20	20
Intercity freight			
Truck	53	59	61
Rail	197	206	209
Water (domestic)	276	282	288
Pipeline	307	329	339
Air (domestic)	5	5	5

[a]Based on imported crude oil price of $7.00/bbl.

[b]Based on average load factors.

Source: Federal Energy Administration, *Project Independence Report, Project Independence* (Washington, D.C.: U.S. Government Printing Office, 1974), App. A1, table AIII-1, p. 92.

5. See Jack Faucett Associates, Inc., *Project Independence and Energy Conservation: Transportation Sectors* (Washington, D.C.: August 1974).

miles per gallon of fuel required; for the freight nodes, in ton-miles per gallon—with higher values representing greater energy efficiency. These projections demonstrate very small gains in energy efficiency in each mode by 1985. Unfortunately, current trends also suggest that there will continue to be a general shift away from the more energy efficient modes toward the less efficient in both the passenger and freight sectors.[6] Table 35-8 provides a summary of the most recent data on fuel consumption by the various passenger modes.

A Concluding Point

Transportation—especially the private automobile, the taxicab, and the truck—is responsible for substantial amounts of urban air pollution and energy consumption. In most major cities the transport modes contribute to the air about 95 percent of all carbon monoxide, 50 percent of hydrocarbons, 25 percent of nitrogen oxides, and 20 percent of toxic particulates. So little is known about the true energy efficiencies of alternative transportation modes, both urban and intercity, that the present state of the art on this topic is rather embryonic. The prospects are that this topic, perhaps by necessity, may be the most important area of research in transportation during the coming decade.

6. Federal Energy Administration, *Project Independence Report, Project Independence* (Washington, D.C.: U.S. Government Printing Office, November 1974), App. A-1, pp. 92-94.

Table 35-8
Passenger Transportation: 1975 Fuel Consumption[a]

	Average Seat-Miles per Gallon
Rail:	
3,000 hp. locomotive, turbocharged, 9 coaches for locomotive, 60-80 seats each	270-360
2,250 hp. E-8, nonturbocharged, 4-5 coaches per locomotive, 60-80 seats each	150-250
Rail diesel car (Budd) 75-85 seats	250
Bus:	
Intercity (Greyhound), 47 seats	282
Urban, 50 seats	180-230
Automobile:	
Urban, subcompact, 4 seats, 24 mpg	96
Urban, compact, 5 seats, 18 mpg	90
Urban, standard, 6 seats, 14.4 mpg	86.4
Urban, luxury, 6 seats, 9 mpg	54
Intercity, subcompact, 4 seats, 30 mpg	120
Intercity, compact, 5 seats, 22.5 mpg	112.5
Intercity, standard, 6 seats, 18 mpg	108
Intercity, luxury, 7 seats, 12 mpg	72
Air:	
Twin engine turbofan, 68-106 seats	
Short-stage length (250 mi.)	30-38
Medium-stage length (500 mi.)	37-47
3 & 4 engine turbofan, 131-200 seats	
Medium-stage length (500 mi.)	35-41
Long-stage length (1,000 mi.)	44-51
3 & 4 engine turbofan, widebody, 256-385 seats	
Medium-stage length (500 mi.)	44-51
Long-stage length (1,000 mi.)	54-60

[a]Based on seating capacity and average fuel use rates for selected pieces of equipment.

Source: U.S. Department of Transportation, *Report to the Congress on the Rail Passenger Service Act* (Washington, D.C.: July 1974), pp. 41-42.

36 Perspectives on National Transportation Policy

During periods of general economic stability, policy changes are difficult to implement. Institutions are usually so well-established that with the political stability typically found in these situations some kind of crisis is necessary to evoke any kind of meaningful change. Forces appear to be mobilized and compromises more readily reached during crisis periods than during calmer ones. For better or for worse, a period of significant crisis now looms inevitable for several transportation industries in the United States. The recent bankruptcies of several eastern railroads is one problem that appears can only be solved through a major reorganization. This factor hopefully will be resolved within the next few years. A second factor is the environmental concern that should be ubiquitous to our cities. This factor will inevitably have a major impact on the use of the automobile, on the utilization of trucking and on urban goods movements. Likewise, energy shortages, and the consequential changes in the price of fuel relative to other factors, threaten major changes in the basic economics of the transport modes and in the use of transportation relative to other activities.

Threatening as these situations may be, a remarkably good opportunity exists for initiating major new directions in national transportation policy and for emphasizing the required changes in the institutions that determine the overall efficiency of the transportation and distribution system of this country. It is the purpose of this chapter to examine certain current issues of national transportation policy and to propose some steps required to implement major improvements in the existing policy of the federal government.

What is National Transportation Policy?

Every domestic transportation service must be produced and offered by either a business firm or governmental agency. Regardless of which agent offers the service, the performance and viability of a transportation system are measured and evaluated in terms of economic factors, including costs, revenues, and profits. If costs exceed revenues over time, then the firm withdraws from the market, or it receives subsidies, or another agency must take over the operations and also provide a subsidy. This problem is pervasive to all transportation activities and numerous practical and contemporary examples can be provided as documentary evidence. The extent to which certain firms are subsidized (either by direct outlays or with loan guarantees) and to which certain governmental agencies receive priorities in funding is the subject matter of what is loosely labeled "national transportation policy."

Public policy is also a term that has been mentioned several times during the course of this book. In many ways it is the proximate purpose for which economic analysis should be used. While economic analysis reflects the science of economics, public policy (in our case, transportation policy) reflects the use of judgment or prescription for which economic analysis should be used. Transportation policy can be applied to numerous areas: federal, state, and local; executive, legislative, and judicial; statutory and "ad hoc"; regulatory and administrative; multimodal and modal; and for the enterprise–transportation policies that affect maintenance, operations, and finance. Because of its widespread applications, the term often loses its meaning and thereby its impact. For our purposes in this chapter let us assume that national transportation policy refers to matters of national, legislative, and multimodal interests.

Even though national transportation policy is an extremely important matter, its exact nature is difficult to identify. Congress initially promulgates national transportation policy through its action in appropriating funds, in establishing and authorizing regulatory commissions and administrative boards, and in announcing policy guidelines. The executive branch influences natural transportation policy principally through its power of appointment and through the U.S. Department of Transportation.

The original Act to Regulate Interstate Commerce in 1887 was the first attempt to prescribe a general national transportation policy.[1] The earliest form of a modern policy appeared in the Transportation Act of 1920, which subjected the railroads to the complex regulation in the public utility mold that had been adopted by many states to combat the practices of local utilities. Regulation existed at that time allegedly for the purpose of controlling monopoly and restricting competition among the railroad companies. Between 1920 and 1935 technological advances changed the national transportation structure drastically so that transportation no longer remained a monopoly of the railroads. During the era of the Great Depression, the basis for national transportation policy became the restriction of and protection against competition. This philosophy was embodied in the Motor Carrier Act of 1935, the Civil Aeronautics Act of 1938, and the Transportation Act of 1940 as applied to water common carriers. The numerous exemptions and exceptions to these pieces of legislation reflected the obvious discomfort experienced by each of the industries covered by their respective statutory policies. The litigation arising from interpretations of these statutes has continued at an increasing pace to the present time. Needless to say, the economic costs associated with the litigation have been substantial.

The role of the common carrier in transportation is not nearly so great as it

1. Dudley F. Pegrum, *Economics of Transportation*, 7th ed. (Homewood, Ill.: Richard D. Irwin, Inc., 1972).

was in earlier decades. At the present time federal economic regulation affects 100 percent of rail and air freight, 95 percent of air passenger services, 80 percent of pipeline tonnage, 41 percent of motor trucking, and only 7 percent of domestic water carriers. With the advent of various forms of noncommon carriage and other innovative endeavors, there are at least three main national policy issues that relate to the current activities of the common carrier. As suggested by Dudley F. Pegrum, these issues include:

1. The degree of protection that should be afforded common carriers against each other, regardless of mode
2. The protection to be afforded common carriers from those that cannot be forced into this category
3. The question of whether common carriers should be confined to common carrier transport[2]

The ultimate resolutions of these issues will depend on the effectiveness of the institutional arrangements among the carriers, the regulatory agencies, the Department of Transportation, and in some instances, the Department of Justice. As an example of formal statutory policy, consider the following criteria originally stated in the Act to Regulate Commerce (1887) Sec. 5(2)(C) and amended by the Transportation Act of 1940, Sec. 5(2):

1. The effect of the proposed transaction upon adequate transportation service to the public
2. The effect upon the public interest of the inclusion, or failure to include, other railroads in the territory involved in the proposed transaction
3. The total fixed charges resulting from the proposed transactions
4. The interest of the carrier employees affected

In spite of the appealing goals that appear in the statutory proclamations and in spite of the belated recognition of transportation as a systems problem, the impacts of the statutes are unfortunately deficient. The most significant disappointment has been the inability to implement the stated goals into practice. One author has even condensed this deficiency into three adjectives: "incomplete, inconsistent and indefinable."[3] In a broader sense, though, the impacts of national transportation policy are not totally negative. The narrative of the statutes does point in the right direction; awareness is perhaps a necessary first step in a tedious process, the benefits of which may still remain before us. Perhaps more important and more affirmative is that the statutory policy has

2. Dudley F. Pegrum, "Restructuring the Transport System," in Ernest W. Williams, Jr., ed., *The Future of American Transportation* (Englewood Cliffs, N.J.: Prentice-Hall, Inc., 1971), pp. 66-67.

3. Martin T. Farris, "National Transportation Policy: Fact or Fiction?" *Quarterly Review of Economics and Business* 10 (Summer 1970), pp. 7-14.

established a set of standards: ". . . it does set up goals and ideas no matter how unattainable they may be."[4]

In the Department of Transportation Act of 1966 Congress declared that a national transportation policy should be developed to achieve certain goals and objectives. The wording of the legislation was rather general but still emphasized the need for transportation services which were fast, safe, efficient, convenient, and consistent with other national objectives. In support of this legislation the Department of Transportation (DOT) published the first serious document that proposed new approaches in developing policies to achieve transportation objectives. This document was called the *1972 National Transportation Report* and it contained the following five goals:

1. Environmental quality: to increase the benefits derived from the preservation and enhancement of the environmental aesthetic, and social attributes of transportation and its surroundings
2. Safety: to minimize the loss of human life and property and the human suffering due to transportation-related accidents
3. Economic efficiency: to provide that mix of transportation alternatives, including modal systems, related facilities, manpower, research and development, etc., which results in maximum benefits such as service, convenience, comfort, capacity, and speed for a given cost
4. Support of other national interests: to further all other objectives of the federal government whenever they are affected by transportation or whenever the department can perform a particular task more effectively and efficiently
5. Support of local objectives: to facilitate the process of local determination by decentralizing decisionmaking and fostering citizen participation[5]

The report is intended to be updated every few years so that a multimodal analysis, covering all modes of transportation, is sustained by DOT to provide information and recommendations to Congress as provided by legislation.

For individual modes, however, separate policies studies will continue to be undertaken. In fact, two recent documents in the railroad industry have produced (some errors notwithstanding) the most comprehensive analyses of the industry's problems than any heretofore available. These two documents are the *1973 Improving Railroad Productivity* study conducted by a presidential task force[6] and the *1975 Preliminary System Plan* of the eastern and midwestern railroads performed by the United States Railway Association.[7]

4. Ibid., p. 13.

5. U.S. Department of Transportation, Office of the Secretary, 1972 *National Transportation Report* (Washington, D.C.: July 1972), p. 7.

6. National Task Force on Productivity, *Improving Railroad Productivity* (Washington, D.C.: 1973).

7. United States Railway Association, *Preliminary System Plan: Volumes 1 and 2* (Washington, D.C.: February 26, 1975).

Selected Modal Policy Examples

Through the regulatory agencies of the ICC, CAB, and FMC, the federal government can directly influence the structure and performance of the individual transportation industries by imposing regulatory constraints on rates, routes, entry conditions, ownership rights, and the extent of intermodal coordination. The government directly affects the operating costs incurred by the various modes through its roles in providing funds for investment in demonstration projects, operating subsidies, research and development, and the infrastructure. In a similar way, through its more general regulatory role of setting standards for safety, pollution emissions, vehicle sizes, and vehicle weights, the government can also have a direct impact on modal operating costs. The government also directly affects the supply and quality of a broad range of transportation services as an operator of inland waterways, the air traffic control system, Amtrak and ConRail. Finally, as a major user of transportation services, the government (especially the U.S. Department of Defense) can directly affect the allocation of major traffic shipments between modes.

In view of this large number of activities it is not surprising that they remain uncoordinated and often conflicting. The lack of coordination and contradiction are most apparent in the areas of intercity passenger transportation and intercity commodity movements. For example, both the Transportation Act of 1920 and the Federal Highway Act of 1935 committed the federal government to substantial expenditures for inland waterway and highway infrastructures, respectively. These commitments were continued over the years without much regard for these effects on the overall national transportation network. To the extent that these investments have undermined the railroads' comparative advantage in many cases, these earlier pieces of legislation have been inconsistent with the National Transportation Act of 1940 discussed above.

The American railroads never have been the most inspiring examples of heroically independent enterprises. In these halycon days the railroads' relationship with the government was what might be called pragmatic. Especially in the nineteenth century, the existence of cheap prices attached to lanes for rights-of-way (and the methods in which they were determined) contributed substantially to the growth of the industry.[8] There was a period of less than austere principles when railroads "owned" many state legislatures and congressmen. Reciprocity was the law of the land.

The history of the relationship between the railroads and government agencies has been prologue. Only the level of despair has deepened. Federal and state government support now is an undesirable necessity. No community is

8. The extent to which the railroad industry contributed to the development of the West is a matter of debate, while more recent sources have discussed this issue, the classic reference is Robert William Fogel, *Railroads and American Economic Growth: Essays in Econometric History* (Baltimore: The Johns Hopkins Press, 1964).

willing to lose a subsidized rail service and no Congressperson can rebuff such a scheme that would enable his or her acknowledging credit for salvaging (or promoting) a community's rail service. Government involvement in the railroad industry is a hard fact and is typical of the country's current political economy. One must not be deluded, however, in thinking that government subsidies will ever induce private profits, especially in the railroad industry. To the extent that inducements do exist, the ICC has formulated a set of operating criteria or policies for the carriers under its jurisdiction. These criteria have been summarized neatly by Roy Sampson and Martin T. Farris, and are presented in Table 36-1.

The ICC has also been slow to systematize the reporting and disclosure of information to the investing public in connection with offerings of securities by the public owned railroads and motor carriers. In particular, the financial information should show a carrier's relative operations in transportation and nontransportation areas. Other desirable data that should be available to the public are carrier investments in corporate conglomerates and the position of a carrier in relation to subsidiaries and for the corporate parent. Under present Securities and Exchange Commission requirements (form S-1) some of these are available but not in a form that isolates transportation activities.

In the regulation of transportation firms, the commissions need only to regulate profits and rates (as a determinant of profit) as long as effort levels are given and costs are assumed to be minimized.[9] However, if the firms have some degree of X-inefficiency, then regulating profits are insufficient. Higher costs to the firms are no longer an argument for higher rates in conformity with an allowable rate of return (profit), but may be evidence of X-inefficiency and a compelling indicator of a need for a change in management, ownership or both.

In the airline industry, the regulatory policies are promulgated by the CAB while administrative and safety issues are handled by the FAA. The two classic examples of airline modal policy are the *General Passenger Fare Investigation* (GPFI) in 1960 and the *Domestic Passenger Fare Investigation* (DPFI) in 1972. A comparison of the policy issues contained in these two investigations has been made by George W. Douglas and James C. Miller III in a recent article; a sample of these issues appears in Table 36-2.

9. There have been several freight rate increases on the railroad industry during the last few years. These boosts in rates have been proposed in a piecemeal fashion: On August 19, 1973, there was a general freight-rate increase of 3 percent, followed shortly hereafter by three more increases (totaling only 2.8% from October 1973 to March 1974, to assist railroad retirement plans); then a series of fuel surcharges increased freight rates by an additional 3.3 percent by May 1974; on top of these factors were a 4 percent general freight rate increase during May 1974 and a selective 10 percent increase in June 1974; and in October 1974, another 7 percent general freight rate hike was proposed, to be effective January 1975. In their petitions to the ICC the railroad companies claimed that rapidly rising increases in materials and supplies were responsible. When the Chessie System and other southern railroads balked at this proposed increase (in the midst of a severe recession) the application was rejected by the ICC. As one can note by the record, rate policies are not conducted in a consistent and comprehensive way that would be amenable to the needs of a national transportation policy.

Table 36-1
ICC Transportation Policy

I. Elements of transportation monopoly control
  A. Rates and discrimination elements
    1. All rates must be just and reasonable; all unjust and unreasonable rates are illegal. The ICC has power to determine reasonableness and prescribe maximum and minimum rates.
    2. All shippers must be treated equally if they have similar transportation circumstances and conditions (no personal discrimination).
    3. All undue preference and prejudice to any person, locality, or type of traffic is illegal (broad discrimination prohibition).
    4. A carrier may not charge more for a short haul than for a long haul where the short is included in the long haul over the same line and in the same direction. Exceptions allowed by petition.
    5. Rates must be published and available to all. No deviation from the published rate is allowed under penalty of law. Rebates and passes illegal (except for certain exceptions relative to passes).
    6. The general level of rates for carriers as a group are to be so established as to allow the carrier to earn a fair rate of return on a fair value. Excessive individual carrier earnings are to be recaptured in part and made available as loans to carriers earning less than the determined fair level.
    7. Rates may be suspended for a limited time while they are being investigated.
    8. A carrier may not carry its own products in competition with other shippers (except lumber).
    9. Commodity classification procedures may be controlled by the ICC.
    10. Intrastate rates may be raised so as not to discriminate against interstate commerce.
  B. Service elements
    1. Car service rules must be formulated, filed, and approved by the ICC. The commission may control car movement in emergencies.
    2. The ICC may establish through routes and joint rates.
    3. The commission may order joint use of terminals.
    4. All abandonments and extensions must be approved by the ICC.
    5. All pooling or combination must be approved by the ICC (after both were illegal per se for some time).
    6. Labor disputes must progress through a complicated series of time-consuming administrative procedures in an effort to effect settlement of industrial conflict without work stoppage.
  C. Security and financial elements
    1. All accounts must be uniform and open for inspection.
    2. Periodic and detailed financial reports must be rendered.
    3. The ICC may divide revenues from joint rates with the needs of carriers as a standard.
    4. All changes in capital structure and the issuance of securities must be approved by the commission.
    5. All reorganization and bankruptcy must be approved by the ICC. A special procedure is established to facilitate restoration of the carrier to sound financial health.
    6. All consolidations and mergers must fit a master plan and have ICC sanction (after being absolutely illegal for a period).

II. Elements of transportation competition control
  A. Entry controls
    1. Entry is controlled to preserve competitive relationships, insure sale operation, and guarantee adequate financial health of carriers.
    2. Established firms at the date of regulation are preserved by grandfather clauses.

Table 36-1 (cont.)

3. New firms must secure certificates of public convenience and necessity, or permits.
4. New carriers, or those desiring to extend their services, must prove they are "fit, willing, and able" to serve and that the public interest will be served by their entry.
5. Carriers may operate only over specified routes and carry specified commodities.

B. Minimum rate control and inherent advantage
1. Minimum rates are controlled with the goal of limiting intramodal competition.
2. Minimum rates are controlled with the goal of limiting intermodal competition and preserving the inherent advantage of each mode.
3. Minimum rates of one carrier cannot be held up to a particular level to protect the traffic of any other mode.

C. Exemptions and carrier classification
1. For-hire carriers are classified in numerous ways, according to operating characteristics, as common, contract, supplementary, or nonscheduled.
2. Numerous carriers are exempt according to type of commodity hauled, as agricultural commodities, bulk movement by water, newspaper haulers.
3. Numerous carriers are exempt according to geographic operating characteristics, as carriers wholly within one or contiguous municipalities, movement incidental to other transportation, carriers operating in national parks and monuments.
4. Private carriers moving their own goods where the primary business is other than transportation are exempt.

D. Safety and liability controls
1. Control over motor vehicle condition, hours or labor of drivers, and safety devices is allowed.
2. Control over aircraft, pilot training and pilot qualifications is provided.
3. Mandatory insurance provisions to protect shippers and the public are included.

E. Rates and discrimination controls
1. All rates must be just and reasonable. Regulatory bodies may suspend rates, determine reasonableness, and prescribe maximum and minimum rates.
2. Shippers must be treated equally if they have similar transportation circumstances and conditions. Undue preference and prejudice is prohibited.
3. Rates must be published and available to all. Public notice of rate changes is required. No deviation from published rates is allowed and rebates are illegal.

F. Security and financial controls
1. All accounts must be uniform and open for inspection.
2. Periodic and detailed financial reports must be rendered (although some classes of carriers are exempt from this requirement).
3. Changes in capital structure and the issuance of securities must be approved by regulatory authorities (with some exemptions).
4. Consolidations and mergers must be approved by regulatory authorities.

Source: Roy J. Sampson and Martin T. Farris, *Domestic Transportation: Practice, Theory and Policy*, 3rd ed. (Boston: Houghton Mifflin Company, 1971), pp. 334-35 and 364-66.

An important matter of airline industry policy is the issue of supersonic transport travel (SST). The SST controversy hardly will remain dormant. If the French/British Concord or the U.S.S.R.'s TU-144 turns out to be successful, and if antirecessionary fiscal policies in the United States require increased federal government spending in the aerospace or aircraft industries, a renewed effort to build a SST (modified or otherwise) would be forthcoming. Furthermore, continual pressures from Boeing and Lockheed on Washington have resulted in

Table 36-2
A Comparison of CAB Policies, 1960 to 1972

Comparison of Policies: GPFI (1960), Policies Developed During Interim, and DPFI (1972)

Policy Issue (Phase of DPFI)	GPFI (1960)	Policies Developed During Interim	DPFI (1972)
1. Flight Equipment Investment	Straight-line Writeoff	--	Affirmed
2. Leased Aircraft	--	Not Included in Rate Base	Affirmed
3. Deferred Federal Income Taxes	Included as Current Expense	--	Affirmed
4. Joint Fares	--	a. Rate Based on Sum of Local Rates Minus Cost Saving	a. Rate Based on Sum of Local Rates Minus Cost Saving
	--	b. Revenue Division Based on Local Rates	b. Revenue Division Based on Relative Carrier Costs
5. Discount Fares	--	Discriminatory Discounts Encouraged	Discriminatory Discounts Disallowed
6A. Seating Configuration Standards	--	--	Standards Adopted; Regulation Implicit
6B. Load Factor Standards	Rejected	--	Standards Adopted; Regulation Implicit; No Analysis of Price Vs. Quality
7. Fare Level	Unable to Determine Reasonable Fare Level from Record	Fares Based on Actual Costs, Reflecting Carrier "Revenue Need"	Fares Based on Average Cost of Providing Reasonable Quality of Service
8. Rate of Return	a. 10.5 Percent Overall Return, Based on Cost of Capital and Actual Debt Equity Ratio	--	a. 12 Percent Overall Return, Based on Cost of Capital and "Optimal" Debt/Equity Ratio
	b. Some Implication of Guaranteed Return	--	b. "Guarantee" Explicitly Rejected; Actual Return Left to Market Forces; No "Ratchet Effect"
9. Fare Structure	--	Gradual Increase in Fare Taper; Promulgation of Industrywide Fare Formula; No Zone of Reasonableness Fare Flexibility	(Board Decision Not Yet Rendered; Some Preliminary Indication Favoring Cost-based Rates and Limited Pricing Flexibility)

Table 36-2. (cont.)

Sources: CAB Orders E-16068, 70-1-147, 71-1-48, 71-4-54, 71-4-58, 71-4-59, 71-4-60,72-4-42, 72-12-18, 72-5-101, et al.; and George W. Douglas and James C. Miller, III, "The CAB's Domestic Passenger Fare Investigation," *The Bell Journal of Economics and Management Science* 5 (Spring 1974), p. 219.

each manufacturer's continuing planning and design work on supersonic aircraft, in the belief that such an aircraft will be environmentally and economically feasible. Existing airport capacities and sizes certainly can handle a fleet of supersonic aircraft.[10]

Opportunities for Technological and Institutional Change

Perhaps the greatest opportunity for improvements in efficiency of transportation lie in the area of technological and institutional change. Institutional change would appear to be the logical precondition for change in much of today's technology. However, from time to time major shifts in technology will come along and alter the nature of an industry in such a way that institutional change then follows. The jet engine was such a development. For others the technology does not change until reorganization occurs.

A variety of possibilities for reorganization are open to the transportation industries. Railroads are currently Balkanized, which appears to preserve the independence of the ultimate decision-making units while actually preserving all of the bad features of dependence on committee decision making. Virtually the entire industry participates in every decision of consequence. The promotion of end-to-end mergers in the railroad industry may help to promote freely competing railroad companies with their own autonomy, but there are a variety of other organizational forms that remain to be explored.[11]

Integrated intermodal freight transportation companies are one such possibility. By allowing single ownership of both rail and truck facilities, overall coordination is promoted. The same could be said for truck/air combinations or any of the other modes. Efficiency and public equity could be promoted by allowing these larger, integrated companies to compete with each other over the same territory. In Canada, where this policy has been allowed, the results appear to be positive.

10. The world's largest airport is Mirabel, located 34 miles northwest of Montreal. It covers 138 square miles, nearly half the area of New York City and several times the size of the next largest airport, Dallas-Fort Worth International Airport. Mirabel airport includes a unique buffer zone of 111 square miles of airport authority owned land, surrounding the 27 square mile airport proper. By comparison, the world's busiest airport, Kennedy International in New York, is less than eight square miles.

11. Pegrum, *Economics of Transportation.*

Another possibility is the logistics company. The basic concept here is the provision of overall logistics services, including reordering, inventory control, warehousing, transportation, and final distribution of product. There are major economies of scale to be gained in consolidating shipments between points. It remains to be investigated, however, whether companies can trust the inventory management to another company over which they do not have direct control.

An area in which gains can almost certainly be made is the area of freight rate modernization. The current freight rate structure is extremely complex. It cannot be computerized in its current form and is difficult to understand and to analyze. Efficient use of the transport system on the part of the shipper requires that he be heavily staffed with knowledgeable technicians. Perhaps the most glaring fault with the present system however, is the manner in which uneconomic use of the system is promoted. Freight rate discrimination and value of service pricing tend to badly distort the rational use of the overall system. Railroads, for example, have lost much high value commodity tonnage by trying to extract too much for these rates while cutting rates on low rated goods such as sand and gravel.

The treatment of regulation and its overall revamping are areas in which institutional change has long been advocated. The deregulation or partial deregulation of the transport industries has precedence in other countries. Nevertheless, until 1975 there was no strong legislation in the United States to promote deregulation, ease of entry, and joint ownership on the part of carriers.[12] The actual impact of recent activities in regulatory reform, however, does offer some potential for increased efficiency in the transportation sectors.

New technology is an area that generates particular fascination for many people. There is frequently a feeling that any problem can be solved by technological innovation. Although this is an oversimplification, technological innovations may necessitate the reopening of issues relative to supersonic aircraft, solids, pipelines, freight submarines, surface effect ships, long distance conveyors, lighter than air vehicles, and personal rapid transit devices. Although any one of these new modes may not play a major role in transportation in the future, they could nevertheless perform important functions for certain areas, and major developments often emerge when least expected.

Forecasting the economic impacts of transportation activities on urban land use has been a task replete with increasing public and governmental concern in recent years. Most land use/transportation studies during this period have focused on high population density areas for quite obvious reasons. To the extent that the significant problems of urban and metropolitan areas associated with new, modified or abandoned transportation activities have been identified, these studies have been successful in measuring and forecasting short-run impacts with respect to environmental factors, housing, family displacement, real estate

12. A step in the right direction was taken by the ICC in *Ex Parte* No. 279, "Securities Regulation–Public Offerings," which require large carriers to report financial data in a more streamlined fashion. See 344 ICC 167 (September 1973).

values, employment, and traffic congestion. Even though these successes have been implemented in many urban areas across the country, the studies have not been able to shed conclusive evidence on the urban growth process, on the problems of urban sprawl, on the basic justifications of cities themselves, and on the general neglect of smaller cities (low population-density areas).

Without a solid economic-development foundation, without tax-base and job opportunities, and without necessary services and life-supporting commerce, many federally subsidized programs in cities are vacuous. Because of the overriding importance of economic development, the matters of industrial location and land use are far more important to the success of not only low-density transportation services, but also of urban renewal and public housing than most writers and practitioners recognize. In other words, the same degree of awareness that must be paid to the realities of industrial location in central cities also must be applied to business location in low density regions. Since land shortages prevent central cities from providing roots for all types of businesses, industrial decentralization must be accompanied by viable programs to provide low-income housing in exurban and low-density areas where industry has moved or wants to move. This is especially true when such decisions are not based on the proximity to markets, on the existence of better transportation services, on the availability of labor supply, or on other rational economic factors, but increasingly on the irrationalities of tax rate disparities. When the federal government subsidizes one or several industries and maintains some prices (or rates or fares) higher than others, the market mechanism is distorted in the sense that not all of the units in the economy act on the same price ratios.[13] The key for a national transportation policy is to avoid these distortions. If this goal is accomplished, then the question of "balance" so often mentioned in statements of transportation policy is resolved.

Summary

There simply is not a unified policy of economic regulation reflecting the overall needs of the country for a transportation system responsive to the needs of shippers and travelers for the economic, reliable and safe movement of commodities and passengers. While existing regulatory statutes contain pious declarations of policy admonishing the regulators to "coordinate" or "foster" the modes subject to these jurisdictions, the practice has usually been the advocacy by an agency of a policy that benefits a single mode in spite of possible adverse effects on other modes and on the general public. The synthesis of a national transportation policy that would be equitable, efficient, and motivating remains the major challenge in the whole domestic transportation arena.

13. For a recent statement of this classical theorem of welfare economics, see Kunio Kawamata, "Price Distortion and Potential Welfare," *Econometrica* 42 (May 1974), pp. 435-60.

Selected Bibliography: Microeconomic and Econometric Applications to Transportation

Adelman, M.A. "The Measurement of Industrial Concentration," in Heflebower, R.B., and G.W. Stocking, eds., *Readings in Industrial Organization and Public Policy* (Homewood, Ill.: Richard D. Irwin, Inc., 1958).

Agapos, A.M., and Paul M. Dunlap. "The Theory of Price Determination in Government-Industry Relationships," *Quarterly Journal of Economics* 84 (February 1970), pp. 85-99.

Aigner, Dennis J., and S.F. Chu. "On Estimating the Industry Production Function," *American Economic Review* 58 (June 1968), pp. 226-39.

Alberts, William W., and Joel E. Segall, eds. *The Corporate Merger* (Chicago: University of Chicago Press, 1966).

Andrieu, Michel. "Derived Demand, Returns to Scale and Stability," *Review of Economic Studies* 41 (July 1974), pp. 405-17.

Ascel, David H. "Determinants of Executive Compensation," *Southern Economic Journal* 40 (April 1974), pp. 613-17.

Averch, Harvey and Leland L. Johnson. "Behavior of the Firm Under Regulatory Constraint," *American Economic Review* 52 (December 1962), pp. 1052-69.

Bain, Joe S. *Industrial Organization* (New York: John Wiley & Sons, Inc., 2nd ed., 1968).

_______. *Essays on Price Theory and Industrial Organization* (Boston: Little, Brown, and Company, 1972).

Barth, James R., and James T. Bennett. "Economic Determinants of the Regional Allocation of Federal R & D Expenditures." *Land Economics* 50 (February 1974), pp. 100-103.

Baumol, W.J. *Business Behavior, Value, and Growth* (New York: MacMillan, 1959).

_______. "The Theory of Expansion of the Firm," *American Economic Review* 52 (December 1962), pp. 1078-87.

Berg, Sanford, V. "Determinants of Technological Change in the Service Industries," *Technological Forecasting and Social Change* 5 (1973), pp. 407-26.

Blackman, A. Wade Jr. "The Market Dynamics of Technological Substitutions," *Technological Forecasting and Social Change* 6 (1974), pp. 41-63.

Blair, John M. *Economic Concentration* (New York: Harcourt, Brace, Jovanovich, Inc., 1972).

Bloch, Harry. "Advertising and Profitability: A Reappraisal," *Journal of Political Economy* 82 (March/April 1974), pp. 267-86.

Boyle, Stanley E. *Industrial Organization: An Empirical Approach* (New York: Holt, Rinehart and Winston, Inc., 1972).

Branch, Ben. "Research and Development Activity and Profitability: A Distributed Lag Analysis," *Journal of Political Economy* (September/October 1974), pp. 999-1011.

Brozen, Yale. "Concentration and Profits: Does Concentration Matter?" *Antitrust Bulletin* 19 (Summer 1974), pp. 381-99.

Capron, William M., ed. *Technological Change in Regulated Industries* (Washington: The Brookings Institution, 1971).

Carleton, Willard T. "Rate of Return, Rate Base and Regulatory Lag Under Conditions of Changing Capital Costs," *Land Economics* 50 (May 1974), pp. 145-51.

Comanor, William S., and Thomas A. Wilson. *Advertising and Market Power* (Cambridge, Mass.: Harvard University Press, 1974).

Cyert, Richard M., and James G. March. *A Behavioral Theory of the Firm* (Englewood Cliffs, N.J.: Prentice-Hall, Inc., 1963).

Duetsch, Larry L. "Elements of Market Structure and the Extent of Suboptimal Capacity," *Southern Economic Journal* 40 (October 1973), pp. 216-23.

Engwall, Lars. *Models of Industrial Structure* (Lexington, Mass.: Lexington Books, D.C. Heath and Co., 1973).

Forsund, Finn R., and Lennart Hjalmarsson. "On the Measurement of Productive Efficiency," *Swedish Journal of Economics* 76 (June 1974), pp. 141-54.

Glaister, Stephen. "Advertising Policy and Returns to Scale in Markets where Information is Passed between Individuals," *Economica* 41 (May 1974), pp. 139-56.

Gold, Bela. *Explorations in Managerial Economics: Productivity, Costs, Technology and Growth* (New York: Basic Books, 1971).

Goldberg, Lawrence G. "Conglomerate Mergers and Concentration Ratios," *Review of Economics and Statistics* 55 (August 1974), pp. 303-9.

Gorecki, Paul K. "The Measurement of Enterprise Diversification," *Review of Economics and Statistics* 55 (August 1974), pp. 399-403.

Grabowski, Harry, and Dennis Mueller. "Industrial Organization: The Role and Contribution of Econometrics," *American Economic Review* 60 (May 1970), pp. 100-108.

Griliches, Zvi. "Hybrid Corn: An Exploration of the Economics of Technological Change," *Econometrica* 25 (October 1967), pp. 501-22.

Harris, Maury N. "Restricting by 'Internal Expansion': The Case for Limiting Mergers into Oligopoly Industries," *Antitrust Law and Economics Review* 7 (1974), pp. 37-48.

Haugen, Robert A., and Dean W. Wichern. "The Elasticity of Financial Assets," *Journal of Finance* 29 (September 1974), pp. 1229-40.

Hellman, Darly A. "Agglomeration Economies: A Model of Regional Export Activity," *Growth and Change* 5 (January 1974), pp. 12-17.

Hexter, J.L., and John W. Snow. "Mergers, Asymmetry and Antitrust," *Antitrust Bulletin* 19 (Summer 1974), pp. 401-19.

Higgins, Robert C., and Lawrence D. Schall. "Corporate Bankruptcy and Conglomerate Mergers," *Journal of Finance* 30 (March 1975), pp. 93-113.

Hirschman, Albert O. *Exit, Voice and Loyalty: Responses to Decline in Firms, Organizations, and States* (Cambridge, Mass.: Harvard University Press, 1972).

Hunt, H.G. *Industrial Economics* (London: Pergamon Press, 1965).

Ijiri, Yugi, and Herbert Simon. "Interpretations of Departures from the Pareto Curve Firm-Size Distributions," *Journal of Political Economy* 82 (March/April 1974), pp. 315-32.

Imel, Blake, Michael R. Behr, and Peter G. Helmberger. *Market Structure and Performance: The U.S. Food Processing Industries* (Lexington, Mass.: Lexington Books, D.C. Heath and Co., 1972).

Jackson, Raymond. "The Consideration of Economies in Merger Cases," *Journal of Business* 43 (October 1970), pp. 439-47.

Karni, Edi. "The Value of Time and the Demand for Money," *Journal of Money, Credit and Banking* 6 (February 1974), pp. 45-64.

Kelly, Eamon M. *The Profitability of Growth Through Mergers* (University Park, Pa.: Pennsylvania State University, 1967).

Klevorick, Alvin K. "The 'Optimal' Fair Rate of Return," *The Bell Journal of Economics and Management Science* 2 (Spring 1971), pp. 122-53.

Kochen, Manfred, and Karl W. Deutsch. "A Note on Hierarchy and Coordination: An Aspect of Decentralization," *Management Science* 21 (September 1974), pp. 106-14.

Kuenne, Robert E. *Microeconomic Theory of the Market Mechanism: A General Equilibrium Approach* (New York: Macmillan, 1968).

Lancaster, Kelvin J. "A New Approach to Consumer Theory," *Journal of Political Economy* 75 (April 1966), pp. 132-57.

Larner, Robert J. *Management Control and the Large Corporation* (Cambridge, Mass.: Dunellen, 1970).

Leibenstein, Harvey. "Organizational or Frictional Equilibria, X-Efficiency, and the Rate of Innovation," *Quarterly Journal of Economics* 83 (November 1969), pp. 600-623.

Mann, H.M. "Seller Concentration, Barriers to Entry and Rates of Return in Thirty Industries, 1950-60," *Review of Economics and Statistics* 48 (August 1966), pp. 296-307.

Mansfield, Edwin. "Size of Firm, Market Structure, and Innovation," *Journal of Political Economy* 121 (December 1963), pp. 556-76.

_______, ed. *Monopoly Power and Economic Performance: The Problem of Industrial Concentration* (New York: W.W. Norton and Co., Inc., 1964).

_______. "Industrial Research and Development Expenditures," *Journal of Political Economy* 122 (June 1964), pp. 319-40.

_______, ed. *Defense, Science and Public Policy* (New York: W.W. Norton and Co., Inc., 1968).

Mansfield, Edwin. *The Economics of Technological Change* (New York: W.W. Norton and Co., Inc., 1968).

_______. *Industrial Research and Technological Innovation* (New York: W.W. Norton and Co., Inc., 1968).

_______, ed. *Microeconomics: Selected Readings* (New York: W.W. Norton and Co., Inc., 1971).

Marcus, M. "Advertising and Changes in Concentration," *Southern Economic Journal* 36 (October 1969), pp. 117-21.

Marris, Robin. *The Economic Theory of "Managerial" Capitalism* (1964; rpt. New York: Basic Books, 1968).

Marris, Robin, and Adrian Wood, eds. *The Corporate Economy: Growth, Competition and Innovative Potential* (Cambridge, Mass.: Harvard University Press, 1971).

Martin, David D. "The Uses and Abuses of Economic Theory in the Social Control of Business," *Journal of Economic Issues* 8 (June 1974), pp. 271-85.

Mason, Edward S., ed. *The Corporation in Modern Society* (Cambridge, Mass.: Harvard University Press, 1961).

McGuire, Joseph W. *Theories of Business Behavior* (Englewood Cliffs, N.J.: Prentice-Hall, Inc., 1963).

McNicol, David L. "The Comparative Statics Properties of the Theory of the Regulated Firm," *The Bell Journal of Economics and Management Science* 4 (Autumn 1973), pp. 428-53.

Meehan, James W., Jr., and Thomas D. Duchesneau. "The Critical Level of Concentration: An Empirical Analysis," *Journal of Industrial Economics* 22 (September 1973), pp. 21-36.

Migué, Jean-Luc, and Gérard Belanger. "Toward a General Theory of Managerial Discretion," *Public Choice* 17 (Spring 1974), pp. 27-43.

Mueller, Dennis. "The Firm Decision Process: An Econometric Investigation," *Quarterly Journal of Economics* 81 (February 1967), pp. 58-87.

Mueller, Willard F., and Larry G. Hamm. "Trends in Industrial Market Concentration, 1947 to 1970," *Review of Economics and Statistics* 56 (November 1974), pp. 511-20.

Naylor, Thomas J., and John M. Vernon. *Microeconomics and Decision Models of the Firm* (New York: Harcourt, Brace and World, Inc., 1969).

Nelson, Richard R., Merton J. Peck, and Edward D. Kalachek. *Technology, Economic Growth and Public Policy* (Washington: The Brookings Institution, 1967).

Nordhaus, William D. *Invention, Growth and Welfare: A Theoretical Treatment of Technological Change* (Cambridge, Mass.: the M.I.T. Press, 1969).

Phillips, Almarin. *Market Structure, Organization and Performance; An Essay on Price Fixing and Combinations in Restraint of Trade* (Cambridge, Mass.: Harvard University Press, 1962).

Porter, Michael E. "Consumer Behavior, Retailer Power and Market Performance in Consumer Goods Industries," *Review of Economics and Statistics* 56 (November 1974), pp. 419-34.

Posner, Richard A. "Exclusionary Practices and the Antitrust Laws," *University of Chicago Law Review* 41 (Spring 1974), pp. 506-35.

Rosenberg, Nathan. "Science, Invention and Economic Growth," *Economic Journal* 84 (March 1974), pp. 90-108.

Rubin, Paul H. "The Expansion of Firms," *Journal of Political Economy* 81 (July/August 1973), pp. 936-49.

Schall, Lawrence D. "The Lease-or-Buy and Asset Acquisition Decisions," *Journal of Finance* 29 (September 1974), pp. 1203-14.

Scherer, F.M. *Industrial Market Structure and Economic Performance* (Chicago: Rand McNally and Co., 1970).

_______. "The Determinants of Multi-Plant Operation in Six Nations and Twelve Industries," *KYKLOS* 27 (1974), pp. 124-39.

Schmalensee, Richard. *The Economics of Advertising* (Amsterdam: North-Holland Publishing Company, 1972).

Schmookler, Jacob. *Invention and Economic Growth* (Cambridge, Mass.: Harvard University Press, 1966).

_______. *Patents, Invention and Economic Change: Data and Selected Essays*, edited by Zvi Griliches and Leonid Hurwicz (Cambridge, Mass.: Harvard University Press, 1972).

Shashua, L., and Y. Goldschmidt. "An Index for Evaluating Financial Performance," *Journal of Finance* 29 (June 1974), pp. 797-814.

Shepherd, William G. *Market Power and Economic Welfare* (New York: Random House, 1970).

Sherman, Roger. *Oligopoly: An Empirical Approach* (Lexington, Mass.: Lexington Books, D.C. Heath and Co., 1972).

Simon, Herbert H., and C.P. Bonini. "The Size Distribution of Firms," *American Economic Review* 48 (September 1958), pp. 607-17.

Smyth, David J., William J. Boyes, and Dennis E. Peseau. "The Measurement of Firm Size: Theory and Evidence for the United States and the United Kingdom," *Review of Economics and Statistics* 62 (February 1975), pp. 111-14.

Sutton, C.J. "Advertising, Concentration and Competition," *Economic Journal* 84 (March 1974), pp. 56-69.

Theil, Henri. "A Theory of Rational Random Behavior," *Journal of the American Statistical Association* 69 (June 1974), pp. 310-14.

Tilton, John E. *International Diffusion of Technology: The Case of Semiconductors* (Washington: The Brookings Institution, 1971).

Trebing, Harry M. "Realism and Relevance in Public Utility Regulation," *Journal of Economic Issues* 8 (June 1974), pp. 209-33.

Varian, Hal R. "Equity, Envy, and Efficiency," *Journal of Economic Theory* 9 (September 1974), pp. 63-91.

Vernon, John M. *Market Structure and Industrial Performance: A Review of Statistical Findings* (Boston: Allyn and Bacon, Inc., 1972).

Vernon, John M., and Robert E.M. Nourse. "Profit Rates and Market Structure of Advertising Intensive Firms," *Journal of Industrial Economics* 22 (September 1973), pp. 1-20.

Weston, J. Fred. *The Role of Mergers in the Growth of Large Firms* (Berkeley, Cal.: University of California Press, 1953).

Weston, J. Fred, and Stanley I. Ornstein, eds. *The Impact of Large Firms on the U.S. Economy* (Lexington, Mass.: Lexington Books, D.C. Heath and Co., 1973).

Weston, J. Fred, and Sam Peltzman, eds. *Public Policy Toward Mergers* (Pacific Palisades, Cal.: Goodyear, 1969).

Williamson, Oliver E. "The Vertical Integration of Production: Market Failure Considerations," *Papers and Proceedings of the American Economic Association* 61 (May 1971), pp. 112-23.

_______. *The Economics of Discretionary Behavior: Managerial Objectives in a Theory of the Firm* (Chicago: Markham, 1967).

_______. *Corporate Control and Business Behavior* (Englewood Cliffs, N.J.: Prentice-Hall, Inc., 1970).

Winter, S.G. "Satisficing, Selection and the Innovating Remnant," *Quarterly Journal of Economics* 85 (November 1971), pp. 237-61.

Yarrow, G.K. "Managerial Utility Maximization Under Uncertainty," *Economica* 40 (May 1973), pp. 155-73.

Zajac, E.E. "A Geometric Treatment of Averch-Johnson's Behavior of the Firm Model," *American Economic Review* 60 (March 1970), pp. 117-25.

Selected Statistical References

Aigner, D.J., and S.M. Goldfeld. "Estimation and Prediction from Aggregate Data When Aggregates Are Measured More Accurately than their Components," *Econometrica* 42 (January 1974), pp. 113-34.

Bry, Gerhard. "The Rationale of Short Term Economic Forecasting Techniques," *Business Economics* 9 (September 1974), pp. 72-77.

Fogler H. Russell. "A Pattern Recognition Model for Forecasting," *Management Science* 20 (April 1974), pp. 1178-89.

Friedman, James W. "Concavity of Production Functions and Non-increasing Returns to Scale," *Econometrica* 41 (September 1973), pp. 981-84.

Griliches, Zvi. *Economies of Scale and the Form of the Production Function* (Amsterdam: North-Holland Publishing Co., 1971).

Howrey, E. Philip, Lawrence R. Klein, and Michel D. McCarthy. "Notes of Testing the Predictive Performance of Econometric Models," *International Economic Review* 15 (June 1974), pp. 366-83.

Kuh, Edwin, and John Meyer. "Correlation and Regression Estimates When The Data Are Ratios," *Econometrica* (October 1955), pp. 400-416.

MacKinnon, Ross D. "Lag Regression Models of the Spatial Spread of Highway Improvements," *Economic Geography* 50 (October 1974), pp. 368-74.

Mardsen, James, David Pingry, and Andrew Whinston. "Engineering Foundations of Production Functions," *Journal of Economic Theory* 9 (October 1974), pp. 124-40.

Meyer, R.A., and K.R. Kadiyala. "Linear and Nonlinear Estimation of Production Functions," *Southern Economic Journal* 40 (January 1974), pp. 463-72.

Silberman, I.H. "On Lognormality as a Summary Measure of Concentration," *American Economic Review* 57 (December 1967), pp. 807-30.

U.S. Department of Transportation, Federal Railroad Administration. *Rail Passenger Statistics in the Northeast Corridor 1973* (Washington: June 1974).

Westin, Richard B. "Predictions from Binary Choice Models," *Journal of Econometrics* 2 (May 1974), pp. 1-16.

Zellner, Arnold, ed. *Readings in Economic Statistics and Econometrics* (Boston: Little, Brown and Company, 1968).

Zellner, Arnold, and Franz Palm. "Time Series Analysis and Simultaneous Equation Econometric Models," *Journal of Econometrics* 2 (May 1974), pp. 17-54.

Appendix A: Glossary of Transportation Terms

This glossary provides a brief description of the most frequently used terms in transportation economics. The terms are separated into the conventional modal categories of:

Air transportation
Road transportation
  Bus
  Motor trucking
Local transit
Water transport
Railroads
Oil pipeline

Most of these terms and their descriptions are extracted from U.S. Department of Transportation Office of the Secretary, *Summary of National Transportation Statistics* (Washington, D.C.: November 1973), pp. 103-11.

Air Transportation

Airborne Speed: Often called "wheels-off wheels-on speed." The average speed of an aircraft while airborne, in terms of great-circle airport-to-airport distance.

Aircraft Revenue Miles: The miles (computed in airport-to-airport distances) for each interairport hop completed, whether or not performed in accordance with the scheduled pattern. For this purpose, operation to a flag stop is a hop completed, even though a landing is not actually made.

Certificated Route Air Carriers: One of a class of air carriers holding certificates of public convenience and necessity issued by the CAB, authorizing the performance of scheduled air transportation over specified routes and a limited amount of nonscheduled operations. This general carrier grouping includes the all-purpose carriers (i.e., the so-called passenger/cargo carriers) and the all-cargo carriers, and comprises all of the airlines certificated by the board, except the supplemental air carriers. Certificated route air carriers are often referred to as "scheduled airlines," although they also perform nonscheduled service.

Domestic Operations: Effective January 1, 1970, in accordance with the new 50-states concept, the 50 states of the United States and the District of

Columbia including operations between states separated by foreign territory or major ex-certificated trunk carriers and Pan American and the operations of the local service, helicopter, intra-Alaska, intra-Hawaii, domestic all-cargo and "other carriers" are classified under this operation. The other carriers classification now contains the territorial passenger/cargo category. In addition, any transborder operations conducted on the domestic route segments of United States air carriers are shown as domestic operations.

International and Territorial Operations: Effective January 1, 1970, in accordance with the new 50-states concept, those operations between the 50 states of the United States and foreign points includes both the combination passenger/cargo carriers and the all-cargo carriers engaged in international and territorial operations.

Nonscheduled Service: Revenue flights not operated in regular scheduled service, principally contract and charter operations.

Operating Expenses: Expenses incurred in the performance of air transportation, which includes direct aircraft operating expenses and ground and indirect operating expenses.

Operating Revenues: Includes *transport* revenues from the carriage of all classes of traffic in scheduled and nonscheduled services including the performance of aircraft charters, which includes passenger, freight, express, mail, excess baggage, and other transport revenues; and *nontransport* revenues consist of federal subsidy (where applicable) and incidental revenues, net revenues less related expenses from services incidental to air transportation.

Revenue Passenger Load Factor: The percent that revenue passenger-miles are of available seat-miles in revenue passenger services, presenting the proportion of aircraft seating capacity that is actually sold and utilized.

Revenue Passenger-Mile: One revenue passenger transported one mile in revenue service. Revenue passenger-miles are computed by summation of the products of the revenue aircraft-miles flown on each interairport flight stage and multiplied by the number of passengers carried on that flight stage.

Revenue Ton-Mile of Freight: One short ton of freight transported one statute mile. Ton-miles are computed by summation of the products of the aircraft-miles flown on each interairport flight stage multiplied by the number of tons carried on that flight stage.

Scheduled Service: Transport service operated over an air carrier's certificated routes, based on published flight schedules, including extra sections and related nonrevenue flights.

Supplemental Air Carriers: One of a class of air carriers now holding certificates, issued by the CAB, authorizing them to perform passenger and cargo charter services supplementing the scheduled service of the certificated route air carriers. Supplemental air carriers are often referred to as "nonskeds," that is, nonscheduled carriers.

Road Transportation

Auto Passenger-Miles: This movement covers the total travel of passengers riding within passenger automobiles and taxis movement of 1 miles.

Federal Expenditures: Federal expenditures equals the intergovernmental payments to the states, District of Columbia, and local governments plus direct expenditures for capital outlay, maintenance, administration, and research.

Interstate Highway System: 42,500 miles of specifically designed interconnected highways, as prescribed in the 1956 Interstate Highway Act and Amendments thereto.

Local Rural Roads: The vehicle-miles traveled upon roads in the local vicinity of the suburban areas.

Main Rural Roads: The vehicle-miles traveled upon main thoroughfares leading into the metropolis.

Municipal Mileage: This mileage is computed from traffic on any road inside the city municipal district or boundary.

Rural Mileage: This mileage is computed from traffic on any roads outside the city municipal district or boundary.

State and Local Expenditures: State and local expenditures equals the sum of disbursements for capital outlay, maintenance and traffic surfaces, administration, and research, highway law enforcement and safety, and interest on debt.

State Primary System: Refers to highways that had been officially designated by states and the "primary system."

State Secondary Roads: Mileage for "state secondary systems" is reported in the tables from the states (taken from the *Highway Statistics 1970 Bulletin*) that have designated both a primary and a secondary system.

Vehicle-Miles: The vehicle-miles of an automobile are computer based on gasoline tax and the miles per gallon.

Vehicle-Miles–Streets: This distance covers the total number of miles (by millions) of a passenger car, taxi, and motorcycle on an average regular intracity route.

Bus

These figures cover the total operation and maintenance, insurance, depreciation, operating taxes, licenses, and operating rents of school buses.

Average Speed for Commercial Bus on Main Rural Roads: This average is the speed of free-flowing bus traffic along level sections of a highway.

Commercial Bus: A motor carrier (coach) used to carry multiple passengers for a fare.

Intercity Bus: This total equals class I, II, and III carriers reporting to the ICC and intrastate car carriers.

Intercity Bus–Class I Carriers: A class I motor carrier of passengers is defined by the commission as having average annual gross operating revenues of $1,000,000 or more during interstate service.

Number of Revenue Passengers: The total number of passengers in revenue transportation services.

Revenue Passenger-Miles: One revenue passenger transported one mile.

School and Nonrevenue Bus: These motor carriers are used to carry multiple passengers without a fare for the destination carried.

Vehicle-Miles Operated: This term covers the total of miles during regular-route intercity service, local and suburban service, charter and special service.

Motor Trucking

Average Length of Haul (Miles): The total number of ton-miles divided by tons of revenue freight carried.

ICC-Regulated and Non-ICC-Regulated: An ICC-regulated carrier is a truck company operating in interstate commerce under ICC authority for hire carrier. A non-ICC-regulated carrier is a private carrier hauling only for itself.

Operating Expenses of Class I Intercity Motor Carriers: This is the cost of truck operations by service functions.

Operating Revenues of Class I Intercity Motor Carriers: The amount of money which a carrier becomes entitled to receive or achieved to its benefit for transportation and services incidental thereto.

Revenues: The amount of which the carrier becomes entitled to receive for transportation and services incidental thereto.

Ton-Miles: The transportation of a ton of freight a distance of one mile.

Vehicle-Miles: This term covers miles operated by power units upon urban streets, main rural streets, and local rural roads.

Local Transit

Dial-a-Ride: A computerized system of small vehicles (10 to 30 passengers including jitneys) incorporating demand responsive features, operating in more than 50 medium-size United States cities.

Line Mileage: This mileage is computed from point to point. It begins with mileage gained from leaving the garage on a regular route and ending back at the garage.

Operating Expenses: This category includes all equipment, maintenance, wages, fuel, advertisement, taxes, licenses, insurance, rent, etc.

Operating Revenue: Passengers carried in revenue service of local motor-buses, subway and elevated, surface rail, and trolley coach services.

Passenger Revenue: Revenue from the transportation of passengers upon the basis of fares.

Personal Rapid Transit (PRT): New technological innovations, attempting to stress the needs of individual passengers.

Revenue Vehicle-Miles: Bus-miles represented as operated in revenue service.

Subway and Elevated: These modes are classified as rapid rail transit.

Surface Rail: This mode is classified as a street car.

Trolley Coach: Coach on rubber wheels but powered by a running overhead electrical wire.

Water Transport

Class A and Class B Carriers by Inland and Coastal Waterways: Class A water carriers are ones with an annual operating revenue above $500,000. Class B water carriers have an annual operating revenue greater than $100,000 but less than $500,000.

Coastwise/Coastal Waterways; These terms apply to domestic traffic receiving a carriage over the ocean, or the Gulf of Mexico, for example, New Orleans to Baltimore, New York to Puerto Rico, San Francisco to Hawaii, and Puerto Rico to Hawaii. Traffic between Great Lakes ports and seacoast ports, when having a carriage over the ocean, is also termed "coastwise." The Chesapeake Bay and Puget Sound are considered internal bodies of water rather than arms of the ocean and therefore traffic confined to these areas is "internal" rather than "coastwise."

Domestic Freight: All commodities being shipped waterborne between points in the United States and its territorial waters (Puerto Rico and the Virgin Islands) consisting of bulk materials–grains, sugar, molasses, logs and lumber, coal and coke iron ore, iron and steel, sand gravel, stone chemicals, and related products.

Domestic Passenger: Any person traveling on a public conveyance within United States territorial waters.

Dry Cargo Barges and Scows: Both are large, flat-bottomed boats used to transport dry bulk materials; the scow is chiefly used for transporting sand, gravel, or refuse.

Internal Waterways: This term applies to traffic between ports or landings wherein the entire movement takes place on inland waterways. Also termed internal are movements involving carriage on both inland waterways and waters of the Great Lakes; inland movements that cross short stretches of open waters that link inland systems, marine products, sand, and gravel taken directly from beds of the oceans, the Gulf of Mexico and important arms thereof; and movements between offshore installations and inland waterways.

International Freight: All movements waterborne between the United States and foreign countries and between Puerto Rico and the Virgin Islands, United States, and foreign countries are considered as international freight, consisting of: petroleum and products, coal and coke, iron ore, and iron and steel, grains, and chemicals.

International Passenger: Any person traveling on a waterborne public conveyance between the United States and foreign countries and between Puerto Rico and the Virgin Islands, United States, and foreign countries is considered an international passenger.

Lakewise/Great Lakes: This term applies to traffic between United States ports on the Great Lakes system. The Great Lakes system is treated as a separate system rather than as part of the inland system.

Maritime: Those carriers engaging in waterborne trade in the same capacity as inland water carriers, differing only in that maritime carriers commerce takes place on the sea.

Maritime Revenue: Revenue received for the carriage of freight in international shipping and trade on oceans.

Nonselfpropelled: This term applies to vessels not containing within themselves the means for their own propulsion.

Self-propelled Towboats and Tugs: This towboat is a compact shallow-draft boat with squared bow and towing knees for pushing tows of barges on inland waterways; and a tug is a strongly built boat used for towing and pushing, also termed as towboat. Both of these vessles have within their structure the means for their own propulsion.

Tank Barges: This term applies to flat barges that travel on inland waterways, have no engine, and must be pulled by a towboat, and that usually carry fluid such as oil.

Tons of Freight Hauled: This covers the total number of tons of freight hauled across domestic waterways carrying both imports and exports.

Railroads

Arrival/Departure Time: Clock time when a train arrives/departs.

Average Haul: In applying to freight, it is the average distance in miles one ton is carried, computed by dividing the number of ton-miles by the number of tons carried, whether for an individual railway or for a group of railways, in either case representing the haul per railway. For the United States as a whole, it is also computed by dividing the total ton-miles by the tons of freight originated, thus giving effect to the fact that some freight originates on one railway and reaches its destination on another.

Average Passenger Trip Length: Calculated by dividing the number of revenue passenger-miles by the number of passengers carried.

Car Mileage: The miles run by an individual car in a unit carrying freight or a passenger a distance of one mile.

Class I Railroads: These railways have an annual operating revenue greater than $5,000,000.

Commutation: Passenger traffic handled between designated points at less than the basic fare per trip. It does not include traffic moving on basic rates of round trip, half rates, clergy, charity, military, special excursions, and other special-rated traffic.

Delay Time: The sum of all delay minutes encountered by a train on a single trip, including intermediate yard stop time.

Express Revenue: Revenue from transportation of express matter and from use of facilities on trains and at stations incidental to such transportation.

Freight Revenue: Revenue from the transportation of freight and from transit, stop, diversion, and reconsignment arrangements, upon the basis of tariffs.

Inbound/Outbound Train: A train that is moving into/out of a yard.

Line Haul: The portion of the rail activity pertaining to movements on the links (the portion of a train's trip in going from its origin to destination point, excluding yard activities).

Line Mileage: The miles run by a complete unit of all car equipment carrying freight or passenger a distance of one mile.

Link: A rail segment connecting two nodes.

Locomotive Mileage: The miles run by a locomotive in freight or passenger train service.

Locomotives: These are self-propelled units of equipment or combinations of units operated under a single control, and designed solely for moving other equipment.

Mail Revenue: Revenue from the transportation of mail at established rates, and for the services and facilities provided in connection with the handling of United States mail.

Mechanical and Electrical (M&E) Delay Time: Delay time due to failures in motive power, braking systems, electrical systems, etc.

Network: The total configuration of rail nodes and links.

Node: An origin or destination point.

Operating Delay Time: Delay time due to meets and passes, and other traffic interferences.

Operating Expenses: Expenses of furnishing transportation service including the expense of maintenance and depreciation.

Other Than Commutation: Passenger traffic other than that handled between designated points at less than the basic fare per trip. It does not include traffic moving on basic rates of round trips, half rates, clergy, charity, military, special excursions, and other special-rated traffic.

Other Revenue: A general heading on the income statement under which are grouped revenues from miscellaneous operations, income from lease of road and equipment, miscellaneous rent income, income from nonoperating property, profit from separately operated properties, dividend income, interest income, income from sinking and other reserve funds release of premium on funded debt, contributions from other companies, and miscellaneous income.

Passenger: A person traveling on a train by right of fare or pass, or a person lawfully on the premises of a carrier incidental to traveling on a train.

Passenger and Pullman Cars: Car units that provide areas for sitting and sleeping.

Passenger Revenue: Revenue from the transportation of passengers upon the basis of tariffs, including the carrier's portion of through fares, extra fares on limited trains, additional railway fares for the exclusive use of space, mileage and script coupons honored, and revenue from the transportation of corpses.

Revenue Passengers Carried: Passengers who pay fares for transportation services.

Revenue Passenger-Mile: One revenue passenger transported one mile.

Revenue Ton-Mile: The movement of one ton (2,000 pounds) of revenue freight a distance of one mile.

Running Time: Trip time minus delay time (the time during which a train is actually in movement).

Train Mileage: The miles run by a train in passenger or freight service.

Trip Time: Time difference between a train's actual departure and arrival time.

Yard Time: Time spent in a yard (hump yard or flat yard); or time spent switching at intermediate points.

Oil Pipeline

ICC-Regulated Carriers: These carriers report to ICC all operating revenues, because of needed authority from ICC to operate in interstate commerce, if a pipeline crosses states or if a pipeline is receiving oil from another state.

Nonregulated Carriers: These carriers are not required to report to ICC any revenues received for transportation and services because they do not engage in interstate commerce.

Operating Expenses: The cost of pipeline operation by service functions.

Operating Revenues: The amount of revenue a carrier is entitled to receive for transportation and services incidental thereto.

Index

About the Author

James T. Kneafsey is an economic consultant to the Center for Transportation Studies of the Massachusetts Institute of Technology. After receiving the Ph.D. degree in economics from the Ohio State University in 1971, Dr. Kneafsey developed and taught transportation and microeconomics courses in the Department of Economics at the University of Pittsburgh and in the Department of Civil Engineering at the Massachusetts Institute of Technology. His teaching and research interests center on transportation economics, industrial organization, and applied econometrics. His articles and books—including *The Economics of the Transportation Firm* (Lexington Books, 1974)—cover the industrial organization of the transportation industries, mergers, and reorganizations in the railroad industry, air transport economics, and a wide range of multimodal studies in transportation systems planning. Dr. Kneafsey also has been a consultant to various regulatory commissions, research firms, and business corporations that are involved in transportation problems.